Palaeopathology

Paleopathology is designed to help bone specialists with diagnosis of diseases in skeletal assemblages. It suggests an innovative method of arriving at a diagnosis in the skeleton by applying 'operational definitions'. The aim is to ensure that all those who study bones will use the same criteria for diagnosing disease, which will enable valid comparisons to be made between studies. This book is based on modern clinical knowledge and provides background information so that readers understand the natural history of bone diseases, which will enable them to draw reliable conclusions from their observations. Details of bone metabolism and the fundamentals of basic pathology are also provided, as well as a comprehensive and up-to-date bibliography. A short chapter on epidemiology provides information on how best to analyze and present the results of a study of human remains.

Professor Tony Waldron teaches paleopathology at the Institute of Archaeology, University College London. The author of about 300 peer-reviewed papers in medical, scientific and archaeology journals, as well as books on occupational medicine and paleoepidemiology, Waldron is co-founder of the *International Journal of Osteoarchaeology* and served as co-editor for its first decade. He is a Fellow of the Royal College of Physicians of London, the Royal Society of Medicine, the Institute of Biology and the Royal Anthropological Institute.

Cambridge Manuals in Archaeology

General Editor
Graeme Barker, *University of Cambridge*

Advisory Editors
Elizabeth Slater, *University of Liverpool*
Peter Bogucki, *Princeton University*

Cambridge Manuals in Archaeology is a series of reference handbooks designed for an international audience of upper-level undergraduate and graduate students and professional archaeologists and archaeological scientists in universities, museums, research laboratories and field units. Each book includes a survey of current archaeological practice alongside essential reference material on contemporary techniques and methodology.

Books in the Series

Pottery in Archaeology, CLIVE ORTON, PAUL TYRES and ALAN VINCE
Vertebrate Taphonomy, R LEE LYMAN
Photography in Archaeology and Conservation, 2nd edition, PETER G DORRELL
Alluvial Geoarchaeology, A G BROWN
Shells, CHERYL CLAASEN
Sampling in Archaeology, CLIVE ORTON
Excavation, STEVE ROSKAMS
Teeth, 2nd edition, SIMON HILLSON
Lithics, 2nd edition, WILLIAM ANDREFFSKY JR
Geographical Information System in Archaeology, JAMES CONOLLY and MARK LAKE
Demography in Archaeology, ANDREW CHAMBERLAIN
Analytical Chemistry in Archaeology, A M POLLARD, C M BATT, B STERN and S M M
   YOUNG
Zooarchaeology, 2nd edition, ELIZABETH J REITZ and ELIZABETH S WING
Quantitative Paleozoology, R LEE LYMAN

Palaeopathology

Tony Waldron *Institute of Archaeology, University College London*

CAMBRIDGE
UNIVERSITY PRESS

CAMBRIDGE UNIVERSITY PRESS
Cambridge, New York, Melbourne, Madrid, Cape Town, Singapore, São Paulo, Delhi

Cambridge University Press
32 Avenue of the Americas, New York, NY 10013-2473, USA

www.cambridge.org
Information on this title: www.cambridge.org/9780521678551

First published 2009

A catalog record for this publication is available from the British Library.

Library of Congress Cataloging in Publication Data
Waldron, T. (Tony)
Palaeopathology / Tony Waldron.
  p. ; cm. – (Cambridge manuals in archaeology)
Includes bibliographical references and index.
ISBN 978-0-521-86137-3 (hardback) – ISBN 978-0-521-67855-1 (pbk.)
1. Paleopathology.   I. Title.   II. Series.
[DNLM: 1. Paleopathology. QZ 11.5 W167p 2009]
R134.8.W354   2009
616.07–dc22   2008018710

ISBN   978-0-521-86137-3 hardback
ISBN   978-0-521-67855-1 paperback

CONTENTS

LIST OF FIGURES

PREFACE

I entered palaeopathology via a very circuitous route, having previously had a back-ground in anatomy, toxicology and epidemiology, although an interest in pathology was always present, having been greatly stimulated by the subject during my time as a medical student. My first hands-on experience with bones, however, was in collecting specimens for lead analysis when I was working at the University of Birmingham. We undertook the analysis of many hundreds of specimens until it became clear that the variation in lead levels that we were finding owed much more to contamination from the soil than to exposure during life, and I formed the view that it would be more profitable to see what information could be obtained from the bones themselves. When I moved to London to work at the London School of Hygiene and Tropical Medicine (LSHTM), I became very active in examining skeletal assemblages and some mummified material, and I had the good fortune to become acquainted with Don Brothwell at the Institute of Archaeology, which was just a few minutes walk around the corner from the LSHTM. He not only kindly gave me a corner of a desk, but invited me to take part in the teaching of the undergraduates and post-graduates at the Institute. I have had the great pleasure of teaching at the Institute now for many years, and this book is based very largely on the course of lectures in palaeopathology that I give to those taking the master's courses.

Perhaps I should try to explain what this book is *not*. It is not a review of the palaeopathological literature, although, of course, references to this source are made as appropriate. Rather, the purpose of the book is to provide enough information to those who have no medical training to enable them to understand the nature and natural history of those diseases that they may encounter when they examine a collection of skeletons or other human remains. The book ought also to help them to recognise at least the majority of these conditions and perhaps allow them to categorise the most common. The text is firmly based on clinical evidence, because this is the only reliable source of information that permits us to differentiate normal from abnormal. I do not subscribe to the view of some of my medical colleagues that those without medical training have no business dabbling in bone pathology, even in those long dead, but I do consider that medical training is not actually a hindrance in doing so. There are, however, great differences in arriving at a diagnosis in those long dead, compared with the living, and it is my experience that the significance of this difference is not always appreciated by those who come from non-medical backgrounds. I have tried to emphasize these difficulties and to suggest that it might be best if palaeopathologists were guided in their attempts at diagnosis by so-called operational definitions. These are more often used by epidemiologists than clinicians – although the latter use other guides such as flow charts or algorithms to help them. In the text I discuss, and attempt to justify, the use of operational definitions and, where possible, propose some which I consider helpful. I am not so naïve as to believe that bone specialists will fall on these operational definitions with relief if not with joy, and I am perfectly willing to discuss moderations of those that I have proposed and consider new definitions for some of the conditions that presently lack them. The definitions must, of course, be based on clinical evidence. Those who think otherwise are seriously in error, for if we do not use the signs that clinicians use to formulate disease states, what are we to fall back on? A disease that exists only in the mind of a particular palaeopathologist cannot really be said to exist anywhere else.

Many of my students and colleagues have helped to moderate or change my views over the years. One of the pleasures of teaching the young is that they come with uncluttered minds and are generally willing to be challenging and to question dogma; in this way both student and teacher learn. It was Harry S Truman who said that 'the only things worth learning are the things you learn after you know it all', and this is certainly true of most university lecturers, some more than others. I have learnt much from my students and from many colleagues but most especially from the late Dr David Birkett; Professors Don Brothwell, Simon Hillson and Don Ortner; and Dr Ann Stirland; I must reserve particular thanks for the late Dr Juliet Rogers with whom I had the very great pleasure of working and collaborating until her untimely death in 2001. I must also express my gratitude to Dr Don Resnick, whom I regret I have met only once, but whose monumental work on bone and joint radiology[1] has seldom been on my shelves while writing this book. It is one of the three very best textbooks that I have ever read,[2] and many unattributed opinions in this book have their origin in his pages. On this account, I would like to say that he is responsible

---

[1] D Resnick and G Niwayama, *Diagnosis of bone and joint disorders*. Philadelphia, WB Saunders, 1988.
[2] The other two are Bradford Hill's *Principles of medical statistics* and Donald Hunter's *Diseases of occupations*.

for the errors that appear in *these* pages but lack the courage, and so I will have to do the decent thing and accept responsibility for them myself. Perhaps there may be an opportunity to correct them in the future.

I must also thank my long-suffering family, whose home life was – again – interrupted to an unconscionable degree while I was writing the book, despite assurances that it would never happen again. Virtually every flat surface in the house was covered with piles of paper, which increased in size as time went on, and dark mutterings were the normal means of communication for several months. At last, normality has returned, and we can all eat around the dining table again. I am grateful to my son Richard who has taken time out from his burgeoning career as a pop star to draw two illustrations for me, and special thanks, as always, go to Gill, who valiantly read every word, who found a good deal of amusement from the draft and who corrected spelling and grammar assiduously. She also gamely supported the author through dark patches and always encouraged and stimulated; I dedicate this book to her with all my love.

London, 2008

Introduction and Diagnosis

The study of disease in earlier societies stands firmly in the purview of the discipline of the history of medicine. There are a number of ways in which the subject can be approached, such as from the study of extant medical texts or of pictorial or plastic art and artefacts. However, the most direct approach is from the examination of the physical remains of our ancestors. Each approach has its limitations and calls for different skills. The preservation of documentary evidence is subject to random vagaries, at least as great as the preservation of human remains. The medical historians must be able to set their interpretation of the written word in the context of the various theories of disease extant at the time the original was written. Medical historians will also almost certainly need to be proficient in some languages other than their own. Those who attempt to diagnose disease from paintings, pots or sculpture will need to be familiar with the artistic conventions of the artists whose artefacts they study.

Palaeopathologists have the advantage of being able to study directly the remains of the diseased, although usually only in part, and this ability may be the only factor in their favour. The principal disadvantage that constrains palaeopathologists is that their study is restricted largely to those diseases that affect the skeleton – preserved soft tissues being decidedly unusual in most parts of the world. Skeletal diseases are uncommon, as most diseases affect the soft tissues; this is certainly the case for the killing diseases. Thus, it is generally impossible for palaeopathologists to determine the cause of death of those they examine, which is a great pity because the knowledge of how the causes of death might have changed over the centuries would add greatly to our understanding of the history of disease.[1]

---

[1] This problem does not, of course, solely affect palaeopathologists. Even though they have written accounts of disease and, in more recent times, mortality statistics, historians also find it difficult to determine the causes of death of our ancestors. One cause of the difficulty is due to the inability to recognise precisely what diseases earlier authors were actually describing. There is considerable scepticism among many historians

The other major problem is that there is no agreed system for diagnosing disease in the skeleton to which all (or even the majority of) palaeopathologists subscribe, thus rendering comparisons between different studies somewhat arbitrary at best, and invalid at worst. The problem is not alleviated at all by the fact that most palaeopathologists have no medical training and so have not been subject to the discipline of the diagnostic treadmill and are not always inclined to base their diagnosis on clinical evidence, or rein in their imaginations. On this account it seems appropriate to meet the difficulty with diagnosis head on and dispatch it with all haste.

DIAGNOSIS IN PALAEOPATHOLOGY

In the clinical setting, medical students are taught the traditional, formalised approach to diagnosis, which begins by taking a detailed history from the patient, eliciting all the present complaints, followed by the past medical history and family, social and occupational histories. Any drugs that are being taken are noted and then the patient is examined to discover any abnormal signs in the various organ systems. The next step is to compile a list of all the conditions that might conceivably cause the signs and symptoms, beginning with the most likely and proceeding downwards to the esoteric and frankly improbable. In practice, such a list – the so-called differential diagnosis – is seldom created except for special purposes, such as writing up, or presenting a case report, when the aim is then to astonish the audience with the brilliance of the presenter. It is much more likely that following the first steps in the procedure, the clinician will have a good idea of the problem and will then arrange for a series of investigations by which the provisional diagnosis can be confirmed. Ancillary investigations may include *inter alia* blood tests, biochemistry, radiology (plain X-rays and scans), virology, bacteriology, ultrasound, endoscopy, biopsy and, as a last resort, invasive surgery. As the results roll in, the provisional diagnosis may be – and frequently is – revised.[2] To aid diagnosis, a number of algorithms, flow

about the reliability of death registration (G Alter and A Carmichael, Studying causes of death in the past. Problems and models, *Historical Methods*, 1996, 29, 44–48).

[2] This procedure may sound familiar to those with a knowledge of Bayes' theorem and, indeed, the claim has been made that clinicians are natural bayesians (CJ Gill, L Sabin and CH Schmidt, Why clinicians are natural bayesians, *British Medical Journal*, 2005, 330, 1080–1083). Bayes' theorem states that the pre-test probability of an hypothesis being true multiplied by the likelihood ratio (the weight of new evidence) produces the post-test probability. Clinicians certainly do change their minds about the probability of a diagnosis being true as new evidence emerges to improve the odds of being correct, but the similarity to the formal Bayesian

charts and various other aids have been designed to make the procedure both more reliable and more consistent.[3]

The purpose of a diagnosis is – as it has always been – to offer the patient a prognosis and, where indicated, some treatment. For the latter purposes, it is immaterial what name is attached to the disease that affects the patient. Diagnostic nomenclature is a rag-bag of terms, some descriptive, some anatomical, some denoting a specific infection, some with virtually no meaning at all. Old and new terms are frequently mixed in a miscellany that has been likened to a room full of furniture from different periods, from Georgian sideboards to glass coffee tables. However, because the aim of the clinician is simply to say, you have a disease that I will treat with such and such a drug, from which you will recover completely, the illogicality of diagnosis causes scarcely a ripple on the medical mill pond.[4]

There are few clinicians who will readily admit to the fact that diagnosis is a rather hit-and-miss affair that tends to be conducted at a subliminal level. The clinician is apt to recognise a diagnosis by its 'jizz'; this is a term that bird watchers use to refer to what one might call the 'totality' of a bird. Bird watchers recognise a marsh harrier, for example, by the sum of its appearance and behaviour. Most clinicians do the same with disease. They recognise its salient features and then expend their energy substantiating their hunch. Most lay people are somewhat disillusioned when (or if) they learn that diagnosis remains more art than science; they are even more alarmed when (or, again, if) they find out how prone the procedure is to error.

There have been many studies of the accuracy of diagnosis, most frequently by comparing a clinical diagnosis with that determined at autopsy. The results have never been very reassuring. In one recent study of fifty-three previously published reports, it was found that up to half of all diagnoses were seriously in error, and

procedure is more apparent than real and it is not very likely, in fact, that most clinicians would consider themselves bayesians (MW Cooper, Should physicians be bayesian agents? *Theoretical Medicine*, 1992, 13, 349–361).

[3] See, for example, those published by the American Academy of Family Physicians (aafp.org). There is now a web site which will offer diagnoses in response to a list of symptoms (www.isabelhealth.com) and some doctors are now using Google as an aid to diagnosis.

[4] In truth, doctors are not much interested in discussing disease and diagnosis in any philosophical sense and, indeed, have some difficulty in saying what precisely they mean by 'disease' or its antithesis 'health'. These matters are discussed in detail in: *What is disease?* (edited by JM Humber and RF Almeder), Humana Press, Totowa, 1997 and *Health, disease and illness* (edited by AL Caplan, JJ McCartney and DA Sisti), Georgetown University Press, Washington, 2004. The allusion to diagnostic furniture is from RE Kendall, *The role of diagnosis in psychiatry*, Blackwell, Oxford, 1975, p 20. Despite its age, this is still probably the best account of the state of diagnosis in medicine. For some more recent thinking on models of disease see C Del Mar, J Doust and P Glasziou, *Clinical thinking. Evidence, communication and decision-making*, Oxford, Blackwell, 2006, pp 27–37.

Table 1.1. *Error rates in clinical diagnosis detected at autopsy*

Type of patient	Number of studies	Overall error rate (%)	Class I error rate (%)*
General inpatients	13	12.6–38.0	1.5–12.0
Adult medical	5	14.0–41.0	7.0–16.0
Adult intensive care	7	19.8–27.9	7.0–12.0
Surgical	5	15.7–49.8	2.6–20.7
Paediatric	3	6.4–13.1	4.3–6.5
Neonatal or paediatric intensive care	5	0.3–28.0	2.1–11.8
Others	5	4.1–33.3	0–9.5

* Errors that might have affected outcome

Data from Shojania et al. (2003)[5]

that in up to one-fifth, the error was sufficiently serious that the patient received the wrong treatment (see Table 1.1). The authors of the review did not believe that the errors had resulted in many avoidable deaths, but overall, their conclusions were not a boost for diagnostic acumen and do little to instil confidence in the procedure.

Now, if clinicians, with a host of information at their disposal get their diagnoses wrong so frequently, how much more likely is it that palaeopathologists will fare any better when they have so *little* information on which to base their conclusions? The answer should be, not very likely at all, although one is not infrequently astonished by the certainty that some authors attach to their diagnoses, sometimes seeming to possess gifts denied to most of us.

If one looks at the clinical criteria for diagnosing a common condition, osteoarthritis (OA) of the knee, that have been developed by the American College of Radiologists[6] (Table 1.2), it is immediately obvious that this is only a minimal help to the palaeopathologist. There is no way in which pain or stiffness can be determined in the skeleton; crepitus cannot be elicited; osteophytes as a lone phenomenon are not necessarily indicative of OA; and even deciding that a skeleton may be that of

[5]   KG Shojania, EC Burton, KM McDonald and L Goldman, Changes in rates of autopsy-detected diagnostic errors over time. A systematic review, *Journal of the American Medical Association*, 2003, 289, 2849–2856.

[6]   R Altman, E. Asch, D. Bloch, D. Bole, K. Borenstein, K. Brandt, W Christy, TD Cooke, R Greenwald, M Hochberg, D Howell, D Kaplan, W Koopman, S Longley, H Mankin, DJ McShane, R Medsger, R Meenan, W Mikkelsen, R Moskowitz, W Murphy, B Rothschild, M Segal, L Sokoloff and F Wolfe, Determination of criteria for the classification and reporting of osteoarthritis: classification of osteoarthritis of the knee, *Arthritis and Rheumatism*, 1986, 29, 1039–1049.

Table 1.2. *Clinical criteria for the classification of osteoarthritis of the knee*

Clinical and radiological	Clinical
Knee pain	Knee pain
+	+
at least one of the following:	at least three of the following
Age >50 years	Age >50 years
Stiffness for less than 30 minutes	Stiffness for less than 30 minutes
Crepitus	Crepitus
+	Bony tenderness
osteophytes	Bony enlargement
	No palpable warmth

Data from Altman et al. (1986)[7]

a man or woman aged over fifty at death is not always a straightforward matter to determine. What is true for OA of the knee is true for many other diseases that affect the skeleton. Thus, another strategy must be adopted for diagnosing lesions in the skeleton, albeit firmly based on clinical evidence.[8]

The palaeopathologist can obtain a limited amount of information about his 'patients'. The skeleton can be examined directly, or at least as much of it as is present,[9] and the visual inspection can be supplemented by radiography, although this is often not as informative as one might hope because it is a relatively insensitive technique.[10] It may also be possible to carry out a small number of ancillary tests, such

[7] R Altman, E. Asch, D. Bloch, D. Bole, K. Borenstein, K. Brandt, W Christy, TD Cooke, R Greenwald, M Hochberg, D Howell, D Kaplan, W Koopman, S Longley, H Mankin, DJ McShane, R Medsger, R Meenan, W Mikkelsen, R Moskowitz, W Murphy, B Rothschild, M Segal, L Sokoloff and F Wolfe, Determination of criteria for the classification and reporting of osteoarthritis: classification of osteoarthritis of the knee, *Arthritis and Rheumatism*, 1986, 29, 1039–1049.
[8] Those who espouse the quaint notion that clinical evidence may not be suitable for use in palaeopathology will probably wish to read no further, but continue along the primrose path with their like-minded colleagues (M Brickley and M Ives, Skeletal manifestations of infantile scurvy, *American Journal of Physical Anthropology*, 2006, 129, 163–172).
[9] Unfortunately that is often by no means the whole skeleton. It is a regrettable fact of the palaeopathologist's life that the most interesting skeletons (pathologically) are often the least complete, sometimes because the disease affecting the bones makes them more liable to post-mortem damage. (The factors affecting bone preservation are considered by CM Stojanowski, RM Seidermann and GH Doran, Differential skeletal preservation at Windover Pond: causes and consequences, *American Journal of Physical Anthropology*, 2002, 119, 15–26.)
[10] Juliet Rogers and her colleagues, for example, found that radiography was much less able to detect osteoarthritic changes than direct examination. For example, changes were noted in sixteen knees by direct examination but radiographically in only two (J Rogers, I Watt and P Dieppe, Comparison of visual and radiographic detection of bony changes at the knee joint, *British Medical Journal*, 1990, 300, 367–368).

as histology (usually not very helpful)[11] and ancient DNA (aDNA) analysis (which may be helpful in confirming the diagnosis of some infectious diseases)[12] and that is about it. The diagnosis, therefore, is almost always based solely on the morphology and distribution of the changes found in the skeleton on direct examination.[13]

To make a diagnosis based on this meagre information and to ensure conformity, I suggest that the palaeopathologist should use what epidemiologists refer to as an operational definition (see Chapter 13). An operational definition would take the form of a set of criteria that must be fulfilled in order for the disease to be recognised, similar to the criteria set out for the clinical diagnosis of OA of the knee shown in Table 1.2. However, there would be no criteria relating to symptomatology. In a few cases the appearances of the lesion, or the radiological signs, are so characteristic that they are said to be pathognomonic of the condition, that is, they fit this, and only this disease. Not many bone diseases have pathognomonic signs. Therefore, one might say, for example, that disease D would be said to be present if two major criteria were fulfilled, or three of five minor criteria.

[11] Not usually very helpful because of alterations in the bone substance after death, so-called diagenetic change. (See, for example, J Zapata, C Pérez-Sirvent, MJ Martínez-Sánchez and P Tovar, Diagenesis not biogenesis: Two late Roman skeletal examples, *Science of the Total Environment*, 2006, 369, 357–368). The processes that underlie diagenesis are by no means completely understood (REM Hedges, Bone diagenesis: an overview of processes, *Archaeometry*, 2002, 44, 319–328).

[12] DNA generally survives well only in those bones that have preserved their normal microscopic structure (AN Marinho, NC Miranda, V Braz, AK Ribeiro-Dos-Santos and SM de Souza, Paleogenetic and taphonomic analysis of human bones from Moa, Beirada, and Zé Espinho Sambaquis, Rio de Janeiro, Brazil, *Memórias do Instituto Oswaldo Cruz*, 2006, 101 Suppl 2, 15–23).

[13] It is possible that other techniques will find an application in palaeopathology. For example, micro-CT scanning can provide information on trabecular structure (F Peyrin, M Salome, P Cloetens, AM Laval-Jeanet, R Ritman and P Rüegsegger, Micro-CT examinations of trabecular bone samples at different resolutions: 14, 7 and 2 micron level, *Technology and Health Care*, 1998, 6, 391–401) and can provide information about diseased bone (FJ Rühli, G Kuhn, R Evison, R Müller and M Schultz, Diagnostic value of micro-CT in comparison with histology in the qualitative assessment of historical human skull bone pathologies, *American Journal of Physical Anthropology*, 2007, 133, 1099–1111) although it cannot distinguish woven from lamellar bone, for which polarised light microscopy is needed (G Kuhn, M Schultz, R Müller and FJ Rühli, Diagnostic value of micro-CT in comparison with histology in the qualitative assessment of historical human postcranial pathologies, *Homo*, 2007, 58, 97–115). Backscatter electron microscopy can provide qualitative information on the distribution of bone mineral within a section (AL Boskey, Assessment of bone mineral and matrix using backscatter electron imaging and FTIR imaging, *Current Osteoporosis Reports*, 2006, 4, 71–75) while Raman spectroscopy can supply information on the structure of bone crystals (JS Yerramshetty and O Akkus, The association between mineral crystallinity and the mechanical properties of human cortical bone, *Bone*, 2008, 42, 476–482) and nonlinear resonant ultrasound spectroscopy (NRUS) can be used to assess micro-damage in bone (M Muller, A Sutin, R Guyer, M Talmant, P Laugier and PA Johnson, Nonlinear resonant ultrasound spectroscopy (NRUS) applied to damage assessment in bone, *Journal of the Acoustical Society of America*, 2005, 118, 3946–3952). These techniques may soon find application for research purposes but being mostly expensive and confined to specialist laboratories, none is likely to become widely available to the jobbing palaeopathologist.

To date, few operational definitions have been proposed for use in palaeopathology, and none has been universally agreed upon. The procedure by which diseases are diagnosed in the skeleton often remains something of a mystery, which does little to advance the discipline and nothing to help in making between-study comparison. One of the most interesting aspects of palaeopathology is the potential for comparing the frequency of disease at different times and in different places. With a knowledge of environmental or social factors it might even be possible to suggest how the natural history of some diseases has been influenced by those, or indeed, other factors. It might also conceivably shed some light on the aetiology of diseases of the skeleton. Unless the same criteria are used for diagnosis, however, comparisons are invalid and a great deal of potentially useful information is wasted.

There is no doubt that an operational definition will tend to underestimate the true prevalence of disease in a skeletal assemblage because signs in the skeleton often develop late in the history of a disease, and the early stages are very likely to be overlooked. This deficiency, however, would be more than compensated for by observing strict rules for diagnosis, thereby ensuring the validity of any comparisons that *are* made.

What is required for palaeopathology is a set of operational definitions on the lines of the manual produced, for example, by the American College of Psychiatry which is used for both clinical and epidemiological purposes. The present manual makes no claim to be a comprehensive account of skeletal disease. I have, however, suggested operational definitions for some of those diseases in the hope that this will at least promote discussion or perhaps, even acceptance; however, in this last respect, like Corydon, I am unlikely to get what I hope for.[14]

OTHER COMPARISONS

Apart from making comparisons with other contemporary studies on skeletons, it is useful to be able to make comparisons with modern-day data and with data published in bone reports from earlier periods. There is, alas, little prospect of being able to do so. Modern studies almost always use different criteria for making a diagnosis and are carried out on very different populations. For example, some recent studies of the epidemiology of fractures have used referrals to a tertiary trauma

---

[14] G Mackie, *The eclogues of Virgil, translated into English verse, line for line*, Quebec, Gilbert Stanley, 1847, pp 8–10.

centre,[15] hospital discharge registers,[16] the general population of a city[17] and a general practice research database[18] as their study base. It can scarcely be expected that the incidence or prevalence data that are thereby calculated will have any direct relation to those that might be obtained from the study of a skeletal assemblage or, indeed, with each other. Data from modern epidemiological studies will, therefore, rarely be directly comparable with palaeopathological data in a quantitative sense, although it may be possible to draw some qualitative inferences.[19] For example, suppose one were able to study the distribution of secondary bone tumours, let's say by examining many assemblages using radiography as an aid in collecting cases. If this sort of study were possible, one could compare the distribution of the tumours with that found in a clinical study. Suppose further that the clinical study showed that the major proportion of secondaries from lung and breast tumours concentrated in the thoracic region, followed in order of frequency by the vertebrae, pelvis, upper and lower limbs and the skull.[20] It would then be perfectly reasonable to compare the order in which these regions were represented in the skeletal assemblages, even though the actual percentages may vary due to different methods of investigation. If inconsistencies were found, this might reflect some difference in the behaviour of tumours over time; alternatively the distribution might be found to be so similar that it was reasonable to conclude that the mode of spread showed no substantial differences between the two groups, ancient and modern. One might wish to carry

[15] T Throckmorton and JE Kuhn, Fractures of the medial end of the clavicle, *Journal of Shoulder and Elbow Surgery*, 2007, 16, 49–54.
[16] E Lonnroos, H Kautiainen, P Karppi, T Huusko, S Hartikainen, I Kiviranta and R Sulkava, Increased incidence of hip fractures. A population based-study in Finland, *Bone*, 2006, 39, 623–627.
[17] A Lešić, M Jarebinski, T Pekmezović, M Bumbasirević, D Spasovski and HD Atkinson, Epidemiology of hip fractures in Belgrade, Serbia Montenegro, 1990–2000, *Archives of Orthopaedic and Trauma Surgery*, 2007, 127, 179–183.
[18] F de Vries, C de Vries, C Cooper, B Leufkens and TP van Staa, Re-analysis of two studies with contrasting results on the association between statin use and fracture risk: the General Practice Research Database, *International Journal of Epidemiology*, 2006, 35, 1301–1308.
[19] An additional factor that needs to be stressed here is that modern epidemiological data – certainly those that are published in major journals – are obtained largely from patients or others living and working in the developed countries of Europe, North America and Japan. They will have been following an urban life style which would be about as unlike anything experienced by the majority of past societies studied as can be imagined. Data from rural populations in developing countries who might provide a more suitable comparison group are very hard to come by. Autopsy studies, which probably provide the most reliable data on cause of death – although they cannot provide population incidence or prevalence data – are likely to become increasingly rare in the United Kingdom because of the provision of the *Human Tissue Act 2004* (A Mavroforou, A Giannoukas and E Michalodimitrakis, Consent for organ and tissue retention in British law in the light of the Human Tissue Act 2004, *Medical Law*, 2006, 25, 427–434).
[20] MA Wilson and FW Calhoun, The distribution of skeletal metastases in breast and pulmonary cancer: concise communication, *The Journal of Nuclear Medicine*, 1981, 22, 594–597.

out studies on other diseases to see how similarly they behave qualitatively in a contemporary population.

When trying to make comparisons with old material (that is, those printed more than fifty years ago), there is an immediate problem with nomenclature. Thus, in 1920, R Stockman used four synonyms when discussing osteoarthritis – arthritis deformans, senile arthritis, morbus coxae senilis and spondylitis deformans.[21] When he refers to the history of osteoarthritis, he points out that many other terms were used by even earlier authors, including rheumatic gout, rheumatic arthritis and hypertrophic arthritis.[22] It will not be immediately obvious when reading old reports to which modern condition the author is actually referring, especially if there are no illustrations.

Finally, remember that some diseases that are recognised today will not appear at all in old (or even relatively modern) texts. This is particularly well illustrated by the development of the joint diseases for which fresh entities have been recognised, especially with the development of better means of laboratory diagnosis. If, for example, one reads successive editions of a standard textbook, such as that written by WSC Copeman, it is possible to see how the understanding of the erosive joint diseases was continuously in flux, and to witness the gradual emergence and acceptance of terms such as rheumatoid factor and sero-negative disease.[23] To expect to find an account of the sero-negative joint diseases from prior to the 1970s, therefore, will be met only with grave disappointment.

A NOTE ON HEALTH . . .

Among those who examine human remains, there is frequent reference to the 'health' of the assemblage. This seems to be a reflection of our present obsession with using health as a synonym for disease. The United Kingdom has a Department of Health whose prime responsibility is to offer services to deal with illness, and there are now health, rather than medical, records, as though this will somehow shield the population from the unpleasant business of having to contemplate disease even

---

[21] R. Stockman, *Rheumatism and arthritis*, W Green & Son, Edinburgh, 1920, chapter IX.
[22] *Ibid*, pp 118–120.
[23] WSC Copeman, *Textbook of the rheumatic diseases*, Livingstone, Edinburgh, 1948. Reference to rheumatoid factor first appears in the third (1964) edition. Not until the fourth (1969) edition, however, is its nature 'so well established that it is no longer necessary to discuss the several arguments against it' (p 187). It is in this edition that the first reference to the term sero-negative is given.

though it is manifestly disease, rather than health, that is of major concern. However one defines health – the World Health Organisation's notion of it being 'a state of complete physical, mental and social well being and not merely the absence of disease or infirmity' does not seem in the least realistic[24] – it is certain that an examination of the skeleton is not going to enable anything to be said about health, even in its most basic form as being the absence of disease. It may very well be the case that there is little evidence of bone or joint disease in an assemblage. However, to then infer that the individuals were in good health seems perverse, given that they are all dead and that it is probable that at least a third to a half of them will have died prematurely; this is a very strange notion of health. Perhaps other indicators of health could be adduced? The expectation of life might show that one assemblage enjoyed a greater expectation of life than another and might therefore be considered healthier, but anyone who relied on such data, given the virtual impossibility of assigning an accurate age at death to a skeleton, would be a brave soul indeed.

There is, in fact, no means of knowing the state of health during life of the individuals who come to comprise an assemblage of skeletons, especially because what determines their actual state of health depends not only upon the diseases that affected their internal organs, but their mental state, their diet[25] and many other environmental and social factors, about which there is little to be known from the state of their bones. It is best to recognise that all palaeopathologists can comment upon is disease and settle for that; it may be less than desirable but it is what we have.

... AND MUMMIES

In this book, most of the emphasis is on human skeletal remains because these are much more common in most contexts than mummified material. This is especially true of those countries in which the majority of palaeopathologists work. Even when mummified material is available, it is often not as informative as one might think. For example, the internal organs may have been removed during mummification or

---

[24] R Saracci, The World Health Organisation needs to reconsider its definition of health, *British Medical Journal*, 1997, 314, 1409–1410.

[25] It is possible to deduce whether the diet of an individual contained a lot of meat or fish, or neither. Originally this was based on trace-element analysis of bone (see, for example, KB Byrne and DC Parris, Reconstruction of the diet of the Middle Woodland Amerindian population at Abbott Farm by bone trace-element analysis, *American Journal of Physical Anthropology*, 1987, 74, 373–384) but this method was susceptible to contamination from the soil, and more reliable results are now obtained from analysis of the stable isotopes of carbon and nitrogen found in collagen (S Lösch, G Grupe and J Peters, Stable isotopes and dietary adaptations in humans and animals at pre-pottery Neolithic Nevalli Cori, southeast Anatolia, *American Journal of Physical Anthropology*, 2006, 131, 181–193).

are not amenable to study without radiography, scanning or endoscopy. Similarly, the joints cannot be directly examined, and often the death rictus also prevents the teeth from being fully examined. Mummies may also be a disappointment from the epidemiological point of view, often being present in such small numbers that no worthwhile prevalence – or other – data can be obtained. Despite this, useful and important information can sometimes be gleaned. I refer to this information especially in Chapter 11.

2

Bone Metabolism and Pathology

The majority of bones in the skeleton first appear in the fetus as cartilage models that calcify and ossify. The exceptions to this are the bones of the cranial vault and the clavicles, the primordal of which are formed by mesenchymal cells.[1] Long bones grow in length at the growth plates situated at the junction of the shaft (diaphysis) and the ends of the bone (the epiphyses). Circumferential growth is achieved by the laying down of bone beneath the periosteum[2] which covers the entire outer surface of all bones except that covered by articular cartilage. Bone is also laid down under the endosteum, which lines the inner surface of the bones. The entire process from cartilage formation, calcification, mineralisation, joint formation and remodelling is controlled by a plethora of genetic and molecular systems which are still by no means completely understood.[3]

TYPES OF BONE

Macroscopically, two types of bone can be distinguished in the skeleton, dense cortical (or compact) bone, such as forms the shaft of the femur and the humerus, for example, and cancellous (or spongy) bone, which occupies *inter alia* the ends of the long bones and the vertebral bodies. Cancellous bone is formed from trabeculae,

---

[1] This is known as membranous ossification. The ossification of the mandible differs again, in that it forms in the fibrous mesenchymal tissue around Meckel's cartilage (SK Lee, YS Kim, HS Oh, KH Yang, EC Kim and JG Chi, Prenatal development of the human mandible, *Anatomical Record*, 2001, 263, 314–325).

[2] F Rauch, Bone growth in length and width: the Yin and Yang of bone stability, *Journal of Musculoskeletal and Neuronal Interaction*, 2005, 5, 194–201.

[3] G Karsenty and EF Wagner, Reaching a genetic and molecular understanding of skeletal development, *Developmental Cell*, 2002, 2, 389–406.

bars and plates of bone arranged in a honeycomb manner which convey considerable strength to the region of the bone containing them, but also provides a huge surface area for metabolic reactions. The space between the trabeculae is filled with haemopoietic bone marrow and cancellous bone is always covered by a shell of cortical bone.

Microscopically, three broad categories can be distinguished: woven bone, primary bone and secondary bone.[4] Woven, or trabecular bone, is less dense than primary bone and the collagen fibres within it are arranged more or less randomly. It is formed in the fetus and during the healing phase following a fracture, when it is referred to as a callus (see Chapter 8).

Primary bone can also be divided into three broad categories: primary lamellar, plexiform and primary osteons. Lamellar bone is dense, strong, multi-layered and arranged circumferentially around the endosteal and periosteal surfaces. Plexiform bone resembles highly organised cancellous bone and is found in rapidly growing animals. When lamellar bone is arranged around a central canal which conveys a blood vessel, it forms a concentric structure – like growth rings in a tree trunk – referred to as an osteon.

The arrangement of the cortical osteons is often referred to as a Haversian system after the splendidly named seventeenth-century English anatomist Clopton Havers (1655–1702) who first described them. The Haversian systems branch and anastomose and are supplied with blood which run both in the central canal and in the so-called Volkmann canals.[5] The Volkmann canals carry blood vessels originating from the periosteum which anastomose with the Haversian vessels.[6]

Primary osteons are formed in early life and subsequently replaced by secondary osteons during the process of remodelling, when bone is resorbed and re-deposited (see below). The secondary osteons so formed are larger than the primary and surrounded by an irregular cement line which represents the boundary between resorption and re-deposition; between the secondary osteons small, irregular areas of lamellar bone (interstitial bone) can be found but not between primary osteons. In trabecular bone, the osteons are saucer shaped and are stacked in layers but without the regular arrangement of those in cortical bone.

---

[4] One of the best accounts of the micro-structure of bone is that written by Alan Boyd and Sheila Jones in *Gray's Anatomy*, 38th edition (London, Churchill-Livingstone, 1995, pp 452–480) although this section in the book is not directly attributed to them.

[5] Named after Wilhelm Volkmann, 1801–1877.

[6] M Chanavaz, Anatomy and histopathology of the periosteum: quantification of the periosteal blood supply to the adjacent bone with 85^{Sr} and gamma spectrometry, *Journal of Oral Implantology*, 1995, 21, 214–219.

THE BONE MATRIX

The bone matrix[7] consists mainly of type I collagen fibres, with a number of other proteins including osteonectin, osteocalcin and osteopontin. Collagen is a fibrous protein. The fibres are arranged concentrically in cortical bone and in a virtually random fashion in the trabeculae. Within and around the collagen fibres, and in the surrounding matrix, crystals of hydroxy-apatite $[3Ca_3(PO_4)_2.(OH)_2]$ are found which tend to be orientated in the same direction as the collagen fibres. This mixture of collagen fibres and hydroxy-apatite crystals enables bone to resist both shear and compressive forces extremely well, much in the way that reinforced concrete is able to do.

BONE CELLS AND CYTOKINES

There are three principal types of cell in bone: osteoblasts, osteoclasts and osteocytes, and there are epithelial-like lining cells that cover inactive bone surfaces that are not undergoing remodelling. The function of the osteoblasts and osteoclasts is to form and resorb bone, respectively, while osteocytes appear to have a signalling function. The development and function of the osteoblasts and osteoclasts is regulated by hormones, such as parathyroid hormone, thyroid hormone and growth hormone and a host of factors known collectively as cytokines. In addition, the differentiation and formation of the osteoblast and osteoclast are closely coupled in a system described in the following section.[8]

> *Cytokines:* Cytokines are proteins released by a variety of cells, and have signalling functions. They act in one of three ways: autocrine, paracrine or endocrine. Autocrine cytokines affect the cells that release them, paracrine cytokines affect adjacent cells and endocrine cytokines, distant cells. Once released, they bind to specific receptor sites on their target cells and produce a change in their activity or differentiation.

Cytokines may be classified into six broad groups: interleukins, colony-stimulating factors, tumour necrosis factor, interferons, growth factors and chemokines. These six group can be broken down into several sub-groups.

---

[7] PG Robey and AL Boskey, Extracellular matrix and biomineralization of bone, In: *Primer of the metabolic bone diseases and disorders of mineral metabolism*, 6th edition, Washington, American Society for Bone and Mineral Research, 2006, pp 12–19.

[8] DJ Hadjidakis and II Androulakis, Bone remodelling, *Annals of the New York Academy of Sciences*, 2006, 1092, 385–396.

The cytokines are concerned in the inflammatory response and may perform either a pro-inflammatory,[9] or an anti-inflammatory role,[10] that is, they either stimulate the inflammatory process or they suppress it. Interleukin 1 (IL-1) and tumour necrosis factor (TNF) are pro-inflammatory, whereas other interleukins (IL-4, IL-6, IL-10, IL-11, IL-13) and interleukin-1 receptor antagonist (IL-1ra) are anti-inflammatory. The situation is considerably confused, however, since most cytokines are pleiotropic, that is, they have many functions and they may be both pro- and anti-inflammatory, depending on local conditions. The one exception seems to be IL-1ra which is though to have a purely anti-inflammatory effect. One of the many functions of the cytokines is to regulate the differentiation and function of the osteoblasts and osteoclasts so that they may either encourage the laying down of bone, or its removal.

The chemokines, of which there are four sub-families, secrete factors that attract other cells into damaged or inflamed areas.

Osteoblasts: Osteoblasts are formed from mesenchymal stem cells derived from the bone marrow or periosteum.[11] They are found lining active bone surfaces and their function is to secrete collagen I and bone matrix proteins to form unmineralised osteoid. The osteoblasts also initiate mineralisation through the release of small vesicles, called matrix vesicles, which provide the optimum conditions for mineralisation by concentrating calcium and phosphate ions and inhibitors of substances such as pyrophosphate and proteoglycan found in the bone matrix and which may prevent mineralisation from taking place.[12] Osteoblasts are rich in bone-specific alkaline phosphatase which is used clinically as a marker of osteoblast activity.

After they have finished a phase of bone formation between 50–70% of the osteoblasts die by apoptosis – that is, programmed cell death – while others are incorporated in the bone substance to become osteocytes. Yet others become flattened and remain on the surface as bone lining cells. The bone lining cells are thought to regulate the flow of ions in and out of the extra-cellular fluid surrounding the bone, but they may also revert back to functional osteoblasts under the stimulation of parathyroid hormone (PTH) or mechanical forces.

---

[9] CA Dinarello, Proinflammatory cytokines, *Chest*, 2000, 118, 503–508.
[10] SM Opal and VA DePalo, Anti-inflammatory cytokines, *Chest*, 2000, 117, 1162–1172.
[11] TCA Phan and MH Zheng, Interaction between osteoblast and osteoclast: impact on bone disease, *Histology and Histopathology*, 2004, 19, 1325–1344.
[12] The process of mineralisation is also very dependent on the presence of the so-called SIBLING (Small Integrin-Binding Ligand N-linked Glycoproteins) (AL Boskey, Mineralization of bones and teeth, *Elements*, 2007, 3, 385–391).

Osteoclasts: Derived from bone marrow macrophages, osteoclasts are large, multi-nucleated cells which are seen to have an extensive ruffled border under the electron microscope. This ruffled border is formed when the cells contact bare bone, as is an actin ring that acts to seal the rim of the osteoblast on the bone surface.[13] The osteoclasts require RANK-L (receptor activator of nuclear factor-κB ligand), colony stimulating factor (CSF-1), IL-1 and IL-6, and hormones, including PTH and vitamin D, and calcitonin for their development.[14] They secrete hydrochloric acid and a number of enzymes that dissolve and digest bone mineral and they sit in depressions on the bone surface called Howship's[15] lacunae, or within cylindrical tunnels in cortical bone. Osteoclasts are the only cells that can dissolve bone which they do by secreting hydrochloric acid onto the surface of the basic hydroxyapatite, releasing calcium and phosphate ions and water, as follows:[16]

$$[Ca_3(PO_4)_2]_3Ca(OH)_2 + 8H^+ = 10Ca^{++} + 6HPO_4^{--} + 2H_2O.$$

There is an intimate relationship between the osteoclast and the osteoblast and the osteoblast regulates the differentiation and formation of the osteoclast through the secretion of RANK-L. RANK-L binds to RANK on macrophages, stimulating them to assume the osteoclast phenotype. The process can be down-regulated if the osteoblast secretes osteoprotegerin (OPG) which is a decoy receptor that competes with RANK-L for RANK.

Osteocytes: Osteocytes are the most abundant type of cell in bone, outnumbering the osteoblast (the next most numerous) by a factor of about ten. They are formed from osteoblasts that have become embedded in the bone matrix; however, little is known about this transformation.[17] Osteocytes have long processes that run in canaliculi throughout the bone and they communicate with each other through the bone matrix, forming a network somewhat analogous to a neural network. They seem to respond to mechanical stimuli and it is thought

---

[13] SL Teitelbaum, Osteoclasts: what do they do and how do they do it? *American Journal of Pathology*, 2007, 170, 427–435.
[14] S Roux and P Orcel, Bone loss. Factors that regulate osteoclast differentiation: an update, *Arthritis Research*, 2000, 2, 451–456; M Asagiri and H Takayanagi, The molecular understanding of osteoclast differentiation, *Bone*, 2007, 40, 251–264.
[15] John Howship 1781–1841.
[16] MM Cohen, The new bone biology, *American Journal of Medical Genetics*, 2006, 140A, 2646–2706.
[17] TA Franz-Odendall, BK Hall and PE Witten, Buried alive: how osteoblasts become osteocytes, *Developmental Dynamics*, 2006, 235, 176–190.

that they have an important signalling function in the regulation of local bone mass.[18]

BONE MASS

The total bone mass, that is, the mass of the entire skeleton, increases throughout childhood, adolescence and early adult life, reaching a maximum at about age 25–35.[19] There are a number of factors that determine the magnitude of the maximum or peak bone mass (PBM) including genetics, sex, ethnicity and physical activity.[20] Following the achievement of PBM, bone mass is lost at varying rates but always relatively more quickly in females than in males, and especially quickly after the menopause when the bone-sparing effects of oestrogen are lost.

Although bone appears to be an inert substance it is, in fact, in what AM Cooke[21] called a state of 'ceaseless activity' which describes the process of constant resorption and renewal. This constant flux of bone substance results in the turnover of the entire skeleton every ten years or so.

REMODELLING

The ceaseless activity of bone is achieved through the process of bone remodelling in which bone is removed by the osteoclast and replaced by the osteoblast. Remodelling may be initiated to repair small defects or cracks in the bone,[22] in response to strain,[23] or to release calcium ions required by other metabolic processes,[24] the bone being

[18] J Lein-Nulend, PJ Nijweide and EH Burger, Osteocyte and bone structure, *Current Osteoporosis Research*, 2003, 1, 5–10. They achieve this control, at least in part, by secreting sclerostin, a protein expressed by the Sost gene, and which antagonises other proteins including BMP and Wnt, that stimulate the formation of osteoblasts. (T Bellido, Osteocyte control of bone formation via Sost/sclerostin, *Journal of Musculoskeletal and Neuronal Interaction*, 2006, 6, 360–363)

[19] SA Abrams, Normal acquisition and loss of bone mass, *Hormone Research*, 2003, 60, Supplement 3, 71–76.

[20] SA New, Exercise, bone and nutrition, *Proceedings of the Nutrition Society*, 2001, 60, 265–274. In addition to these factor, the Wnt family of proteins are also thought to have a significant effect on regulating bone mass (V Krishnan, HU Bryant and OA Macdougald, Regulation of bone mass by Wnt signalling, *Journal of Clinical Investigation*, 2006, 116, 1202–1209).

[21] AM Cooke, Osteoporosis, *Lancet*, 1955, 1, 878–882.

[22] D Taylor, JG Hazenberg and TC Lee, Living with cracks: damage and repair in human bones, *Nature Materials*, 2007, 6, 262–268.

[23] TM Skerry, One mechanostat or many? Modifications of the site-specific response of bone to mechanical loading by nature and nurture, *Journal of Musculoskeletal and Neuronal Interaction*, 2006, 6, 122–127.

[24] LG Raisz, Physiology and pathophysiology of bone remodelling, *Clinical Chemistry*, 1999, 45, 1353–1358.

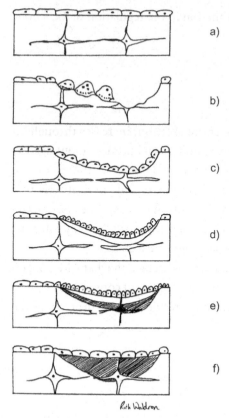

a)

b)

c)

d)

e)

f)

Rick Waldron

FIGURE 2.1. Diagram to show different phases of bone remodelling. (a) Resting surface covered with lining cells; (b) resorption taking place through the action of osteoclasts; (c) end of resorption and formation of cement line; (d) formation of osteoid by osteoblasts; (e) mineralisation of osteoid; (f) mineralisation complete and new packet of bone formed, covered with lining cells. (Drawing by Richard Waldron.)

the major repository of calcium in the body; however, much remodelling appears to take place in a completely random manner.[25]

Remodelling is achieved by the sequential action of the osteoclast and the osteoblast which together form what is referred to as a bone remodelling unit (BRU) or cutting cone. There are four phases in a remodelling cycle, activation, resorption, reversal and formation (Figure 2.1). Activation involves the recruitment of osteoblast precursors which infiltrate the lining cells and form mature osteoblasts which attach firmly to the naked bone surface. Resorption ends with apoptosis of the osteoclast and pre-osteoblasts are then attracted to the site during the reversal phase by growth factors released by the osteoclast from the bone matrix. These growth factors include TGF-, insulin-like growth factors 1 and 2 (IGF 1 and 2), bone morphogenic proteins

[25] DB Burr, Targeted and non-targeted bone remodelling, *Bone*, 2002, 30, 2–4.

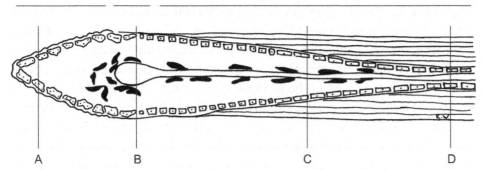

FIGURE 2.2. Diagram of remodelling unit. I represents the cutting cone; II, the reversal zone; and III, the closing cone. At A, the resorption cavity is being formed; at B, it is fully formed; at C, Haversian systems are being formed; and at D, they are fully formed. (Drawing by Richard Waldron.)

(BMP), platelet derived growth factor (PDGF), and fibroblast growth factor (FGF). The osteoblast in turn acts to stimulate or inhibit osteoblast activity through the RANK-L/OPG system. The BRU forms a cylinder within cortical bone (Figure 2.2) but on the trabeculae it lies on the surface and is, in effect, a cortical BRU cut in half. The process, however, is identical in both types of bone.[26] The end result of the remodelling cycle is to form a new, secondary osteon.

The rate of removal and formation of bone is referred to as the bone balance. It is slightly positive on periosteal surfaces, so that with increasing age the circumference of cortical bone increases; this is especially the case with increasing strain on the bone, a fact that is generally referred to as Wolff's Law.[27] On endosteal surfaces there is a net negative balance so that the medullary canal enlarges with age; the loss on the endosteal surface generally exceeds the gain on the periosteal surface so that there is a loss of cortical thickness with age. Similarly, the trabeculae tend to be in negative balance and they also lose substance with increasing age.[28]

BONE PATHOLOGY

Diseases that affect bone perturb the normal remodelling balance and the net effect is that bone is either formed or lost in excess (or sometimes both); that is, bone diseases

[26] AM Parfitt, Osteonal and hemiosteonal remodelling: the spatial and temporal framework for signal traffic in adult bone, *Journal of Cellular Biochemistry*, 1994, 55, 273–276.

[27] HM Frost, A 2003 update on bone physiology and Wolff's Law for clinicians, *Angle Orthodontist*, 2004, 74, 3–15. (Julius Wolff 1836–1902.)

[28] HM Frost, *Intermediary organization of the skeleton*, Boca Raton, CRC Press, 1986.

tend either to be mainly proliferative or erosive. Bone may also be lost when normal bone tissue is replaced by abnormal tissue, such as inflammatory tissue, or tumour tissue. These mechanisms underlie virtually all the changes seen in diseased bone. The role of the periosteum in bone disease is also important.[29] The periosteum is a two-layered structure, the outer layer being composed of fibrous connective tissue while the inner layer contains bone forming cells.[30] It is well supplied with blood vessels and nerve endings and is anchored down to the bone by strong collagenous fibres known as Sharpey's[31] fibres. In addition to covering all external bone surfaces except those covered by articular cartilage, the periosteum is reflected for some distance over the end of tendons that insert into bone at the point known as the enthesis. The periosteum has only one response to any stimulus and this is to form bone and this is a concomitant of many pathological conditions as will be seen in later chapters. It should be noted even at this stage, that there is a great deal of confusion about the nature and cause of periosteal new bone in the minds of many palaeopathologists and I hope that I will be able to clarify this in Chapter 6.

Inflammation plays an important part in several bone diseases and a brief and extremely simplistic description of the process is warranted. It is the response of the body to the introduction of foreign material, infection or trauma and has been recognised for centuries by the classic rubric of rubor, tumor, calor and dolor,[32] that is, redness, swelling, heat and pain. These symptoms will have been familiar to most at some time in their lives.

Inflammation is initiated by the immune system, and the first response is the infiltration into the affected area by white blood cells which phagacytose bacteria and cellular debris, or other foreign material.[33] Cytokines and chemokines are released to regulate the increase of inflammatory cells – neurophils, monocytes and lymphocytes – from dilated blood vessels in affected areas. In acute inflammation, granulocytic white blood cells predominate, whereas in chronic infection monocytes and macrophages are most in evidence. The factors released during inflammation include histamine, prostaglandin, TNF-, IL-1 and antibodies.[34]

---

[29] MR Allen, JM Hock and DB Burr, Periosteum: biology, regulation, and response to osteoporosis therapies, *Bone*, 2004, 35, 1003–1012.

[30] KH Włodarski, Normal and heterotopic periosteum, *Clinical Orthopaedics and Related Research*, 1989, 241, 265–277.

[31] William Sharpey 1802–1880.

[32] This description is generally attributed to the Roman physician Celsus who flourished in the first century AD.

[33] It is important to understand that inflammation is not synonymous with infection, although it is often used this way.

[34] For a much more complete account of inflammation see, for example, I Roitt, J Brostoff and D Male, *Immunology*, 6th edition, St Louis, Mosby, 2002.

Acute inflammation may end in complete resolution; in scarring, especially following trauma; in the formation of an abscess, especially following infection with a pyogenic organism such as *Staphylococcus aureus*; or in chronic inflammation which may persist for years, as may happen with skeletal tuberculosis, for example.

PATHOLOGY, PSEUDOPATHOLOGY AND NORMAL VARIATION[35]

Grossly diseased bone is easy to recognise by anyone with even the most modest knowledge of bony anatomy. Spectacular fractures can be spotted even by the most casual observer and skulls riddled with holes are evidently not normal, although knowing what caused them – what was in the holes – is by no means as simple. Deciding whether it was an excavator's pick, a bullet, syphilis or a tumour may tax the most experienced palaeopathologist from time to time. Indeed, deciding the most probable cause for any lesion found in the skeleton is frequently perplexing and often inconclusive, and the beginner may be frustrated at the apparent inability of those who have been in the field for years immediately (or ever) to come up with a definitive diagnosis for abnormalities presented to them; as in the medical specialties, however, the more you know, the more you know you don't know! It is sensible at the beginning to accept that there will be many lesions that you are unable to diagnose and that there is no disgrace in admitting to this, either when giving a presentation or writing a bone report or publishing a paper. The person to be wary of in most cases is not the most cautious but the most confident. For many of the lesions that one sees, the most that can be done is to provide a good description, a drawing or a photograph, and – if confidence allows – a range of possibilities as to cause (eg, this is most likely an infectious disease, perhaps tuberculosis or brucellosis or some other non-pyogenic infection) or give a generic diagnosis (eg, this is an erosive arthropathy, but no further refinement is possible.

As a general rule, the certainty of a diagnosis is in direct relation to the amount of the skeleton present and its state of preservation. The more complete the skeleton and the better its condition, the more likely it is that lesions can be identified. As we will see, there are some elements of the skeleton that *must* be present for some diseases to be diagnosed, irrespective of how suggestive signs elsewhere may appear.

Sometimes it is not clear when a feature on a bone is pathological or not. A small amount of periosteal new bone may be normal, especially on children's bones, and

---

[35] Those who wish to learn more about general pathology, and about the way in which modern pathologists look at diseases of the bones and joints should consult Ed Friedlander's web site, www.pathguy.com.

deciding when the rubicon of pathology has been crossed may be extremely taxing and is something that will come only when great familiarity with the huge range of normal variety in skeletal form has been achieved. This familiarity is achieved by examining dozens, preferably hundreds, of skeletons. Some areas of the skeleton are especially prone to a variety of form. The carpals and tarsals, and the occipito-axial and lumbro-sacral junctions of the spine are notable examples. There are also a number of other variants to be aware of, the so-called non-metric traits, including the septal aperture in the distal humerus or the sternal aperture[36] which may be confused with pathological holes; the bipartite patella that may be confused with a patellar fracture; or the supra-condylar process on the medial side of the distal humerus, which might imply soft tissue trauma.[37] Although some of these non-metric traits are relatively common, familiarity with large numbers of skeletons will, nevertheless, be necessary to recognise their true nature without mistake.

Another trap into which the tyro may readily fall is to mis-identify those holes that normally appear in bone as manifestations of joint disease, or occasionally, malignant disease. There are many foramina in the base of the skull though which blood vessels and nerves pass, and the ends of the long bones may be perforated by dozens of holes allowing the access of blood vessels to the metabolically active trabeculae and bone marrow beneath the cortex. There may also be small cortical defects, especially on the concave aspects of joints. The proximal surface of the first phalanx of the foot is a common site and is sometimes referred to as pseudo-erosions because they can be confused with true erosions that accompany some forms of joint disease (see Chapter 4).

Pseudo-pathology: Calvin Wells (1908–1978) was active in palaeopathology during the 1950s, 1960s and early 1970s and for much of this period – certainly during the 1950s and 1960s – he was one of only a handful of people working in the field in the United Kingdom. Thus, he accounted for the greater number of citations in the palaeopathological literature. His over-interpretive style has now largely fallen out of fashion, especially among those palaeopathologists who require some

---

[36] The sternal aperture presents a hazard for acupuncturists as an acupuncture point used for treating lung disease lies over the place where the aperture is usually found (in up to 10% of individuals). Inserting a needle through the aperture may well pierce the underlying right ventricle and blood pulsing up around the needle will not be a welcome sight to either patient or operator; deaths have been noted. See: TB Halvorsen, SS Anda, AB Naess and OW Levang, Fatal cardiac tamponade after acupuncture through congenital sternal foramen, *Lancet*, 1995, 1, 1175. I am grateful to Mrs Ann Beavis, herself an acupuncturist, for bringing this hazard to my attention.

[37] The tip of the supracondylar process may be joined to the medial epicondyle by a band of fibrous tissue – the ligament of Struthers – beneath which the brachial artery and the median nerve may pass, and pressure symptoms in the hand may ensue; unfortunately, it is impossible to know whether this was the case in the skeleton. (Sir John Struthers 1823–1899.)

evidence on which to base their judgements, but his concept of pseudo-pathology is extremely useful and long lasting.[38] Pseudo-pathology may be produced by the physico-chemical changes that take place after death, by post-mortem damage, by gnawing from rodents or other animals, or by the pressure of roots forming what seem to be the markings of abnormal blood vessels on the surface of the bone. All must be recognised for what they are and not confused with true pathological changes.

[38] He refers to this in his well-known book, *Bones, bodies and disease* (London, Thames and Hudson, 1964) which gives a very good impression of his general style of palaeopathology.

3

Diseases of Joints, Part 1

There are several different types of joint in the skeleton (Table 3.1). The synovial joints are the most numerous and the only ones commonly affected by disease. Some joints change their appearance with age and these changes are often used by physical anthropologists to help age a skeleton. The pubic symphysis and the auricular surface of the ilium are particularly useful in this regard.

The structure of a typical synovial joint is shown in Figure 3.1. In this type of joint the articulating ends of the bone are held in place by a capsule which is composed externally of a layer of fibrous tissue that varies in thickness partly due to the attachment of ligaments of tendons. The inner layer is composed of the synovial membrane. The capsule is well supplied with blood vessels, lymphatics and nerve endings which may extend down to the synovial membrane.

The articulating ends of the bone are covered with cartilage which varies in thickness from 1–7 mm; it is thicker in larger than in small joints and in joints under considerable stress, such as those of the leg. The cartilage is avascular, has no lymph vessels and is not innervated. The cartilage-forming cells (the chondrocytes) obtain their nutrients by diffusion from fluid within the joint. Articular cartilage provides a moveable surface with an extremely low coefficient of friction, much less than that of two opposing Teflon-coated surfaces.[1] Because it is transparent to X-rays, it does not show up on a radiograph and the apparent displacement between the ends of the bones is referred to by radiologists as the joint space.

The bone immediately beneath the articular cartilage is referred to as the subchondral bone plate and is usually made up of trabeculae that curve around the inferior surface of the cartilage. Immediately above subchondral plate there is a calcified zone of cartilage that is known as the tide mark.

---

[1] The static coefficient of friction of a synovial joint is 0.01 and the kinetic equivalent is 0.003. For comparison, the coefficient of friction of Teflon, both static and kinetic, is 0.04.

Table 3.1. *Types of joints*

Type of joint	Properties	Examples
Suture	Bone joined by connective tissue. Immobile	Skull
Syndesmosis	Fibrous joint where articulating bones are joined by ligaments. Minor degrees of movement permitted by stretching of ligaments	Distal tibiofibular joint
Gomphosis	Special type of fibrous articulation fixing teeth in the jaws	Teeth
Symphysis	Bones joined by fibrocartilaginous or fibrous connective tissue. Very small degree of movement permitted	Symphysis pubis; intervertebral disc; sternomanubrial joint
Synchondrosis	Temporary joints composed of hyaline cartilage existing only during growth phase of the skeleton. Eventually obliterated by bony union	Growth plates; neurocentral joint; spheno-occipital joint
Synovial	Joints containing a synovial membrane. Fully mobile	Large and small joints of the extremities; facet joints of spine; costovertebral and costotransverse joints; sternoclavicular joint

All bone contained within a joint is covered with periosteum except for that covered by articular cartilage. The joint capsule is firmly attached to the periosteum and variable lengths of non-articular bone may be present within the capsule. The synovial membrane covers all structures within the joint except for the cartilage and the non-articular bone. It attaches around the rim of the cartilage, at the so-called joint margin; the region of non-articular bone within a joint is called the bare area.[2]

The synovial membrane is a delicate, highly vascular structure which has two layers: a cellular inner layer – the intima – and an outer, vascular layer, the sub-intima that merges with the fibrous part of the capsule. The intima contains two types of cell, type A, which are like macrophages and probably have a phagocytic function, and type B that secrete hyaluronic acid which helps lubricate the joint. The function of the synovial membrane is to secrete synovial fluid which provides nutrition to

---

[2] Further details of the structure of joints can be found in any standard text book of anatomy.

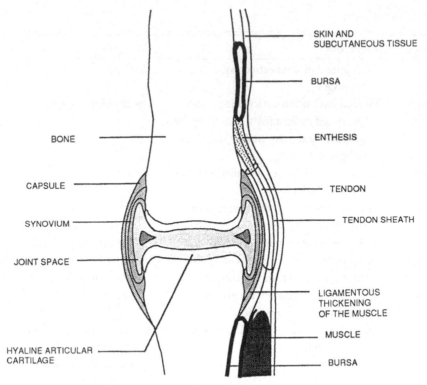

FIGURE 3.1. Diagram of normal synovial joint.

the chondrocytes, lubrication to the joint surfaces and removes micro-organisms or debris arising from the wear and tear of the joint surfaces.[3]

Some synovial joints contain additional structures, including fibro-cartilaginous discs, fat pads or ligaments. The knee joint contains the best known of these intra-articular structures in the form of the menisci and cruciate ligaments whose injury is dreaded by all athletes.[4]

OSTEOARTHRITIS

Osteoarthritis (OA) is the most common condition seen in the skeleton, apart from dental disease. It is a disease of considerable antiquity and affects all animals with

[3] P Barland, AB Novikoff and D Hamerman, Electron microscopy of the human synovial membrane, *Journal of Cell Biology*, 1962, 14, 207–220.
[4] Other joints with intra-articular structures include the temporo-mandibular joint, sterno-clavicular joint, hip, shoulder and the distal radio-ulnar joint.

synovial joints.[5] Osteoarthritis is primarily a disease of the articular cartilage which breaks down as the disease progresses. Three stages in this process can be recognised beginning with an enzymatic breakdown of the cartilage matrix. During this stage, the metabolism of the chondrocytes is affected, leading to the release of enzymes, including metalloenzymes, that further break down the matrix. The chondrocytes also release enzyme inhibitors but in insufficient quantities to counteract the proteolytic effect.

During the second stage, the cartilage starts to fibrillate both horizontally and vertically. The surface of the cartilage becomes eroded, leading to the release of fragments of collagen and proteoglycan (one of the constituents of the matrix) into the joint cavity. These breakdown products initiate the third phase during which an inflammatory response in the synovial membrane leads to the production of inflammatory cytokines including IL-1, TNF- and metalloproteinases which can either diffuse into the matrix or directly destroy it with the release of yet further proteolytic enzymes. The inflammation in the synovial membrane is accompanied by the formation of new blood vessels due to the generation of vascular endothelial growth factor (VEGF) by the synovium.[6] The bone within the joint responds by producing bone in an attempt to affect repair.[7] The changes that subsequently take place in the articulating bones are well understood and include:

1. the formation of new bone around the margins of the joint, so-called marginal osteophyte;
2. the formation of new bone on the joint surface due to the vascularisation of the subchondral bone;
3. pitting on the joint surface manifested as a series of holes on the joint surface, some of which may communicate with sub-chondral cysts;
4. changes in the normal contour of the joint, often widening and flattening of the contour; and
5. the production of eburnation, a highly polished area on the joint surface, usually sharply demarcated from the non-eburnated surface. The eburnated surface is

[5] The appearances in arthritic joints in animals are precisely the same as in humans; see *Jubb, Kennedy and Palmer's Pathology of Domestic Animals, 5th edition* (edited by M Grant Maxie), Philadelphia, WB Saunders, 2007, volume 1.

[6] L. Haywood, DF McWilliams, CI Pearson, SE Gill, A Ganesan, D Wilson and DA Walsh, Inflammation and angiogenesis in osteoarthritis, *Arthritis and Rheumatism*, 2003, 48, 2173–2177.

[7] Since the changes seen in OA represent an attempt at repair, it is preferable not to refer to it as a degenerative condition, although this is still very commonly done, and is almost universally the case in the older (and not so old) clinical and palaeopathological literature.

sometimes scored or grooved in the direction of movement of the joint, presumably due to the presence of debris, or perhaps crystals, between the two articulating surfaces.[8]

Eburnation is the most important of these changes to the palaeopathologist. It develops in areas of the joint where the articular cartilage has been completely lost and bare bone rubs on bare bone to produce a surface as shiny as a billiard ball. Eburnation can be taken as pathognomonic of osteoarthritis because although it may occur in some other joint diseases, there is no difficulty in differentiating them from OA and confusion should not arise.

PRECIPITANTS OF OSTEOARTHRITIS

The cause of OA is not known with any certainty but a number of factors are known to be important precipitants. These factors include age, genetics, sex, race, obesity and trauma and, most importantly, movement. Movement is a *sine qua non* for the production of OA; joints that do not move, do not develop OA. Age is important, and both incidence and prevalence increase with increasing age, such that, in extreme old age, there is scarcely anyone left with a completely normal set of joints. A genetic predisposition has also been demonstrated from studies with heterozygous twins which have shown that this can account for a considerable amount of the variance seen in the development of OA; up to 65% for OA of the knee, 60% for OA of the hip and 70% for OA of the spine.[9] Genes that may be implicated in conferring susceptibility have been found on several chromosomes including the X chromosome.[10] There are racial differences in both the prevalence and outcome of OA,[11] while the disease is slightly more common in females, especially elderly females, than in males.[12] Obesity has been found to be highly correlated with OA of

[8] Crystals containing calcium, such as calcium pyrophosphate or apatite, are commonly found within arthritic joints but whether they are the cause or the effect of the disease is unclear; there is ample evidence to support both points of view (see AK Rosenthal, Calcium crystal deposition and osteoarthritis, *Rheumatic Diseases Clinics of North America*, 2006, 32, 401–412).

[9] TD Spector and AJ MacGregor, Risk factors for osteoarthritis: genetics, *Osteoarthritis and Cartilage*, 2004, 12 Supplement A, S39–44.

[10] J Loughlin, Genetic epidemiology of primary osteoarthritis, *Current Opinion in Rheumatology*, 2001, 13, 111–116.

[11] KL Dominick and TA Baker, Racial and ethnic differences in osteoarthritis: prevalence, outcomes and medical care, *Ethnicity and Disease*, 2004, 14, 558–566.

[12] There is a suggestion that OA may be an atheromatous disease of subchondral bone, and that even if vascular changes do not initiate the disease, they may, nevertheless, accelerate its progress (PG Conaghan, H Vanharanta and P Dieppe, Is progressive osteoarthritis an atheromatous vascular disease? *Annals of the*

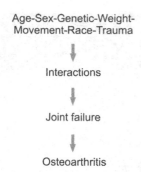

Age-Sex-Genetic-Weight-
Movement-Race-Trauma

↓

Interactions

↓

Joint failure

↓

Osteoarthritis

FIGURE 3.2. Model of aetiology of osteoarthritis. Various precipitating factors are shown, any number of which may interact to produce joint failure, the end result of which is the combination of pathological signs that is referred to as osteoarthritis.

the knee,[13] less strongly with OA of the hand, and weakly, if at all, with OA of the hip, suggesting that mechanical factors may not be entirely to blame, but that systemic factors may also play a role.[14]

One or more of these precipitants, and most likely other factors presently unknown, will initiate or interact to initiate the chain of events that leads to joint failure, and produce the morphological appearances that are referred to as OA (Figure 3.2). When there is no obvious direct cause, the disease is referred to as primary OA. There is no means of knowing from the appearance of the joint which of the precipitants was the proximate cause. Indeed, given that it is most likely to be multifactorial in origin, this should come as no surprise, and attempts that are sometimes made to attribute an occupation to a skeleton on the basis of the presence and distribution of OA are – of course – futile and doomed to failure.

Rheumatic Diseases, 2005, 64, 1539–1541). There is a further hypothesis that an intact neural pathway may also be necessary for the production of OA (TJ Tait and HA Bird, Asymmetrical osteoarthritis in a patient with Ehlers-Danlos syndrome and poliomyelitis, *Clinical and Experimental Rheumatology*, 1994, 12, 425–427). Alexander calls for a complete change in the standard paradigm that sees the disease as essentially catabolic, preferring instead to consider idiopathic OA as an entity separate from secondary OA, and resulting from synovial stasis, in essence resurrecting an old idea put forward over fifty years ago by Harrison and his colleagues (CJ Alexander, Idiopathic osteoarthritis: time to change paradigms? *Skeletal Radiology*, 2004, 33, 321–324; MHM Harrison, F Schajowicz and JT Trueta, Osteoarthritis of the hip: a study of the nature and evolution of the disease, *Journal of Bone and Joint Surgery*, 1953, 35B, 598–626).

[13] Obesity also speeds up the progression of the disease.

[14] DT Felson, Epidemiology of hip and knee osteoarthritis, *Epidemiologic Reviews*, 1988, 10, 1–28; DT Felson and CE Chaisson, Understanding the relationship between body weight and osteoarthritis, *Bailliere's Clinical Rheumatology Clinical Rheumatology*, 1997, 11, 671–681; T Strümer, K-P Günther and H Brenner, Obesity, overweight and patterns of osteoarthritis: the Ulm osteoarthritis study, *Journal of Clinical Epidemiology*, 2000, 53, 307–313; CB Eaton, Obesity as a risk factor for osteoarthritis: mechanical versus metabolic, *Medicine and Health, Rhode Island*, 2004, 87, 201–204; SC Wearing, EM Hennig, NM Byrne, JR Steele and AP Hills, Musculoskeletal disorders associated with obesity: a biomechanical perspective, *Obesity Reviews*, 2006, 7, 239–250.

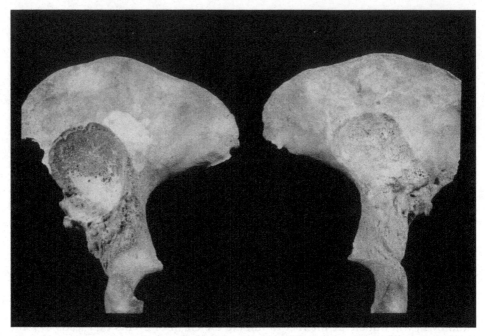

FIGURE 3.3. Secondary osteoarthritis of the hip. The heads of both femurs have been displaced from the acetabulum and false joints (pseudoarthroses) have formed on the iliac crest with the production of new bone and eburnation. The fact that eburnation is present shows that there was movement at the false joint and the individual was probably able to get around reasonably well.

Where a cause for OA *is* evident, this is referred to as secondary OA (Figure 3.3). This may occur in the context of other joint diseases such as rheumatoid arthritis, or following trauma. If a fracture extends into a joint it is almost certain that OA will eventually supervene unless the normal anatomy of the joint can be restored, usually by surgery. Similarly if a long bone fracture is not reduced, the resultant deformity may alter the mechanics of the joint above or below the fracture, again leading to the development of OA several years later.

THE NATURAL HISTORY OF OSTEOARTHRITIS

Osteoarthritis may affect a single joint (monoarticular) or many joints (polyartic-ular) and there may be a great production of new bone (hypertrophic), or very little (atrophic). OA of the hip in elderly females is commonly of the atrophic form, whereas hypertrophic OA is common in the so-called bone formers, and in individuals with DISH (see Chapter 5). Rarely the changes seen in a joint with OA may reverse,[15] but in the great majority of cases they are irreversible and often progressive. Osteoarthritis does not necessarily produce significant symptoms and there may be little correlation between the morphological appearances of a joint and the symptoms experienced by a particular patient.[16] Palaeopathologists should resist the temptation to make clinical inferences from the changes seen in a joint, not only because of the weak relationship between these changes and symptoms, but also because they have no prospect of being able to validate their conclusions.

Osteoarthritis is uncommon under the age of about forty[17] but the incidence and prevalence increases considerably thereafter. Osteoarthritis should never be used as an ageing criterion for the skeleton, however, as there are no other means to calculate age-specific prevalences which are necessary when comparing frequency between studies (see Chapter 13).

In modern clinical practice, OA is said to occur most commonly in the knee, hip and hands (Figures 3.4 and 3.5). There is also a form that particularly affects older women known as generalised osteoarthritis. Although there is no general agreement as to its precise definition, the Ulm criteria require OA of the thumb base and either the proximal or distal inter-phalangeal joints be present.[18] Other definitions also require OA of one large joint – the hip or the knee – to be affected.[19] Generalised OA is uncommon in skeletal assemblages, and the disease is most commonly found in the acromio-clavicular joint (ACJ), the facet joints of the spine, and the hands. The difference between skeletal appearances and clinical experience may be because OA of the knee – and especially of the medial compartment – and of the hip and

---

[15] JH Bland, The reversibility of osteoarthritis: a review, *American Journal of Medicine*, 1983, 14, 16–26.

[16] See, for example, O Bruyere, A Honore, LC Rovati, G Giacovelli, YE Henrotin, L Seidel and J-YL Reginster, Radiologic features poorly predict clinical outcomes in knee osteoarthritis, *Scandinavian Journal of Rheumatology*, 2002, 31, 13–16 and S Dahaghin, SMA Bierma-Zeinstra, AZ Ginai, HAP Polis, JMW Hazes and BW Koes, Prevalence and pattern of radiographic hand osteoarthritis and association with pain and disability (the Rotterdam study, *Annals of the Rheumatic Diseases*, 2005, 64, 682–687). Likewise, there is often little or no relationship between radiographic appearances and the signs or symptoms in a particular patient (I Watt, Bone disorders: a radiological approach, *Balliere's Clinical Rheumatology*, 2000, 14, 173–199).

[17] An exception to this occurs in Kashin-Beck disease, a form of endemic osteoarthritis found in areas of the world with a deficiency of selenium in the diet including Siberia, parts of China, Korea and Tibet. In this condition, children as young as four or five may be affected (WH Zhang, J Neve, JP Xu, J Vanderpass and ZL Wand, Selenium, iodine and fungal contamination in Yulin District (People's Republic of China) endemic for Kashin-Beck disease, *International Orthopaedics*, 2001, 25, 188–190).

[18] KP Günther, T Stürmer, I Zeissig, Y Sun, S Kessler, HP Scharf, H Brenner and W Puhl, Prevalence of generalised osteoarthritis in patients with advanced hip and knee arthritis, *Annals of the Rheumatic Diseases*, 1998, 57, 717–723.

[19] E Vignon, Hand osteoarthritis and generalized osteoarthritis: a need for clarification, *Osteoarthritis and Cartilage*, 2000, Supplement A, S22–24.

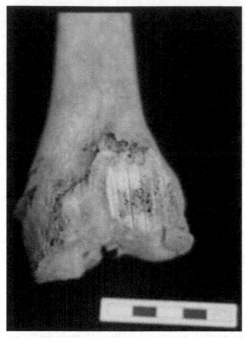

FIGURE 3.4. Osteoarthritis of the patello-femoral compartment of the knee showing marginal osteophyte, eburnation and pitting on the joint surface. Scoring in the direction of movement of the joint is clearly seen on the eburnated area.

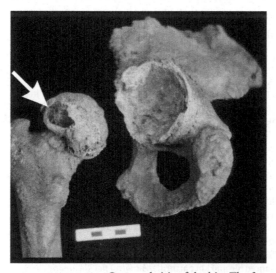

FIGURE 3.5. Osteoarthritis of the hip. The femoral head shows relatively little change, but the acetabulum is widened with a large collar of marginal osteophyte and new bone on the joint surface. The femoral head has a large area of postmortem damage (arrowed).

thumb base tend to be painful and often disabling, and so disease in these joints tends to cause patients to seek treatment. OA of the ACJ and the facet joints are often less painful and most often found as concomitants of other conditions such as rotator cuff disease or intervertebral disc disease (qv).

Not all the synovial joints are equally prone to develop OA. Thus, the ankle and elbow joints are rarely affected and when the elbow is affected, it is invariably only in the radio-humeral compartment. The predilection for the disease to affect the radial side of the hand preferentially is striking and the reason obscure, although Hutton's ingenious suggestion that it may be due to impact loading on joints that have come into use late in evolutionary development is persuasive.[20]

DIAGNOSIS OF OSTEOARTHRITIS

Clinicians make the diagnosis of OA largely on the basis of pain and swelling in the affected joint. In addition, many patients complain of short-lasting stiffness but this is of minor importance compared with the pain that is experienced. If the capsule of the joint is thickened this may be felt when palpating the joint and if an arthritic joint is moved, a sense of crackling, known as crepitus, can be felt in the overlying hand. Radiologists rely on joint space narrowing, (indicating that the articular cartilage is thinning), the presence of marginal osteophytes and sclerosis[21] when they make the diagnosis.

Of these clinical and radiological criteria, only the presence of marginal osteophytes and eburnation (sclerosis) are available to the palaeopathologist and an operational definition should be adopted as shown in the "Operational definition for osteoarthritis" box. Osteoarthritis can be said to be present if eburnation can be demonstrated, or as least two of the following exist: marginal osteophyte, new bone on the joint surface, pitting on the joint surface or an alteration in the joint contour. The condition should *not* be diagnosed in the presence of only *one* of the minor criteria. Relying on the presence of marginal osteophyte to make the diagnosis, as is sometimes done, is particularly to be avoided as it can occur as an independent age-related phenomenon, or as a concomitant of other diseases. In practice there is very little to be said against relying solely on the presence of eburnation since this should at least ensure comparability between observers.

---

[20] CW Hutton, Generalised osteoarthritis: an evolutionary problem, *The Lancet*, 1987, 1, 1463–1465.
[21] Sclerosis in a radiological context refers to a line or area of increased radio-density. In a joint with OA, sclerosis is produced by sub-chondral bone thickening and is equivalent to eburnation.

Operational definition for osteoarthritis

Presence of eburnation,

OR

at least *two* of the following:

marginal osteophyte
new bone on the joint surface
pitting on the joint surface
alteration in joint contour

Although eburnation in large joints is often immediately obvious even to a casual observer, it is not always so clear in small joints, such as the proximal or distal interphalangeal joints (pips or dips). The joint surfaces should always be examined under a strong light and they must be clean. If the joint surface is moved around under a lamp, light will be seen to be reflected off the shiny eburnated surface. It is often useful to 'polish' the surface with your thumb as this may highlight the eburnated area.

OSTEOARTHRITIS AT INDIVIDUAL SITES

Temporo-mandibular joint: The temporo-mandibular joint is notable for the presence of a disc that separates the head of the mandible from the mandibular fossa and temporal eminence, and divides the joint into superior and inferior parts. The superior part is between the temporal bone and the disc, and the inferior, between the disc and the mandibular condyle; both are synovial. Osteoarthritis most often develops in response to internal derangement of the disc.[22] It is common[23] and the changes are the same as in other joints but it may be erosive[24] although ankylosis rarely follows. It seems to occur frequently in cultures

---

[22] G Dimitroulis, The prevalence of osteoarthritis in cases of advanced internal derangement of the temporo-mandibular joint: a clinical, surgical and histological study, *International Journal of Oral and Faciomaxillary Surgery*, 2005, 34, 345–349.

[23] E Engel, S Lachmann and D. Axmann-Kremar, The prevalence of radiologic TMJ findings and self-reported pain in a patient group wearing implant dentures, *International Journal of Prosthodontics*, 2001, 14, 120–126.

[24] L Flygare, M Rohlin and S Akerman, Microscopy and tomography of erosive changes in the temporo-mandibular joint. An autopsy study, *Acta Odontologica Scandinavica*, 1995, 53, 297–303.

that use their teeth as tools,[25] and has also been found to be related to excessive tooth wear.[26]

Acromio-clavicular joint (ACJ): OA of the acromio-clavicular joint (ACJ) is often found as part of the rotator cuff disease complex (qv), but it also occurs commonly as a separate entity[27] and may be an overlooked cause of shoulder pain.[28] ACJ is also one of the joints that may be affected in patients with chronic kidney disease.[29] Disease of this joint is almost universal in the elderly and is one of those found to be most commonly affected in the skeleton.

Sterno-clavicular joint: The sterno-clavicular joint is also separated into two by a fibrocartilaginous disc, which attaches to the medial end of the clavicle and inferiorly to the first costal cartilage. The joint is not commonly affected by OA and when it is, the changes are generally not as marked as in the ACJ and they are generally more noticeable on the clavicular side of the joint.[30] Men are affected more commonly than women.[31]

Spine: The facet joints of the spine are very commonly the seat of OA. It particularly affects the cervical and lumbar regions,[32] although the lower thoracic region is also affected in females.[33] This pattern does not seem to have changed over time.[34] Osteoarthritis of the lumbar spine is often associated with pain[35] but

[25] RA Roberts-Thompson and PJ Roberts-Thompson, Rheumatic disease and the Australian aborigine, *Annals of the Rheumatic Diseases*, 1999, 58, 266–270.

[26] CJ Griffin, R Powers and R Krszynski, The incidence of osteo-arthritis of the temporomandibular joint in various cultures, *Australian Dental Journal*, 1979, 24, 94–106; DC Hodges, Temporomandibular joint osteoarthritis in a British skeletal population, *American Journal of Physical Anthropology*, 1991, 85, 367–377. Note that in the first reference, the authors are calculating prevalence, not incidence as suggested in the title. This is a mistake that is commonly made in both the clinical and palaeopathological literature (see Chapter 13).

[27] R Peetrons, OS Rasmussen, V Creteur and RK Chem, Ultrasound of the shoulder joint: non "rotator cuff" lesions, *European Journal of Ultrasound*, 2001, 14, 11–19; C Martinoli, S Biachi, N Prato, MP Zamarani, M Vell and LE Derchi, US of the shoulder: non rotator-cuff disorders, *Radiographics*, 1993, 23, 381–401.

[28] CJ Buttaci, TP Stitik, PP Yonclas and PM Foye, Osteoarthritis of the acromio-clavicular joints. A review of the anatomy, biomechanics, diagnosis, and treatment, *American Journal of Physical Medicine and Rehabilitation*, 2004, 83, 791–797.

[29] C Shih, KH Chen, CY Chang, JF Jim and T Chang, Articular manifestations of renal osteodystrophy, *Zhonghua Yi Xue Za Zhi*, 1993, 52, 373–377.

[30] M Silberberg, EL Frank, S Jarrett and R Silberberg, Aging and osteoarthritis of the human sterno-clavicular joint, *American Journal of Pathology*, 1959, 35, 851–865.

[31] JS Noble, Degenerative sterno-clavicular arthritis and hyperostosis, *Clinics in Sports Medicine*, 2003, 22, 407–422.

[32] A Prescher, Anatomy and pathology of the aging spine, *European Journal of Radiology*, 1998, 27, 181–195.

[33] PA Kramer, Prevalence and distribution of spinal osteoarthritis in women, *Spine*, 2006, 15, 2843–2848.

[34] HA Waldron, Prevalence and distribution of osteoarthritis in a population from Georgian and early Victorian London, *Annals of the Rheumatic Diseases*, 1991, 50, 301–307.

[35] D Borenstein, Does osteoarthritis of the lumbar spine cause chronic low back pain? *Current Rheumatology Reports*, 2004, 6, 14–19.

it is unclear whether this is also always the case when the disease affects the cervical region.[36] The costo-transverse joints may also become arthritic with the typical changes seen elsewhere[37] but these joints seem very seldom to come to the attention of the palaeopathologist and this is certainly an area that merits further attention.

Shoulder: Osteoarthritis of the gleno-humeral joint is uncommon in the absence of local trauma, and when it does occur, women are more often affected than men.[38] When it is found in the skeleton, the eburnation is found on the surface that articulates directly with the glenoid. Eburnation on the superior pole of the humeral head is a complication of rotator cuff disease (qv). A rim of osteophyte around the head of the humerus and around the attachment of the labrum to the glenoid is an almost invariable accompaniment of gleno-humeral OA. There is an uncommon form of OA of the shoulder which is atrophic and rapidly destructive;[39] the destruction may involve not only the glenohumeral joint, but the ACJ, and the head and neck of the humerus.[40] It mainly affects elderly women and is accompanied *inter alia* by the presence of basic calcium phosphate (BCP) crystals in the joint, but whether the presence of the crystals is related to the aetiology of the condition is unclear.[41]

Elbow: In the absence of trauma, OA of the elbow is very rare although it has been found more frequently in some occupational groups[42] and a high prevalence has been found in some skeletal assemblages[43] When it does occur, the changes are invariably confined to the radio-ulnar joint and the right arm is more often affected than the left.[44]

Wrist and carpal bones: The wrist joint, that is the joint between the distal radius and the lunate and scaphoid is commonly affected by OA[45] while in the carpus, the general rule is observed, that is, that the joints on the radial side of the hand

---

[36] C Peterson, J Bolton, AR Wood and BK Humphrey, A cross-sectional study correlating degeneration of the cervical spine with disability and pain in United Kingdom patients, *Spine*, 2003, 28, 129–133.

[37] D Resnick, Degenerative diseases of the vertebral column, *Radiology*, 1985, 156, 3–14.

[38] Y Nakagawa, K Hyakuna, S Otani, M Hashitani and T Nakamura, Epidemiological study of glenohumeral osteoarthritis with plain radiography, *Journal of Shoulder and Elbow Surgery*, 1999, 8, 580–584.

[39] VD Nguyen, Rapid destructive arthritis of the shoulder, *Skeletal Radiology*, 1996, 25, 107–112.

[40] GV Campion, F McCrae, W Alwan, I Watt, J Bradfield and PA Dieppe, Idiopathic destructive arthritis of the shoulder, *Seminars in Arthritis and Rheumatism*, 1988, 17, 232–245.

[41] AK Rosenthal, Update in calcium deposition diseases, *Current Opinion in Rheumatology*, 2007, 19, 158–162.

[42] DT Felson, Do occupation-related physical factors contribute to osteoarthritis? *Baillière's Clinical Rheumatology*, 1994, 8, 63–77.

[43] L Debon, B Mafart, E Jeusel and G Guipert, Is the incidence of elbow osteoarthritis underestimated? Insights from paleopathology, *Joint Bone Spine*, 2004, 71, 397–400.

[44] M Doherty and B Preston, Primary osteoarthritis of the elbow, *Annals of the Rheumatic Diseases*, 1989, 48, 743–747.

[45] AP Weiss, Osteoarthritis of the wrist, *Instructional Course Lectures*, 2004, 53, 31–40.

are more often affected than those on the ulnar side;[46] the trapezium is often described as being at the centre of osteoarthritic change in the carpus.

Hand: The thumb base is an extremely common site for OA in the hand, and so are the distal and proximal interphalangeal joints (dips) and (pips).[47] The swellings that accompany OA of the dips are referred to as Heberden's nodes, while those on the pips are known as Bouchard's nodes.[48] When the metacarpophalangeal (MCP) joints are affected, the first three bear the main brunt of the disease. The disease may be secondary to trauma.[49] There appear to have been some changes over time in the number of joints involved in the hand. Prior to 1500 the disease was most likely to affect only a single joint, or set of joints, whereas there was an increasing tendency for more than one joint to be affected after that date.[50]

Knee: The knee is a compound joint with three compartments, the patellofemoral, and the medial and lateral tibiofemoral. The patellofemoral joint is most commonly affected, followed by the lateral and medial tibiofemoral joints in that order. Females are more likely to be affected than males[51] and OA of the knee is very strongly correlated with obesity.[52] Patients are more likely to complain of pain and loss of function if more than one compartment is affected[53] and this joint may be one in which clinical symptoms correlate more closely with radiographic change than is usually the case.[54]

[46] GD Brown, MS Roh, RJ Strauch, MP Rosenwasser, GA Ateshian and VC Mow, Radiography and visual pathology of the osteoarthritic scaphotrapezio-trapezoidal joint, and its relationship to trapeziometacarpal osteoarthritis, *Journal of Hand Surgery,* 2003, 28A, 739–743.

[47] JU Poole, VD Pellegrini, Arthritis of the thumb basal joint complex, *Journal of Hand Therapy,* 2000, 13, 91–107; S Kessley, J Stove, W Puhl and T Sturmer, First carpometacarpal and interphalangeal osteoarthritis of the hands in patients with advanced hip or knee OA. Are there differences in the aetiology? *Clinical Rheumatology,* 2003, 22, 409–413.

[48] William Heberden 1710–1801; Charles-Joseph Bouchard 1837–1915.

[49] P Feldon and MR Belsky, Degenerative diseases of the metacarpophalangeal joints, *Hand Clinics,* 1987, 3, 429–447. Osteoarthritis of the second and third mcpjs may occur as a complication of haemochromatosis, a disorder of iron metabolism (MR Schumacher, Haemochromatosis, *Baillière's Best Practice & Research. Clinical Rheumatology,* 2000, 14, 277–284).

[50] T Waldron, Changes in the distribution of osteoarthritis over historical time, *International Journal of Osteoarchaeology,* 1995, 5, 383–389.

[51] MI O'Connor, Osteoarthritis of the hip and knee: sex and gender differences, *Orthopedic Clinical of North America,* 2006, 37, 559–568.

[52] D Coggon, I Reading, P Croft, M McLaren, D Barrett and C Cooper, Knee osteoarthritis and obesity, *International Journal of Obesity and Related Metabolic Disorders,* 2001, 25, 622–627.

[53] B Szebenyi, AP Hollander, P Dieppe, B Quilty, J Duddy, S Clarke and J Kirwan, Association between pain, function and radiographic features in osteoarthritis of the knee, *Arthritis and Rheumatism,* 2006, 54, 230–235.

[54] R Duncan, G Peat, E Thomas, E Hay, I McCall and P Croft, Symptoms and radiographic osteoarthritis: not as discordant as they are made out to be? *Annals of the Rheumatic Diseases,* 2007, 66, 86–91.

Hip: Osteoarthritis of the hip is more common in females than in males but there is only a weak association with obesity, suggesting that stress on this joint may not be a major component in the aetiology.[55] Various patterns of involvement can be recognised; eburnation is most common on the superior pole, somewhat less common on the medial pole,[56] and very uncommon on the axial pole.[57] Eburnation of the superior pole (sometimes also called proximal arthropathy) is usually unilateral whereas eburnation of the axial pole is usually bilateral. Various other conditions are well known to predispose to the development of OA of the hips including congenital hip dislocation, slipped capital femoral epiphysis and Legg-Calvé-Perthes disease.[58] Acetabular dysplasia has been considered of aetiological importance; however, more recent studies suggest that this may not be the case.[59] Other findings that may be associated with OA of the hip include acetabular protrusion[60] and increased or decreased anteversion of the femur.[61] In addition to new bone being found on the femoral head, it may also be found around the rim of the fovea.[62]

Ankle: In the absence of trauma, OA of the ankle is extremely uncommon, although it is subjected to more weight-bearing force per square centimetre than any other joint in the body. Osteoarthritis of the ankle is approximately nine times less frequent than OA of the hip or knee.[63] Various explanations have been put forward for this difference, including differences in joint movement, thickness of the articular cartilage and some evolutionary changes.[64]

Foot: OA in the foot is almost exclusively limited to the first toe, affecting either the first tarsometarsal joint[65] or the first metarsophalangeal joint where it might

[55] AM Lievense, SM Bierma-Zeinstra, AP Verhagen, ME van Baar, JA Verhaar and BW Koes, Influence of obesity on the development of osteoarthritis of the hip: a systematic review, *Rheumatology*, 2002, 41, 1155–1162.

[56] HU Cameron and I McNab, Observations on osteoarthritis of the hip joint, *Clinical Orthopaedics and Related Research*, 1975, 108, 31–40.

[57] D Resnick, Patterns of migration of the femoral head in osteoarthritis of the hip, *American Journal of Roentgenology, Radium Therapy and Nuclear Medicine*, 1975, 124, 62–74.

[58] Arthur Thornton Legg 1874–1939; Jacques Calvé 1875–1954; Georg Clement Perthes 1869–1927.

[59] NE Lane, MC Nevitt, C cooper, A Pressman, R Gore and M Hochberg, Acetabular dysplasia and osteoarthritis of the hip in elderly white women, *Annals of the Rheumatic Diseases*, 1997, 56, 627–630.

[60] This refers to an internal displacement of the medial wall of the acetabulum into the pelvis.

[61] D Tönnnis and A Heinecke, Acetabular and femoral anteversion: relationship with osteoarthritis of the hip, *Journal of Bone and Joint Surgery*, 1999, 81A, 1747–1770.

[62] This is the site of attachment of the ligament of the head of the femur (ligamentum teres) which attaches distally to both sides of the acetabular notch, blending with the transverse ligament. New bone around the fovea is by no means only found with OA of the hip. It may be found in an otherwise apparently normal hip and presumably reflects either repeated micro-trauma to, or inflammation of the ligamentum teres.

[63] RH Thomas and TR Daniels, Ankle arthritis, *Journal of Bone and Joint Surgery*, 2003, 85A, 923–936.

[64] K Huch, KE Kuettner and P Dieppe, Osteoarthritis in ankle and knee joints, *Seminars in Arthritis and Rheumatism*, 1997, 26, 667–674.

[65] KD Brandt, Osteoarthritis, *Clinical Geriatric Medicine*, 1988, 4, 279–293.

give rise to hallux rigidus.[66] In the joints of the tarsus, OA usually only follows trauma and may be common in some occupational groups who put excessive stress on their feet, such as ballet dancers.[67]

THE ASSOCIATION BETWEEN OSTEOARTHRITIS AND OTHER CONDITIONS

Osteoarthritis is the most common of the joint diseases and so it is not surprising that it is sometimes found in association with other conditions that affect the joints. Many of these associations are obviously coincidental but there are at least two conditions where it seems more than this, Paget's disease of bone and osteoporosis.

Paget's disease of bone: Paget's disease (PDB) is considered in its own right in chapter 7; suffice it to say here that it is a disease of the elderly in which there is an increased production of abnormal, disorganised bone. There is plenty of evidence to suggest that osteoarthritis may be a complication of PDB[68] and that it may actually accelerate its progress.[69] The presence of OA may be the main reason that patients with PDB complain of pain. There are a number of reasons that PDB might induce OA, including bone enlargement, softening of the subchondral bone or alteration of normal joint dynamics.[70] This association does not seem to have been examined in skeletal assemblages, probably because PDB is not very common and may be difficult to recognise or diagnose in the skeleton.

Osteoporosis: Clinical studies have shown that there is a direct relationship between OA and bone density; that is, patients with OA tend to have a higher bone density than those without.[71] Although this association has been known for many years, the reasons for it are still poorly understood[72] but may have some relationship to the release of cytokines (especially TNF-β) into arthritic joints.[73] When the association between directly measured bone density and

[66] D Karasick and KL Wapner, Hallux rigidus deformity: radiologic assessment, *American Journal of Roentgenology*, 1991, 157, 1029–1033.

[67] CN van Dijk, LS Lim, A Poortman, EH Strubbe and RK Marti, Degenerative joint disease in female ballet dancers, *American Journal of Sports Medicine*, 1995, 23, 295–300.

[68] RW Whitehouse, Paget's disease of bone, *Seminars in Musculoskeletal Radiology*, 2002, 6, 313–322.

[69] PS Helliwell, Osteoarthritis and Paget's disease, *British Journal of Rheumatology*, 1995, 34, 1061–1063.

[70] RD Altman, Paget's disease of bone: rheumatologic complications, *Bone*, 1999, 24 (Supplement), 47S–48S.

[71] J Dequiker, S Boonen, J Aerssens and R Westhovens, Inverse relationship osteoarthritis-osteoporosis: what is the evidence? What are the consequences? *British Journal of Rheumatology*, 1996, 35, 813–820.

[72] J Dequeker, J Aerssens and FP Luyten, Osteoarthritis and osteoporosis: clinical and research evidence of inverse relationship, *Aging Clinical and Experimental Research*, 2003, 15, 426–439.

[73] NE Lane and MC Nevitt, Osteoarthritis, bone mass, and fractures: how are they related? *Arthritis and Rheumatism*, 2002, 46, 1–4.

osteoarthritis was examined in a skeletal assemblage from London, it was found that there was no relationship in males but that in females, bone density was *lower* in those with OA than in those without.[74] The reason these results differ from those in the contemporary population are not known but may have something to do with differences in nutritional status; this is clearly something that would warrant further investigation.

ROTATOR CUFF DISEASE AND INTERVERTEBRAL DISC DISEASE

It is convenient to consider rotator cuff disease and intervertebral disc disease here since in the case of the first, osteoarthritic change is part of the total picture, and in the second, some of the minor changes found in OA are present.

> *Rotator cuff disease (RCD):* The shoulder joint is an extremely complex joint which allows for a very great range of movement,[75] but on this account, it sacrifices stability. The gleno-humeral joint is very shallow but its depth is increased somewhat by the presence of a fibrous labrum that attaches to the rim of the glenoid. It is also stabilised to some extent by the tendons of four muscles that arise from the scapula and insert into the lesser and greater tuberosities of the humerus, forming part of the joint capsule. These muscles are (from anterior to posterior in the order in which they insert into the humerus) subscapularis, supraspinatus, infraspinatus and teres minor. The long head of biceps takes its origin from the labrum and runs through the joint and in the bicipital groove[76] on the front of the humerus, filling the gap between the subscapularis and the supraspinatus tendons. The four muscles act as rotators of the humerus and the combined tendinous structure around the shoulder joint is referred to as the rotator cuff.

Rotator cuff disease (RCD) is extremely common and is a frequent cause of shoulder pain,[77] especially in the elderly. RCD seems to be a true degenerative disease,[78] the

---

[74] M Brickley and T Waldron, Relationship between bone density and osteoarthritis in a skeletal population from London, *Bone*, 1998, 22, 279–283.

[75] CA Petersilge, DH Witte, BO Sewell, E Bosch and D Resnick, Normal regional anatomy of the shoulder, *Magnetic Resonance and Imaging Clinics of North America*, 1997, 5, 667–681.

[76] RO Cone, L Danzig, D Resnick and AB Goldman, The bicipital groove: radiographic, anatomic, and pathologic study, *American Journal of Roentgenology*, 1983, 141, 781–788.

[77] G Tytherleigh-Strong, A Kirahara and A Miniaci, Rotator cuff disease, *Current Opinion in Rheumatology*, 2001, 13, 135–145.

[78] T Hashimoto, K Nobuhara and T Hamada, Pathologic evidence of degeneration as a primary cause of rotator cuff disease, *Clinical Orthopedics*, 2003, 415, 111–120; JD Rees, AM Wilson and RL Wolman, Current concepts in the management of tendon disorders, *Rheumatology*, 2006, 45, 508–521.

Table 3.2. *Causes of rotator cuff disease*

Extrinsic factors	Intrinsic factors
Traumatic tear in tendons from a fall or other accident	Poor blood supply
	Normal attrition and degeneration with ageing
Over-use injuries from repetitive lifting, pushing, pulling or throwing	Calcification of tendons

Note that RCD is often due to a combination of extrinsic and intrinsic factors.

prevalence of which increases markedly with age and there are a number of intrinsic and extrinsic causes (see Table 3.2). RCD is associated with over-use, such as occurs in some occupational groups,[79] and it may be a complication of os acromiale (qv).[80]

All the elements around the shoulder may be involved in RCD and changes may be found on the acromion, the coracoid process,[81] the ACJ[82] and the bicipital groove.[83] As the disease progresses, a tear may develop in the subscapularis tendon and the action of the deltoid muscle may then cause the head of the humerus to become displaced upwards to impinge on the undersurface of the acromion. Tears in subscapularis have been associated with variations in the morphology of the acromion. One variety in particular, the so-called 'keeled' acromion, in which there is a central, downward-facing spur on the undersurface of the acromion has been said to place patients at risk of a tear.[84] This is something that could easily be investigated in the skeleton since RCD is common and the acromion often survives well.[85]

RCD is easily recognised in the skeleton and the changes seem to conform precisely to those found in contemporary populations. The changes are seen in the insertions of the rotator cuff muscles. These changes include pitting, alteration in normal contour and the presence of enthesophytes. Moreover it is easy to tell which of the

---

[79] M Hagberg and DH Wegman, Prevalence rates and odds ratios of shoulder-neck disease in different occupational groups, *British Journal of Industrial Medicine*, 1987, 44, 602–610; P Frost and JH Anderson, Shoulder impingement syndrome in relation to shoulder intensive work, *Occupational and Environmental Medicine*, 1999, 56, 494–498.

[80] JG Park, JK Lee and CT Phelps, Os acromiale associated with rotator cuff impingement: MR imaging of the shoulder, *Radiology*, 1994, 193, 255–257.

[81] S Ogata and HK Uhtoff, Acromial enthesopathy and rotator cuff tear. A radiologic and histologic post-mortem investigation of the coracoacromial arch, *Clinical Othopedics*, 1990, 254, 39–48.

[82] DC Hardy, JB Vogler and RH White, The shoulder impingement syndrome: prevalence of radiographic findings and correlation with response to treatment, *American Journal of Roentgenology*, 1986, 147, 557–561.

[83] AM Murtagh, CL Vosburgh and TJ Neviaser, The incidence of pathologic changes in the long head of biceps, *Journal of Shoulder and Elbow Surgery*, 2000, 9, 382–385.

[84] TJ Tucker and SJ Snyder, The keeled acromion: an aggressive acromial variant – a series of 20 patients with associated rotator cuff tears, *Arthroscopy: The Journal of Arthroscopic and Related Surgery*, 2004, 20, 744–753.

[85] There is considerable confusion over the terms used to describe the morphology of the acromion; some clarification is to be found in: AFW Chambler and RJH Emery, Acromial morphology: the enigma of terminology, *Knee Surgery, Sports Traumatology, and Arthroscopy*, 1997, 5, 268–272.

tendons has been involved and this should normally be recorded. New bone may also be found on the coracoid, and on the acromion, and the ACJ is frequently involved. If the impingement syndrome was present, eburnation may be found on the superior pole of the humerus and on the undersurface of the acromion. If the bicipital tendon has been involved, new bone may also be found in the bicipital groove.[86] The operational definition for RCD and impingement is shown in the "Operational definition of rotator cuff disease and impingement syndrome" box.

Operational definition of rotator cuff disease and impingement syndrome

Rotator cuff disease

Pitting on insertion of rotator cuff muscles

AND

New bone on or around insertion

OR

alteration in contour of insertion

Impingement syndrome

Eburnation on superior pole of head of humerus

OR

Eburnation on undersurface of acromion

RCD may be accompanied by new bone on the acromion, coracoid, and in the bicipital groove and by OA of the acj.

Intervertebral disc disease: The vertebrae are articulated through the medium of the intervertebral disc which is formed from an outer fibrous part (the annulus fibrosus) which surrounds a central part (the nucleus pulposus). The annulus is composed largely of type I collagen fibres which are laid down obliquely in a series of lamellae, the orientation of the fibres alternating between lamellae.

---

[86] There is sometimes a ridge that extends from the lesser tuberosity upwards onto the joint surface, the so-called supratubercual ridge. It is said that this may act as a hypomochlion which may irritate or damage the intra-articular portion of the biceps tendon; it is a structure worth looking out for in the skeleton, especially in the presence of RCD. A hypomochlion is a structure that forces a tendon or a muscle to change its direction. (See: A Nidecker, C. Gückel and A von Hochstetter, Imaging the long head of biceps tendon – a pictorial essay emphasising magnetic resonance, *European Journal of Radiology*, 1997, 25, 177–187).

The nucleus consists of a proteoglycan and water gel which is held together loosely by type II collagen and elastin fibres. The cells in the annulus are elongated like fibroblasts whereas those in the nucleus are rounded, often situated within a capsule.[87] The disc is held firmly in place by Sharpey's fibres which insert around the margin of the vertebral body. Degeneration of the disc is particularly associated with aging and occurs equally in both sexes. It is rare below the age of 40 and extremely common above the age of 70. The changes within the nucleus and the annulus result in the nucleus bulging outwards and the annulus collapsing[88] with joint space narrowing on X-ray. These changes have been likened to the disc behaving like a flat tyre.[89] They are accompanied by the formation of marginal osteophyte and by pitting on the superior or inferior surfaces of the vertebrae most commonly seen in the lower cervical and lumbar regions (Figure 3.6).[90] Many alterations in metabolism have been described; however, their role in the aetiology of disc degeneration is poorly understood.[91]

Operational definition of intervertebral disc disease

Pitting on the inferior or superior surface of the vertebral bodies

AND

Marginal osteophyte

Intervertebral disc disease is very easy to recognise in the spine and the operational definition is shown in the "Operational definition of intervertebral disc disease" box. It is very common in skeletal assemblages and, as expected, is found especially in the cervical and lower lumbar regions. Thus, it conforms with modern experience extremely well, suggesting that its aetiology has probably not changed much over the years.

---

[87] S Roberts, H Evans, J Trivedi and J Menage, Histology and pathology of the human intervertebral disc, *The Journal of Bone and Joint Surgery*, 2006, 88A (Supplement 2), 10–14.

[88] MA Adams and PJ Roughley, What is intervertebral disc degeneration, and what causes it? *Spine*, 2006, 31, 2151–2161.

[89] P Brinkman and H Gootenburg, Change of disc height, radial disc bulge, and intradiscal pressure from discectomy. An in vitro investigation on human lumbar discs, *Spine*, 1991, 16, 641–646.

[90] It is important to remember that marginal osteophytes are found in other conditions, and as an isolated, aging phenomenon. See: MD Jones, MJ Pais and B Omiya, Bony overgrowths and abnormal calcifications of the spine, *Radiologic Clinics of North America*, 1988, 26, 1213–1234; TW O'Neill, EV McCloskey, JA Kanis, AK Bhalla, J Reeve, DM Reid, C Todd, AD Woolf and AJ Silman, The distribution, determinants, and clinical correlates of vertebral osteophytosis: a population based survey, *Journal of Rheumatology*, 1999, 26, 842–848.

[91] BH Guiot and RG Fessley, Molecular biology of degenerative disc disease, *Neurosurgery*, 2000, 47, 1034–1040.

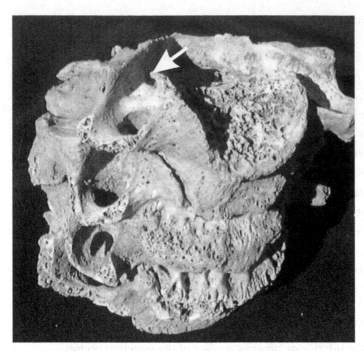

FIGURE 3.6. Cervical vertebrae (C3–C5) with disc disease. Note the presence of marginal osteophyte and pitting and new bone formation on the superior surface of C3 and the small osteophyte (white arrow) which is protruding into the intravertebral foramen. If the exiting nerve root had been compressed, symptoms would have been noticed around the neck and in the skin overlying the upper fibres of the trapezius muscle.

Intervertebral disc disease and neurological complications: In some cases of inter-vertebral disc disease (IVD) in the cervical region, an osteophyte may been seen protruding into the intervertebral foramen (IVF) and can sometimes be seen to decrease the size of the IVF when the vertebrae are articulated.[92] Where this occurs it is probable that the nerve root which exits through the IVF behind the vertebral artery in the neural groove was compressed. Compression of nerve roots in the cervical region[93] may give rise to symptoms in the hand or arm. A knowledge of

[92] The intervertebral foramen has been described as the doorway between the spinal canal and the periphery. The anatomy of the structures that enter and leave it is extremely interesting and complex, and important in understanding the pathological changes that may result from their damage or compression (RV Gilchrist, CW Slipman and SM Bhagia, Anatomy of the intervertebral foramen, *Pain Physician*, 2002, 5, 373–378). The widths of the IVF are greater in females than in males, but are not related to age, stature or lateralisation (FJ Rühli, M Müntener and M Henneberg, Human osseous intervertebral foramen width, *American Journal of Physical Anthropology*, 2006, 129, 177–188).

[93] In clinical practice root compression is related to herniation of the annulus and the condition, known as cervical spondylitis, is most commonly found in the C6 and C7 distribution (K Radhakrishnan, WJ Litchy, WM O'Fallon and LT Kurland, Epidemiology of cervical radiculopathy. A population based study from Rochester, Minnesota, 1976 through 1990, *Brain*, 1994, 117, 325–335). In skeletal assemblages, osteophytes impinging on the IVF may be found at higher levels up to C3.

which root is involved by IVD and reference to a dermatome chart[94] permits the palaeopathologist to postulate where symptoms might have been experienced during life; this is an unusual circumstance and one that ought not to be missed.

SCHMORL'S NODES

Schmorl's[95] nodes are formed when damage to the vertebral endplate decompresses the adjacent nucleus, transferring the load onto the annulus, resulting in it herniating into the damaged part of the endplate. Schmorl's nodes are extremely common, especially in the lower thoracic and lumbar regions and are readily recognised in the skeleton as impressions in the surfaces of the vertebrae lined with cortical bone. Schmorl's nodes can take a variety of shapes and may appear serpiginous on occasions. The nodes may appear in almost any position on the vertebral surface, sometimes extending into the vertebral canal. Radiologically, they are frequently surrounded by a sclerotic margin showing that some degree of remodelling has taken place.[96] If they are placed in a very anterior position and the herniation is large, they may cause angular kyphosis, a condition that is referred to as Scheuermann's disease.[97]

A number of causes have been suggested for the generation of Schmorl's nodes and they are particularly common in those who impose great stresses on their lower spine, including, for example, elite athletes.[98] Modern research seems to imply that Schmorl's nodes are secondary to ischaemic necrosis of trabecular bone beneath the endplate.[99] There is no prospect of determining the proximate cause in the excavated skeleton.

---

[94] Dermatome charts, which show the areas of skin supplied by each of the sensory nerve roots, can be found in any textbook of neurology or clinical anatomy.

[95] Christian Georg Schmorl 1861–1932.

[96] D Resnick and G Niwayama, Intervertebral disk herniations: cartilaginous (Schmorl's) nodes, *Radiology*, 1978, 126, 57–65.

[97] Holger Werfel Scheuermann 1877–1960. See: RM Ali, DW Green and TC Patel, Scheuermann's kyphosis, *Current Opinion in Pediatrics*, 1999, 11, 70–75.

[98] L Sward, The thoracolumbar spine in young elite athletes. Current concepts on the effects of physical training, *Sports Medicine*, 1992, 13, 357–364.

[99] B Peng, W Wu, S Hou, W Shang, X Wang and Y Yang, The pathogenesis of Schmorl's nodes, *Journal of Bone and Joint Surgery*, 2003, 85B, 879–882.

4

Diseases of Joints, Part 2

The joint diseases can be simply divided into those in which the major feature is the proliferation of new bone and those in which the loss of bone is the most striking feature; the latter are collectively known as the erosive arthropathies. A simplified family tree of the joint diseases showing those that are most likely to be found in the skeleton is shown in Figure 4.1.

Osteoarthritis is the archetypal proliferative joint disease but there are many different erosive joint diseases, including an erosive form of OA. However, only a small number of the erosive arthropathies are likely to be encountered during the examination of a skeletal assemblage and it is these that will be discussed here. The most characteristic of the erosive joint diseases is rheumatoid arthritis.

RHEUMATOID ARTHRITIS

Rheumatoid arthritis (RA) is generally considered to have first appeared in the clinical literature in the MD thesis of the French physician Augustin Jacob Landré-Beauvais (1772–1840).[1] The thesis described the clinical findings in a group of nine patients whom Landré-Beauvais attended at the Salpêtrière hospital in Paris. The signs and symptoms differed in a number of ways from those found in other forms of gout, the rubric under which the joint diseases were all included at the time. It was more common in women, involved many joints from the onset and ran a chronic course. Landré-Beauvais was certain that he had discovered a new form of joint

---

[1] AJ Landré-Beauvais, *Doit-on admettre une nouvelle espèce de goutte sous la denomination goutte asthénique primitive*, MD Thesis, Paris. A complete translation of the thesis was published in *Joint Bone Spine*, 2001, 68, 130–143 (The first description of rheumatoid arthritis. Unabridged text of the doctoral dissertation presented in 1800). The size of this thesis will no doubt astonish those who have presented their own in more recent times!

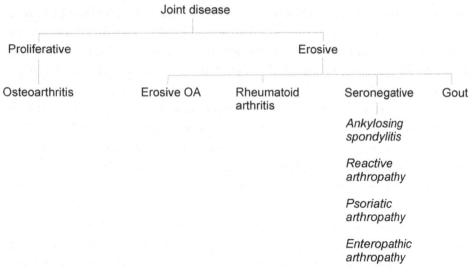

FIGURE 4.1. Diagram to show relationship of the different joint diseases.

disease, which he called primary asthenic gout (goutte asthénique primitive). Some of the features of RA are so characteristic, especially the deformities in the hands, that it would be surprising if physicians before Landré-Beauvais had failed to recognise it. Thus, many considered it a new disease although there have been suggestions that a number of historical figures suffered from it, including Mary Queen of Scots, but most of these attributions are disputed.[2] There is also palaeopathological evidence for a much greater antiquity. Cases have been found from the mediaeval and post-mediaeval periods in England[3] and seventh- to ninth-century France.[4] There is nothing to support the view that the disease originated in the New World and became widespread only after the colonisation of North America by Europeans.[5] The disease affects women more often than men and the prevalence in Europe

[2] WW Buchan and WF Kean, Rheumatoid arthritis: beyond the lymphocytes, *Journal of Rheumatology*, 2001, 28, 691–693.

[3] T Waldron, J Rogers and I Watt, Rheumatoid arthritis in an English post-medieval skeleton, *International Journal of Osteoarchaeology*, 1994, 4, 165–167; P Hacking, T Allen and J Rogers, Rheumatoid arthritis in a medieval skeleton, *International Journal of Osteoarchaeology*, 1994, 4, 251–255.

[4] J Blondiaux, A Cotton, C Fontaine, C Haenni, A Bera and R-M Flipo, Two Roman and medieval cases of symmetric erosive polyarthropathy from Normandy: anatomicopathological and radiological evidence of rheumatoid arthritis, *International Journal of Osteoarchaeology*, 1997, 7, 451–466. Even older cases have been reported from the final Jomon period in Japan (3,400–2,400 years BP); see: K Inoue, S Hukuda, M Nakai, K Katayama and J Huang, Erosive peripheral polyarthritis in ancient Japanese skeletons: a possible case of rheumatoid arthritis, *International Journal of Osteoarchaeology*, 1999, 9, 1–7.

[5] FJ Aceves-Avila, F Medina and A Fraga, The antiquity of rheumatoid arthritis: a reappraisal, *Journal of Rheumatology*, 2001, 28, 691–693.

and North America is between 0.5 and 1%[6] but is higher in older than in younger age groups.[7] There is good evidence that since the 1960s both the prevalence and incidence of the disease are falling in the developed nations, the disease is increasing, however, in sub-Saharan Africa[8] although it tends to run a milder course in the developing countries.[9]

The proximate cause of RA is unknown but it seems to depend upon a mixture of genetic, environmental and immune factors. Genetic factors are clearly important and contribute substantially to the pathogenesis as judged from twin studies.[10] A substantial proportion of patients show the presence of the HLA-DR4 antibodies[11] and many proinflammatory cytokines and chemokines can be found in tissue from joints affected by RA.[12] In the majority of patients (about 70%) with RA there is an antibody in the serum that reacts with the Fc portion of IgG and which is referred to as rheumatoid factor (RF). After RF was discovered, it was found that patients with some of the other forms of erosive joint disease lacked this antibody and these conditions were referred to thereafter as seronegative arthropathies which will be discussed later.[13]

It is rather interesting to follow the history of RF through the text books of rheumatology. In Copeman's text book,[14] for example, the term does not appear until the third edition published in 1964, but it is not until the fourth (1969) edition that the author states that the nature of the rheumatoid factor 'is so well established that it is no longer necessary to discuss the several arguments against it'.[15] More

---

[6] Y Alamanos and AA Drosos, Epidemiology of adult rheumatoid arthritis, *Autoimmunity Reviews*, 2005, 4, 130–136.

[7] TK Kvien, Epidemiology and burden of illness of rheumatoid arthritis, *Pharmacoeconomics*, 2004, 22 (Supplement 2), 1–12.

[8] PE McGill and GO Oyoo, Rheumatic disorders in Sub-saharan Africa, *East Africa Medical Journal*, 2002, 79, 214–216.

[9] AA Kalla and M Tikly, Rheumatoid arthritis in the developing world, *Best Practice & Research Clinical Rheumatology*, 2003, 17, 863–875.

[10] RR de Vries, TW Huizinga and TE Toes, Redefining the HLA and RA association: to be or not to be anti-CCP positive, *Journal of Autoimmunity*, 2005, 25 (Supplement), 21–25.

[11] A Ebringer and C Wilson, HLA molecules, bacteria and autoimmunity, *Journal of Medical Microbiology*, 2000, 49, 305–311.

[12] These include TNFα, IL-1, IL-6, IL-8 and GM-CSF which are all proinflammatory. Some anti-inflammatory cytokines and cytokine inhibitors are also found, including IL-10, TGFβ, IL-1ra and soluble TNF-R but they are not in sufficient quantity to counteract the activity of the others (see: M Feldmann, FM Brennan and RN Maini, Role of cytokines in rheumatoid arthritis, *Annual Review of Immunology*, 1996, 14, 397–440.

[13] Rheumatoid factor is not specific for RA; it can be found in some other conditions, and in some other rheumatological disorders, including Sjögren's syndrome and systemic lupus erythematosis. There is some suggestion that RF-negative and RF-positive RA are different disorders (OMR Westwood, PN Nelson and FC Hay, Rheumatoid factors: what's new? *Rheumatology*, 2006, 45, 379–385).

[14] WSC Copeman, *Textbook of the rheumatic diseases*, E&S Livingstone, Edinburgh, 1948.

[15] *Ibid*, 4th edition, p 187.

recently, auto-antibodies to citrullinated[16] cyclic proteins have been demonstrated in patients with RA. This occurrence has provoked considerable interest not only because it is a more sensitive indicator of the disease, but their presence during the early stages of the disease is associated with a significantly greater number of erosions at follow up.[17] It is now suggested that the anti-CCP positive (a-CCP+) and anti-CCP negative (a-CCP-) types of RA may be aetiologically distinct.[18] In particular, it is postulated that in the a-CCP+ type, the symptoms of RA may be triggered by smoking.[19] We have tried without success to extract rheumatoid factor from bones which we were certain had RA on morphological grounds but to date, there have been no attempts to try to extract anti-CCP antibodies. This is clearly something that will be done at some time in the future.

THE NATURAL HISTORY OF RHEUMATOID ARTHRITIS

It seems highly probable that the progenitor of RA is an inflammatory arthropathy which may evolve into RA or perhaps some other inflammatory arthropathy, or resolve depending on the interaction of a variety of genetic, environmental and personal factors (see Figure 4.2). Once established, RA may remit, in perhaps 10–30% of cases, or become persistent, again depending on interactions similar to those acting earlier in the course of the disease.[20]

There are three distinct phases in the history of the disease:

1. infiltration of the synovial membrane by cells derived from the bone marrow; this phase seems to be common to a number of the inflammatory arthropathies;
2. an amplification phase, the progression of which is highly dependent on the genotype of the patient; and

---

[16] Citrulline is an amino acid that is not normally present in protein. It formed as an intermediate in the conversion of ornithine to arginine in the urea cycle. It gained its name from the fact that it was first extracted from a water-melon, the Latin name of which is *citrullus*.

[17] WJ van Venrooij and LBA van de Putte, Is assaying autoantibodies useful for diagnosing early rheumatoid arthritis? *Nature Clinical Practice Rheumatology*, 2005, 1, 4–5; T Mimori, Clinical significance of anti-CCP antibodies in rheumatoid arthritis, *Internal Medicine Tokyo*, 2005, 44, 1122–1126.

[18] C Deighton and LA Criswell, Recent advances in the genetics of rheumatoid arthritis, *Current Rheumatology Reports*, 2006, 8, 394–400.

[19] L Klareskog, L Padyukov, J Ronnelid and L Alfredsson, Genes, environment and immunity in the development of rheumatoid arthritis, *Current Opinion in Immunology*, 2006, 18, 650–655.

[20] WER Ollier, B Harrison and D Symmond, What is the natural history of rheumatoid arthritis? *Best Practice & Research Clinical Rheumatology*, 2001, 15, 27–48.

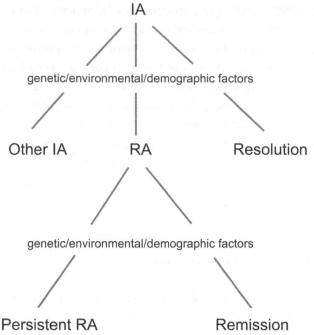

FIGURE 4.2. Model of aetiology of rheumatoid arthritis. The condition probably begins as an undifferentiated inflammatory arthropathy (IA) which may either resolve under the influence of various factors, or evolve into rheumatoid arthritis (RA) or some other inflammatory arthropathy. The condition may then either persist or remit, again depending on genetic and environmental influences.

3. chronic inflammation with unregulated cytokine production leading to the formation of a pannus, the release of bone destroying enzymes, and increased vascularisation.

Pannus is the name given to the abnormal synovial membrane which gradually encroaches across the joint, destroying the articular cartilage in its wake. Marginal erosions are found in the proximal joints of the hands and feet – the proximal interphalangeal (PIP) and the metacarpophalangeal (MCP) and metatarsophalangeal (MTP) joints – in the majority of patients, probably appearing in the feet before the hands. The erosions usually appear in the first two years of the disease.[21] Erosions are symmetrical and may spread to involve other joints, including the wrist, elbow, hips, knees, ankles and ACJ and they usually have a sclerotic margin on X-ray. Erosions may also affect the spine. Erosions of the odontoid peg are particularly significant since they may lead to instability of the atlanto-axial junction with potentially serious

---

[21] D McGonagle, PG Conaghan, R Wakefield and P Emery, Imaging the joints in early rheumatoid arthritis, *Best Practice & Research Clinical Rheumatology*, 2001, 15, 91–104.

neurological sequelae.[22] The damage to the joints tends to progress throughout the disease and accounts for much of the disability caused by it.[23]

The development of the erosions is dependent upon the production and activation of osteoclasts by inflammatory cytokines, including TNFα, IL-1 and IL-6, and the production of RANK-L.[24] Osteoporosis is noted around affected joints and bony ankylosis may also supervene. Generally the sacroiliac joint (SIJ) is spared and there is very little new bone formed and spinal fusion does not occur.

As the disease progresses, the hands and feet may develop a number of deformities including ulnar deviation of the fingers at the MCP joints, which may sometimes be inferred from the skeleton owing to the changes in the contours of the metacarpal heads and the proximal joint of the proximal phalanges.[25]

> *Erosions:* Recognising a true erosion, and differentiating it from other holes in bones is central to being able to diagnose an erosive arthropathy in the skeleton. Erosions may be found at the joint margin, in the centre of a joint, or in para-articular tissues (Figure 4.3). They are characterised by the following features:
> - cortical destruction;
> - undercut edges;
> - exposed trabeculae;
> - sharp or scalloped ridges; and
> - a scooped floor.

Any hole in a bone in which the cortex is intact *cannot* be an erosion. Holes which may be caused by the spread of a tumour, for example, will show some of the features of an arthropathic erosion, including cortical destruction and undercut edges, but it is very unlikely that they will be found in or around joints and there

[22] DH Kim and AS Hilibrand, Rheumatoid arthritis in the cervical spine, *Journal of the American Academy of Orthopaedic Surgeons*, 2005, 13, 463–474.
[23] DL Scott, K Pugner, K Kaarela, DV Doyle, A Woolf, J Holmes and K Hieke, The links between joint damage and disability in rheumatoid arthritis, *Rheumatology*, 2000, 39, 122–132.
[24] MJ Green and AA Deodhar, Bone changes in early rheumatoid arthritis, *Best Practice & Research Clinical Rheumatology*, 2001, 15, 105–123.
[25] The other changes in the hands and feet are extremely unlikely to be recognised in the skeleton. In well-preserved mummies, however, it *may* be possible to recognise these changes as was the case in a sixteenth-century female mummy from Italy (R Caranni, F Garbini, E Neri, L Melai, L Giust and G Fornaciari, The "Braids Lady" of Arezzo: a case of rheumatoid arthritis in a 16th century mummy, *Clinical and Experimental Research*, 2002, 20, 745–752). The French neurologist Jean-Martin Charcot (1825–1893) gave the first complete description of the changes in the hand. The description, together with illustrations of the changes can be found in *Œuvres complete de J.M. Charcot. Tome 7 Maladies des vieillards, goutte et rheumatisme*, Lescrosnier et Babe, Paris, 1890). One of the illustrations from this volume appears on the front cover of the August 2001 volume of *Arthritis Care and Research* and there are a number of illustrations in *Arthritis and allied conditions: a textbook of rheumatology* (edited by WJ Koopman and LW Morland), Lippincott Williams and Wilkins, Baltimore, 2005, pp 1170–1173 and 1178.

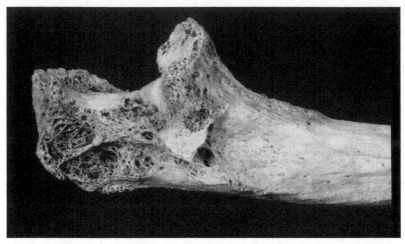

FIGURE 4.3. Rheumatoid arthritis of the elbow. Most of the normal joint surface has been destroyed and the joint is heavily eroded. The cortex of the joint has largely disappeared and trabeculae are evident. Scalloped ridges and scooped floors are also clearly seen.

should be no difficulty in making the differentiation. Post-mortem damage to a joint may sometimes simulate an erosion but if the damage is recent, the colour of the damaged cortex will be lighter than the rest and this will make the cause obvious. Other destructive processes, including rodent gnawing should also present no difficulty. On X-ray, a true erosion will often have a sclerotic margin, showing that some remodelling has taken place during life; sclerosis will *never* be found with a pseudo-erosion or other post-mortem artefact.

Operational definition for rheumatoid arthritis

Symmetrical marginal erosions of small joints of hands and/or feet

AND

Sparing of sacroiliac joints

Minimal new bone formation

Absence of spinal fusion

Erosions may be found in other joints in both spinal and extra-spinal locations; osteoporosis may be found around affected joints

---

The operational definition of rheumatoid arthritis is shown in the "Operational definition for rheumatoid arthritis" box. Note that the disease *cannot* be diagnosed with any certainty if the hands and/or the feet are not present. On this account, it is certain that the true prevalence of the disease in skeletal assemblages is under-estimated. This underestimation might be rectified if it proves possible in the future to extract RF or aCCP antibodies from bone in cases with suspicious erosions.

SERO-NEGATIVE ARTHROPATHIES

Following the discovery of rheumatoid factor, it was found that many of the conditions that had previously been referred to as atypical forms of rheumatoid arthritis were not associated with this factor, that is, they were sero-negative, and in this way a new concept in rheumatology was established.

The sero-negative arthropathies include cases of sero-negative RA and erosive OA. Another group of the sero-negative arthropathies which share a number of features in common, including sacroiliitis and some degree of fusion of the spine, are known as the spondylarthropathies, a term first introduced by Moll and his colleagues in 1974.[26] In addition, the group contains a number of undifferentiated disorders. Sero-negative RA can not be differentiated from sero-positive RA in the skeleton but erosive OA can be recognised as a separate entity. Spondylarthropathies can also be differentiated as described later in this text.

EROSIVE OSTEOARTHRITIS

Erosive osteoarthritis (EOA) has been known for more than forty years, since Crain and Washington gave the first full description of it, and it forms the bridge between the proliferative and inflammatory arthropathies.[27] However, Crain and Washington were not the first to use the term.[28] EOA occurs almost exclusively in women and often runs a particularly aggressive course. The disease has been found to affect between 4–15% of those with OA of the hands,[29] so it is not that uncommon. The

[26] JM Moll, I Haslock, IF McCrae and V Wright, Associations between ankylosing spondylitis, psoriatic arthritis, Reiter's disease, the intestinal arthropathies, and Behçet's syndrome, *Medicine (Baltimore)*, 1974, 53, 343–364.

[27] DC Crain and DC Washington, Interphalangeal osteoarthritis characterised by painful, inflammatory episodes resulting in deformity of the proximal and distal articulations, *Journal of the American Medical Association*, 1961, 175, 1049–1053.

[28] This seems to be due to Peters and his colleagues: JB Peters, CM Pearson and L Marmor, Erosive osteoarthritis of the hands, *Arthritis and Rheumatism*, 1966, 9, 365–388.

[29] M Pattrick, S Aldrige, E Hamilton, A Manhire and M Doherty, A controlled study of hand function in nodal and erosive osteoarthritis, *Annals of the Rheumatic Diseases*, 1989, 48, 978–982; M Cobby, J Cushnagen, P Creamer, P Dieppe and I Watt, Erosive osteoarthritis: is it a separate disease entity? *Clinical Radiology*, 1990, 42, 258–262; F Cavain, L Punzi, M Pianon, F Oliviero, P Sfriso and S Todesco, Prevalenza dell'atrosi erosive delle mani. Studio in una popolazione del Veneto, *Reumatisomo*, 2004, 56, 46–50.

Table 4.1. *Some features of the erosive arthropathies*

Type of arthropathy	Erosions	Sacroiliitis	Spinal fusion	Proliferation
Ankylosing spondylitis	Symmetric, para-articular	Bilateral, symmetrical	Continuous from below; no skip lesions	+
Psoriatic	Asymmetric or symmetric, hands and feet, especially dips	May be unilateral and asymmetric	Skip lesions; paravertebral bridging	+
Reactive	Asymmetric, mainly in lower limbs	May be unilateral and asymmetric	Skip lesions; paravertebral bridging	+
Enteropathic	Usually monoarticular, especially affects the knees	Bilateral, symmetrical	No skip lesions	±
Erosive OA	Asymmetric, hands only	–	–	+
Rheumatoid arthritis	Symmetric	Rare	–	–
Gout	Asymmetric	Any form	–	–

erosive changes, which are confined to the hands, are most frequently seen in the interphalangeal joints, although the thumb base may also be affected and, less commonly, other joints of the hand.[30] The typical changes of OA are, of course, also present in the hand but there is, in addition, a severe synovitis and there is recent evidence that IL-1 may play a role in the pathogenesis of the disease.[31] The sacro-iliac joints are not affected, and there is no spinal involvement (see Table 4.1).

The changes seen radiographically are a mixture of proliferation and erosions, the erosions first appearing in the central portion of the joints. So-called 'crumbling'

[30] GE Ehrlich, Erosive osteoarthritis: presentation, clinical pearls, and therapy, *Current Rheumatology Reports*, 2001, 3, 484–486.
[31] AG Stern, MRC de Carvalho, GA Buck, RA Adler, TPS Rao, D Disler and G Moxley, Association of erosive hand osteoarthritis with a single nucleotide polymorphism on the gene encoding interleukin-1 beta, *Osteoarthritis and Cartilage*, 2003, 11, 394–402.

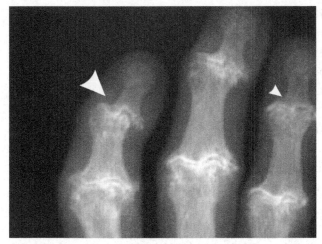

FIGURE 4.4. Radiograph of erosive osteoarthritis with gull-wing (small arrow head) and saw-tooth (large arrow head) lesions.

erosions may be found and as the erosions progress, they may lead to the formation of the 'gull-wing' deformity which is caused by marginal sclerosis and osteophytes on the distal sides of the joints with central erosion and collapse or thinning on the proximal side. The gull wing deformity is characteristic of EOA as is the 'saw-tooth' lesion, formed by a series of erosions in line, which is found particularly in the PIPs (Figure 4.4). EOA is the only form of osteoarthritis in which bony ankylosis in the hands is at all likely to be found.[32]

Operational definition for erosive osteoarthritis

Presence of eburnation in any of the joints of the hand

AND

Asymmetrical central erosions of the pips and dips

The 'gull wing' sign and/or the 'saw tooth' signs may be present on x-ray

---

EOA has seldom been reported in the skeleton[33] but in a recent series of skeletons from the town of Barton-on-Humber in Lincolnshire dating from between 950–1850, three cases were found, giving a prevalence of 2.65% (with a 95% confidence interval

[32] L Punzi, R Romonda and P Sfriso, Erosive osteoarthritis, *Best Practice & Research Clinical Rheumatology*, 2004, 18, 739–758.
[33] J Rogers, T Waldron and I Watt, Erosive osteoarthritis in a mediaeval skeleton, *International Journal of Osteoarchaeology*, 1991, 1, 151–153.

of 0.91–7.52%)[34] which agrees well with modern prevalence data, suggesting that there may not have been much change in the frequency of this type of OA over time. The operational definition for EOA is shown in the "Operational definition for erosive osteoarthritis" box.

THE SPONDYLOARTHRITIDES[35]

The sero-negative spondyloarthritides (SpA) are a group of diseases that share a number of morphological and immunological or genetic features in common. The group includes ankylosing spondylitis, reactive arthropathy (Reiter's syndrome), psoriatic arthropathy and enteropathic arthropathy. There are also other forms that fail to conform with the criteria established for definite entities and they are referred to as the undifferentiated spondyloarthritides.[36] The true prevalence of the spondyloarthritides as a whole is not known with any certainty, although there are reasonable data for the main sub-groups[37] but it is probably about double that of ankylosing spondylitis.[38]

Although several different forms of SpA are differentiated, in some respects they represent a continuum which is linked by an association with the presence of the HLA-B27 antigen,[39] sacroiliitis, asymmetrical peripheral joint involvement, spinal fusion and enthesitis.[40] The forms that are differentiated are done so mainly on the basis of their aetiology or their association with other conditions. The prevalence of the SpA reflects the prevalence of HLA-B27 in the general population but it is interesting that although the majority of patients with SpA have HLA-B27, by no

---

[34] The 95% confidence interval represents the values between which the 'true' prevalence will be found in 95 of 100 estimations (see also chapter 13).

[35] The consensus now is that the term spondyloarthritis (plural arthriditides) should be used instead of spondyloarthropathy to better reflect the inflammatory nature of these conditions.

[36] H Zeidler, W Maw and MA Khan, Undifferentiated spondylarthropathies, *Rheumatic Disease Clinics of North America*, 1992, 18, 187–202.

[37] The lack of epidemiological information has been hindered by the lack of adequate criteria for classifying the various sub-groups (I Olivieri, A van Tubergen, C Salvarani and S van der Linden, Seronegative spondyloarthritides, *Best Practice & Research Clinical Rheumatology*, 2002, 16, 723–739).

[38] J Sieper, M Rudwaleit, MA Khan and J Braun, Concepts and epidemiology of spondyloarthritis, *Best Practice & Research Clinical Rheumatology*, 2006, 20, 401–417.

[39] The HLA (human leucocyte antigen) B27 is part of the major histocompatibility complex (MHC) of the immune system. The MHC comprises a series of proteins that bind to fragments of antigens. The class I proteins present antigens to cytotoxic T lymphocytes. The HLA-B27 allotype is encoded for by the B locus of the MHC complex on chromosome 6. (An allotype is the protein product of an allele which may be detected as an antigen in an animal of the same species.) For further details see: AL Hughes, Molecular evolution of the vertebrate immune system, *Bioessays*, 1997, 19, 777–786.

[40] MA D'Agostino and I Olivieri, Enthesitis, *Best Practice & Research Clinical Rheumatology*, 2006, 20, 473–486.

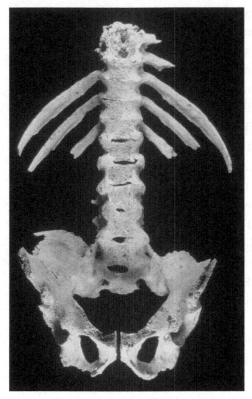

FIGURE 4.5. Ankylosing spondylitis. The sacroiliac joint are fused bilaterally and fusion extends the whole length of the spine with no skip lesions. Many of the ribs are fused but some have been damaged or broken off post mortem.

means all those with this antigen develop an arthritis; the reason for this is the subject of much debate.[41]

ANKYLOSING SPONDYLITIS

Ankylosing spondylitis (AS) is the most common of the SpA and probably the easiest to recognise in the skeleton (Figure 4.5). It seems to have been described first by the Irish physician Bernard Connor (1666–1698) who gave an account of an unusual skeleton that had been found in cemetery close to where he was demonstrating anatomy in France.[42] The pelvis, sacrum, lumbar and most of the thoracic spine,

[41] JD Reveille, The genetic basis of spondyloarthritis, *Current Rheumatology Reports*, 2004, 6, 117–125.
[42] The claim has been made that Colombo described AS about a hundred years previously in his *De Re Anatomica* (published in Venice in 1559) but Connor's was certainly the first most complete description.

and a number of ribs were all joined together so that they made one continuous bone. Connor described this case in a letter to Sir Charles Walgrave in 1695 and in the *Philosophical Transactions* of the Royal Society.[43] A plate, showing this specimen, and an ankylosed knee from another case, has been reproduced by Blumberg and Blumberg.[44] AS is a condition of great antiquity having been reported in some of the Egyptian pharaohs[45] but it is also certain that some cases have been confused with diffuse idiopathic skeletal hyperostosis DISH.[46] The disease has had many eponyms in the past, including Marie-Strümpel disease and von Bechterew's syndrome; however AS has become the most common usage.[47]

The disease begins most frequently in the third decade of life and men are affected two or three times more often than women. Approximately 90% of patients have one or other of the subtypes of HLA-B27.[48] The prevalence of AS in Europe is about 1% but there are very large variations in other countries, depending on the prevalence of HLA-B27 in the general population.[49] The disease is virtually unknown in Japan, for example, where the prevalence of HLA-B27 is extremely low, conversely the prevalence is 4.5% in Canadian Haida Indians where half the population is antigen positive.[50]

The disease typically affects entheses, with erosions and bony ankylosis also being prominent features.[51] In addition, osteoporosis may develop and greatly increase the risk to the patient of a vertebral fracture,[52] most commonly occurring in the cervical

43 B Connor, An extract of a letter to Sir Charles Walgrave, published in French at Paris: Giving an account of an extraordinary humane (sic) skeleton, whose vertebrae of the back, the ribs and several bones down to the os sacrum, were all firmly united into one solid bone, without joynting or cartilage, *Philosophical Transactions*, 1695, 19, 21–27.
44 BS Blumberg and JL Blumberg, Bernard Connor (1666–1698) and his contribution to the pathology of ankylosing spondylitis, *Journal of the History of Medicine and Allied Sciences*, 1958, XIII, 349–366.
45 E Feldtkeller, EM Lemmel and AS Russell, Ankylosing spondylitis in the pharaohs of ancient Egypt, *Rheumatology International*, 2003, 23, 1–5.
46 RK Chhem, P Schmit and C Faurè, Did Ramesses II really have ankylosing spondylitis? A reappraisal, *Canadian Association of Radiologists' Journal*, 2004, 55, 211–217.
47 Pierre Marie (1853–1940); Ernst Adolf Gustav Gottfried von Strümpel (1853–1925); Vladimir Mikhailovich Bekhterev (1857–1927) – he is much better known by the German form of his name, Wladimir von Bechterew.
48 At least 23 subtypes of HLA-B27 have been identified; AS and the other SpAs occur in those with the first ten (EJ Ball and MA Khan, HLA-B27 polymorphism, *Joint Bone Spine*, 2001, 68, 378–382).
49 There is good evidence that non-MHC genes are also involved in conferring susceptibility to AS (MA Brown, Non-major-histocompatibility-complex genetics of ankylosing spondylitis, *Best Practice & Research Clinical Rheumatology*, 2006, 20, 611–621).
50 I Oliveiri, L Barozzi, A Padula, M De Matteis and P Paclica, Clinical manifestations of seronegative spondylarthropathies, *European Journal of Radiology*, 1998, 27, S3–S6.
51 J Sieper, J Braun, M Rudwaleit, A Boonen and A Zinc, Ankylosing spondylitis: an overview, *Annals of the Rheumatic Diseases*, 2002, 61 Supplement III, iii8–iii18.
52 JB Jun, KB Joo, MY Her, TH Kim, SC Bae, DH Yoo and SK Kim, Femoral bone mineral density is associated with vertebral fractures in patients with ankylosing spondylitis: a cross-sectional study, *Journal of Rheumatology*, 2006, 33, 1637–1641.

region sometimes with dire neurological consequences. The disease most often begins with sacroiliitis and the SIJs may become symmetrically fused. Spinal fusion is common with the formation of syndesmophytes which are ossifications in the annulus fibrosus of the intervertebral discs. If the development of syndesmophytes is extensive, the spine may take on an undulating contour which is described by the radiologists as a 'bamboo spine'. Spinal fusion extends inexorably upwards with no normal vertebrae interspersed between those that are fused – no skip lesions, in other words – but the anterior surface of the vertebrae is relatively smooth since osteophytosis is not a prominent feature. The fusion may stop at any level or go on to involve the entire spine from top to bottom. As the disease progresses, the spine may show a considerable degree of kyphosis; this was very likely to have been the end result in the past before the course of the disease could be modified by treatment. It is less likely to occur nowadays with modern treatment.

In the thoracic region, the costovertebral joints may be involved, in which case the ribs become fused to the vertebrae, and calcification and ossification of interspinous and supraspinous ligaments is common. Extra-spinal enthesophytes are not common, but may be found around the calcaneum at either the insertion of the Achilles tendon posteriorly, or the plantar fascia on the inferior surface.[53]

Erosions are present in the vertebral bodies and they may be central or peripheral but will not be well seen in skeletons in which the spine is ankylosed but they may be apparent if the spine is X-rayed. Peripheral erosions are not as prominent in AS as in other forms of SpA although they may eventually be present in half of all cases. The large joints are generally the first affected, especially the hip and the shoulder, although other joints can also be involved.

Operational definition for ankylosing spondylitis

Symmetrical fusion of both sacroiliac joints

AND

Spinal fusion with no skip lesions

{Erosions may be seen in the spine and in peripheral joints, especially the shoulder and hip}

Bamboo spine may be evident on x-ray

---

[53] CZ Erdem, S Sarikaya, LO Erdem, S Ozdolap and S Gundogdu, MR Imaging features of foot involvement in ankylosing spondylitis, *European Journal of Radiology*, 2005, 53, 110–119.

The diagnosis of a full-blown case of AS presents little difficulty in the skeleton since the pelvis and spine will be fused into a single unit and it is very likely that many of the ribs, or at least those that are extant, will also be fused to the vertebrae. The operational definition is shown in the "Operational definition for ankylosing spondylitis" box.

REITER'S SYNDROME (REACTIVE SPONDYLOARTHROPATHY)

In 1916, Hans Reiter (1881–1946) described the case of a young German army officer with bloody dysentery who presented with a combination of urethritis, conjunctivitis and arthritis which he believed was the result of an unusual form of syphilis.[54] A similar combination of symptoms was described in the same year by Fiessinger and Leroy in a group of four French soldiers[55] but the term Reiter's syndrome has persisted, at least in the English literature. The condition existed long before the first modern clinical descriptions of it appeared, however, and the arthritis associated with venereal disease was common in the nineteenth century and was said to have accounted for 3% of all admissions to three of the largest hospitals in London.[56]

A variety of infections is now known to trigger the condition and in order to emphasise its immunological basis, Ahvonen and his colleagues suggested in 1969 that the term, reactive arthritis (ReA) should be used.[57] ReA is now the term generally preferred, although some authorities still persist in using Reiter's syndrome for those cases which present with the classic triad of urethritis, conjunctivitis and arthritis.

There is no doubt that HLA-B27 predisposes to developing the disease and at least 50% of those with the condition are positive for this antigen. In these, the most common precipitating event is an infection with *Campylobacter*, *Chlamydia*, *Clostridium*, *Salmonella*, *Shigella* or *Yersinia* species. In those who are HLA-B27

[54] H Reiter, Über ein bisher unbekannte Spirochäten-infektion (Spirochätosis arthritica), *Deutsche Medizinische Wochenschrift*, 1916, 42, 1535–1536.

[55] N Fiessinger and E Leroy, Contribution á l'étude d'une épidemie de dysenterie dans la Somme, *Bulletin et Mémoires de la Soceité Médicale des Hôpitaux de Paris*, 1916, 40, 2030–2069. In the French literature, the condition is still often referred to as Fiessinger-Leroy, or Fiessinger-Leroy-Reiter syndrome. (Noël Fiessinger 1881–1946; Emile Leroy b 1873.)

[56] GO Storey and DL Scott, Arthritis associated with venereal disease in nineteenth century London, *Clinical Rheumatology*, 1998, 17, 500–504.

[57] P Ahvonen, K Sievers and K Aho, Arthritis associated with *Yersinia enterocolitica* infection, *Acta Rheumatological Scandinavica*, 1969, 15, 232–253.

negative, a much wider spectrum of infectious agents may trigger the condition.[58] The symptoms of joint disease may appear within two or four weeks of the infection, but may also appear after the infection has cleared up. It seems that once the immunological tap has been turned on, it cannot be turned off. The prevalence of ReA is not known with any precision, and different authors give different figures; it is certainly low, however, not more than 0.5 per thousand. Nor is it clear exactly how many of those with triggering infections develop an arthritis but it might be as many as a half, although a lower figure is more likely.

Operational definition for reactive arthropathy

Asymmetric fusion of one or both sacroiliac joints

AND

Spinal fusion with paravertebral bridging and skip lesions

AND

Asymmetric erosions of small joints of the feet

Enthesophytes may be present, especially in the lower limbs and feet, and there may be proliferation of new bone

---

The development of the joint symptoms is precipitated by the presence of bacterial antigens, or sensitised lymphocytes in the joints, as shown in Figure 4.6.[59] The outcome is usually good although a quarter of patients may go on to develop chronic arthritis.

In ReA sacroiliitis is asymmetrical; extra-spinal lesions are more extensive than in AS and typically affect the lower extremities; enthesopathy is common and there is a good deal of new bone produced.

The changes in the SIJs may be bilateral or unilateral and the changes within the joint are asymmetrical. In the spine, fusion begins in the lower thoracic or upper lumbar region and may proceed upwards, but normal vertebrae are interspersed between the fused ones, forming so-called 'skip' lesions. The vertebrae are joined by osseous bridges that appear on the lateral aspects of the vertebrae in the paravertebral

---

[58] T Hannu, R Inman, K Granfors and M Leirisalo-Repo, Reactive arthritis or post-infectious arthritis? *Best Practice & Research Clinical Rheumatology*, 2006, 20, 419–433.

[59] A Toivanen and P Toivanen, Reactive arthritis, *Best Practice & Research Clinical Rheumatology*, 2004, 18, 689–703.

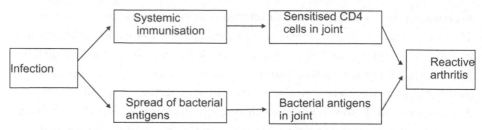

FIGURE 4.6. Model to show aetiology of reactive arthritis. The condition begins with an infection which may result in the spread of bacterial antigens which gain entrance to joints, or in systemic immunisation with sensitised CD4 (T lymphocyte) cells entering the joints; in either case, the end result is inflammatory change in the joint.

position. These outgrowths of bone are asymmetric, they extend across the disc space and they may be well defined or fluffy in outline. Early in the disease, a clear space may be seen between the bony bridges and the vertebral bodies but they eventually fuse with the vertebral body as the disease progresses. Enthesophytes can be found at many sites, most particularly around the pelvis, lower legs and feet. The calcaneum is a favoured site and a calcaneal spur may be present. Fluffy new bone may be present on the metatarsal or metacarpal shafts and around the ankle and knee. Erosions are asymmetric and most often involve the MTP and interphalangeal joints of the feet, the first MTP joint being especially favoured. There is a rare form of the disease in which there is subluxation and deformity of the MTP joints; this is sometimes known as Launois's deformity.[60]

The diagnosis of ReA in the skeleton is difficult except in a full-blown case with a very complete skeleton. ReA cannot, of course, be differentiated from classic Reiter's syndrome and it is probably best to refer to the condition as ReA when discussing this type of spondyloarthritis in the skeleton. An operational definition is shown in the "Operational definition for reactive arthropathy" box.

PSORIATIC ARTHROPATHY

Psoriasis is a common skin condition that affects approximately 1–3% of the general population. It is mediated through the immune system and T-cells and TNF- are both intimately connected with its pathogenesis.[61] The manifestations of joint disease

---

[60] Pierre-Emile Launois 1856–1914.

[61] WA Myers, AB Gottlieb and P Mease, Psoriasis and psoriatic arthritis: clinical features and disease mechanisms, *Clinics in Dermatology*, 2006, 24, 438–447.

Table 4.2. *Subsets of psoriatic arthritis in order of frequency*

Order of frequency	Subset
1	Asymmetric oligoarthritis
2	Symmetric arthritis similar to rheumatoid arthritis
3	Distal interphalangeal joints predominantly involved
4	Spondylitis predominant
5	Arthritis mutilans

*From Veale et al (1994)[62]

occur predominantly in those whose nails are affected and are noted especially in the distal interphalangeal joints of the hand, the sacroiliac joints and the spine; both sexes are equally affected. There is no consensus on the proportion of patients with psoriasis who will develop arthritis but it may be up to a third.[63] There is the usual link with HLA-B27, particularly in those with spinal disease[64] and there is an excess of males with the disease who are antigen positive.[65] Because both psoriasis and joint disease are relatively common there has been some discussion as to whether or not psoriatic arthropathy (PsA) is a separate entity or merely the occurrence of two common conditions coincidentally in the same patient. After a lengthy review of the matter, Fitzgerald and Dougados concluded that PsA was, indeed, a condition in its own right.[66]

A variety of clinical subsets of PsA have been described depending on how many joints are affected and the distribution of the joint changes (see Table 4.2). In the majority of cases, the disease presents as an asymmetric oligoarthritis[67] or a symmetrical polyarthritis similar to RA.[68] The variable nature of PsA makes it very difficult to diagnose in the skeleton, and it is almost certainly the third subset – in which the dips are affected – about which the palaeopathologist could feel most

[62] D Veale and O Fitzgerald, Psoriatic arthritis, *Best Practice & Research Clinical Rheumatology*, 2002, 16, 523–535.

[63] H Zachariae, Prevalence of joint disease in patients with psoriasis: implications for treatment, *American Journal of Clinical Dermatology*, 2003, 4, 441–447.

[64] D Veale and O Fitzgerald, Psoriatic arthritis, *Best Practice & Research Clinical Rheumatology*, 2002, 16, 523–535.

[65] R Queiro, C Sarasqueto, J Beizunegui, C Gonzalez, M Figueroa and JC Torre-Alonso, Psoriatic spondyloarthropathy: a comparative study between HLA-B27 positive and HLA-B27 negative disease, *Seminars in Arthritis and Rheumatism*, 2002, 31, 413–418.

[66] O Fitzgerald and M Dougados, Psoriatic arthritis: one or more diseases? *Best Practice & Research Clinical Rheumatology*, 2006, 20, 435–450.

[67] That is, having four or fewer joints affected.

[68] D Veale, S Rogers and O Fitzgerald, Classification of clinical subsets in psoriatic arthritis, *British Journal of Rheumatology*, 1994, 33, 133–138.

confident. It may be this difficulty that has resulted in so few cases appearing in the palaeopathological literature.[69]

Operational definition for psoriatic arthropathy

Sacroiliitis

AND

Spinal fusion with skip lesions

AND

Erosions of dips of hands or feet with tuftal resorption in hands

There may be bony ankylosis, proliferation of new bone, and appearance of the 'cup and pencil' sign on X-ray

---

The best-known feature of PsA is the destructive change seen in the dips of the hands. Erosions begin at the joint margin but may proceed centrally and their distribution may be unilateral, bilateral, symmetric or asymmetric. Resorption of the distal tufts of the phalanges is characteristic of PsA and progressive bone resorption may result in a much shortened phalanx. The proximal joint surface of the distal phalange may be widened and this, associated with osteolysis of the middle phalanx, gives rise to the so-called 'cup and pencil' sign on X-ray. Proliferation of new bone is a common feature, especially on the metacarpal or metatarsal shafts, or around eroded joints, subluxation at the MCP joints may occur rather in the fashion of RA, and bony ankylosis is common. Arthritis mutilans is the name given to the very rapidly progressive osteolysis that causes severe deformity in the hands.[70] Changes in the feet are similar to those in the hands, and extensive destruction of the interphalangeal joint of the big toe is characteristic of PsA.

Changes in the sacroiliac joint may be bilateral, unilateral, symmetric or asymmetric, although bilateral, symmetric changes are the most common. Erosions may be present within the joint and sclerosis can be demonstrated on X-ray. The sacroiliac joint is probably affected less often in PsA than in the other forms of SpA.

In the spine, fusion is accomplished by the formation of paravertebral bony bridges, often starting in the lower thoracic and upper lumbar spine, as in ReA.

[69] J Zias and P Mitchell, Psoriatic arthropathy in a fifth-century Judean Desert monastery, *American Journal of Physical Anthropology*, 1996, 101, 491–502.
[70] JH Rose and MR Belsky, Psoriatic arthritis in the hand, *Hand Clinics*, 1989, 5, 137–144.

Fusion may extend upwards, but with skip lesions and the bony bridges may take on the appearance of 'chunky' syndesmophytes.[71] One feature of PsA is that the cervical spine may be strikingly involved with erosions, the formation of syndesmophytes, erosion of the odontoid peg and subluxation of the atlanto-axial joint, and bony ankylosis.[72] Almost any other joint may also be involved, but changes in the shoulder and hip joints are relatively unusual.

Skeletons with PsA are likely to be friable and the pathological small joints of the hands and feet are liable to be damaged during excavation and post-excavation procedures, which will add to the already considerable difficulty of coming to a definite diagnosis; an operational definition is shown in the "Operational definition for psoriatic arthropathy" box.[73]

ENTEROPATHIC ARTHROPATHY

The association between joint disease and some gastro-intestinal diseases has been recognised for well over a hundred years since White described it in *Lancet* in 1895.[74] It occurs most frequently in patients with inflammatory bowel disease (IBD) such as ulcerative colitis and Crohn's disease.[75] The joint changes develop some months after the onset of the bowel disease and may be exactly similar to those seen in ankylosing spondylitis, although other non-specific changes of SpA may appear in a greater number of patients.[76] The association between HLA-B27 and the ankylosing spondylitis of IBD is not as strong as in the idiopathic form.[77] Although it is probable that both ulcerative colitis and Crohn's disease occurred in the past, it is not very likely that those who contracted either would have survived

[71] PS Helliwell, P Hickling and V Wright, Do the radiological changes of classic ankylosing spondylitis differ from the changes found in the spondylitis associated with inflammatory bowel disease, psoriasis, and reactive arthritis? *Annals of the Rheumatic Diseases*, 1998, 57, 135–140.

[72] K Laiho and M Kauppi, The cervical spine in patients with psoriatic arthritis, *Annals of the Rheumatic Diseases*, 2002, 61, 650–652.

[73] A simplified scheme for differentiating between the major forms of erosive arthropathy is shown in figure 4.6.

[74] WH White, Colitis, *Lancet*, 1895, i, 537–541.

[75] CN Bernstein, JF Blanchard, P Rawsthorne and N Yu, The prevalence of extraintestinal diseases in inflammatory bowel disease: a population-based study, *American Journal of Gastroenterology*, 2001, 96, 1116–1122.

[76] N Turkcapar, M Toruner, I Soykan, OT Aydintug, H Cetinkaya, N Duzgun, A Ozden and M Duman, The prevalence of extraintestinal manifestations and HLA association in patients with inflammatory bowel disease, *Rheumatology International*, 2006, 26, 663–668.

[77] M Rudwaleit and D Baeten, Ankylosing spondylitis and bowel disease, *Best Practice & Research Clinical Rheumatology*, 2006, 20, 451–471.

very long. In any case, there is no prospect that cases of enteropathic arthritis could be differentiated either from classical AS or other undifferentiated forms of SpA.

UNDIFFERENTIATED SPONDYLOARTHRITIDES

Individuals with undifferentiated spondyloarthritis (uSpA) are put into this category if they fail to fulfil the criteria for any of the four other main categories, although some do progress to develop AS. This group of SpA is probably as common as AS and – of course – they share many of the clinical, pathological and radiological features of the differentiated SpAs.[78] It is almost certain that the majority of cases of erosive arthritis with SIJ and spinal involvement seen in a skeletal assemblage will fall into this undifferentiated category, and this will be especially the case when joint changes are seen in a poorly preserved or incomplete skeleton. There will also be many occasions when erosions are seen around a joint which cannot be put into any neat diagnostic box and the most that the palaeopathologist can do then is preferably photograph the lesion(s) and simply record it as an erosive arthropathy (or arthritis), not further classified. It is possible that we will be able to extract biomarkers of joint disease from bone in the future, including perhaps rheumatoid factor, anti-CCP antibodies or HLA-B27 which may help to provide a putative diagnosis but there is no sign that this is likely in the near future. There should be no shame in being unable to classify erosive joint disease in every case. Palaeopathologists can hardly expect to do better than their clinical colleagues, and they – as we have seen – are far from perfect.

JUVENILE ARTHRITIS

I have said nothing about arthritis in juveniles although it is recognised and may be RF positive, in which case it is often referred to as Still's disease,[79] or a form of spondylarthropathy. Virtually all forms of chronic arthritis in children are subsumed under the rubric of juvenile idiopathic arthritis (JIA) but there is a form that is associated with psoriasis.[80] The prevalence of JIA is about 1 per 1000;[81] girls are

---

[78] J Zochling, J Brandt and J Braun, The current concept of spondyloarthritis with special emphasis on undifferentiated spondyloarthritis, *Rheumatology*, 2005, 44, 1483–1491.

[79] Sir George Frederick Still 1861–1941.

[80] ML Stoll and PA Nigrovic, Subpopulations within juvenile psoriatic arthritis: a review of the literature, *Clinical and Developmental Immunology*, 2006, 13, 377–380.

[81] KG Oen and M Cheang, Epidemiology of chronic arthritis in childhood, *Seminars in Arthritis and Rheumatism*, 1996, 26, 575–591.

more often affected than boys and there are two major peaks of onset, between the ages of 1 and 2, and 9 and 15.[82] Cases of juvenile arthritis are rarely reported in the archaeological record and the diagnosis needs the assistance of a clinical paediatric rheumatologist if any certainty is to be attached to it.[83] An excellent review of JIA has recently been published by Borchers and her colleagues and those who wish to know about the subject could hardly do better than refer to it.[84]

GOUT

Gout is one of the oldest diseases to be recorded in the medical literature and many acute clinical observations were recorded in the Hippocratic corpus. It has afflicted many historical figures. One of the best descriptions of the effects of an attack of acute gout was provided by Thomas Sydenham (1624–1689) who was himself a sufferer.[85] James Gilray's cartoon of gout as an evil devil attacking the big toe, published (1799) at a time when gout was a common affliction would have been thought close to the truth by those who suffered from it at the time. Many blame the widespread contamination of wine with lead for the increase in gout during this period.[86]

Gout is a disorder of uric acid metabolism in which the production of uric acid is increased or its excretion through the kidney decreased. Whatever the cause, the result is an increase in the concentration of uric acid in the blood.[87] Uric acid is a by-product of purine metabolism, being formed from xanthine under the influence of the enzyme, xanthine oxidase. In most animals, uric acid is further metabolised to allantoin but humans lack the enzyme, urate oxidase, that catalyses this step.

[82] L Berntson, GB Andersoon, A Fasth, T Herlin, J Kristinsson, P Lahdenne, G Marhaug, S Nielsen, P Pelkonen and M Rygg, Incidence of juvenile idiopathic arthritis in the Nordic countries, *Journal of Rheumatology*, 2003, 30, 2275–2282.
[83] BM Rothschild, I Herskovitz, L Bedford, B Latimer, O Dutour, C Rothschild and LM Jellema, Identification of childhood arthritis in archaeological material: juvenile rheumatoid arthritis versus juvenile spondyloarthropathy, *American Journal of Physical Anthropology*, 1997, 102, 249–264. The *Portrait of a youth* by Botticelli, painted *ca* 1483 shows a young man with what appear to be swellings of the wrist, mcp and pip joints and these have been interpreted as being due to juvenile RA (D Alarcón-Segovia, A Laffón and J Alcocer-Varela, Probable depiction of juvenile arthritis by Sandro Botticelli, *Arthritis and Rheumatism*, 1983, 26m 1266–1269).
[84] AT Borchers, C Selmi, G Cheema, CL Keen, Y Shoenfeld and ME Gershwin, Juvenile idiopathic arthritis, *Autoimmunity Reviews*, 2006, 5, 279–298.
[85] G Nuke and PA Simkin, A concise history of gout and hyperuricemia and their treatment, *Arthritis Research and Therapy*, 2006, 8 (Supplement 1) S1–S5.
[86] GV Ball, Two epidemics of gout, *Bulletin of the History of Medicine*, 1971, 45, 401–408.
[87] KY Kim, HR Schumacher, E Hunsche, AI Wertheimer and SX Kong, A literature review of the epidemiology and treatment of gout, *Clinical Therapeutics*, 2003, 25, 1593–1617.

The incidence of gout is directly related to the serum uric acid level but only about a fifth of all those with a high uric acid actually develop gout. There are obviously other factors involved, notably genetic factors and a number of enzyme abnormalities.[88] Gout is more common in males than in females.[89] The prevalence was about 3 per 1000 in the 1970s but was found to be much greater in the mid 1990s[90] and there is evidence that it is increasing rapidly worldwide.[91]

The arthropathy is due to the precipitation of uric acid crystals in structures either within or around a joint, inducing inflammatory changes in them.[92] The disease starts with an acute attack which, in most cases, affects the first MTP joint. Acute attacks are self-limiting and are followed by an asymptomatic period that may last from months to years, but about half of patients then enter into the phase of chronic gout which is characterised by the formation of tophi which are agglomerations of inflammatory tissue and uric acid crystals and may settle in almost any tissue, including the synovial membrane, articular cartilage and periarticular tissues. Tophi deposited within or around joints will cause erosions which may be intra-articular, para-articular or situated some distance away from the joint. The erosions are usually well defined, round or oval in shape, and usually orientated in the long axis of the bone. They may have a punched out appearance which is accentuated by a sclerotic margin.[93] The erosions often have an overhanging edge which is referred to as a Martel hook (Figure 4.7)[94] and represents bone which has formed over the tophus.[95] Osteoporosis does not occur and ankylosis is extremely uncommon. Chronic gout may be polyarticular, but is asymmetric and the most commonly affected sites are the foot, ankle, knee, hand and wrist. The shoulder sternoclavicular and sacroiliac joints are less commonly involved, and the spine and hip rarely.

[88] NW McGill, Gout and other crystal-associated arthropathies, *Bailliére's Clinical Rheumatology*, 2000, 14, 445–460.

[89] This is true of so-called primary gout but not of secondary gout which is a concomitant of other diseases, especially those that affect renal function, or caused by drugs, particularly some classes of diuretics.

[90] CM Harris, DCEF Lloyd and J Lewis, The prevalence and prophylaxis of gout in England, *Journal of Clinical Epidemiology*, 1995, 48, 1153–1158.

[91] R Zaka and CJ Williams, New developments in the epidemiology and genetics of gout, *Current Rheumatological Reports*, 2006, 8, 215–223.

[92] E Pascual and T Pedraz, Gout, *Current Opinions in Rheumatology*, 2004, 16, 282–286.

[93] A Gentili, Advanced imaging of gout, *Seminars in Musculoskeletal Radiology*, 2003, 7, 165–174.

[94] W Martel, The overhanging margin of bone: a roentgenologic manifestation of gout, *Radiology*, 1968, 91, 755–756.

[95] JU Monu and TL Pope, Gout: a clinical and radiologic review, *Radiology Clinics of North America*, 2004, 42, 169–184.

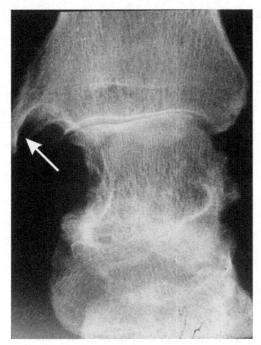

FIGURE 4.7. Radiograph of ankle showing destruction of part of the medial malleolus and the talus with a Martel hook (arrowed), a shell of bone covering the underlying tophus.

Operational definition for gout

Asymmetric erosions in articular or para-articular tissues

with

Overhanging margins (Martel hook)

Erosions may have sclerotic margins; interosseous calcification is rare; osteoporosis does not occur

---

The diagnosis of gout in the skeleton relies on finding erosions within or around joints, the latter often involving both bones around the joint. Radiology is very helpful in this condition since it may well demonstrate sclerotic margins, the presence of a Martel hook or, rarely, interosseous calcification. If the palaeopathologist is very lucky, uric acid crystals may be present in a lesion, as was the case with the terminal phalanx of the fifth finger of the Emperor Charles V who died in

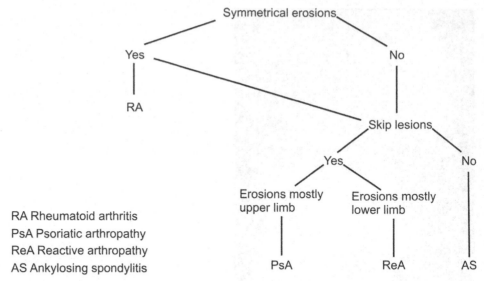

FIGURE 4.8. Simplified diagram to show the differentiation between the various forms of erosive arthropathy.

1556.[96] Otherwise, gout seems to figure much less often in the skeleton than one would suppose in the light of its history, and especially in assemblages from the eighteenth century when we know that the disease was very common and unequivocal cases are uncommon.[97] An operational definition is shown in the "Operational definition for gout" box.[98]

BUNIONS

Bunions do not properly belong in a consideration of joint diseases but they are considered here because their appearance may be confused with that of gout. They seem to result from wearing shoes that are too narrow[99] but this cannot be the whole story since there is a considerable family tendency to the condition. The condition begins with a weakening of the tissues on the medial side of the first MTP joint and flattening of the ridge on the inferior surface of the metatarsal head between the first and second sesamoids. The result is lateral drift of the proximal phalanx into

[96]   J Ordi, PL Alonso, J de Zulueta, J Esteban, M Velasco, E Mas, E Campo and PL Fernández, The severe gout of Holy Roman Emperor Charles V, *New England Journal of Medicine*, 2006, 355, 516–520.

[97]   C Wells, A palaeopathological rarity in a skeleton of Roman date, *Medical History*, 1973, 17, 399–400.

[98]   A simplified scheme for differentiating the various types of erosive arthropathy is shown in Figure 4.8.

[99]   MJ Coughlin and FM Thompson, The high price of high-fashion footwear, In: *Instructional course lectures* (edited by DW Jackson), American Academy of Orthopedic Surgeons, Rosemont, 1995, pp 371–377.

the so-called valgus position,[100] the deformity being exaggerated by the pull of the adductor hallucis muscle.[101]

The head of the first metatarsal becomes prominent and osteophytes often develop and the overlying bursa may become inflamed and cause cystic lesions to appear on the medial side of the metatarsal head. These lesions may cause some confusion with gout.

Clinically, the degree of hallux valgus is determined by measuring the hallux varus and intermetatarsal angles[102] which cannot be measured with any reliability in a disarticulated skeleton. Instead, reliance has to be placed on finding cysts in the metatarsal head which are unlike true erosions in that the cortex is intact and they do not have overhanging margins, or in finding sloping surfaces on the first metatarsal and proximal phalanx. This will not be possible if only one of these two bones is present, although it is permissible to diagnose bunions from the presence of cysts in the metatarsal head. Bunions seem to have become more common in the latter part of the medieval period when the fashion for narrow, pointed shoes came into vogue.[103]

> *Bunionette*: This is a valgus deformity of the fifth metatarsal with hypertrophy of the metatarsal head. It was once common in tailors who sat cross-legged to sew. Bunionette generally causes little problem although pressure on the metatarsal head may cause inflammation or infection.[104] These complications might draw attention to the presence of the disease in the skeleton.

---

[100] Valgus refers to the orientation of one part of the body away from the mid-line of the body relative to the part immediately proximal to it. The opposite condition, varus, is when one part of the body is angled towards the mid-line relative to the part immediately proximal to it.

[101] AHN Robinson and JP Limbers, Modern concepts in the treatment of hallux valgus, *Journal of Bone and Joint Surgery*, 2005, 87B, 1038–1045.

[102] A Gentili, S Masih, L Yao and LL Seeger, Pictorial review: foot axes and angles, *British Journal of Radiology*, 1996, 69, 968–974.

[103] SA Mays, Paleopathology of hallux valgus, *American Journal of Physical Anthropology*, 2005, 126, 139–149.

[104] A Ajis, M Koti and N Maffulli, Tailor's bunion: a review, *Journal of Foot and Ankle Surgery*, 2005, 44, 236–245.

5

Bone Forming and DISH

BONE FORMING AND BONE FORMERS

Within any skeletal assemblage there seems to be a proportion who apparently had a tendency to ossify soft tissues, especially the entheses, that is, the point at which tendons insert into bone, probably in response to minimal repetitive trauma. The result is the production of bony spurs at these points, which are referred to as enthesophytes. We alluded to these individuals as bone formers[1] but our original definition was later modified by Rogers and her colleagues.[2] Rogers and colleagues examined the sites of a series of entheses in the skeleton (fourteen in total[3]) to see which showed the presence of an enthesophyte. The total number of enthesophytes was then divided by the number of sites examined and if the score was equal to, or greater than 0.3, that was considered evidence of bone forming. Bone formers are probably more likely than others to produce heterotopic ossification and to calcify or ossify costal cartilages, the thyroid cartilage and other soft tissues. It is not certain what proportion of the population are bone formers but it may be up to a fifth. There are several skeletal diseases in which bone forming is a feature – some joint diseases, some infections and Paget's disease, for example – and it is likely that the production of bone in these conditions will be particularly exuberant if the individual is also a

---

[1] T Waldron and J Rogers, An epidemiologic study of sacroiliac fusion in some human skeletal remains, *American Journal of Physical Anthropology*, 1990, 83, 123–127.

[2] J Rogers, L Shepstone and P Dieppe, Bone formers: osteophyte and enthesophyte formation are positively associated, *Annals of the Rheumatic Diseases*, 1997, 56, 85–90. For a critique of the concept of bone forming see: DT Felson and T Neogi, Osteoarthritis: is it a disease of cartilage or bone? *Arthritis and Rheumatism*, 2004, 50, 341–344.

[3] There are several other entheses in both the arm and the leg; for a complete list see tables 1 and 2 in: M Benjamin and D McGonagle, The anatomical basis for disease localisation in seronegative spondyloarthropathy at entheses and related sites, *Journal of Anatomy*, 2001, 199, 503–526.

bone former. There are two other conditions that will be mentioned in this chapter, diffuse idiopathic skeletal hyperostosis (DISH) and hyperostosis frontalis interna (HFI).

DIFFUSE IDIOPATHIC SKELETAL HYPEROSTOSIS (DISH)

DISH probably represents the extreme end of bone forming and it is characterised by the exuberant production of new bone into the anterior longitudinal ligament of the spine with calcification or ossification of extra-spinal entheses and ligaments, and other soft tissues. The changes in the spine were first recorded by Forestier and Rotés-Quérol;[4] who noticed that the changes were usually confined to those beyond middle age and that the prevalence increased markedly with age. Later, when Resnick and his colleagues examined those with what by then had become known as Forestier's disease, they noticed many extra-spinal manifestations and they coined the term DISH to account for these.[5]

The changes in the spine are the result of ossification into the anterior longitudinal and other ligaments, although the posterior longitudinal ligament is often not involved, at least in those living in the western world. In its most florid form, the new bone may look like melted candle wax down the front of the vertebrae (Figure 5.1). The whole of the spine may be involved and bony ankylosis results, although the disc spaces and the facet joints are normal unless they are involved in some concomitant pathological condition. The changes in the thoracic region are unique in that they occur only on the right-hand side of the vertebral bodies. For many years it was supposed that this was due to the presence of the descending aorta on the left-hand side and this view was confirmed when, in a patient with the rare condition of situs inversus, in which the heart and the great blood vessels are inverted so that the descending aorta lies on the right of the vertebral bodies, the changes of DISH were observed on the *left*.[6]

The ossification of extra-spinal entheses produces spurs of bone which are especially prominent around the calcaneum and the patella, and at the insertion of the

[4] J Forestier and J Rotés-Quérol, Senile ankylosing hyperostosis of the spine, *Annals of the Rheumatic Diseases*, 1950, 9, 321–330.

[5] D Resnick, SR Shaul and JM Robbins, Diffuse idiopathic skeletal hyperostosis (DISH): Forestier's disease with extraspinal manifestations, *Diagnostic Radiology*, 1975, 115, 513–524.

[6] A Ciocci, Diffuse idiopathic skeletal hyperostosis (DISH) and situs viscerum inversus. Report of a single case, *Clinical and Experimental Rheumatology*, 1987, 5, 159–160.

FIGURE 5.1. Thoracic spine of Giso, the last Anglo-Saxon Bishop of Wells showing extensive fusion and right-sided osteophyte formation.

triceps muscle into the olecranon. Ligamentous ossification of, for example, the sacroiliac ligaments may result in fusion of the sacrum to the ilium but the sacroiliac joint can be seen to be normal, either directly or on X-ray.

DISH is more common in men than in women and rarely occurs below the age of 40; above this age the condition is found in about 4% of men and 2.5% of women.[7] In modern populations, DISH is found in association with obesity and late onset (type II) diabetes,[8] an association with abnormal vitamin A metabolism has also been noted.[9] Those with DISH have higher levels of serum uric acid than normal.[10] In addition, serum levels of growth hormone and IGF-I are higher in patients with

---

[7] S Mata, PR Fortin, MA Fitzcharles, MR Starr, L Joseph, CS Watts, B Gore, E Rosenberg, RK Chen and JM Esdaile, A controlled study of diffuse idiopathic skeletal hyperostosis. Clinical features and functional status, *Medicine (Baltimore)*, 1997, 76, 104–117.

[8] H Julkunen, OP Heinonen and K Pyörälä, Hyperostosis of the spine in an adult population, *Annals of the Rheumatic Diseases*, 1971, 30, 605–612.

[9] M Abiteboul and J Arlet, Retinonol-related hyperostosis, *American Journal of Roentgenology*, 1985, 144, 435–436.

[10] C Kiss, M Szilágyi, A Paksy and G Poór, Risk factors for diffuse idiopathic skeletal hyperostosis: a case-control study, *Rheumatology*, 2002, 41, 27–30.

symptomatic DISH than normal controls.[11] Denko and his colleagues believe DISH is most likely a multisystem hormonal disorder.[12]

Most patients with DISH are asymptomatic and for this reason, Hutton suggested some years ago that it should be called a 'state' rather than a disease.[13] Some patients complain of bone or joint pain,[14] and some may have some stiffness in the back but the prevalence of back pain is no greater than in those without the condition.[15] There is some evidence that DISH may predispose to the development of intervertebral disc disease[16] and this is something that could easily be examined in the skeleton. Before dismissing it completely out of hand as a clinical nonentity, however, it is worth noting those rare cases in which spinal fracture has occurred in the thoracic or cervical regions, sometimes in response to minimal trauma[17] and sometimes with devastating neurological sequelae.[18] There is also some recent epidemiological evidence that DISH is associated with an increased incidence of risk factors for stroke and other cerebrovascular disease, such as stenosis or occlusion of a major cerebral artery.[19]

One particularly interesting feature of DISH is that the prevalence is considerably increased in those who followed the monastic way of life in the medieval period, or who were otherwise apparently of high status. This was first suggested in an article in a Christmas issue of the *British Medical Journal*[20] which usually allows authors to air amusing or slightly unusual views. Since then, this association has

[11] CW Denko, B Boja and CJ Malemud, Growth hormone and insulin-like growth factor-I in symptomatic and asymptomatic patients with diffuse idiopathic skeletal hyperostosis (DISH), *Frontiers in Bioscience*, 2002, 7, a37–a43.

[12] CW Denko, B Boja and RW Moskowitz, Growth promoting peptides in osteoarthritis and diffuse idiopathic skeletal hyperostosis – insulin, insulin-like growth factor-I, growth hormone, *Journal of Rheumatology*, 1994, 21, 1725–1730.

[13] C Hutton, DISH ... a state not a disease? *British Journal of Rheumatology*, 1989, 28, 277–278.

[14] P Utsinger, D Resnick and R Shapiro, Diffuse skeletal abnormalities in Forestier disease, *Archives of Internal Medicine*, 1976, 136, 763–768.

[15] P Schlapbach, C Beyeler, NJ Gerber, S van der Linder, U Burgi, WA Fuchs and H Ehrengruber, Diffuse idiopathic skeletal hyperostosis (DISH) of the spine: a cause of pain? A controlled study, *British Journal of Rheumatology*, 1989, 28, 299–303.

[16] C di Girolamo, N Pappone, C Rengo, E Miniero, C Crisci and I Olivieri, Intervertebral disc lesions in diffuse idiopathic skeletal hyperostosis (DISH), *Clinical and Experimental Rheumatology*, 2001, 19, 310–312.

[17] RW Hendrix, M Melany, F Miller and LF Rogers, Fracture of the spine in patients with ankylosis due to diffuse idiopathic skeletal hyperostosis: clinical and imaging findings, *American Journal of Roentgenology*, 1994, 162, 899–904.

[18] S Sreedharan and YH Li, Diffuse idiopathic skeletal hyperostosis with cervical spine cord injury – a report of 3 cases and a literature review, *Annals of the Academy of Medicine of Singapore*, 2005, 34, 257–261.

[19] N Miyazawa and I Akiyama, Diffuse idiopathic skeletal hyperostosis associated with risk factors for stroke – a case-control study, *Spine*, 2006, 31, 225–229.

[20] T Waldron, DISH at Merton Priory; evidence for a 'new' occupational disease? *British Medical Journal*, 1985, 291, 1762–1763.

been confirmed[21] and the reason is almost certainly related to the diet enjoyed by the monks. At Westminster Abbey, for example, on an average day outside Advent or Lent, the monks had an allowance of 6,207 calories; during Advent the allowance was 5,291 calories *per diem*, and during Lent, 4,870 calories.[22] Of course the monks would not consume their entire allowance, but even assuming that they consumed only 60% of it, and the rest was left for the poor at the gate, this would still leave them with an average daily allowance of 3,723 calories, more than enough to get by on. The variety of the monastic diet was at times, wonderfully impressive. Fish was abundant during this period, as was all manner of game – capons, chicken, ducks, geese, egret, herons, pheasant, partridge, pigeons, quail, teal and swan are all mentioned in the account books of the fourteenth century Abbot of Westminster. And in 1372, this same abbot gave a dinner at which beef, mutton, four small pigs, five ducks, one swan, six geese, six capon, nine fowl, two woodcock and a milk cream cheese were all served, washed down with a plentiful supply of wine or ale.[23] One visiting scholar was offended by the huge quantity of food on offer at Canterbury when no less than sixteen dishes were served, all with stimulating sauces and an accompaniment of beer, ale, claret, new wine, mead and mulberry wine.[24] Thus, there seems little reason to doubt the association between DISH and the state of nutrition of those who enjoyed high status, but care should be taken not to assume that every skeleton found with DISH must necessarily be that of a monk or some other high-status individual as is sometimes done.[25]

There is no difficulty in recognising a full-blown case of DISH in the skeleton, the right-sided ossification in the thoracic region does not occur in any other condition, but the inexperienced might confuse DISH with the osteophytosis that occurs in disc disease or the appearances in some of the sero-negative arthritides. A distinction is still sometimes made between Forestier's disease (in which the spine is fused) and DISH (in which spinal fusion is accompanied by extra-spinal enthesopathy). There seems little to be gained by maintaining this distinction in palaeopathology; this is especially so in an incomplete skeleton where it may be difficult to determine that there are extra-spinal manifestations. The diagnosis depends on finding fusion in four contiguous vertebrae but some thought may have to be given to the case

[21] J Rogers and T Waldron, DISH and the monastic way of life, *International Journal of Osteoarchaeology*, 2001, 11, 357–365; HAM Janssen and GJR Maat, *Canons buried in the 'Stiftskapel' of the Saint Servaas Basilica at Maastricht AD 1070–1521. A palaeopathological study*, Barge's Anthropologica No 5, Leiden, Barge's Anthropologica.

[22] B Harvey, *Living and dying in England 1100–1540. The monastic experience*, Oxford, Clarendon Press, 1993.

[23] F Gasquet, *Monastic life in the middle ages*, London, G Bell, 1922.

[24] M Bishop, *The Pelican book of the middle ages*, London, Penguin, 1983.

[25] TJD Bruntjes, Diffuse idiopathic skeletal hyperostosis (DISH). A 10th century AD case from the St Servaas church at Maastricht, *Bone*, 1987, 1, 23–28.

in which fewer vertebrae are preserved. So long as right-sided ossification can be demonstrated in the thoracic region, the diagnosis can be made since this appearance is pathognomonic of DISH. It might be worth distinguishing between what one might call early DISH (eDISH) in cases where the typical appearances are present in the spine, but fewer than four vertebrae are fused. The operational definition is shown in the "Operational definition for DISH" box.

Operational definition for DISH

Ossification and fusion of four contiguous vertebrae, confined to the right side of the vertebral bodies in the thoracic region

AND

Ossification into extra-spinal entheses and ligaments
Early DISH may be diagnosed if fewer than four vertebrae are fused

---

OSSIFICATION IN THE POSTERIOR LONGITUDINAL LIGAMENT

Ossification of the posterior longitudinal ligaments (OPLL) occurs in the cervical and thoracic regions and it may cause pressure symptoms on the spinal cord and nerve roots that need surgical correction.[26] It is common in Japan and some other Asian countries, where, conversely, DISH is rare. The same association with obesity and type II diabetes is noted, and the condition is more common in males than females. Genetic factors, particularly those related to collagen synthesis, and some cytokines (including BMP-2 and TGF-) seem to be involved.[27] Although OPLL is said to be rare outside Japan, it has been found in a considerable proportion of patients undergoing spinal surgery[28] and it is well worth looking for both in skeletons with DISH and those without. If a large osteophyte is found protruding into the spinal canal, it would be reasonable to suppose that it had caused neurological complications during life, the nature of which would have depended on the level at which the spinal cord was compressed.

---

[26] MH Schmidt, A Quinones-Hinojosa and WS Rosenberg, Cervical myelopathy associated with degenerative spine disease and ossification of the posterior longitudinal ligament, *Seminars in Neurology*, 2002, 22, 143–148.

[27] J Inamasu, BH Guilot and DC Sachs, Ossification of the posterior longitudinal ligaments: an update on its biology, epidemiology, and natural history, *Neurosurgery*, 2006, 58, 1027–1039.

[28] NE Epstein, The surgical management of ossification of the posterior longitudinal ligament in 43 North Americans, *Spine*, 1994, 19, 664–672.

HYPEROSTOSIS FRONTALIS INTERNA

Hyperostosis frontalis interna (HFI) is a condition in which there is a thickening of the internal table of the frontal bone. The changes are usually bilateral but it is sometimes unilateral[29] and it may spread beyond the confines of the frontal bone to include much of the internal table of the skull. The thickening may take several forms and different types were distinguished by Perou in what remains still the classic work on the subject.[30] Indeed, HFI may be part of a continuum of hyperostotic changes within the skull that can be subsumed under the single term, hyperostosis cranii.[31]

The first account of the disease was made by Morgagni (1682–1771) in 1719 who described it in an elderly female in association with obesity and hirsutism.[32] This triad of signs came to be looked upon as a discrete syndrome and was rediscovered much later, and with the addition of some psychiatric features, by Stewart and by Morel; it is still sometimes referred to as Morgagni-Stewart-Morel disease. In the older clinical literature it was reported to have an association with acromegaly, toxic goitre and diabetes – the so-called Troell-Junet syndrome,[33] and to be more common in diabetics.[34]

Today, HFI is found predominantly in older women[35] but there is some evidence that this was not the case in the past[36] although it is probable that an apparent male excess in skeletal assemblages is an artefact of small numbers and because the true prevalence has never been established. In modern practice the condition is generally noted as an incidental finding when the skull is X-rayed. It may sometimes be confused with Paget's disease or acromegaly, and it may form part of the rare Alstrom syndrome,[37] but is generally asymptomatic unless the formation of new bone is so extensive that it causes compression of the underlying cerebral cortex, in which case the patient may present with some cognitive impairment[38] or other

[29]   T Hasegawa, H Ito, S Yamamoto, K Haba and H Murata, Unilateral hyperostosis frontalis interna. A case report, *Journal of Neurosurgery*, 1983, 59, 710–713.
[30]   ML Perou, *Cranial hyperostosis*, Springfield, CC Thomas, 1964.
[31]   W Dihlmann, Computerized tomography in typical hyperostosis cranii (THC), *European Journal of Radiology*, 1981, 1, 2–8.
[32]   GB Morgagni, *Adversaria anatomica*, Padua, 1719.
[33]   S Moore, The Troell-Junet syndrome, *Acta Radiologica*, 1953, 39, 485–493.
[34]   S Dann, Metabolic craniopathy: a review of the literature with report of a case with diabetes, *Annals of Internal Medicine*, 1951, 34, 163–202.
[35]   W Devriendt, MD Piercecchi-Marti, P Adalian, A Sanvoisin, O Dutour and G Leonettit, Hyperostosis frontalis interna: forensic issues, *Journal of Forensic Science*, 2005, 50, 143–146.
[36]   FJ Ruhli, T Bone and M Hennenberg, Hyperostosis frontalis interna: archaeological evidence of possible microevolution of human sex steroids? *Homo*, 2004, 55, 91–99.
[37]   P Maffei, V Munno, JD Marshall, C Scandellai and N Sicolo, The Alstrom syndrome: is it a rare or unknown disease? *Annali Italiani di Medicina Interna*, 2002, 17, 221–228.
[38]   GI de Zubicaray, JB Chalk, SE Rose, J Semple and GA Smith, Deficits on self ordered tasks associated with hyperostosis frontalis interna, *Journal of Neurology, Neurosurgery and Psychiatry*, 1997, 63, 309–314.

psychiatric symptoms.[39] The aetiology of the condition is unknown[40] but it is not part of a general bone-forming condition, being no more common in bone formers than in others.

It is certain that the condition is of considerable antiquity[41] and sporadic cases are reported in the palaeopathological literature. It is also certain that the prevalence has generally been underestimated in the past because it will be seen only in skulls that have been broken. For a better estimate, it is necessary to examine the interior of the skull using an endoscope or by radiography when the prevalence will appear to be considerably greater, although still less than in modern populations.[42] Finding new bone on the inside of the frontal bone is pathognomonic of the condition but when found, the temptation to assume that the individual was a hairy woman[43] is to be avoided at all costs to avoid error or even ridicule. There is also very little justification for considering that finding the condition in two skeletons with similar morphology implies that it is likely to have a genetic basis.[44] These are both examples of what might be called 'wrong end reasoning' (see Chapter 13).

HETEROTOPIC OSSIFICATION

Heterotopic ossification is the formation of bone in the soft tissues[45] as the result of trauma or wounding,[46] surgery,[47] burns,[48] prolonged immobility[49] and a number of central nervous system disorders. It is often asymptomatic but may be extensive

[39] G Chaljub, RF Johnson III, RF Johnson Sr and CW Sitton, Unusually exuberant hyperostosis frontalis interna: MRI, *Neuroradiology*, 1999, 41, 45–45.
[40] R She and J Szakacs, Hyperostosis frontalis interna: case report and review of the literature, *Annals of Clinical Laboratory Science*, 2004, 34, 206–208.
[41] PR Šikanjić, Analysis of human skeletal remains from Nadin iron age burial mound, *Collegium Anthropologicum*, 2006, 30, 795–759.
[42] G Barber, I Watt and J Rogers, A comparison of radiological and palaeopathological diagnostic criteria for hyperostosis frontalis interna, *International Journal of Osteoarchaeology*, 1997, 7, 157–164.
[43] E Lazer, quoted in: L Dayton, The fat hairy women of Pompeii, *New Scientist*, 1994, September 24, p 10.
[44] H Glab, K Szostek and K Kaczanowski, Hyperostosis frontalis interna, a genetic disease? Two medieval cases from Southern Poland, *Homo*, 2006, 57, 19–27.
[45] EF McCarthy and M Sunderam, Heterotopic ossification: a review, *Skeletal Radiology*, 2005, 34, 609–619.
[46] BK Potter, TC Burns, AP Lacap, RR Granville and DA Gajewski, Heterotopic ossification following traumatic and combat-related amputations. Prevalence, risk factors, and preliminary results of excision, *Journal of Bone and Joint Surgery*, 2007, 89A, 476–486.
[47] PJ Tortolani, BW Cunningham, M Eng, PC McAfee, GA Holsapple and KA Adams, Prevalence of heterotopic ossification following disc replacement. A prospective, randomized study of two hundred and seventy-six patients, *Journal of Bone and Joint Surgery*, 2007, 89A, 82–88.
[48] A Gurr, M Sinclair, E Caruso, G Peretti and D Zaleske, Heterotopic ossification around the elbow following burns in children: results after excision, *Journal of Bone and Joint Surgery*, 2003, 85A, 1538–1543.
[49] SJ Hudson and SJ Brett, Heterotopic ossification – a long-term consequence of prolonged immobility, *Critical Care*, 2006, 10, 174.

FIGURE 5.2. Two large plaques of heterotopic bone, thought to have been formed in one of the larger muscles of the body, perhaps the quadriceps femoris.

enough to impair joint function – if it were to cause ankylosis of a joint, for example.[50] The pathogenesis is incompletely understood but probably results from the formation and activation of bone-forming cells in traumatised tissues under the influence of cytokines or other factors.[51]

Heterotopic ossification (HO) is relatively often seen in the skeleton, usually manifesting itself by the presence of irregularly shaped pieces of bone attached to the long bones. Sometimes plaques of bone are found which were presumably formed within the larger muscles of the body (Figure 5.2). In the palaeopathological literature, the condition has most often been referred to as myositis ossificans, sometimes modified by the suffix, traumatica. This is an unfortunate name as it may cause confusion with the genetic condition, fibrodysplasia (myositis) ossificans progressive

---

[50] L Vanden Bossche and G Vanderstraeten, Heterotopic ossification: a review, *Journal of Rehabilitation Medicine*, 2005, 37, 129–136.

[51] TA Balboni, R Gobezie and HJ Mamon, Heterotopic ossification: pathophysiology, clinical features, and the role of radiotherapy in prophylaxis, *International Journal of Radiation Oncology, Biology, Physics*, 2006, 66, 1597–1598.

(FOP) in which the soft tissues become extensively ossified along fascial planes resulting in profound disability.[52] It is better to use the term heterotopic ossification (with the suffix traumatica, if that seems appropriate) in a palaeopathological context, unless FOP really is being described.

In the skeleton, it is usually assumed that HO is the result of soft tissue trauma and that bone has formed in a haematoma that has been produced by damage to muscle or periosteum. It might not be possible to rule out other causes, such as burns, if the HO were found on bones which might have been damaged by a burn, being relatively close to the surface.

> *Ossification of the ligamentum flavum:* The ligamentum flavum is composed of
> elastic fibres which give it its yellowish colour; it joins the laminae of adjacent
> vertebrae, attaching on the superior edge and postero-superior surface of the
> vertebra below and the inferior edge and antero-inferior surface of the one
> above.[53] Although it is generally described as continuous in the midline, this
> is not always the case.[54] Ossification in this ligament was thought at one time
> thought to be confined to the countries of East Asia but this is now known not
> to be so.[55] It may be a concomitant of ageing[56] and may also enlarge to such a
> degree as to cause compression of the spinal cord or the nerve roots.[57]

Ossification of the ligamentum flavum is commonly seen in the skeleton, recognised by spikes of bone arising from its insertions in the laminae. It is most common in the lower thoracic and lumbar regions but the prevalence and distribution have not been determined with any precision and this in another task that awaits further attention. The prevalence is higher in those who engage in activities that require a lot of bending as was the case in the skeletons from the *Mary Rose,* where it was

---

[52] FOP is due to a mutation in the ACVR1 gene (J Couzin, Bone disease gene finally found, *Science*, 2006, 312, 514–515) and is most likely to result from the disregulation of the BMP-4 signalling pathway (FS Kaplan, J Fiori, LS De La Pena, J Ahn, PC Billings and EM Shore, Dysregulation of the BMP-4 signaling pathway in fibrodysplasia ossificans progressive, *Annals of the New York Academy of Sciences*, 2006, 1068, 54–65).

[53] AD Olszewski, MJ Yaszemski and AA White, The anatomy of the human lumbar ligamentum flavum: new observations and their surgical importance, *Spine*, 1006, 21, 2307–2312.

[54] P Lirk, M Moriggl, J Colvin, C Keller, L Kirchmai, J Rieder and C Kolbitsch, The incidence of lumbar ligamentum flavum midline gaps, *Anesthesia and Analgesia*, 2004, 98, 1178–1180. (As is so often the case, the authors have determined the prevalence and not the incidence in this paper!)

[55] J Inamasu and BH Guiot, A review of the factors predictive of surgical outcome for ossification of the ligamentum flavum of the thoracic spine, *Journal of Neurosurgery Spine*, 2006, 5, 133–139.

[56] M Benoist, Natural history of the aging spine, *European Spine Journal*, 2003, 12 (Supplement 2), S86–S89.

[57] P Trivedi, S Behari, L Paul, D Banerji, VK Jain and DK Chhabra, Thoracic myelopathy secondary to ossified ligamentum flavum, *Acta Neurochirurgica (Wien)*, 2001, 143, 775–782.

assumed the high prevalence found was related to activities undertaken aboard ship that placed an excessive load on the spine.[58]

OSTEOPETROSIS

Osteopetrosis will be considered in Chapter 10, with other disorders of growth and development.

---

[58] AJ Stirland and T Waldron, Evidence for activity related markers in the vertebrae of the crew of the *Mary Rose, Journal of Archaeological Science*, 1997, 24, 329–335.

6

Infectious Diseases

Most experts believe that infectious diseases were common in the past and that many of the deaths of the very young seen in skeletal assemblages would have resulted from gastro-intestinal infections, as is the case in developing countries today.[1] Almost all forms of infection spread by the faeco-oral route must have been common in the past and almost unavoidable before there was any way to separate drinking water from sewage. Unfortunately for the palaeopathologist, the infections that are likely to have accounted for the death of children leave no stigmata on the skeleton and until and unless we are able to extract bacterial or viral DNA or RNA from the bones of their victims, we will remain ignorant of if, and how often, infectious diseases might have caused death.

Those living in tropical climates would have almost certainly died from malaria and other tropical infections, probably at no less a rate than at present, while at various times the plague, smallpox and cholera all accounted for terrible, episodic periods of mortality in tropical and non-tropical climes.[2] For most infections to be sustained, a large population is required and so the acute bacterial and viral

---

[1] About a fifth of deaths in children in developing countries are estimated to be caused by diarrhoea (RE Black, SS Morris and J Bryce, Where and why are 10 million children dying every year? *Lancet*, 2003, 361, 2226–2234).

[2] One important aspect of infectious diseases is that they may alter in virulence from time to time, giving rise to some of the epidemics that have occurred in the past. An epidemic may also be produced because the host has no immunity, as happened when Europeans brought novel infections to the native peoples they met or conquered often with devastating results for those newly infected. There is a constant interaction between parasite and host in which the host evolves new immunological mechanisms to rid itself of the parasite, and the parasite, in its turn, evolves defence mechanisms to ensure that its residence in the host is unimpeded. This is sometimes referred to as the Red Queen effect; the Red Queen told Alice that 'it takes all the running you can do, to keep in the same place'. Joseph Lederberg has noted how infectious disease is on the rise again and warns that the rules of engagement are changing, implying they are changing in favour of the parasites (Infectious history, *Science*, 2000, 288, 287–293). For an examination of the evolutionary interaction between parasite and host see: RM Anderson, Evolutionary pressure in the spread and persistent of infectious agents in vertebrate populations, *Parasitology*, 1995, 111, S15–31.

infections are not likely to have assumed significant threats to life on a large scale before populations became settled and grew in numbers. For the hunter gatherers, and other nomadic peoples, the main burden of infectious diseases would have been from parasites living in the gut, which survive for long periods in their hosts and reproduce asexually *in situ* or lay eggs that can be picked up from the environment by uninfected hosts.[3]

Since most infectious diseases primarily affect the soft tissues, it is no surprise that there are few signs on the skeleton. The number of infections that affect the skeleton is small and includes osteomyelitis, tuberculosis, syphilis, leprosy and polio. There are some fungal and viral infections that may involve the skeleton in some parts of the world and a considerable number of infections that may very rarely have a skeletal component[4] and some soft tissue infections may cause change in bones if the periosteum is involved.

OSTEOMYELITIS

Osteomyelitis is a term that can be used to encompass any form of infection of bone and bone marrow which results in the inflammatory destruction of bone. The infection may result from one of three sources: haematogenous spread, that is through the bloodstream; by direct spread from an infection in an overlying or adjacent organ; or by direct implantation by penetrating injuries or animal bites, for example, or following a compound fracture. Haematogenous spread is the most common means by which bones become infected. Any individual infection is invariably caused by a single organism, *Staphylococcus aureus* being responsible for the greatest number of

---

[3] The origin of human infectious diseases makes for fascinating speculation. There is an influential school of thought that many have evolved from diseases that were transmitted from animals, as is thought to have happened in recent times with respect to infection with HIV which may have been contracted from chimpanzees. Aidan Cockburn, who was one of the founders of the Paleopathology Association was particularly interested in this matter and although it is now rather old and somewhat outdated, his *Evolution and eradication of infectious diseases* (Baltimore, Johns Hopkins University Press, 1963) still makes for interesting reading. Some more recent work finds less unequivocal evidence for the passage of disease from domestic animals and lays more emphasis on environmental change (JM Pearce-Duvet, The origin of human pathogens: evaluating the role of agriculture and domestic animals in the evolution of human disease, *Biological Reviews of the Cambridge Philosophical Society*, 2006, 81, 369–382). The animal-derived hypothesis is given support, however, in an authoritative review by Wolfe and his colleagues, which includes an account of the five stages through which an animal pathogen must pass to become an exclusively human one (ND Wolfe, CP Dunavan and J Diamond, Origins of major human infectious diseases, *Nature*, 2007, 447, 279–283). One important infection that seems almost certainly *not* to have been derived from an animal form is human tuberculosis, as we shall see.

[4] ME Abd El Bagi, BM Sammak, MS Al Shahed, BA Yousef, OA Demuren, M Al Jared and MA Al Thagafi, Rare bone infections "excluding the spine", *European Radiology*, 1999, 9, 1078–1087.

Table 6.1. *Common causes of osteomyelitis*

Staphylococcus aureus
Streptococci
Enterococci
Pseudomonas sp
Enterobacter sp
Proteus sp
Escherichia coli
Serrotia sp
Anaerobic bacteria (*Peptostreptococcus* sp; *Clostridium* sp; *Bacteroides fragilis*)

infections but many other bacteria have been isolated (see Table 6.1).[5] *S aureus* is a pyogenic organism, that is, pus-producing and it predominantly causes localised skin infections. It is from such skin infections that spread to other organs, including the skeleton, generally takes place. Pyogenic osteomyelitis is most common in children and the age of onset is most often between the ages of 3 and 15. The organisms tend to settle out at the growing ends of bones. The proximal tibia is a favoured site because here the capillaries loop up to supply the growth plate[6] and the bacteria settle out like silt at the bend of a meandering river. Once the bacteria gain access to the bone marrow, they find themselves in what is in effect a wonderful culture medium, where they rapidly multiply, stimulating a brisk immunological response. A good deal of pus is produced and the increased volume of material within the medullary cavity raises the intra-medullary pressure. The bone may increase in size, and drainage channels called cloacae are formed, through which the pus drains from the bone to the outside, through sinuses[7] that are formed in the overlying soft tissues. In the meantime, the presence of organisms under the periosteum stimulates the formation of new bone which may be very exuberant, sometimes forming a thick sheath of new bone around the shaft of the infected bone which is known as an involucrum (Figure 6.1). Interruption of the blood supply to the cortex, or disruption of the supply from the main nutrient artery, may result in areas of necrosis with pieces

---

[5] *S aureus* owes its name to the fact that it appears as grape-like clusters under the microscope and forms golden colonies when it is cultured. It has gained a good deal of notoriety as the MRSA (methicillin-resistant *S aureus*) in recent years because it has become resistant to most antibiotics, causing potentially lethal infections in hospital patients.

[6] SS Shim and G Leung, Blood supply of the knee joint. A microangiographic study in children and adults, *Clinical Orthopaedics and Related Research*, 1986, 208, 119–125.

[7] In this context a sinus means a passage leading from a pus-filled cavity; not to be confused with the sinuses (air-filled spaces) in the skull, or venous sinuses (large blood-filled vessels).

FIGURE 6.1. Posterior view of left femur with osteomyelitis. The distal part of the bone is slightly swollen, there is periosteal new bone on the shaft and a large cloaca (arrowed) is clearly seen.

of dead bone becoming isolated from the cortex and forming sequestra[8] within the medullary cavity. Sequestra may remain hidden within an infected bone although they may sometimes be seen through a large cloaca, and they will also be evident on X-ray. This combination of an involucrum, cloacae and sequestra is pathognomonic of pyogenic osteomyelitis and although the most likely infectious agent is *S aureus*, it is impossible to be certain about this since other pyogenic organisms will produce similar effects.[9]

Untreated osteomyelitis can persist for years and several complications may follow. The shaft of the bone may undergo substantial osteolysis and pathological fractures occur through weakened areas of the shaft and there may be substantial damage to the growth plate. In particularly unfortunate individuals, malignant change may supervene in the tract of the sinus,[10] and there may be deposition of an unusual protein material called amyloid in the kidney.[11] Death is likely to follow either event.

[8]   Singular, sequestrum.
[9]   There is no reason to suppose that aDNA of *S aureus* will not be isolated from bones with osteomyelitis, particularly since the genome has been completely elaborated.
[10] M Altay, M Arikan, Y Yildiz and Y Saglik, Squamous cell carcinoma arising in chronic osteomyelitis in foot and ankle, *Foot and Ankle International*, 2004, 25, 805–809.
[11] ZO Alabi, OS Ojo and WO Odesanmi, Secondary amyloidosis in chronic osteomyelitis, *International Orthopaedics*, 1991, 15, 21–22.

Table 6.2. *Common causes of osteomyelitis in open fractures*

Staphylococcus aureus
β-haemolytic streptococci
Clostridium sp
Bacillus sp
Stenotrophomonas maltophilia
Nocardia sp
Aspergillosus sp
Rhizopus sp
Mucor sp

Death may also ensue if the infection spreads to other organs. Infection of the brain or meninges would inevitably have been rapidly fatal. The majority of cases of osteomyelitis seen in skeletal assemblages are found in adults which presumably indicates that they had survived for several years with the condition. There was no cure for the disease until the advent of effective antibiotics but it became one of the indications for amputation when the operation passed from military into general surgical practice in the eighteenth century.

SPECIAL FORMS OF OSTEOMYELITIS

There are a number of special forms of osteomyelitis that might be met with in the skeleton and which deserve a mention of their own.

> *Compound fracture osteomyelitis:* A compound, or open, fracture presents an easy means of access to infectious organisms. The tibia is the most frequent site of infection in this case, mostly in young men who engage in sport or other hazardous pursuits. The infection may come from normal skin flora, organisms in the soil or by those tending to the injury. The infection is often polymicrobial and staphylococci and gram-negative bacilli are most frequently implicated (Table 6.2).[12] It is said that between 3 and 25% of compound fractures become infected. There is no reason to suppose that this was not also the case in the past. It is striking how few fractures in the past appear to have been infected, however, but this may simply be that relatively few are compound.

[12] IG Sia and EF Berbari, Osteomyelitis, *Best Practice & Research Clinical Rheumatology*, 2006, 20, 1065–1081.

Phossy jaw: Osteomyelitis of the jaw was a much-feared occupational disease in the nineteenth-century workers who used white phosphorus to make strike-anywhere matches, commonly known as Lucifers. Phosphorus particles in the air were taken into the mouth and gained entry to the bone through diseased teeth or gums. The effects could be horrible in the extreme and there was no cure except for surgical removal, the prospect of which could not have been much less feared than the disease itself. In England, the Salvation Army set up a factory in London that used non-toxic red phosphorus instead of white phosphorus and the disease eventually came to an end when it became uneconomic to use white phosphorus.[13] When cemeteries containing late nineteenth-century burials are excavated as they are certain to be in the future, cases of mandibular osteomyelitis may well come to light.

Vertebral osteomyelitis: Vertebral osteomyelitis is more common in adults than in children and most infections are due to *S aureus*.[14] Infection usually follows haematogenous spread and infection may spread to adjacent vertebrae through the intervertebral disc or behind the anterior longitudinal ligament. Considerable destruction of the vertebral body may result, with vertebral collapse and kyphosis.[15] Other complications include subluxation of the vertebrae, new bone formation and bony ankylosis. Radiologically, extensive sclerosis may be present. The result may mimic malignant disease[16] and in the skeleton the disease needs to be differentiated from other infectious causes of spinal collapse, including tuberculosis and brucellosis. This differentiation is sometimes difficult.

Discitis: The intervertebral disc has a limited blood supply in children but the adult disc is avascular and infections spread to it from infected vertebrae above or below. In children, there is some evidence for haematogenous spread to the disc with erosion of the subchondral bone plate and sclerosis without concomitant osteomyelitis.[17]

Brodie's abscess:[18] Brodie's abscess is a chronic abscess arising from single or multiple infections that occurs commonly in children, especially boys, and has a

[13]   JS Felton, Classical syndromes in occupational medicine: phosphorus necrosis – a classical occupational disease, *American Journal of Industrial Medicine*, 1982, 3, 77–120.

[14]   N Stefanovski and LP van Voris, Pyogenic vertebral osteomyelitis: report of a series of 23 patients, *Contemporary Orthopedics*, 1995, 31, 159–164.

[15]   B Jeanneret and F Mageri, Treatment of osteomyelitis of the spine using percutaneous suction/irrigation and percutaneous external spinal fixation, *Journal of Spinal Disorders*, 1994, 7, 185–205.

[16]   I Kayani, I Syed, A Saifuddin, R Green and F MacSweeney, Vertebral osteomyelitis without disc involvement, *Clinical Radiology*, 2004, 59, 881–891.

[17]   HA Peterson, Disk-space infection in children, *Instructional Course Lectures*, 1983, 32, 50–60.

[18]   Sir Benjamin Collins Brodie 1783–1862. For an account of Brodie's original cases see: JF Brailsford, Brodie's abscess and its differential diagnosis, *British Medical Journal*, 1938, 2, 11 9–123.

predilection for the distal tibia. On X-ray, it appears as a translucent area, surrounded by sclerotic bone. There is often a tortuous channel connecting the lesion to the growth plate which may be important in making the diagnosis, and there may be overlying periosteal new bone, although this is often negligible.[19] The affected bone may be swollen, which may highlight the lesion in the skeleton;[20] otherwise they may well go undetected.

Chronic recurrent multifocal osteomyelitis: Chronic recurrent multifocal osteomyelitis (CRMO) is an inflammatory disease found in children with systemic symptoms. CRMO is often accompanied by the appearance of skin lesions, including acne and pustules on the palms and soles. Females are twice as often affected as males.[21] Lesions are found in the long bones adjacent to the growth plate, in the clavicle and the vertebrae. The radiographic appearances are of lytic lesions which become surrounded by a sclerotic margin as the condition progresses. There are no sequestra and no periosteal new bone and cultures of fluid drawn from the lesions are invariably sterile. The causative agent is presently unknown.[22] The lesions are only likely to come to light in the skeleton if the long bones of children are routinely X-rayed and even then, the yield will be low given the rarity of the condition.

Septic arthritis: Infection may spread to a joint by any of the routes considered for osteomyelitis; however, as with osteomyelitis, haematogenous spread is the most common, and *S aureus* the most common causative agent. The bacteria infiltrate the synovium and from there are presumably shed into the lumen of the joint.[23] The synovium becomes swollen and inflamed, the articular cartilage is destroyed, erosions form within the joint and if the infection is untreated – as would have normally been the case in the past – bony ankylosis is almost inevitable. Almost any joint is susceptible to infection by one route or the other but in children, the hip and the knee are common targets for haematogenous spread. Penetrating injuries may potentially affect any joints, while in conditions in which there is sensory loss, such as diabetes or leprosy, the joints of the foot are particularly susceptible, especially in those who walked barefoot or with flimsy footwear. Treatment was unavailable unless the surgeon felt able to drain the joint, or advised amputation.

---

[19] NH Harris and WH Kirkaldy-Willias, Primary subacute pyogenic osteomyelitis, *Journal of Bone and Joint Surgery*, 1965, 47B, 526–532.

[20] R Lagier, C-A Baud and C Kramer, Brodie's abcess (sic) in a tibia dating from the Neolithic period, *Virchow's Archiv A. Pathology, Anatomy and Histopathology*, 1983, 401, 153–157.

[21] W Handrick, D Hörmann, A Voppmann, R Schille, P Reichardt, RB Tröbs, R Möritz and M Borte, Chronic recurrent multifocal osteomyelitis – report of eight patients, *Pediatric Surgery International*, 1998, 14, 195–198.

[22] AG Jurik, Chronic recurrent multifocal osteomyelitis, *Seminars in Musculoskeletal Radiology*, 2004, 8, 243–253.

[23] S Nade, Septic arthritis, *Best Practice & Research Clinical Rheumatology*, 2003, 17, 183–200.

TUBERCULOSIS

Tuberculosis (TB) is thought nowadays to infect about a third of the world's population although only about 5–10% of those infected develop the disease. Nevertheless, almost two million people a year die from tuberculosis, most of them in Africa.[24] In the past, TB was an equally efficient killer of men. John Graunt, a London haberdasher, published an account of the *London Bills of Mortality*[25] in which causes of death were examined for the years between 1629 and 1660 and found that consumption was by far the major cause of death in non-plague years.[26] Deaths occurring in the London parishes were reported to the sexton who then informed the searchers ('antient Matrons sworn to their office'[27]) who would visit the corpse to ascertain the cause of death as best they could. Those who died of consumption were reported to be 'very lean and worn away'[28] and while there is no doubt that some of those who died in this condition would have done so as a result of other wasting diseases such as malignant disease, diabetes or thyrotoxicosis, there seems little reason to doubt that the majority of deaths were really due to TB. The high death rate persisted throughout the eighteenth century and for the first half of the nineteenth when, for reasons that are still poorly understood, it began to decline steeply. Only in more recent times has it begun a resurgence, due in substantial part to concomitant infection with HIV.[29]

TB is caused by a bacterium of the genus *Mycobacterium*, two of which may infect humans, *M tuberculosis* and *M bovis*.[30] Although the result of bone infection is identical irrespective of which is the causative organisms, the route of infection differs substantially. *M tuberculosis* is responsible for the so-called human form of the disease. Infection is spread through the medium of infected droplets and the primary infection develops in the lungs. What follows then depends very largely on the individual's ability to mount an effective cell-mediated immune reaction to the bacteria. Once inhaled, the infective droplets are engulfed by macrophages in which the bacteria continue to multiply if they are not killed immediately. Those cells in which the

[24]   World Health Organisation, *Tuberculosis. Fact sheet 104* (www.who.int/mediacentre/factsheets).

[25]   The *Bills* were first published in 1592 following an outbreak of plague but rapidly fell into disuse; they were revived in 1602 following another episode of plague. They were published weekly on a Thursday with a yearly compilation published on the Thursday before Christmas.

[26]   John Graunt, *Natural and political observations mentioned in a following index, and made upon the Bills of Mortality*, London, Thomas Rycroft and Thomas Dicas, 1662.

[27]   *Ibid*, p 13.

[28]   *Ibid*, p 14

[29]   For a history of tuberculosis, see: TM Daniel, *Captain of death, the story of tuberculosis*, Rochester, University of Rochester Press, 1997.

[30]   These two bacteria form part of what is known as the *M tuberculosis* complex. The two other bacteria in the complex that may rarely cause tuberculosis are *M africanum* and *M microti*.

bacterial multiply are killed and the bacteria released to be engulfed by other macrophages which release cytokines and chemokines to attract other phagocytic cells. With adequate immunity, lesions known as granulomas (or tubercles[31]) are formed. These are comprised of T-cells and macrophages, the latter of which fuse to form giant cells known as Langerhans[32] giant cells, surrounded by lymphocytes and often with central necrosis. Within the granulomas, CD4+ (helper) T cells secrete cytokines including interferon-γ which activate macrophages to kill the bacteria they contain.[33] There are also CD8+ (killer) T cells present which can destroy bacteria directly.[34]

In about 90% of those infected, the infection is contained and the primary lesion may become walled off and calcified, when it is known as a Ghon[35] focus which may be discovered coincidentally on chest X-ray. In those unable to mount an adequate immune response,[36] the disease may spread unchecked. The bacteria can also be reactivated in those who have previously contained the infection, either because host immunity wanes or because the bacteria start to replicate again,[37] and at this stage the disease is characterised by spreading, coalescing tubercles with necrotic centres containing a cheese-like material.[38] Those at particular risk of re-activating the disease include the elderly, those who are malnourished, particularly those without an adequate protein intake, and those who may have concomitant disease. Tuberculosis is *par excellence* a disease of poverty, overcrowding and malnutrition. From the lungs, the disease may spread through the blood stream to distant organs, including bone. The proportion of those with TB who develop skeletal lesions is variable but always a minority, probably no more than 2%.[39]

---

[31] The word tubercle was first used by Franciscus Sylvius of Leyden (1614–1672) in the seventeenth century; the name tuberculosis was given to the disease much later, by Johann Schönlein (1793–1864) in the 1830s. (See: ERN Grigg, Historical and bibliographical review of tuberculosis in the mentally ill, *Journal of the History of Medicine and Allied Sciences*, 1955, X, 58–108.)

[32] Paul Langerhans 1847–1888.

[33] SH Kaufmann, Protection against tuberculosis: cytokines, T cells, and macrophages, *Annals of the Rheumatic Diseases*, 2002, 61, Supplement 2, ii54–ii58.

[34] EN Houben, L Nguyen and J Pieters, Interaction of pathogenic mycobacteria with the host immune system, *Current Opinion in Microbiology*, 2006, 9, 76–85.

[35] Anton Ghon 1866–1936.

[36] Immunity seems to be conferred by a specific gene; see: H Pan, BS Yan, M Rojas, YV Shebzukhov, H Zhou, L Kobzik, DE Higgins, MJ Daly, BR Bloom and I Krammick, Ipr1 gene mediates innate immunity to tuberculosis, *Nature*, 2005, 434, 767–772.

[37] BM Saunders and WJ Britton, Life and death in the granuloma: immunopathology of tuberculosis, *Immunology and Cell Biology*, 2007, 85, 103–111.

[38] The macrophages that mount the immune response are also responsible for much of the tissue damage caused by the infection. They liberate hydrogen peroxide and toxic enzymes which not only kill the bacteria but also destroy host tissue.

[39] E Pertuiset, J Beaudreuil, F Liote, A Horusitzsky, F Kemiche, P Richette, D Clerc-Wyel, I Cerf-Payraste, H Dorfmann, J Glowinski, J Crouzet, T Bardin, O Meyer, A Dryll, JM Ziza, MF Kahn and D Kuntz, Spinal tuberculosis in adults. A study of 103 cases in a developed country, 1980–1994, *Medicine (Baltimore)*, 1999,

Conversely, about a third of those with skeletal lesions have a history of pulmonary tuberculosis.[40]

Bovine tuberculosis is caused by *M bovis* which also infects a great many other species. The disease in cattle was probably never common before the start of herding but one assumes that it must have been a considerable cause of morbidity and mortality thereafter. Tuberculosis is a primary lung disease in cattle but the organism is excreted in milk and humans contract the disease by eating or drinking infected milk or milk products, although those who may spend a large amount of time in cattle sheds may also contract it from infected droplets spread by diseased cows. From the gut, the bacteria gain entry to the lymphatic system and infect lymph nodes which enlarge and may suppurate. Tuberculosis of the cervical lymph nodes gained a certain notoriety during the seventeenth century, particularly when it was known as scrofula, or the King's evil. A touch by the King was thought to bring about a cure, no doubt to the great disappointment to the many who seem to have been 'stroaked' by the monarch.[41]

It has been suggested that the human form of the bacterium evolved from the bovine form[42] but analysis of the DNA of many species of mycobacteria suggests that this is very unlikely and it seems much more likely that *M tuberculosis* existed before the *M bovis* lineage split off from the common ancestor.[43] There has been further speculation that tuberculosis might have been introduced into the Americas by Europeans during their various periods of exploration, conquest and colonisation, but the finding of the disease, including ancient DNA, in pre-Columbian mummies, for example, has put this notion firmly to bed.[44]

78, 309–320; SH Liyange, CM Gupta and AR Cobb, Osteoarticular tuberculosis: current diagnosis and treatment, *American Journal of Therapy*, 2000, 7, 393–398; NC Mkandawire and E Kaunda, Bone and joint TB at Queen Elizabeth Hospital Centre 1986 to 2002, *Tropical Doctor*, 2005, 35, 14–16.

[40] B Autzen and JJ Elberg, Bone and joint tuberculosis in Denmark, *Acta Orthopedica Scandinavica*, 1988, 59, 50–52.

[41] IE Willetts, John Knight and the King's healing, *Journal of the Royal Society of Medicine*, 1994, 87, 756–757. Samuel Johnson was taken to London when he was 2½ years old to be touched by Queen Anne but without the benefit of a cure (LC McHenry and R MacKeith, Samuel Johnson's childhood illnesses and the King's evil, *Medical History*, 1966, 10, 386–399).

[42] WW Stead, KD Eisenach, MD Cave, ML Beggs, GL Templeton, CO Thoen and JH Bates, When did *Mycobacterium tuberculosis* first occur in the New World? An important question with public health implications, *American Review of Respiratory and Critical Care Medicine*, 1995, 151, 1267–1268.

[43] R Brosch, SV Gordon, M Marmiesse, P Brodin, C Buchreiser, K Eiglmeier, T Garnier, C Gutierrez, G Hewinson, K Kremer, LM Parsons, AS Pym, S Samper, D van Sooingen and ST Cole, A new evolutionary scenario for the *Mycobacterium tuberculosis* complex, *Proceedings of the National Academy of Sciences*, 2002, 99, 3684–3698. See also: MC Gutierrez, S Brisse, R Brosch, M Fabre, B Omaïs, M Marmiesse, P Supply and V Vincent, Ancient origin and gene mosaicism of the progenitor of *Mycobacterium tuberculosis*, *PloS Pathogens*, 2005, 1, e5.

[44] WL Salo, AC Aufderheide, J Buikstra and TA Holcomb, Identification of *Mycobacterium tuberculosis* DNA in a pre-Columbian Peruvian mummy, *Proceedings of the National Academy of Sciences of the United States*

FIGURE 6.2. Thoracic spine with tuberculosis. The central vertebral body has been almost completely destroyed and the spine has collapsed to form the characteristic angular kyphosis. The posterior elements of the spine are not involved.

Irrespective of which organism causes the skeletal lesions, the morphology is exactly the same and there is no truth in the statement that the bovine form is more likely to affect bone than the human. In half those with skeletal TB, the spine, especially the lumbar spine, is affected (Figure 6.2). The disease is largely confined to the vertebral bodies, with the posterior elements of the vertebrae usually, but not invariably, spared.[45] The infection may spread up and down the spine from the primary focus either through the intervertebral discs, or behind the anterior longitudinal ligament, and soft tissues around the vertebrae may also become involved. There is very little new bone formed and there are no cloacae as in pyogenic osteomyelitis but infection of lumbar vertebrae may result in an abscess forming beneath the fascia of the psoas muscle[46] which may extend to the groin where it points and is recognised

of America, 1994, 91, 2091–2094; BT Arriaza, W Salo, AC Aufderheide and TA Holcomb, Pre-Columbian tuberculosis in northern Chile: molecular and skeletal evidence, American Journal of Physical Anthropology, 1995, 98, 37–45; N Konomi, E Lebwohl, K Mowbray, I Tattersall and D Zhang, Detection of mycobacterial DNA in Andean mummies, Journal of Clinical Microbiology, 2002, 40, 4738–4740.

[45] RS Narlawar, JR Shah, MK Pimple, DP Patkar, T Patankar and M Castillo, Isolated tuberculosis of posterior elements of spine: magnetic resonance imaging findings in 33 patients, Spine, 2002, 27, 275–281.

[46] The psoas muscle takes its origin from the transverse processes of the lumbar vertebrae and inserts into the lesser trochanter of the femur.

as a cold abscess;[47] the abscess may also calcify and it is possible that the remnants of a calcified abscess presenting in the lumbar region could be recognised in a burial. Progression of the disease results in considerable loss of bone tissue with subsequent weakening of the affected vertebral bodies and, eventually, collapse and ankylosis. The result is to produce a marked angular kyphosis of the spine which is known as Pott's disease[48] which may be complicated by paraplegia or other neurological conditions.[49] This disease is of considerable antiquity and has been recognised in human remains at least as long ago as ancient Egypt.[50] A well-known case was described by Elliot Smith and Ruffer in a mummy from the tweny-first dynasty.[51]

When Pott's disease is established, it is relatively easy to diagnose tuberculosis in the skeleton; however, in earlier cases, the diagnosis may have to depend upon finding lytic lesions in the vertebral body with no new bone formation. Occasionally, one may find vertebrae with lesions on the front of the body which have resulted from infection beneath the anterior longitudinal ligament. Outside the spine, the lesions are generally solitary but this is not always the case and in the tropics especially, extraspinal lesions are more likely to be multifocal.[52] Lytic lesions are again the norm with little or no new bone formation and any bone may be affected and there is a form in children in which the fingers are involved, so-called tuberculous dactylitis. The term *spina ventosa* refers to the cyst-like swelling of the infected finger, often with cortical destruction but no periosteal new bone formation.[53] Tuberculosis also affects single joints; the hip and knee are commonly involved and so is the wrist.[54] Spread to a joint is usually from infection in an adjacent bone, but primary involvement of the synovial membrane does occur, most often in the knee. Proliferation of new bone is not extensive and ankylosis is almost inevitable as the disease progresses unchecked by treatment. Some authors have diagnosed pulmonary tuberculosis in the skeleton on the basis of finding new bone on the inner surface of the ribs, presumably those

[47] R Maron, D Levine, TE Dobbs and WM Geisler, Two cases of pott disease associated with bilateral psoas abscess: case report, *Spine*, 2006, 15, 561–564.
[48] Percival Pott 1714–1788.
[49] AK Jain, Treatment of tuberculosis of the spine with neurologic complications, *Clinical Orthopaedics and Related Research*, 2002, 398, 75–84.
[50] G Palfí, O Dutour, G Deák and I Hutás, *Tuberculosis: past and present*, Budapest, Golden Book Publishers, 1999.
[51] G Elliot Smith and MA Ruffer, Pott'sche Krankheit in einer ägyptischer Mumie, aus der Zeit der 21 Dynastie, um 1000 vor Chr., Heft 3 of Sudhoff and Sticker's Historische Biologie der Krankheitserreger, Giessen, 1910.
[52] AN Aggarwal, IK Dhammi and AK Jain, Multifocal skeletal tuberculosis, *Tropical Doctor*, 2001, 31, 219–220.
[53] S Adronikou and B Smith, "Spina ventosa" – tuberculous dactylitis, *Archives of Disease in Childhood*, 2002, 86, 206.
[54] AN Malaviya and PP Kotwal, Arthritis associated with tuberculosis, *Best Practice & Research Clinical Rheumatology*, 2003, 17, 319–343.

overlying peripheral lesions.[55] There is now good evidence that patients dying from pulmonary tuberculosis are likely to produce new bone on the ribs, especially on the vertebral ends;[56] and biomarkers of TB have been recovered from ribs from skeletons with morphological evidence of the disease elsewhere in the skeleton.[57] Unfortunately, these changes are not specific to tuberculosis and cannot be used for making a diagnosis without some confirmatory evidence. An operational definition for tuberculosis is shown in the "Operational definition for tuberculosis" box.

Operational definition for tuberculosis

Spinal: Lytic lesions predominantly affecting the vertebral bodies with sparing of the posterior elements

With

Virtually no new bone formation
There may be ankylosis, vertebral collapse and angular kyphosis.
Extra-spinal: Unifocal lytic lesions with virtually no new bone formation
Dactylitis: Cystic lesions in the fingers with swelling, cortical erosion but no periosteal new bone
Tuberculous arthritis: Unifocal joint fusion with little or now new bone formation
The diagnosis in all forms can be *confirmed* by detecting mycobacterial DNA, or mycolic acids in bone

---

In many cases, the diagnosis of TB in the skeleton is difficult but it can be made for certain if mycobacterial DNA can be recovered from the bone as has now been done on many occasions.[58] Moreover, bacterial DNA has been recovered from bones with non-specific lesions and even from bones that appear normal.[59] Further help with

[55] MA Kelley and MS Micozzi, Rib lesions in chronic pulmonary tuberculosis, *American Journal of Physical Anthropology*, 1984, 65, 381–386.
[56] V Matos and AL Santos, On the trail of pulmonary tuberculosis based on rib lesions: results from the Human Identified Skeletal Collection from the Museu Bocage (Lisbon, Portugal), *American Journal of Physical Anthropology*, 2006, 130, 190–200.
[57] AM Gernaey, DE Minnikin, MS Copley, RA Dixon, JC Middleton and CA Roberts, Mycolic acids and ancient DNA confirm an osteological diagnosis of tuberculosis, *Tuberculosis (Edinburgh)*, 2001, 81, 259–265; J Raff, DC Cook and F Kaestle, Tuberculosis in the New World: a study of ribs from the Schild Mississippian population, West-Central Illinois, *Memoria do Instituto Oswaldo Cruz*, 2006, 101, Supplement 2, 25–27.
[58] See AR Zink, W Grabner and AG Nerlich (Molecular identification of human tuberculosis in recent and historic bone tissue samples: the role of molecular techniques for the study of historic tuberculosis, *American Journal of Physical Anthropology*, 2005, 126, 32–47) for references.
[59] AR Zink, W Grabner, U Reischl, H Wolf and AG Nerlich, Molecular study on human tuberculosis in three geographically distinct and time delineated populations from ancient Egypt, *Epidemiology and Infection*, 2003, 130, 239–249.

the diagnosis can be made because the mycobacteria have waxy sheaths which are largely composed of mycolic acids that can readily be extracted and identified as to species[60] and they have been recovered from human bones.[61] Finding either aDNA or mycolic acids in bone with a putative case of TB would confirm the diagnosis, but absence of either could not rule out the possibility because neither might have survived after death and burial.

> *Brucellosis:* Brucellosis is a disease of animals that is readily passed to humans and it is considered here because it affects the skeleton and may easily be confused with tuberculosis. Four species of brucella are pathogenic to human, each with a different animal host; *Brucella abortus* is found in cattle, *Br melitensis* in goats, *Br suis* in pigs, and *Br canis* in dogs. In northern Europe most infections are contracted from cattle, especially from handling infected blood, or meat. While in warmer climates, where goats are herded, infection with *Br melitensis* is more common, with infection coming from drinking contaminated milk. Infection with *Br suis* occurs mainly in North America while infection with the canine species is rare and provokes only a mild reaction. The skeletal effects include sacroiliitis and there is often a monoarticular arthritis.[62] The spine is affected in up to a third of those with the infection, most commonly the lumbar spine, although all areas may be involved.[63] Destructive lesions are noted in the vertebrae on the superior and inferior surfaces but these may spread to involve deeper parts of the vertebral body. There is an attempt at repair early in the course of the disease and new bone formation is a feature of brucellosis while radiographs of affected vertebrae show dense sclerosis around and beneath lesions, an important point that may be used to differentiate brucellosis from tuberculosis. Vertebral collapse and kyphosis is not common but ankylosis does occur.

There seems little reason to doubt that brucellosis was common in the past. It might have been contracted readily by assisting cows in labour, for example, when there would inevitably have been considerable contact with blood, or from drinking

---

[60] E Garza-Gonzalez, M Guerrero-Olazaran, R Tijerina-Menchaca and JM Viader-Salvado, Identification of mycobacteria by mycolic acid patterns, *Archives of Medical Research*, 1998, 29, 303–306.

[61] AM Gernaey *et al*, 2001. *op cit.*

[62] A Pourbagher, MA Pourbagher, L Savas, T Turunc, YZ Demiroglu, I Erol and D Yalcintas, Epidemiologic, clinical and imaging findings in brucellosis patients with osteoarticular involvement, *American Journal of Roentgenology*, 2006, 187, 873–880.

[63] H Bodur, A Erbay, A Colpan and E Akinci, Brucellar spondylitis, *Rheumatology International*, 2004, 24, 221–226.

infected goat's milk.[64] The number of cases recorded in human remains is insignif-icant[65] and it is probable that some cases thought to be tuberculosis were, in fact, brucellosis. The index of suspicion should be high in putative cases of TB in which new bone formation is prominent and an X-ray would be very helpful in these cases. There is no reason bacterial DNA could not be recovered from bone, and if this were successfully achieved, then the diagnosis would be certain.

LEPROSY

Leprosy is a mycobacterial disease like tuberculosis and the clinical effects are again dependent on the immunological status of the host. Like tuberculosis, it is of great antiquity; it is thought to have originated in Eastern Africa or the Near East and spread throughout Europe, reaching the Americas within the past 500 years.[66] It apparently became common in Europe during the Middle Ages when it is supposed that it had been introduced from the Middle East, the bacillus – to use one author's graphic phrase – shuttling back and forth between Europe and the Near East.[67] The disease reached its peak during the twelfth to fourteenth centuries in Europe and then began to disappear, perhaps because of an increase in the prevalence of tuberculosis which confers some immunity to leprosy.[68]

Lepers were hated, persecuted and ostracized, and the physical stigmata 'were regarded as outward manifestations of inner sinfulness and likened to heresy in its

[64] Brucellosis is still a significant occupational risk for vets, meat handlers and laboratory workers, for example: AJ Reid, Brucellosis – a persistent occupational hazard in Ireland, *International Journal of Occupational and Environmental Health*, 2005, 11, 302–304.

[65] L Capasso, Brucellosis at Herculaneum (79AD), *International Journal of Osteoarchaeology*, 1999, 9, 277–288. This author later examined some carbonized cheese from Herculaneum and found evidence for the presence of bacteria, some of which seemed morphologically like brucella (Bacteria in two-millennia-old cheese, and related epizoonoses in Roman populations, *Journal of Infection*, 2002, 45, 122–127).

[66] M Monot, N Honoré, T Garnier, R Araoz, J-Y Coppée, C Lacrois, S Sow, JS Spencer, RW Truman, DL Williams, R Gelbar, M Virmond, B Flageul, S-N Cho, B Ji, A Paniz-Mondolfi, J Convit, S Young, PE Fine, V Rasolfo, PJ Brennan and ST Cole, On the origin of leprosy, Science, 2005, 308, 1040–1042.

[67] MF Leachat, The palaeoepidemiology of leprosy: an overview, *International Journal of Leprosy*, 1999, 67, 460–470.

[68] There is archaeological evidence for the co-occurrence of both leprosy and tuberculosis in the same individual, or in individuals buried together which is taken as evidence supporting this notion. (See: HD Donaghue, A Marcsik, C Matheson, K Vernon, E Nuorala, JE Molto, CL Greenblatt and M Spigelman, Co-infection of *Mycobacterium tuberculosis* and *Mycobacterium leprae* in human archaeological samples: a possible explanation for the historical decline of leprosy, *Proceeding Biological Sciences The Royal Society*, 2005, 272, 389–394; N Tayles and HR Buckley, Leprosy and tuberculosis in Iron Age Southeast Asia? *American Journal of Physical Anthropology*, 2004, 125, 239–256. Because of the cross-immunity with tuberculosis, BCG vaccine has been used to treat and prevent leprosy (MS Setia, C Steinmaus, CS Ho and GW Rutherford, The role of BCG in prevention of leprosy: a meta-analysis, *The Lancet Infectious Diseases*, 2006, 6, 162–179).

pernicious effects'.[69] It is difficult to know exactly what the prevalence of leprosy was during the Middle Ages but it may not have been as common as is sometimes supposed. Richards, for example, suggests that at its peak in the fourteenth century there were at most 3,000–4,000 people with the disease in Britain, in a population of about three million. Although, there were about 200 leper hospitals in Britain, they mostly catered to a tiny numbers of patients, often no more than ten with a staff of three to care for them.[70]

Probably not all those said to have the disease actually did. The disease was often confused with other skin diseases such as psoriasis, eczema, erysipelas, or pustular acne, while deforming joint diseases such as psoriatic arthropathy or rheumatoid might also have done their bit to muddy the diagnostic waters. Although it was suggested that the medieval physicians actually confused the disease with syphilis, a view propounded particularly by Holcomb[71] and effectively demolished by Demaitre.[72] The evidence from archaeology suggests that, in fact, the physicians got the diagnosis right in the majority of cases. For example, over three-quarters of those buried at the leper hospital at Naestved in Denmark had the characteristic lesions of the disease, indicating a high degree of diagnostic precision.[73]

The disease is caused by a mycobacterium, *M leprae* which is also sometimes known as Hansen's bacillus, after the Norwegian physician who identified it as the cause of leprosy.[74] The disease is thought to be transmitted by the airborne spread of nasal secretions which are taken up through the mucosal lining of the nose and respiratory tract. It is not very infectious and the disease cannot be contracted by touch.[75] The effects of infection are determined by the immune response mounted by the host. There is a wide spectrum of effect and the disease has been classified into a number of clinical types[76] (see Table 6.3). There is a long interval between infection and the appearance of symptoms. Males are affected more frequently than females by about 2:1. The organism is an obligate intracellular parasite, that is, it can survive only inside other cells, and it has a special predilection for skin macrophages

[69] M Goodrich, *Other middle ages. Witnesses at the margins of medieval society*, Philadelphia, University of Pennsylvania Press, 1998, pp 10–11; 111.

[70] P Richards, Leprosy: myth, melodrama and mediaevalism, *Journal of the Royal College of Physicians of London*, 1990, 24, 55–62.

[71] RC Holcomb, The antiquity of congenital syphilis, *Bulletin of the History of Medicine*, 1941, 10, 148–167.

[72] L Demaitre, The description and diagnosis of leprosy by fourteenth century physicians, *Bulletin of the History of Medicine*, 1985, 59, 327–344.

[73] JG Anderson, Studies in the mediaeval diagnosis of leprosy in Denmark, MD Thesis, University of Copenhagen.

[74] Gerhard Henrick Armauer Hansen 1841–1912.

[75] WJ Britton and DNJ Lockwood, Leprosy, *Lancet*, 2004, 363, 1209–1219.

[76] DS Ridley and WH Jopling, Classification of leprosy according to immunity: a five group system, *International Journal of Leprosy*, 1966, 34, 255–273.

Table 6.3. *Classification of leprosy and main clinical features**

Classification	Clinical features
Tuberculoid	Single, small skin lesions; solitary enlarged peripheral nerves
Borderline tuberculoid	Many skin lesions; asymmetric irregular enlargement of several large peripheral nerves
Borderline lepromatous	Multiple skin lesions, all sizes; symmetrical involvement of many peripheral nerves
Borderline	Many small skin lesions; diffuse thickening of the skin; asymmetrical thickening of peripheral nerves with loss of sensation of weakness
Lepromatous	Innumerable confluent skin lesions; diffuse thickening of the skin; symmetrical peripheral neuropathy

Note: This classification is not always used in the clinical literature, as some workers prefer a simplified classification in which patients are referred to as having a paucibacillary or a multibacillary form; these correspond to the tuberculoid and lepromatous forms, respectively.
*Based on: DNJ Lockwood, Leprosy, *Medicine*, 2005, 33, 26–29.

and the Schwann cells which cover myelinated neurones. Additionally, it prefers to reside in the cooler parts of the body, such as the skin and the periphery.[77]

The two extremes of the clinical spectrum are the tuberculoid and the lepromatous forms. In the tuberculoid form, the cell-mediated immune response is good. Granulomas are formed but contain few bacteria. Activated CD4+ T-cells are abundant in the centre of the granulomas and they produce interferon-γ which stimulates macrophages to contain the growth of the organisms. The CD4+ cells also secrete IL-2 which upregulates the further production of CD4+ cells. On the periphery of the granuloma, CD8+ cells lurk to prevent expansion of the granuloma and tissue destruction. Conversely, in the lepromatous form, the immune response is poor, granulomas are poorly formed and huge numbers of bacteria are present. CD8 cells secrete cytokines that enhance the growth of the bacteria and suppress CD4 activity; IL-4 seems to be important in this respect.

Leprosy is a predominantly a disease of the nervous system and the skin (as can be seen from Table 6.3). The effects of the skeleton are confined largely to those with lepromatous or long-standing tuberculoid leprosy[78] and by no means all patients with

[77] The bacterium cannot be grown in normal culture media and the nine banded armadillo (*Dasypus novemcinctus*) is the only other animal in which the disease occurs, although genetically altered mice can also be induced to grow the organism in the laboratory.

[78] SPW Kimarasinghe, Some useful clinical clues and techniques in the diagnosis of tuberculoid leprosy, *International Journal of Dermatology*, 2001, 40, 299–304.

the disease have skeletal involvement. While it has been estimated that up to 88% of patients may be affected[79] much lower prevalences are generally quoted. The maximum prevalence is probably much lower, and certainly considerably less than half.[80]

The bone changes in leprosy may be classified as either specific or secondary. Specific changes are due to the direct infection of bone with the bacterium, often the bones of the hands or the feet,[81] whereas the secondary changes result from other effects which do not involve direct infection.[82] The secondary changes are complex and include concentric loss of bone from the phalanges of the hands and feet, osteomyelitis, predominantly of the bones of the feet, great destruction of joints of the leg (Charcot joints) and a group of changes in the skull that have been called the rhino-maxillary syndrome. The skeletal changes were described by Møller-Christensen who examined human remains from Aebelholt and Naestved in Denmark. Møller-Christensen's publications on leprosy constitute one of the classics of palaeopathology and represent one of the few occasions on which the study of bones has aided modern understanding of a disease.[83] Møller-Christensen coined the term 'facies leprosa' to describe the changes in the skull but since this is thought to have clinical connotations, the alternative, rhino-maxillary syndrome has come to supersede it.

The concentric loss of cortical bone in the hands and feet begins peripherally and proceeds proximally with great destruction of the hands and feet, although the metacarpals and metatarsals are generally spared. The most distal affected bone may be tapered and American radiologists sometimes refer to this as the 'licked candy sign'. The cause of this loss of bone is not known for certain but is probably due to denervation of the digits. Osteomyelitis is the direct result of sensory loss, so that cuts are sustained without the individual being aware of the fact, and infection follows. It is obvious that unshod feet are particularly liable to be damaged and the foot bones subsequently infected. Charcot's joints are also the result of sensory loss and are produced by a combination of bony fragmentation, fracture and dislocation.[84]

[79] DE Paterson, Bone changes in leprosy, their incidence, progress, prevention and arrest, *International Journal of Leprosy*, 1961, 29, 393–422.

[80] R Jurado and CA Agudelo, Of skin and bones, *Journal of Clinical Rheumatology*, 2001, 7, 211–212.

[81] S Dave, AV Nori, DM Thappa and N Siddaraju, Leprous ossteitis presenting as bone cyst and erosions, *Dermatology Online Journal*, 2004, 10, 17

[82] P Moonot, N Ashwood and D Lockwood, Orthopaedic complications of leprosy, *Journal of Bone and Joint Surgery*, 2005, 87B, 1328–1332.

[83] The most important are probably: V Møller-Christensen, *Bone changes in leprosy*, Copenhagen, Munksgaard, 1961; *Leprosy changes of the skull*, Odense, Odense University Press, 1978; New knowledge of leprosy through paleopathology, *International Journal of Leprosy*, 1965, 33, 6S03–S610.

[84] E Trepman, A Nihal and MS Pinzur, Current topics review: Charcot neuroarthropathy of the foot and ankle, *Foot and Ankle International*, 2005, 26, 46–63.

The end result is a highly disorganised joint; in leprosy the joints of foot and ankle are most likely to be affected.[85]

The rhinomaxillary syndrome is pathognomonic of lepromatous or borderline lepromatous leprosy and comprises the following:[86]

Operational definition for leprosy

Rhinomaxillary syndrome

OR

Concentric loss of bone from phalanges of hands or feet
There may also be osteomyelitis of the bones of the feet or neuropathic change in the joints of the feet or ankles.

---

1. Resorption of the alveolar process in the centre of the maxilla (the prosthion) with extension and eventual loss of the central incisors;
2. destruction of the anterior nasal spine;
3. resorption and remodelling of the margins of the nasal aperture;
4. pitting on the palatine process of the maxilla;
5. resorption of the nasal septum; and
6. pitting on the nasal conchae and their eventual destruction to give the appearance of an 'empty nose'.

Presented with a skull with the full-blown rhinomaxillary syndrome, or hands and feet with concentric loss of bone, there should be little difficulty in making a diagnosis. The nature of palaeopathology, however, is such that things may not be this clear cut but where the thought of leprosy strays into the mind, it might be possible to confirm a suspicion by the extraction of mycobacterial DNA.[87] Otherwise, the operational definition is shown in the "Operational definition for leprosy" box.

[85] Jean-Martin Charcot 1825–1893. It should be noted that these so-called neuropathic joints are not unique to leprosy. Charcot described them in patients with tertiary syphilis, but they may be found in any condition in which there is a sensory peripheral neuropathy including diabetes, alcoholism and syringomyelia.
[86] JG Andersen and K Manchester, The rhinomaxillary syndrome in leprosy: a clinical, radiological and palaeopathological study, *International Journal of Osteoarchaeology*, 1992, 2, 121–129.
[87] See, for example, CJ Haas, A Zink, G Palfi, U Szeimies and AG Nerlich, Detection of leprosy in ancient human skeletal remains by molecular identification of *Mycobacterium leprae*, *American Journal of Clinical Pathology*, 2000, 114, 428–436; R Montiel, C Garcia, MP Canadas, A Isidro, JM Guijo and A Malgosa, DNA sequences of *Mycobacterium leprae* recovered from ancient bones, *FEMS Microbiology Letters*, 2003, 226, 413–414.

VENEREAL SYPHILIS

Venereal syphilis is one of four infectious diseases caused by bacteria of the genus *Treponema*. The four species pathogenic to man are indistinguishable morphologically and in almost every other way, and they are generally regarded all as subspecies of *T pallidum* (see Table 6.4), but they have recently been differentiated on the basis of genetic signatures in three genes.[88]

The treponemes are motile, having between eight and twenty corkscrew spirals, and are often referred to as treponemes. The routes of infection and the clinical conditions differ but there is a school of thought that considers that the various presentations are the result of the bacteria adapting to different environments. Together, they currently infect about 2.5 million people worldwide.[89] The organism of venereal syphilis (syphilis, from this point on)[90] does not survive outside the body and despite what many generations of medical students might have been taught in the past – 'the spirochaete can jump twenty feet' – the infection is spread between adults by sexual contact during which organisms are transferred from an infected, open lesion. Individuals are infectious only during the primary and secondary stages of the disease (see below).[91]

There is also a congenital form which is contracted *in utero* which will be discussed later. The disease has a venerable history[92] but seemed to become particularly common during the eighteenth century and it was commonly treated with mercury, often in the form of calomel (mercurous chloride) administered as an ointment, by mouth or by inhalation as a fumigant. The physician would know when the patient was complying with the treatment when he or she developed typical signs of mercury poisoning, including salivation, blackening of the teeth and a tremor. The medical joke at the time was that an individual might have 'A night with Venus and a lifetime with Mercury'! whether the mercury worked or not is a matter of some debate.

---

[88] A Centurion-Lara, BJ Molini, C Godornes, E Sun, K Hevner, WC Van Voorhis and SA Lukehart, Molecular differentiation of *Treponema pallidum* subspecies, *Journal of Clinical Microbiology*, 2006, 44, 3377–3380.

[89] GM Antal, SA Lukehart and AZ Meheus, The endemic treponematoses, *Microbes and Infection*, 2002, 4, 83–94.

[90] I am using this shorthand since in Europe any skeleton found with a treponemal disease is most likely to have had venereal syphilis; yaws and endemic syphilis will be more likely in other parts of the world and it may prove impossible to differentiate between them on morphological grounds.

[91] RW Peeling and EW Hook, The pathogenesis of syphilis: the Great Mimicker revisited, *Journal of Pathology*, 2006, 208, 224–232.

[92] C Quétel, *History of syphilis*, Baltimore, Johns Hopkins University Press, 1990. It has been suggested that the Neanderthals suffered from syphilis, this accounting for some of their physical characteristics, but the evidence is extremely unconvincing (DJM Wright, Syphilis and Neanderthal man, *Nature*, 1971, 229, 409.

Table 6.4. *Treponemal diseases*

Disease	Causative agent	Occurrence	Mode of spread	Affects bone
Venereal syphilis	*Treponema pallidum*	World wide	Sexual intercourse	Yes
Yaws	*Treponema pallidum subsp pertenue*	Tropics	Direct person-to-person	Yes, indistinguishable from venereal syphilis
Bejel (endemic syphilis)	*Treponema pallidum subsp endemicum*	Countries of the Middle East; West Africa	Mouth to mouth	Yes
Pinta	*Treponema pallidum subsp carateum*	Caribbean, Central and South America	Direct person-to-person	No

Goldwater called it the most colossal medical hoax ever perpetrated,[93] but there is some evidence that it might have been successful, at least in treating infections with low numbers of spirochaetes present.[94]

Clinically, syphilis can be described as having three stages: primary, secondary and tertiary. In the primary stage a painless lesion, called a chancre, develops at the site of inoculation, which is invariably somewhere on the genitalia. It is self-limiting and usually heals – no doubt to great relief – in two to eight weeks. A short while later, the second stage is heralded by a flu-like illness and a widespread rash which may appear on the soles of the feet and the palms of the hands. These symptoms also resolve spontaneously. Just over a third of those infected will enter the tertiary stage after a latent period that may be anything up to thirty years after the initial infection. This stage is characterised by the formation of erosive granulomas called gumma which affect skin and bones. The gumma are similar in appearance to the tubercles of TB but without a necrotic centre.[95]

---

[93] L Goldwater, *Mercury – a history of quicksilver*, Baltimore, York Press, 1972.

[94] JG O'Shea, 'Two minutes with Venus, two years with Mercury' – mercury as an antisyphilitic chemotherapeutic agent, *Journal of the Royal Society of Medicine*, 1990, 83, 392–395.

[95] The manifestations of tertiary syphilis are legion but include general paresis, with psychiatric symptoms and intellectual deterioration; tabes dorsalis, with demyelinization of the sensory neurones in the spinal cord (so-called tabes dorsalis); and the formation of aneurysms on the great vessels; the arch of the aorta being a common site.

THE ORIGINS OF SYPHILIS

Much has been written on the origins of syphilis in Europe, stimulated in part no doubt by the fact that – as Crosby says – it is a 'uniquely historical' disease;[96] that is, we all think we know when it started. There seems little doubt that what seemed to be a 'new' disease erupted during the French invasion of Italy at the start of the sixteenth century, and was on this account, referred to as the 'French disease'.[97] It did not escape notice of later historians either that the outbreak was closely related in time to the return of Columbus from the New World and there has developed a series of suggestions about the origin of the disease which have rather aggrandised by being called 'theories'. These 'theories' are commonsensical suggestions that (1) the disease originated in, and was brought to Europe from the New World (the Columbian theory); (2) it was present in Europe prior to the sixteenth century (the pre-Columbian theory); (3) treponemal disease was present in both the Old and the New Worlds concurrently and developed into developed into syphilis only when the time was ripe (and Columbus and his sailors are innocent – the Unitarian theory); or (4) the disease originated in Africa and spread from there.[98] The Columbian theory has been pushed especially hard by American authors, no doubt hoping this might take our minds off other more recent importations which have done us no good. The paper of Baker and Armelagos was particularly influential in the respect.[99] There does not seem much doubt that a new disease, or perhaps, a novel manifestation of an old one, appeared at the start of the sixteenth century and spread rapidly throughout Europe. One has to say that if Columbus and his men really were responsible, then they must have been extremely busy, given that less than fifty in total returned from America. It is also possible that they were all in the latent period of the disease following their time at sea which would have meant that they were not infectious when they landed.

A recent study of the phylogenetic relations between the treponemes has indicated that yaws was the first disease to emerge (probably evolving from a form that infected apes); that the endemic form derived from the ancestral form in the Middle East

[96]   AW Crosby, The early history of syphilis: a reappraisal, *American Anthropologist*, 1969, 71, 218–227.

[97]   LJ McGough, Syphilis in history: response to 2 articles, *Clinical Infectious Diseases*, 2005, 41, 573–574. The name of the disease derives from the name of the shepherd in the Latin poem of Girolamo Frascatoro (1478–1553), *Syphilis sive morbus gallicus* published in 1530. See: N Thyresson, Girolamo Fracastoro and syphilis, *International Journal of Dermatology*, 1995, 34, 735–739.

[98]   For a more elaborate explanation see: C Meyer, C Jung, T Kohl, A Poenicke, A Poppe and KW Alt, Syphilis 2001 – a palaeopathological reappraisal, *Homo*, 2002, 53, 39–58.

[99]   BJ Baker and GJ Armelagos, The origin and antiquity of syphilis, *Current Anthropology*, 1988, 29, 703–737. At the time, the paper attracted much attention and comments from no fewer than sixteen authors were included with it.

and the Balkans at a later date; and that *T pallidum* was the last to emerge, arising most likely from a progenitor in the New World.[100] Thus, spread from the New World does seem likely, but the evidence for syphilis in the Old World which pre-dates Columbus[101] suggests that Columbus and his men were not culpable.[102] What seems most probable is that the disease increased in virulence towards the end of the fifteenth century and was thereby able to spread much more rapidly than previously, and manifested new symptoms.

CHANGES IN THE SKELETON

Bone changes in primary syphilis are very rare[103] but joint pains may be a feature of secondary syphilis.[104] The most important changes in the skeleton are not found until patients enter the tertiary stage of the disease.

Periosteal new bone formation is very characteristic of syphilis and may appear in the early stages and is especially prominent on bones near the surface, that is, the tibia, frontal bone, ribs and sternum although other bones may be involved. These are non-gummatous changes which persist into the later stages. Periosteal new bone formation may be very considerable, especially on the front of the tibias which take on the appearance of the sabre tibia seen in congenital syphilis (qv). Although the tibia may appear to be bowed, the long axis is, in fact, straight, the bowing being due to the great accumulation of periosteal new bone (PNB) on the subcutaneous surface. The effects in the later stages of the disease are due to the formation of gumma in bones. Bony tissues adjacent to gumma undergo necrosis and are absorbed and this process is termed *caries sicca*.[105] The lesions are most evident on the frontal bone and may heal with remodelling and scarring. On the

---

[100] KN Harper, PS Ocampo, BM Steiner, RW George, MS Silverman, S Bolotin, A Pillay, NJ Saunders and GJ Armelagos, On the original of the treponematoses: a phylogenetic approach, *PLoS Neglected Tropical Diseases*, 2008, 2, e148.

[101] See, for example, C Meyer, C Jung, T Kohl, A Poenicke, A Poppe and KW Alt, Syphilis 2001 – a palaeopatho-logical reappraisal, *Homo*, 2002, 53, 39–58; YS Erdal, A pre-Columbian case of congenital syphilis from Ana-tolia (Nicaea, 13th century AD), *International Journal of Osteoarchaeology*, 2006, 16, 16–33; TE von Hunnius, CA Roberts, A Boylston and SR Saunders, Histological identification of syphilis in pre-Columbian England, *American Journal of Physical Anthropology*, 2006, 129, 559–566 and references therein.

[102] RS Morton and S Rashid, "The syphilis enigma": the riddle resolved? *Sexually Transmitted Infections*, 2001, 77, 322–324.

[103] IA Gurland, L Korn, L Edelman and F Wallach, An unusual manifestation of acquired syphilis, *Clinical Infectious Diseases*, 2001, 32, 667–669.

[104] AJ Reginato, Syphilitic arthritis and osteitis, *Rheumatic Disease Clinics of North America*, 1993, 19, 379–398.

[105] JL Turk, Syphilitic caries of the skull – the changing face of medicine, *Journal of the Royal Society of Medicine*, 1995, 88, 146–149.

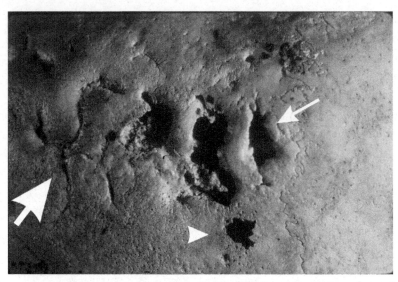

FIGURE 6.3. Frontal bone of skull affected with syphilis. Lesions are seen in all three stages of the disease, active (arrow head), healing (small arrow) and scarring (large arrow). These changes are collectively referred to as caries sicca and are pathognomonic of treponemal disease.

other hand they may be extremely destructive with large areas of the skull destroyed. The lesions in the skull were extensively studied and described by Hackett and his description is another palaeopathological classic.[106] The combination in the skull of active lytic lesions, remodelling and scarring (Figure 6.3) is pathognomonic of treponemal infection. The actual infection cannot be identified but will be decided on probabilistic grounds, depending on the origin of the remains. Neuropathic joint destruction may be found in syphilis. Indeed, Charcot's original description was in the context of tabes dorsalis, and is the result of sensory loss because of damage to the nerve cells in the dorsal columns of the spine.[107]

Congenital syphilis: The treponeme is able to cross the placenta and infect the fetus *in utero* and the infection is a significant cause of stillbirth.[108] The skeleton is

---

[106] CJ Hackett, *Diagnostic criteria of syphilis, yaws and treponarid (treponematoses) and of some other diseases in dry bones (for use in osteo-archaeology)*, Berlin, Springer, 1976.

[107] Some other causes of neuropathic joints, and the joints most likely to be involved are shown in Table 6.5.

[108] DM Judge, N Tafari, RL Naeye and C Marboe, Congenital syphilis and perinatal mortality, *Paediatric Pathology*, 1986, 5, 411–420. Writing in 1908, Clement Lucas noted that 'There is probably no disease responsible for such an enormous destruction of human life in its earlier stages as that caused by syphilitic parentage (R Clement Lucas, An address on inherited syphilis, *Lancet*, 1908, i, 277–279). Congenital syphilis is beginning to manifest itself more commonly in the wake of the great increase in the sexual transmitted diseases and is likely to be a risk particularly for expectant mothers who are unaware that they are infected or do not seek treatment (A Cross, S Luck, M Sharland, P Rice and R Chakraborty, Syphilis in London circa 2004: new challenges from an old disease, *Archives of Disease in Childhood*, 2005, 90, 1045–1046).

Table 6.5. *Features of some fungal diseases of bone*

Disease	Causative agent	Features in bone	Most common sites
Cryptococcosis	*Cryptococcus neoformans*	Lytic lesions with no new bone	Spine, pelvis, ribs, skull and tibia
North American blastomycosis	*Blastomyces dermatitidis*	Lytic lesions with sclerosis and periosteal new bone	Vertebrae, ribs, tibia, wrist and foot
South American blastomycosis	*Paracoccidioides brasiliensis*	Lytic lesions with sclerosis and periosteal new bone	Vertebrae, ribs, tibia, wrist and foot
Coccidioidomycosis	*Coccidioides immitis*	Lytic lesions, often multiple and symmetrical	Spine, ribs and pelvis
Histoplasmosis	*Histoplasma capsulatum and H capsulatum var amboisii*	Cystic lytic lesions with sclerosis and periosteal new bone	Pelvis, skull and ribs
Sporotrichosis	*Sporothrix schenckii*	Single or multiple lytic lesions with no new bone	Tibia, fibula, femur, humerus, hands and feet

invariably involved in secondary syphilis and the affected child may be born with a number of stigmata including a rather characteristic facial appearance consisting of bossing of the frontal bone, a depression of the nose – the so-called saddle nose deformity and underdevelopment of the maxilla. Early signs on the bones include periostitis and osteochondritis which is due to a disturbance of ossification of cartilage at the growing ends of the long bones, and which tends to disappear in the early years of life.[109] Affected individuals may also develop a typical sabre tibia which – as in the acquired form – is due to the apposition of new bone on the front of the tibia. In the case of congenital syphilis, however, the bone shows true anterior bending. Endosteal new bone proliferation leads to enlargement of the bone and the radiological appearances may mimic those of Paget's disease although the sclerotic changes may spare the ends of the bone in syphilis. The best-known features of congenital syphilis, however, are the changes seen in the teeth. These include

[109] SK Hira, GJ Bhat, JB Patel, SN Din, RV Attilil, MI Patel, S Baskarnathan, RS Hira and NN Andu, Early congenital syphilis: clinico-radiological features in 202 patients, *Sexually Transmitted Diseases*, 1985, 12, 177–183.

peg-shaped, notched permanent incisors – Hutchinson's teeth,[110] and changes in the first molar to which the name, mulberry molar or Moon's molar, is usually given.[111]

Diagnosing syphilis in the skeleton can present problems and it should most certainly *not* be diagnosed simply by the presence of periosteal new bone on the tibia. There has been one report (to date) of the extraction of DNA from a 200-year-old skeleton with syphilis[112] but other authors have disputed the validity of this finding and have stated categorically that aDNA analysis cannot be used to study syphilis.[113] The diagnosis has also been made histologically,[114] but the criteria need to be validated clinically before this technique could be regarded as definitive. Both techniques are in need of further work since reliable diagnostic methods would be of great help when studying treponemal disease. Until then, it is not likely that syphilis, either congenital or acquired, can be validly diagnosed in the skeleton in the absence of the skull or a sabre tibia. An operational definition is shown in the "Operational definition of syphilis" box.

Operational definition of syphilis

Acquired: Caries sicca, that is, lesions showing erosion, remodelling and scarring all present together in the skull

OR

Sabre tibia without actual bowing

Congenital: Hutchinson's teeth and/or Moon's or ulberry molars

OR

Sabre tibia with bowing

---

[110] Sir Jonathan Hutchinson 1828–1913.

[111] There are, in fact, two distinct alterations in the molars, one described by Moon and the other by Fournier. There has been a good deal of confusion about this in the literature and the reader should consult the excellent paper by Hillson and his colleagues to obtain clarity: S Hillson, C Grigson and S Bond, Dental defects of congenital syphilis, *American Journal of Physical Anthropology*, 1988, 107, 25–40. (Henry Moon 1845–1892; Jean Alfred Fournier 1832–1914.) Hillson considers that Moon's molars are actually the most characteristic sign of congenital syphilis.

[112] CJ Kolma, A Centurion-Lara, SA Lukehart, DW Owsley and N Tuross, Identification of *Treponema pallidum* subspecies *pallidum* in a 200-year old skeletal specimen, *Journal of Infectious Diseases*, 1999, 180, 2060–2062.

[113] AS Bouwman and TA Brown, The limits of biomolecular palaeopathology ancient DNA cannot be used to study venereal syphilis, *Journal of Archaeological Science*, 2005, 32, 707–713.

[114] TE von Hunnius, CA Roberts, A Boylston and SR Saunders, Histological identification of syphilis in pre-Columbian England, *American Journal of Physical Anthropology*, 2006, 129, 599–566.

POLIOMYELITIS

Poliomyelitis is caused by an RNA enterovirus, one of the family of picornaviruses. It is spread by the faeco-oral route and has a long history. There is, for example, a depiction on the stele for Ruma (or Rem) at the sanctuary of the goddess Astarte at Memphis dating to *ca* 2000 BC[115] but it was not recognised as a distinct entity until the eighteenth century and seems only to have assumed epidemic proportions in the nineteenth.[116] Once ingested, the virus replicates in the throat and intestinal tract before invading the lymphatic system and the blood. In the majority of those infected, the disease is either asymptomatic or no more than a minor ailment. The remainder suffer a relatively mild and self-limiting flu-like illness, sometimes with some muscular pain or stiffness. In approximately 1% of cases, the central nervous system is infected and the motor cells in the ventral horn of the spinal cord may be destroyed and then the muscles supplied by these nerves become paralysed.[117] If the muscles of respiration are affected, death will quickly ensue unless artificial respiration can be given.

The effects on the skeleton will depend on the time of life during which the infection was contracted. If during childhood, when the skeleton is still developing, the bones in the paralysed limb or limbs will be shorter and more gracile than those in the unaffected limb. On the other hand, if the disease is contracted in adult life, the bones in the paralysed limb will be the same length as those on the normal side, but will be likely to be more gracile due to the effect of disuse atrophy (Figure 6.4). There may be additional features which will be of some help with the diagnosis. For example, coxa valga (an increase in the femoral neck angle) may be found in an affected femur, although this is an effect found in other neuromuscular disorders. If the legs are markedly unequal in length, then there may be some degree of spinal curvature and bones from the paralysed limb will become osteoporotic. The diagnosis will be made in the juvenile skeleton on the basis of finding limb bones that are gracile and of unequal length compared with those on the contralateral side. Radiography of the affected limbs will probably show osteoporotic change.

---

[115] RH Major, *A history of medicine*, Springfield, CC Thomas, 1954, illustration on p 43.

[116] DM Horstmann, The poliomyelitis story: a scientific hegira, *Yale Journal of Biology and Medicine*, 1985, 58, 79–90.

[117] JL Melnick, Current status of poliovirus infections, *Clinical Microbiology Reviews*, 1996, 9, 293–300.

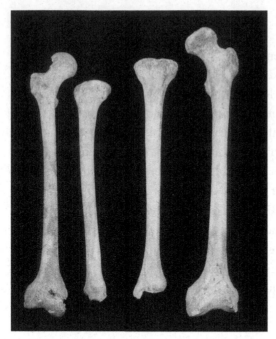

FIGURE 6.4. Left and right tibia and femur from a presumptive case of polio. The bones from the right side are shorter and more gracile than those on the left, suggesting that the individual contracted the disease before growth had finished.

SMALLPOX

Smallpox is of considerable historical importance,[118] not only because it was the first disease for which a vaccine was discovered, but it is also the only one that has

---

[118] Small pox has also been mooted by some as a possible occupational hazard for archaeologists. The scare was first raised by Zuckerman who suggested that all those who excavated sites where there might be the remains of individuals who had died of smallpox should be vaccinated (AJ Zuckerman, Palaeontology of smallpox, *Lancet*, 1984, 2, 1454). This suggestion was quickly condemned on the basis that the risk from vaccination was infinitely greater than the risk of contracting smallpox from a body – which was nil (PL Lewis, Mummified, frozen smallpox: is it a threat? *Journal of the American Medical Association*, 1985, 253, 3095). There the matter rested for a couple of years until the mummy of an Italian child who had died in the sixteenth century was found with skin lesions suggestive of smallpox and in which viral particles were observed with the EM (G Fornaciari and A Marchetti, Intact smallpox virus particles in an Italian mummy of the sixteenth century, *Lancet*, 1986, 2, 625; *Ibid*, Italian smallpox of the sixteenth century, *Lancet*, 1986, 2, 1469–1470). Samples from the mummy were subsequently sent to smallpox reference laboratories and it was confirmed that the virus was not viable (SS Marennikova, EM Shelukhina, OA Zhukova, NN Yanova and VN Loparev, Smallpox diagnosed 400 years later: results of skin lesions examination of 16th century Italian mummy, *Journal of Hygiene, Epidemiology, Microbiology and Immunology*, 1990, 34, 227–231). In the meantime, Meers produced an analysis of some data from a study in which viable viral particles had been obtained from smallpox scabs which had been stored for up to thirteen years (HL Wolff and JJAB Croon, The survival of smallpox virus (Variola Minor) in natural circumstances, *Bulletin of the World Health Organisation*, 1968, 38, 492–493). Extrapolating from these data Meers suggested that smallpox might survive for up to 25 years and perhaps

been eradicated by human endeavour.[119] It was a common cause of death during the eighteenth century, perhaps accounting for up to 20% of all deaths in Europe.[120] In a small number of affected individuals periosteal new bone is formed, in the great majority of cases, on the bones around the elbow, usually bilaterally.[121]

FUNGAL INFECTIONS OF BONE

Fungal infections are relatively common in some areas of the world and at least one – coccidioidomycosis – really is an occupational hazard for archaeologists.[122] Bone is not often involved and the diagnosis of individual infections can be extremely difficult.[123] The most frequent fungal infections and a synopsis of their effects is shown in Table 6.6.

PARASITIC DISEASE

There are not many parasitic diseases that affect bone but it is possible that cases of hydatid disease might occasionally come to light. The disease results primarily from infection with the dog tapeworm *Echinococcus granulosus*. The dog is the definitive host but part of the life cycle of the parasite is carried out in an intermediate

longer in cool, dry conditions, such as a crypt (PD Meers, Smallpox still entombed? *Lancet*, 1985, 1. 1103). Meers also referred to the fact that excavation at the crypt of Christ Church, Spitalfields had been halted by the Health and Safety Executive because a corpse with what appeared to be smallpox had been recovered. I was carrying out the pathological examination of the skeletons from the site at the time and was aware of the anxiety that was created although not actively involved. A colleague of mine was involved, however, and although all the authorities that he asked advised him that there was no risk of contracting smallpox from a body of that age, none would put their advice in writing. Since it was deemed unethical to newly vaccinate the excavators, only those who had already had primary vaccination were permitted to continue with the excavation. Thus, an extra-ordinary amount of fuss was raised about a non-existing risk (*pace* Zuckerman and Meers) and a real hazard, that of lead absorption from working in an enclosed dusty space where lead coffins were quietly disintegrating, was overlooked for a very long time.

[119] EA Belongia and AL Naleway, Smallpox vaccine: the good, the bad, and the ugly, *Clinical and Medical Research*, 20003, 1, 85–86.

[120] AJ Mercer, Smallpox and epidemiological-demographic change in Europe: the role of vaccination, *Population Studies*, 1985, 39, 287–307.

[121] MW Lentz and FR Noyes, Osseous deformity from osteomyelitis variolosa. A case report, *Clinical Orthopaedics and Related Research*, 1979, 143, 155–157.

[122] LR Peterson, SL Marshall, C Barton-Dickson, RA Hajjeh, MD Lindsley, DW Warnock, AA Panackal, JB Shaffer, MB Haddad, FS Fisher, DT Dennis and J Morgan, Coccidioidomycosis among workers at an archaeological site, northeastern Utah, *Emerging Infectious Diseases*, 2004, 10, 637–642. (It is perhaps of some interest that there were more authors of the paper than there were cases!)

[123] R Arkun, Parasitic and fungal disease of bone, *Seminars in Musculoskeletal Radiology*, 2004, 8, 231–242.

Table 6.6. *Some human intestinal parasites that excrete ova in the faeces*

Species	Common name	Pathological
Nematodes		
Ascaris lumbricoides	Large roundworm	In heavy infestations
Ankylostoma duodenale	Hookworm	Yes
Enterobium vermicularis	Pinworm	No
Necator americanis	Hookworm	Yes
Trichuris trichuria	Whipworm	In heavy infestations
Trematodes		
Chlonorchis sinensis	Liver fluke	Yes
Fasciola hepatica	Liver fluke	Yes
Schistosoma haematobium	Bilharzia	Yes
Schistosoma japonica	Bilharzia	Yes
Schistosoma mansoni	Bilharzia	Yes
Paragonimus westermanii	Lung fluke	Yes
Cestodes		
Diphyllobothrium latum	Fish tape worm	Yes
Hymenolepsis nana	Beetle tape worm	No
Taenia saginata	Beef tape worm	Yes
Taenia solium	Pork tape worm	Yes

host. In the United Kingdom, the intermediate host is most commonly the sheep. Therefore, the disease tends to be most prevalent in areas where sheep are reared. The intermediate host is infected by eggs derived ultimately from dog faeces and the parasite then completes part of its life cycle. The definitive hosts become infected by eating raw meat that contains cysts that have developed in the intermediate host and so the cycle continues. Humans become infected by ingesting embryonated eggs, again ultimately derived from dog faeces. Once ingested, the embryos enter a branch of the portal vein and become lodged in the liver capillaries where they may either die, migrate to other organs, or develop into hydatid cysts. In a small number of those infected, cystic lesions develop in bone which may cause swelling on the bone, including the skull, and pathological fractures may occur through the cyst.[124] The cysts are of variable size and have a variety of appearances on X-ray.[125] Dead cysts

---

[124] K Kalinova, V Proichev, P Stafanova, K Tokmakova and E Poriazova, Hydatid bone disease: a case report and review of the literature, *Journal of Orthopaedic Surgery*, 2005, 13, 323–325; P Polat, M Kantarci, F Alper, S Suma, MB Koruyucu and A Okur, Hydatid disease from head to toe, *Radiographics*, 2003, 23, 475–494.

[125] P Polat, M Kantarci, F Alper, S Suma, MB Koruucu and A Okur, Hydatid disease from head to toe, *Radiographics*, 2003, 23, 475–494.

may calcify and it is remnants of calcified cysts that may be found among human remains. Their recognition in the skeleton would depend upon a considerable degree of awareness on the part of the excavator since they are most unlikely to survive intact and may not easily be distinguished from other soil elements. There is – regrettably – nothing unique about the appearances and making the diagnosis would involve a good deal of optimistic deduction. Every palaeopathologist hopes that he or she will uncover something very unusual such as the calcified shell of an hydatid cyst which had developed in the liver, but if hope keeps one looking, most palaeopathologists will be looking for a long time.

Other parasitic diseases, however, can be detected by the presence of ova in archaeological faeces, either coprolites (sometimes from mummified bodies) or more likely, from the debris excavated from latrines (Table 6.6). Eggs from a wide range of species have been recovered, including cestodes, nematodes and trematodes[126] and from both pathogenic and non-pathogenic species.[127] The recovery of these eggs provides valuable information about the geographical spread of parasitic disease, and perhaps the timing of their appearance in humans. The parasite load within individuals will seldom be measurable, however, unless the faeces are obtained from mummified remains,[128] and it will seldom be possible to comment sensibly on the likely clinical effects during life.[129]

NON-SPECIFIC INFECTIONS

Of the non-specific infections that might affect the skeleton, only two will be considered here, sinusitis and periostitis, the latter in order to try to get some order into the rather disordered thought about it that one frequently encounters.

Sinusitis: The paranasal sinuses are air-filled spaces in the bones of the face and skull, all of which communicate through openings known as ostia with the

---

[126] F Boucher, S Harter and M Le Bailley, The state of the art of paleoparasitological research in the Old World, *Memorias do Instituto Oswaldo Cruz*, 2003, 98, Supplement 1, 95–101.

[127] ML Goncalves, A Araujo and LF Ferreira, Human intestinal parasites in the past: new findings and a review, *Memorias do Instituto Oswaldo Cruz*, 2003, 98, Supplement 1, 103–118.

[128] It is possible that ova from other sites might also be recovered from a mummy if the other viscera are present. Occasionally more dramatic evidence of parasite infection is forthcoming from mummies, such as the remains of a Guinea worm (*D medinensis*) in the abdominal wall of the Leeds mummy (E Tapp and K Wildsmith, The autopsy and endoscopy of the Leeds mummy, In: *The mummy's tale* (edited by AR David and E Tapp), London, Michael O'Mara Books, 1992, pp 132–153). A guide to identifying parasite ova, with illustrative slides can be viewed at: www.who.int/wormcontrol/documents/benchaids/training_manual/en/.

[129] DW Crompton and MC Nesheim, Nutritional impact of intestinal helminthiasis during the human life cycle, *Annual Review of Nutrition*, 2002, 22, 35–59.

nasal cavity. There are four: the maxillary (also sometimes known as the antra of Highmore[130]), the frontal, the ethmoid (the collective name for the ethmoid air cells) and the sphenoidal. The maxillary is the largest and the ostium for drainage is situated high on the medial wall, beneath the middle turbinate. The location of the ostium means that when standing upright, the sinus cannot drain properly. The sinuses are in close relation to the orbit and to the anterior cranial fossa.[131]

Acute sinusitis is caused by blockage of one of the ostia, usually that of the maxillary sinus and the great majority of subsequent infections are viral in origin. If the condition becomes chronic, then bacterial infection may supervene and about three-quarters of all chronic infections are caused by three organisms: *Streptococcus pneumoniae, Haemophilus influenzae,* and *Moraxella catarrhalis.*[132] Serious complications of sinusitis are the result of their proximity to the orbit and the brain. About three-quarters of all infections of the orbit spread from the sinuses, especially the ethmoids, while osteomyelitis of the frontal bone – sometimes referred to as Pott's puffy tumour – may be caused by frontal sinusitis which may also spread to cause an intracranial abscess.[133]

Chronic sinusitis is a common modern condition and accounts for a substantial morbidity, especially in areas with much atmospheric pollution.[134] The interior of the sinuses cannot be examined unless the skull is broken, or an endoscope is used (a technique pioneered by Calvin Wells[135]). The maxillary sinuses are most frequently available for view because their anterior walls are thin and liable to be damaged during or after excavation. Chronic sinusitis in the skeleton can be inferred by the presence of new bone on the floor of the sinus. Sometimes it can be seen that the infection has spread into the sinus from an infected molar when one of the roots has penetrated the inferior wall of the sinus. Chronic sinusitis has been diagnosed in mummies using an endoscope[136] and the expected increased prevalence in urban

[130] Nathaniel Highmore 1613–1685
[131] FM Baroody, Nasal and paranasal sinus anatomy and physiology, *Clinical Allergy and Immunology,* 2007, 19, 1–21.
[132] DW Kennedy, Pathogenesis of chronic rhinosinusitis, *Annals of Otology, Rhinology and Laryngology,* 2004, 193, 6–9.
[133] KW Ah-See and AS Evans, Sinusitis and its management, *British Medical Journal,* 2007, 334, 358–361.
[134] VK Anand, Epidemiology and economic impact of rhinosinusitis, *Annals of Otology, Rhinology and Laryngology,* 2004, 193, 3–5.
[135] C Wells, Disease of the maxillary sinus in antiquity, *Medical and Biological Illustration,* 1977, 27, 173–178.
[136] HG Hagedorn, A Zink, U Szeimies and AG Nerlich, Makroskopische und endokopische Untersuchung der Kopf-Hais-Region an altägyptischen Mumien, *HNO,* 2004, 52, 413–422.

compared with rural assemblages has been demonstrated.[137] There is nothing specific about the changes brought about by the various infective agents and so there is no clue as to which organism might have been responsible for any changes seen.

> *Periostitis:* New bone is commonly found on the skeleton, sometimes as a concomitant of well-recognised diseases – osteomyelitis, for example – and sometimes as a lone finding. When interpreting the significance of the latter, clarity of thought is not always the most plentiful commodity on view. This lack of clarity is compounded by the use of the term 'periostitis' to describe new bone, since this implies that it has an inflammatory origin and in much of the palaeopathological literature it is taken to indicate a systemic infection, particularly when found on the bones of juveniles.

The periosteum is a membrane that covers the entire external surface of a bone except where the bone is covered by articular cartilage, the synovial membrane or where it forms part of a non-synovial joint such as the pubic symphysis; it is also reflected for some distance onto entheses. It consists of two discrete layers, an outer fibrous layers which contains blood vessels and Sharpey's fibres that anchor it firmly to the underlying bone, and an inner layer which contains undifferentiated mesenchymal cells with the potential to produce cartilage or bone-forming cells and the growth factors necessary for the formation and remodelling of new bone.[138] The blood vessels in the periosteum are an important source of blood supply to cortical bone and, as we have seen earlier, anastomose with those in the Haversian systems.[139] The periosteum forms bone to enable bones to grow circumferentially, either physiologically as in juveniles, or in response to strains upon them, in the case of adults. It will also respond to any pathological stimulus by laying down bone and on this account it is often referred to as a 'stress' marker although it is clear that it may be laid down in circumstances which are *not* stressful. There are many causes for periosteal new bone formation, both non-inflammatory and non-infectious as may be seen in Table 6.7 and it would be preferable if a more neutral term were used to describe its occurrence in the skeleton – PNB would be preferable since this has no aetiological implications.

---

[137] ME Lewis, CA Roberts and K Manchester, Comparative study of the prevalence of maxillary sinusitis in later medieval urban and rural populations in northern England, *American Journal of Physical Anthropology*, 1995, 98, 497–506.

[138] KN Malizos and LK Paptheodorou, The healing potential of the periosteum. Molecular aspect, *Injury*, 2005, 365, 513–519.

[139] M Chanavez, Anatomy and histopathology of the periosteum: quantification of the periosteal blood supply to the adjacent bone with ^{85}Sr and gamma spectrometry, *Journal of Oral Implantology*, 1995, 21, 214–219.

Table 6.7. *Major causes of periosteal new bone formation*

Physiological in infants
Infantile cortical hyperostosis (Caffey's disease)
Infections
osteomyelitis
syphilis
Trauma
Venous stasis
varicose veins
Haemorrhage
scurvy
Rickets
Burns
Tumours
primary – osteosarcoma
secondary – metastases
Leukaemia
Hypertrophic pulmonary osteoarthropathy (HPO)
Fluorosis
Hypervitaminosis A
Neurofibromatosis
Thyroid acropachy
Some congenital conditions
Menkes' syndrome
Camaruti-Engelmann disease
Overlying soft tissue lesions

Periosteal new bone is found frequently in the skeleton, especially on the middle or distal tibia. In the middle part of the tibia it is often on the subcutaneous surface and probably results from repeated minor trauma. At the ankle it may be the result of movement of the distal tibio-fibular joint and thus is most likely to be an enthesophyte; otherwise PNB around the ankle is most probably due to the presence of varicose veins and on some occasions, a circular raised plaque of new bone signals where the floor of a varicose ulcer was once situated in the overlying soft tissues. Periosteal new bone in actively growing children should be regarded as physiological until proved otherwise. In the living, the diagnosis of the causes of PNB is largely dependent on its X-ray appearances,[140] but radiology is not often helpful

[140] BD Ragsdale, JE Madewell and DE Sweet, Radiologic and pathologic analysis of solitary bone lesions. Part II: Periosteal reactions, *Radiological Clinics of North America*, 1981, 19, 749–783.

for diagnosing PNB in the skeleton since the quantity of new bone is frequently too slight to show up on X-ray. What is abundantly clear, is that in the majority of cases the aetiology of isolated patches of PNB will never be determined and it would be better if the attempt were not made.

New bone on the inner surface of the ribs: I have referred earlier to the suggestion that new bone on the pleural surface of the ribs is indicative of tuberculosis. While it seems true that individuals known to have died from tuberculosis may have new bone on the ribs, the converse is by no means always the case; that is, one cannot argue, as some have done, that finding new bone on the ribs should be taken to indicate tuberculosis.[141] If tuberculous lesions were sited peripherally they may well stimulate the periosteum but so would other peripheral lesions such as a peripheral tumour. The same is also true for lobar pneumonia, while diseases of the pleura such as pleurisy, pleural effusion, or blood or pus in the pleural space might also produce PNB.[142] A knowledge of the surface markings of the lobes of the lungs and the pleura might indicate the cause of PNB on the ribs if the affected ribs could be identified securely. For example, a pleural effusion would be expected to gravitate towards the bottom of the chest and involve the lower ribs on the affected side. If the individual were bed-ridden, the effusion would tend to settle towards the back of the chest. Pneumonia affecting the left-upper lobe of the lung might be deduced from finding PNB on the first four ribs. Diagrams of the surface markings of the lungs and pleura and their relations to the underlying ribs are to be found in any text on clinical anatomy and could be used to map out affected areas provided the ribs are sufficiently well preserved.

[141] CA Roberts, A Boylston, L Buckley, AC Chamberlain and EM Murphy, Rib lesions and tuberculosis: the palaeopathological evidence, *Tuberculosis and other Lung Diseases*, 1998, 79, 55–60.

[142] It is conceivable that PNB on the ribs might be produced as the result of mechanical irritation of the periosteum such as might occur with a persistent, chronic cough. In such a case, the distribution of the PNB would follow no clear pattern.

7

Metabolic Diseases

There are a number of diseases that interfere with the normal metabolism of the skeleton. They include osteoporosis, Paget's disease, rickets and osteomalacia, and scurvy. Some conditions in which there is a hormonal imbalance also affect bone and some of these will be considered in this section.

OSTEOPOROSIS

Until early adult life the skeleton is in positive balance, that is to say, a larger amount of bone is formed than is lost and the total skeletal mass increases until it reaches a maximum at about the age of 25–30. The absolute value of the maximum bone mass (MBM) varies from individual to individual and is dependent on a number of factors including sex, activity, diet and race. After the MBM is achieved the skeletal balance is reversed and there is a net loss of bone during the following years. Women lose bone at a faster rate than men at all ages but their rate of loss increases after the menopause when the depressing effect of oestrogen on the osteoclast is lost. Bone is lost more rapidly at some sites than others, and the rate of trabecular bone loss tends to be greater than the rate of cortical bone loss. If the rate of bone loss becomes too great, and particularly if much trabecular bone is lost, the risk of a fracture occurring is considerable, especially of those bones that contain a great deal of trabecular bone, most notably the distal radius, the femoral neck and the vertebrae. It is this risk of fractures that characterises the condition known as osteoporosis and in the developed countries it is a major cause of morbidity and the prevalence and the cost to the health service is likely to increase *pari passu* with the increasing numbers of elderly individuals in the population.

Osteoporosis is always defined on the basis of a propensity to fracture bones but the diagnosis rests on the measurement of the bone mineral density (BMD) measured as

Table 7.1. *Diagnostic categories of osteoporosis*

Diagnostic category	T-score
Normal	Above –1, that is, not more than 1 SD below that of the young adult mean
Osteopaenia	Between –1 and –2.5. That is BMD lies between 1 and 2.5 SDs below young adult mean
Osteoporosis	Equal or below –2.5. That is BMD is 2.5 or more SDs below young adult mean
Established osteoporosis	Equal of below –2.5 in the presence of one or more osteoporotic fractures

Based on WHO (1994)[1]

grams of bone mineral (hydroxyapatite) per square centimetre. The measurements are usually made over the femoral neck or the lumbar spine, but there are also instruments that can measure the BMD in the calcaneus by propagating a sound wave through it. The BMD obtained in an individual case is converted into either a T- score or a Z-score. The T-score compares the measured BMD with the mean of sex-matched young adults who have achieved maximum bone mass and the result is expressed in terms of the number of standard deviations from the control mean. The Z-score compares the BMD with the mean of age- and sex-matched controls. The various diagnostic criteria are shown in Table 7.1.[2] It is important to note at this stage that osteoporosis is *not* a disease but a risk factor, in the same way that hypertension is not a disease but a measurement of blood pressure that carries a high risk of a stroke. It is this that makes the diagnosis difficult for the palaeopathologist, as we will discuss later.

Osteoporosis is often divided into primary and secondary types, and two further subdivisions of primary osteoporosis have also been suggested, types I and II which have different epidemiological and pathological features, as shown in Table 7.2.[3] Risk factors for developing primary osteoporosis, apart from sex and age, include low MBM, early onset of the menopause, a long postmenopausal interval and inactivity. Potentiating factors include lack of dietary calcium and vitamin D, excessive protein intake, alcohol abuse, smoking and caffeine excess; the first four of these would have

[1] Report of WHO Study Group, WHO Technical Report Series 843, Geneva, World Health Organisation, 1994.
[2] Assessment of fracture risk and its application to screening for postmenopausal osteoporosis. Report of WHO Study Group, WHO Technical Report Series 843, Geneva, World Health Organisation, 1994.
[3] BL Riggs and LJ Melton, Involutional osteoporosis, *New England Journal of Medicine*, 1986, 314, 1676–1686.

Table 7.2. *Types and features of primary osteoporosis*

Features	Type I 55–75 Post-menopausal	Type II Senile
Age	55–75	>70
Sex ratio (F:M)	6:1	2:1
Bone loss	Mainly trabecular	Trabecular and cortical
Type of fracture	Wrist and crush vertebral	Hip, and wedge vertebral

been important at all periods in the past. Factors that contribute to the production of secondary osteoporosis are shown in Table 7.3.[4]

There has been some speculation that osteoporosis is of recent origin. In a paper written in 1994, the author noted that very few general practitioners had ever seen a case.[5] The prevalence depends very much on the definition used and there is no doubt that the introduction of the WHO definition in 1994 and the subsequent availability of machines to measure BMD caused an apparent increase in the prevalence. It would be of very considerable interest to know what the prevalence was in the past and whether it has actually increased in modern times, or whether the increased numbers of those with the condition is just an artefact of screening programmes. To date, however, there is no agreed way in which to diagnose osteoporosis in the skeleton. Studies have been carried to measure cortical thickness of the metacarpals,[6] BMD,[7] bone density directly on skeletal assemblages,[8] and the height at the middle point of the vertebrae;[9] all have generally shown the expected increased loss of bone with age, although the pattern of trabecular loss has been found to differ.[10]

4   Disuse, whether from illness, paralysis or weightlessness, is a well known cause as shown in the table and seems to rely on the reduction in mechanical stress on the bone (a reverse of Wolff's law). It is interesting that bone loss occurs also in most hibernating animals with the exception of the black bear in which bone formation is not impaired during the hibernating period as in other hibernants (SW Donahue, MR Vaughan, LM Demers and HJ Donahue, Bone formation is not impaired by hibernation (disuse) in black bears Ursus americanus, *Journal of Experimental Biology*, 2003, 206, 4233–4239).
5   JA Kanis, Assessment of fracture risk and its application to screening for postmenopausal osteoporosis, *Osteoporosis International*, 1994, 4, 368–381.
6   SA Mays, Age-dependent bone loss in a medieval population, *International Journal of Osteoarchaeology*, 1996, 6, 144–154; Ibid, Age-dependent cortical bone loss in women from 18th and early 19th century London, *American Journal of Physical Anthropology*, 2000, 112, 349–161.
7   B Lees, T Molleson, TR Arnett and JC Stevenson, Difference in proximal femur bone density over two centuries, *Lancet*, 1993, 341, 673–676.
8   M Brickley and PG Howell, Measurement of changes in trabecular bone structure with age in an archaeological population, *Journal of Archaeological Science*, 1999, 26, 151–157.
9   E Gonzalez-Reimers, MA Mas-Pascual, M Arnay-de-la-Rosa, J Velasco-Vázquez, F Santolaria-Fernández and M Machado-Calvo, Noninvasive estimation of bone mass in ancient vertebrae, *American Journal of Physical Anthropology*, 2004, 125, 121–131.
10   SC Agarwal, M Dumitriu, GA Tomlinson and MD Grynpas, Medieval trabecular bone architecture: the influence of age, sex and lifestyle, *American Journal of Physical Anthropology*, 2004, 124, 33–44.

Table 7.3. *Some causes of secondary osteoporosis*

Dietary factors	Malabsorption; starvation; scurvy
Systemic disorders	Diabetes; leukaemia; multiple myelomatosis; rheumatoid arthritis
Endocrine disorders	Cushing's disease; growth hormone deficiency; hyperparathyroidism; hyperthyroidism
Drugs	Glucocorticoids; chemotherapeutic agents; anticonvulsants

These factors would have declined in importance in the past as one goes down the table.

Radiographs of long bones frequently show cortical thinning on X-ray and some authorities have been rumoured to base a diagnosis on the weight of the bone. The difficulty in arriving at a diagnosis of osteoporosis in the skeleton is that most of those who try to do it have forgotten that in clinical practice the diagnosis is made by comparison of BMD with a younger reference group. With the methods used to date, not only are there no data from a reference group but even if there were, who is to say that even a deviation of more than 2.5 standard deviations from the reference mean necessarily implies a greater risk of fracture, as there is no way to validate such an inference. The diagnosis, therefore, tends to be entirely subjective.

It seems the only secure way of diagnosing osteoporosis in the past is by confining the diagnosis to established osteoporosis, that is to say, to diagnose only cases in which an osteoporotic fracture is present. This will necessarily under-estimate the true prevalence but at least the diagnosis would be repeatable and comparable and could be used to measure trends, albeit the numbers likely to be found in any assemblage would be small and the confidence intervals around the prevalence wide.[11]

In the 1970s, Singh and his colleagues introduced a method of diagnosing osteoporosis based on the trabecular pattern in the neck of the femur. They identified six groups of trabeculae; three compressive and three tensile.[12] As the trabeculae are resorbed, the principal compressive and tensile groups are accentuated and Ward's triangle becomes more prominent. The index depends simply upon counting how many of these groups are visible on the X-ray, and six grades are obtained. Grade 6 is the normal appearance, all the trabeculae being visible, while grades 1–3 denote osteoporosis of increasing severity; in grade 1 only the principal compressive group

---

[11]   See Chapter 13 for further details.

[12]   M Singh, AR Nagrath and PS Maini, Changes in trabecular pattern of the upper end of the femur as an index of osteoporosis, *Journal of Bone and Joint Surgery*, 1970, 52A, 457–467; M Singh, BL Riggs, JW Beabout and J Bowsey, Femoral trabecular-pattern index for evaluation of spinal osteoporosis, *Annals of Internal Medicine*, 1972, 77, 63–67.

is visible and the trabeculae are markedly reduced in number.[13] Subsequent authors were not unanimously enthusiastic about the method, some finding no correlation between the index and BMD.[14] Other authors found that it did provide a rough estimate for the mechanical competence of the proximal femur when judged against mechanical properties such as Young's modulus, strength and maximum energy absorption.[15] It did show a greatly increased relative risk of fractures with increasing grade[16] and it has been suggested that it is a useful tool for detecting differences in bone density between and within populations.[17] The consistency of interpretation of the radiographs can apparently be improved by using computer texture analysis.[18]

The Singh index promises to be a useful tool by which palaeopathologists can identify osteoporosis,[19] although it is probably better to restrict its use to comparing prevalence in assemblages rather than making individual diagnoses. For the latter purpose, there seems little alternative to basing the diagnosis on the presence of established fractures unless another method and data against which to measure results can be universally agreed.[20]

PAGET'S DISEASE OF BONE (PDB)

In 1877, Sir James Paget described a chronic inflammation of bone which he called osteitis deformans on account of the swelling and deformation in the affected parts of

---

[13] The method is fully described with clear illustrations in: M Singh, BL Riggs, JW Beabout and J Jowsey, Femoral trabecular pattern index for evaluation of spinal osteoporosis. A detailed methodologic description, *Mayo Clinic Proceedings*, 1973, 48, 184–189.

[14] VCM Koot, SMMJ Kesselaer, GJ Clevers, P de Hooge, T Weits and C van der Werker, Evaluation of the Singh index for measuring osteoporosis, *Journal of Bone and Joint Surgery*, 1996, 78B, 831–834.

[15] NJ Wachter, P Augat, IP Hoellen, GD Krischak, MR Sarkar, M Mentzel, I Kinzl and L Claes, Predictive value of Singh index and bone mineral density measured by quantitative computed tomography in determining the local cancellous bone quality of the proximal femur, *Clinical Biomechanics* (Bristol, Avon), 2001, 16, 257–262.

[16] C Cooper, DJP Barker, J Morris and RSJ Briggs, Osteoporosis, falls, and age in fracture of the proximal femur, *British Medical Journal*, 1987, 295, 13–15.

[17] T Masud, S Jawed, DV Doyle and TD Spector, A population study of the screening potential of assessment of trabecular pattern of the femoral neck (Singh index): the Chingford study, *British Journal of Radiology*, 1995, 68, 389–393.

[18] PP Smyth, JE Adams, RW Whitehouse and CJ Taylor, Application of computer texture analysis to the Singh index, *British Journal of Radiology*, 1997, 70, 242–247.

[19] Our own preliminary observations, using Singh's illustrations on transparencies for grading radiographs have demonstrated that the method is simple and reproducible. The major disadvantage with it, of course, is that is requires access to radiography and on this account might be relatively restricted in its application.

[20] There seems to be very little prospect of being able to validate a T-score in human remains unless a large number of individuals could be found with established osteoporotic fractures. If such a group could be found, then the mean of whatever measure was taken as the 'gold standard' of osteoporosis in the skeleton could perhaps be taken as the 'fracture threshold' and used as a comparator in other skeletons. Alternatively, a Z-score could be derived from groups of age- and sex-matched skeletons but – again – this would give no indication of fracture risk and it might be preferable to use a different term altogether when discussing bone loss in the skeleton – accelerated bone loss (ABL), perhaps.

the skeleton.[21] Paget's disease of bone (PDB) is now the second most common bone disorder in the elderly, with only osteoporosis being more common.[22] The disease is particularly common in northern European populations (or their descendants) and approximately 2% of the population of the United Kingdom over the age of 55 have the disease, although in the majority of individuals it is asymptomatic. The prevalence in parts of the western world has decreased quite considerably in the past thirty years or so. For example, in the 1970s the prevalence in the United Kingdom was 5.4%[23] and the incidence rate was also noted to be falling.[24] A similar trend has been noted in other European countries[25] and in New Zealand [26] and presumably the cause is related to some as yet unknown environmental factor. The suggestion that the disease might actually be *increasing* at the site of Barton-on-Humber from the tenth to the nineteenth centuries[27] was found to be in error after the site had been re-phased and the data recalculated.[28] The prevalence of the disease increases with increasing age and tends to be more common in males than in females.[29]

There is considerable regional variation in the prevalence of PDB, which again suggests that an environmental factor may be important. In France, for example, the prevalence in the over-40s is 1.8% and it is even lower in other countries, most notably in Sweden where the prevalence is only 0.4%.[30] Within England, the disease is more frequent in the north than in the south, and Lancashire is a particular hot spot.[31]

[21] J Paget, On a form of chronic inflammation of bones (osteitis deformans), *Medico-Chirurgical Transactions*, London, 1877, 60, 37–63. (Sir James Paget 1814–1899.)

[22] MA Ankrom and JR Shapiro, Paget's disease of bone (osteitis deformans), *Journal of the American Geriatrics Society*, 1998, 46, 1025–1033. (The disease is often referred to as Paget's disease of bone to differentiate it from Paget's disease of the nipple, an eczematous reaction around the nipple which is invariably associated with an underlying cancer of the breast. Here Paget's disease without qualification refers exclusively to the skeletal variety.)

[23] C Cooper, K Shafheutle, K Dennison, P Guyer and DJ Barker, The epidemiology of Paget's disease in Britain: is the prevalence decreasing? *Journal of Bone and Mineral Research*, 1999, 14, 192–197.

[24] C Cooper, NC Harvey, EM Dennison and TP van Staa, Update on the epidemiology of Paget's disease of bone, *Journal of Bone and Mineral Research*, 2006, 21, Supplement 2, P3–P8.

[25] G Poor, J Donath, B Fornet and C Cooper, Epidemiology of Paget's disease in Europe: the prevalence is decreasing, *Journal of Bone and Mineral Research*, 2005, 21, 1545–1549.

[26] T Cundy, Is the prevalence of Paget's disease of bone decreasing? *Journal of Bone and Mineral Research*, 2006, 21, Supplement 2, P9–P13.

[27] J Rogers, JR Feffrey and I Watt, Paget's disease in an archaeological population, *Journal of Bone and Mineral Research*, 2002, 17, 1127–1134.

[28] HA Waldron, Recalculation of secular trends in Paget's disease, *Journal of Bone and Mineral Research*, 2004, 19, 523.

[29] D Hosking, PJ Meunier, JD Ringe, J-Y Reginster and C Gennari, Paget's disease of bone: diagnosis and management, *British Medical Journal*, 1996, 312, 491–494.

[30] FM Detheridge, PB Guyer and DJ Barker, European distribution of Paget's disease, *British Medical Journal*, 1982, 285, 1005–1008.

[31] DJ Barker, PW Clough, PB Guyer and MJ Gardiner, Paget's disease of bone in 14 British towns, *British Medical Journal*, 1977, 1, 1181–1183.

PDB is primarily a disease of the osteoclasts,[32] although this in turn leads to increased osteoblast activity. Osteoclasts in PDB are increased in number, increased in size and the nuclei contain inclusion bodies, the nature of which has been the subject of considerable debate.[33] Some authorities have considered the inclusion bodies to be derived from the measles virus or other paramyxoviruses,[34] while others have suggested that they are due to the presence of distemper virus[35] and there is an interesting epidemiological association between PDB and dog ownership.[36] This has all led to the hypothesis that PDB is the late result of a viral infection, perhaps derived from dogs or, other animals.[37] Although the debate is vigorous, the issue remains far from settled.[38] There is a strong genetic component to the disease and it tends to run in families.[39] There is clearly an interaction between genetic and environmental factors which together produce the pathophysiological processes and the morphological appearances. The genetic susceptibility to PDB, in some individuals at least, appears to be related to defects in the sequestrosome 1 (SQSTM1) gene.[40] A model for the pathogenesis of PDB is shown in Figure 7.1.[41]

[32]   SV Reddy, N Kurihara, C Menaa and GD Roodman, Paget's disease of bone: a disease of the osteoclast, *Reviews in Endocrine & Metabolic Disorders*, 2001, 2, 195–201.

[33]   MH Helfrich, Osteoclast diseases, Microscopy Research and Technique, 2003, 61, 514–532.

[34]   IB Bender, Paget's disease, *Journal of Endocrinology*, 2003, 29, 720–723.

[35]   AP Mee, JA Dixon, JA Hoyland, M Davies, PL Selby and EB Mawer, Detection of canine distemper virus in 100% of Paget's disease samples by in-situ-reverse transcriptase polymerase chain reaction, *Bone*, 1998, 23, 171–175.

[36]   SA Khan, P Brenna, J Newman, RE Gray, EV McClosky and JA Kanis, Paget's disease and unvaccinated dogs, *Bone*, 1996, 19, 47–50.

[37]   G Lopez-Abente, A Morales-Piga, A Elena-Ibanez, JS Rey-Rey and J Corres-Gonzalez, Cattle, pets and Paget's disease, *Epidemiology*, 1997, 8, 247–251.

[38]   For opposing views see: SH Ralston, MH Helfrich, RP Hobson and TH Pennington, Does Paget's disease really have a viral aetiology? *Journal of Bone and Mineral Research*, 1997, 12, 863–864; BK Rima, Paramyxoviruses and chronic human disease, *Bone*, 1999, 24, 23S–26S.

[39]   ES Siris, R Ottman, E Flaster and JL Kelsey, Familial aggregation of Paget's disease of bone, *Journal of Bone and Mineral Research*, 1991, 6, 495–500.

[40]   SQSTM1 codes for a protein that acts as a scaffold in the RANK (NFκB) signalling pathway (L Sanz, MT Diaz-Meco, H Nakano and J Moscat, The atypical PKC-interacting protein p62 channels NF-kappaB activation by the IL-1-TRAF6 pathway, *EMBO Journal*, 2000, 19, 1576–1586). Actually, this particular genetic defect is found in a minority of those with Paget's disease and there must be other genetic abnormalities awaiting discovery, all of which are presumably involved in the same signalling pathway (GJ Lucas, A Daroszewska and SH Ralston, Contributions of genetic factors to the pathogenesis of Paget's disease of bone and related disorders, *Journal of Bone and Mineral Research*, 2006, 21, Supplement 2, P31–P37. Juvenile Paget's disease is a rare autosomal recessive condition, characterised by a progressive skeletal deformity which starts in childhood and the increased bone turnover involves the entire skeleton by contrast with the adult form (M Rousière, L Michou, F Cornélis and P Orcel, Paget's disease of bone, *Best Practice & Research Clinical Rheumatology*, 2003, 17, 1019–1041). The genetic defect in juvenile Paget's disease involves the mutations in the gene that codes for osteoprotogerin (MP Whyte, Paget's disease of bone and genetic disorders of RANKL/OPG/NF-kappaB signalling, *Annals of the New York Academy of Sciences*, 2006, 1068, 143–164).

[41]   GD Roodman and JJ Windle, Paget disease of bone, *Journal of Clinical Investigation*, 2005, 115, 200–208.

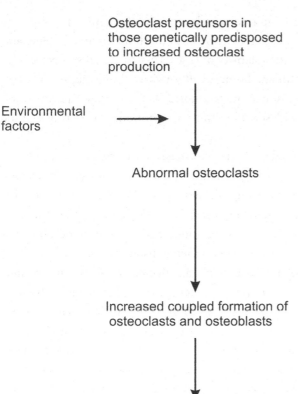

Osteoclast precursors in
those genetically predisposed
to increased osteoclast
production

Environmental
factors

Abnormal osteoclasts

Increased coupled formation of
osteoclasts and osteoblasts

Sclerotic bone

FIGURE 7.1. Model of aetiology of Paget's disease of bone. Environmental factors – the effects of a virus, for example, act to produce abnormal osteoclasts in an individual who is genetically predisposed to increased osteoclast production. Since the production of osteoclasts and osteoblasts is coupled, the increased number of osteoclasts is accompanied by an increased number of osteoblasts which results in rapid bone formation and in time, the production of more and more bone that eventually becomes sclerotic.

PDB is characterised by abnormal bone remodelling – anarchic in the apt phrase of one group of authors[42] – and the disease goes through three stages: a lytic (or active) stage, a mixed lytic and sclerotic stage, and a sclerotic (or inactive) stage. The lytic changes are seen commonly in the skull when radiographs will show well-demarcated lytic areas, a condition referred to as osteoporosis circumscripta. Lysis also takes place in the long bones and invariably begins in the subchondral bone and proceeds upwards or downwards. Affected bones show a V-shaped radiolucent area which is usually called the 'flame' sign. In the sclerotic stage, the affected bones may become enlarged and they feel heavier than their normal counterparts. Cortical

42 Rousière et al (2003), op cit.

thickening, coarsened trabeculae and dense sclerosis are apparent on X-ray. The disease tends to affect the axial skeleton with the skull, lumbar spine, pelvis and proximal femur accounting for the majority of cases. Less commonly affected sites include the tibia, ribs, distal femur and humerus although any bone may be involved. The changes may be found in a single site (monostotic) or in many (polyostotic). The disease tends to be more widespread in those in whom the onset is before the age of 40.[43]

The bone formed in the mixed and sclerotic stages is disorganised, which can clearly be seen in histological sections viewed under polarised light when the chaotic alignment of the collagen fibres is evident. It is also softer than normal and weight-bearing bones, such as the tibia, tend to bow, possibly causing pathological fractures. In the living, Pagetic limbs feel warm to the touch because the blood supply is increased to meet the demands of the increased metabolism.

PDB is easy to miss in the skeleton because not all affected bones appear morphologically abnormal. Additionally, PDB is sometimes discovered coincidentally when bones are X-rayed to investigate some other condition. The lytic phase is particularly likely to be overlooked because there are not likely to be any morphological changes at this stage. Any bones that seem unusually heavy, or are enlarged should be X-rayed. A greatly thickened, heavy skull should immediately alert one to the possibility of PDB. The diagnosis cannot reliably be made without a confirmatory X-ray and it would be preferable if the bone could also be examined histologically to demonstrate the disorganised nature of the affected bone.

Operational definition of Paget's disease

Lytic stage: Radiological osteoporosis circumscripta in the skull

And/Or

Flame sign in tubular bones
Sclerotic stage: Radiological signs of cortical thickening, sclerosis and thickened trabeculae ± areas of radiolucency
Note: confirmation for the condition can be obtained from histological evidence of disorganised bone formation.

There are a number of serious complications of PDB, including deformity, pathological fractures, nerve compression which may affect the nerves leaving or entering

---

[43] S Holgado, D Rotés, M Gumà. J Monfort, A Olivé, J Carbonell and X Tena, Paget's disease of bone in early adult life, *Annals of the Rheumatic Diseases*, 2005, 64, 306–308.

the skull, and approximately 1% of patients will develop osteosarcoma. Primary sarcomas in the skull are almost exclusively related to PDB.[44] In any skeleton with PDB in which the skull or spine is affected it is sensible to try to determine whether nerve compression might have occurred – not forgetting the auditory nerve in the petrous temporal bone – since it would then be reasonable to infer what effects the individual might have experienced during his or her lifetime. Few cases of PDB have been described in the skeleton,[45] and there is no doubt that the prevalence has been greatly under-estimated, a matter that is only likely to improve if skeletons from mature adult skeletons are routinely X-rayed. An operational definition is shown in the "Operational definition of Paget's disease" box; note that this depends principally on characteristic radiological changes.

RICKETS AND OSTEOMALACIA

Rickets is a childhood disease caused principally by a lack of vitamin D but it may also be due to lack of calcium and there are, in addition, three hereditary forms.[46] Vitamin D is formed in the skin by the action of sunlight on 7-dehydrocholesterol, and is obtained from some foods, particularly oily fish. The compound formed in the skin (Vitamin D_3) is inactive and undergoes two chemical transformations, firstly in the liver and then in the kidney. In each case a hydroxyl group is added to the molecule to form successively, 25-hydroxyvitamin D and 1, 25-hydroxyvitamin D which is the active metabolite. The di-hydroxy form is able to enter cells, bind to a vitamin-D receptor which is then able to activate the gene that codes for calcium binding protein which, in turn, mediates the uptake of calcium from the gut.[47] Lack of vitamin D, severe enough to cause rickets, prevents osteoid being mineralized and the bone formed is soft and may bend if the disease occurs during the time the child is weight bearing.

Rickets seems to have been a disease of considerable antiquity, an infant with changes consistent with the disease having been described from a mid-Holocene

---

[44] C Miller and VM Rao, Sarcomatous degeneration in Paget's disease in the skull, *Skeletal Radiology*, 1983, 10, 102–106.

[45] JE Aaron, J Robers and JA Kanis, Paleohistology of Paget's disease in two medieval skeletons, American *Journal of Physical Anthropology*, 1992, 89, 325–331.

[46] Rickets has been found to occur in Nigerian children in whom vitamin D stores are apparently adequate but where levels of calcium in the diet were low (MA Pfitzner, TD Thatcher, JM Pettifor, AL Zoakah, JO Lawson, CO Isichei and PR Fisher, Absence of vitamin deficiency in young Nigerian children, *Journal of Pediatrics*, 1998, 133, 740–744). The genetic forms of rickets are described by RW Chesney, Vitamin D deficiency and rickets, *Reviews in Endocrine & Metabolic Disorders*, 2001, 2, 145–151.

[47] P Lips, Vitamin D physiology, *Progress in Biophysics and Molecular Biology*, 2006, 92, 4–8.

context in Byneskranskop, even though the authors consider that the environment would have ensured that both vitamin D and dietary calcium were plentiful.[48] It was certainly well established in England by the seventeenth century and appears as a cause of death in the *Bills of Mortality* and it was suggested by contemporary commentators that it was a new disease.[49] Several remedies were in current use[50] and it was particularly a disease of those who were wet-nursed for long periods, since with increased lactation, the concentration of calcium in the breast milk declines. Paradoxically, the children of the well-to-do who could afford a wet nurse were often more at risk of rickets than those of poorer families.[51] With the coming of increasing industrialisation and the great palls of smoke that blotted out the sun over the great industrial cities of the north, rickets became epidemic among those who lived in semi-permanent darkness and whose diets were not adequate to compensate for the lack of sunlight. Fortification of milk much later did much to eradicate the disease.[52] One consequence of rickets is deformation of the pelvis which may cause an obstruction to labour in later life and it is often thought that this was a common event in the past. It was certainly the case in Glasgow in the 1870s and 1880s[53] but this seems to have been unusual and maternal mortality from this cause was probably not very great.[54]

Rickets is often found in skeletal assemblages[55] but given that most of those with the disease will recover once they see the sun again, the prevalence must be considerably underestimated. Sometimes the deaths of children are ascribed directly to the disease.[56] This is perhaps rather surprising given that rickets is not usually

---

[48] S Pfeiffer and C Crowder, An ill child among mid-Holocene foragers of Southern Africa, *American Journal of Physical Anthropology*, 2004, 123, 23–29.

[49] JLH O'Riordan, Rickets in the 17th century, *Journal of Bone and Mineral Research*, 2006, 21, 1506–1510.

[50] LM Swinburne, Rickets and the Fairfax family receipt books, *Journal of the Royal Society of Medicine*, 2006, 99, 391–395.

[51] TD Thatcher, Wet-nursing and rickets, *Journal of the Royal Society of Medicine*, 2006, 99, 545–546.

[52] MF Holick, Resurrection of vitamin D deficiency and rickets, *Journal of Clinical Investigation*, 2006, 116, 2062–2072. Worldwide, however, there is still plenty of rickets about. Recent studies show that vitamin D levels are higher in northern Europe than in southern Europe and very low levels have been reported in the Middle East and in countries where people cover themselves up from the sun. The production of vitamin D is less effective in dark-skinned peoples and this is the down-side of having evolved skin colour that protects against the carcinogenic effects of sunlight. It is clear that several factors are involved in determining vitamin D levels other than sunlight (P Lips, Vitamin D status and nutrition in Europe and Asia, *Journal of Steroid Biochemistry and Molecular Biology*, 2007, 103, 620–625).

[53] DA Dow, *The rotten row. The history of the Glasgow Royal Maternity Hospital*, Carnforth, Parthenon Press, 1984, pp 59–70.

[54] I Loudon, Deaths in childbed from the eighteenth century to 1935, *Medical History*, 1986, 30, 1–41.

[55] See, for example, S Mays, M Brickley and R Ives, Skeletal manifestations of rickets in infants and young children in a historic population from England, *American Journal of Physical Anthropology*, 2006, 129, 362–374.

[56] R Larocque, La mortalité en bas âge dans la ville de Québec, XVIIe-XIXe siècles, *Canadian Bulletin of the History of Medicine*, 1999, 16, 341–361.

considered to be a fatal disease but there are two factors that might explain this apparent paradox. Firstly, it is known that children with intestinal malabsorption are susceptible to rickets[57] and so some of those who died with rickets may have died from the effects of malabsorption. Secondly, rickets (or calcium deficiency) predisposes towards the development of pneumonia,[58] and this may also have been a cause of death in children who present in a skeletal assemblage with rickets.

Operational definition for rickets

Enlarged, cupped and fraying or porous epiphysis

And/or

Bowing of leg bones in children who are of an age to weight bear
May also be associated with swelling at the costochondral junctions (rachitic rosary) or areas of thinning in the skull (craniotabes)

The characteristic changes in rickets appear at the growth plate and are most noticeable in regions of most rapid growth. The growth plate is widened and there is widening and cupping of the metaphysis and the bone is often described as 'frayed' or 'porous'. Enlargement at the costo-chondral junctions leads to the condition that is referred to as the 'rachitic rosary' and there may be thinning of the bones of the skull which may have a squared off appearance; this is known as cranio-tabes. Rachitic bones are softer than normal and if the child is walking, the leg bones may bend under the weight. The femurs tend to bend from front to back and the tibiae from side to side, but this configuration is by no means invariable. Forces on the pelvis emanating from the upward thrust of the femurs may cause some deformity which, in the case of girls, may lead to an obstruction of labour in later life. The diagnosis in the skeleton depends upon finding some or all of these abnormalities; see "Operational definition for rickets" box.

So-called healed rickets may sometimes be observed in adult skeletons. It is usually recognised by the presence of bowed femurs or tibias. In the case of the femurs, the bone is frequently buttressed by a bar on the concave surface. Finding bowed tibias alone does not necessarily indicate rickets especially in the presence of other bony anomalies.

---

[57] MJ Pitt, Rickets and osteomalacia are still around, *Radiologic Clinics of North America*, 1991, 29, 97–118.
[58] L Muke, S Lulseged, KE Mason and EAF Simoes, Case-control study of the role of nutritional rickets in the risk of developing pneumonia in Ethiopian children, *Lancet*, 1997, 349, 1801–1804.

OSTEOMALACIA

Osteomalacia is the adult form of rickets and by definition, occurs only after bone growth has ceased. As with rickets, the prevalence shows considerable geographical variation and many of the risk factors for rickets also apply to adults. However, there are also many other diseases in which osteomalacia occurs as a complication, notably gastro-intestinal and renal disorders.[59] Clinically, osteomalacia is said to pass through a number of phases which can be distinguished histologically. In brief, the first phase is manifested by secondary hyperparathyroidism consequent upon the lack of vitamin D; the second by a delay in the mineralisation of osteoid and the third by the complete failure to mineralise osteoid.[60] The bones may become soft in advanced cases with deformities seen most frequently in the ribs and hip bones and rib fractures are not uncommon; radiologically, there may be widespread demineralisation which mimics osteoporosis.[61] The characteristic lesion on X-ray, however, are pseudo-fractures, or Looser's zones, sometimes also referred to as Milkman's syndrome.[62] These are radiolucent areas in the skeleton which are areas of unmineralised osteoid. They appear at right angles to the cortex and are typically bilateral and symmetric.[63] They occur most frequently in the axillary margins of the scapula, the ribs, the superior and inferior pubic rami, and the proximal femur and ulna. They are often surrounded by a sclerotic margin and there may be overlying periosteal new bone.[64] In the absence of bony deformities, there is nothing that would suggest the diagnosis of osteomalacia to the palaeopathologist and cases must go unnoticed if the skeleton is not routinely X-rayed.

SCURVY

Scurvy is caused by a lack of vitamin C, a water-soluble vitamin found in fresh fruit and vegetables. In the body, vitamin C acts as a highly effective antioxidant and as an

---

[59] AJ Reginato and JA Coquia, Musculoskeletal manifestations of rickets and osteomalacia, *Best Practice & Research Clinical Rheumatology*, 2003, 17, 1063–1080.

[60] EB Mawer and M Davies, Vitamin D nutrition and bone disease in adults, *Reviews in Endocrine & Metabolic Disorders*, 2001, 2, 153–164.

[61] AJ Reginato, GF Falasca, R Pappu, B McKnigth and A Agha, Musculoskeletal manifestations of osteomalacia: report of 26 cases and literature review, *Seminars in Arthritis and Rheumatism*, 1999, 28, 287–304.

[62] Nothing to do with the man who used to deliver your milk, but named after LA Milkman.

[63] CN Griffin, Symmetrical ilial pseudofractures: a complication of chronic renal failure. A case report with a review of the literature, *Skeletal Radiology*, 1982, 8, 295–298.

[64] The presence of multiple asymmetrical pseudofractures may be confused with bony metastases (MG Velchik, PT Makler and A Alavi, Osteomalacia. An imposter of osseous metastases, *Clinical and Nuclear Medicine*, 1985, 10, 783–785).

electron donor for enzymes that participate in collagen synthesis.[65] Humans have no ability to synthesize vitamin C and can not store it so that they are dependent upon a constant supply in the diet to avoid scurvy. It is this inability to store the vitamin that made scurvy such a scourge on long sea voyages,[66] during times of famine[67] or in other circumstances when the supply of fresh fruit and vegetables was inadequate. This must presumably have been the case in the past when stocks of stored vegetables were exhausted and before fresh ones were harvested. The disease may still assume epidemic proportions in those parts of the world where the diet remains poor.[68]

In England at least, the name of James Lind is inextricably bound with the history of scurvy because of the experiments he carried out on board *HMS Salisbury* in an attempt to find a cure for the disease. The ship had been at sea for eight weeks when he started his experiment, choosing twelve of the sailors with scurvy as his subjects.[69] The men were given an addition to their common diet. Two men were given two oranges and one lemon a day for six days and they were the only ones fully to recover, although those given cider also derived some benefit.[70] The Admiralty ignored the findings and it is probable that Lind himself did not fully understand their significance since he did not conceive of the disease as being one of nutritional deficit but due to a disorder of digestion and he was seeking ways in which he could restore the digestive system to its optimal condition, not replace lacking essential nutrients.[71] In any event, it was not until 1795, the year after Lind's death that the Royal Navy introduced citrus fruit into seamen's rations with the results that scurvy was abolished aboard ship and the English came to be called 'limeys'.

Infantile scurvy was recognised in the nineteenth century when it was associated particularly with weaning infants onto proprietary foods which were deficient in vitamin C. In this way, it tended to be a middle-class disease, rather than a disease of poverty as it is now. For many years, scurvy and rickets were not clearly distinguished and this was not finally achieved until Barlow clarified the position in 1883.[72]

[65] These enzymes add hydroxyl groups to either proline or lysine which allows the collagen molecule to assume its helical structure (DJ Prockop and KI Kivirikko, Collagens: molecular biology, diseases, and potentials for therapy, *Annual Review of Biochemistry*, 1995, 64, 403–434).

[66] J Watt, Medical perspectives of some voyages of discovery, *Transactions of the Medical Society of London*, 1978–1979, 95, 61–91.

[67] EM Crawford, Scurvy in Ireland during the Great Famine, *Social History of Medicine*, 1988, 1, 281–300.

[68] E Cheung, R Mutahar, F Assefa, MT Ververs, SM Nasiri, A Borrel and P Salama, An epidemic of scurvy in Afghanistan: assessment and response, *Food and Nutrition Bulletin*, 2003, 24, 247–255.

[69] G Sutton, Putrid gums and 'Dead Men's Cloaths': James Lind aboard the Salisbury, *Journal of the Royal Society of Medicine*, 2003, 96, 605–608.

[70] J Lind, *A treatise of the scurvy*, Edinburgh, Kincaid and Donaldson, 1753, pp 191–195.

[71] For an extension of this argument see: M Bartholomew, James Lind's Treatise of the Scurvy, *Postgraduate Medical Journal*, 2002, 78, 695–696.

[72] Sir Thomas Barlow 1845–1945. The skull from one of Barlow's cases, showing extensive plaques of new bone can be seen in the Hunterian Museum of the Royal College of Surgeons of London.

The effects of scurvy are due to defects in collagen, defective formation of osteoid and increased bone resorption.[73] Clinical manifestations include capillary bleeding with bruising and perifollicular haemorrhages, bleeding and swollen gums, sub-periosteal bleeding, tooth loss,[74] and muscle and joint pains. Untreated scurvy is frequently fatal due to effects on the heart causing sudden death. [75] The response to vitamin C is usually rapid, however.

In the adult, osteoporosis is the most prominent radiological sign but in children, the changes interference with growth and characteristic signs can frequently be seen at the ends of the long bones[76] which are often enlarged and may appear porous, as they do in rickets. The radiological signs include osteopaenia with thinning of the cortex, a dense white line in the distal metaphysis (the white line of Fraenkel) with a band of decreased density immediately beneath it (this is the so-called scurvy line or Trümmerfeld zone); small bone spurs adjoining the white line (Pelkan's spur); and a dense rim of calcification around the epiphysis (Wimberger's line).[77] Sub-periosteal bleeding may also be seen surrounded by a line of new bone. The skull may also become bossed with deposits of periosteal new bone on the external surface. The radiographic changes can be related to histopathological findings, as shown in Table 7.4.

Operational definition for scurvy

Characteristic radiological signs at the epiphyses
Sometimes with
Enlarged, porous epiphyses

OR

Deposits of periosteal new bone on the skull

Recognising scurvy in the skeleton is difficult and this accounts for the few reports that have been published in the palaeopathological literature. One would perhaps expect more reports given the mortality associated with scurvy. In the first half of the twentieth century, scurvy accounted for more deaths in children than measles,

---

[73] O Fain, Musculoskeletal manifestations of scurvy, *Joint Bone Spine*, 2005, 72, 124–128.

[74] L Pimental, Scurvy: historical review and current diagnostic approach, *American Journal of Emergency Medicine*, 2003, 21, 328–332.

[75] S Sament, Cardiac disorders in scurvy, *New England Journal of Medicine*, 1970, 29, 282–283.

[76] This is not invariable, however, and cases do arise in which these radiological signs are not present (JD Akikusa, D Garrick and MC Nash, Scurvy: forgotten but not gone, *Journal of Paediatrics and Child Health*, 2003, 39, 75–77).

[77] Y Tamura, DC Welch, JA Zic, WO Cooper, SM Stein and DS Hummell, Scurvy presenting as painful gait with bruising in a young boy, *Archives of Pediatrics and Adolescent Medicine*, 2000, 154, 732–735.

Table 7.4. *Radiological and histopathological correlation of changes seen in scurvy*

Radiological appearances	Histopathological correlate
Dense white line in distal metaphysis – white line of Fraenkel	Thickened zone of provisional calcification
Line of decreased density behind white line of Fraenkel – scurvy line or Trümmerfeld zone*	Decease in number of trabeculae
Metaphyseal or Pelkan's spurs	Lateral extension of zone of provisional calcification with stimulation of periosteal new bone formation
Dense line of calcification around epiphysis – Wimberger's line	Thickened zone of provisional calcification with loss of central trabeculae

* The Trümmmerfeld zone is not – as are the other signs – named after the author who first described it; it is the German word for rubble-field and seems to have been used first by Fraenkel, who was a radiologist working in Vienna.

for example. It has been suggested that the appearance of periosteal new bone on the bones of the skull, especially on the greater wing of the sphenoid is diagnostic of scurvy,[78] but this view lacks clinical validity and I doubt that scurvy in children can be diagnosed in the skeleton without the pathognomonic radiological signs in the long bones and the operational definition would need to include them (see "Operational definition for scurvy" box).

In the skeletons of Dutch whalers buried on the island of Zeeusche, Maat found black staining on the long bones that he considered was the result of sub-periosteal bleeding caused by scurvy.[79] His later demonstration that these deposits contained haemoglobin seems to confirm this diagnosis[80] but if other investigators wish to make the diagnosis on similar grounds, the demonstration of haemoglobin seems mandatory.

OTHER METABOLIC DISEASES

There are a number of other metabolic or endocrine disorders that may affect the skeleton including those affecting the thyroid, parathyroid and pituitary glands,

[78] DJ Ortner and MF Eriksen, Bone changes in human skulls probably resulting from scurvy in infancy and childhood, *International Journal of Osteoarchaeology*, 1997, 7, 212–220.
[79] GJR Maat, Scurvy in Dutch whalers buried at Spitsbergen, Proceedings of the Paleopathological Association 5th European Meeting, Middelburg/Antwerpen, 1982, 82–93.
[80] GJR Maat and HT Uytterschaut, Microscopic observations on scurvy in Dutch whalers buried at Spitzbergen, Proceedings of the Paleopathology Association 6th Meeting, Sienna, 1984, 211–216.

diabetes and some anaemias. Some will be considered briefly here, others are mentioned elsewhere in this book.

Thyroid Disease

Thyroid hormones are essential for normal bone growth and maturation and both under- and over-secretion of thyroid hormone has some effect on the skeleton.[81] Deficiency in childhood results in delayed maturation of the skeleton and an increase in Wormian bones in the cranial sutures.[82] In adults there may be some changes at the thoraco-lumbar junction and T12 and L1 may be smaller than normal and somewhat 'bullet' shaped. Hyperthyroidism results in a condition that mimics osteoporosis and there is an increased risk of fractures, especially of the vertebrae and the femoral neck. Focal bone loss in the skull and ribs may mimic a malignant disease. Thyroid acropachy is a rare complication in which periosteal new bone is laid down symmetrically on the shafts of the small bones of the hands and feet.[83]

Hyperparathyroidism

Parathyroid hormone stimulates the osteoclast to resorb bone and increases the uptake of calcium from the gut. Hyperparathyroidism may be primary, due to a secreting tumour of the parathyroid glands, or secondary to some other disease, most usually, renal disease in which a low serum calcium is produced. The disease is rare, slightly more common in women than in men, and increases with increasing age.[84] The effects on the skeleton are dominated by bone resorption which may be

[81] JH Bassett and GR Williams, The molecular actions of thyroid hormone in bone, *Trends in Endocrinology and Metabolism*, 2003, 14, 356–364. Whether the effect on the skeleton is directly due to thyroid hormone or to the thyroid stimulating hormone (TSH) secreted by the pituitary is something which is still under consideration (TM Galliford, E Murphy, AJ Williams, JH Bassett and GR Williams, Effects of thyroid status on bone metabolism: a primary role for thyroid stimulating hormone or thyroid hormone? *Minerva Endocrinologica*, 2005, 30, 237–246).

[82] Named after Ole Worm (1588–1655). Wormian bones are found in a number of different conditions the mnemonic for remembering which is PORK CHOPS. Unfortunately it is much easier to remember the mnemonic that the conditions it is supposed to remind one of. For those of a curious disposition they are: **P**yknodyostosis, **O**steogenesis imperfecta, **R**ickets in the healing phase, **K**inky hair syndrome, **C**leidocranial dysostosis, **H**ypothyroidism, **O**topalatodigital syndrome, **P**rimary acro-osteolysis, **S**yndrome of Down.

[83] F Capson, F Minonzio, P Sarzi-Puttini, F Atzenie and B Ambrosi, Thyroid acropachy: an unusual rheumatic manifestation of Graves' disease, *Clinical and Experimental Rheumatology*, 2005, 23, 125–126.

[84] R Jorde, KH Bønaa and J Sundsfjord, Primary hyperparathyroidism detected in a health screening. The Tromsø study, *Journal of Clinical Epidemiology*, 2000, 53, 1164–1169.

Table 7.5. *Sites of bone resorption in hyperparathyroidism*

Type of bone resorption	Sites affected	Appearance
Subperiosteal	Phalanges of hands and feet, wrists	Marginal erosions with cortical thinning and tuftal osteolysis
Subchondral	Symphysis pubis; sacroiliac, sterno-clavicular and acromio-clavicular joints; vertebrae; extra-spinal joints	Subchondral erosions sometimes with vertebral collapse
Subligamentous	Trochanters of femur; ischial tuberosities; deltoid tuberosity of humerus; insertion of plantar fascia on calcaneus; insertion of conoid ligament on inferior surface of distal clavicle	Bone erosions with new bone formation

subperiosteal, subchondral or subligamentous and which affects different parts of the skeleton preferentially (see Table 7.5).

The disease is sometimes referred to as osteitis fibrosa cystica which is characterised by a combination of subperiosteal bone resorption, osteopaenia and brown tumours.[85] Subperiosteal bone resorption is virtually pathognomonic of hyperparathyroidism and is seen most frequently in the phalanges of the hand, especially along the radial side.[86] Osteolysis of the tufts of the terminal phalanges may occur very early in the disease.

Brown tumours are not malignant but in life appear as reddish-brown, friable masses that are composed of fibrous tissue, macrophages which may contain haemosiderin, a breakdown product of haemoglobin, and osteoclasts. Brown tumours are most common in the pelvis, ribs and long bones and if multiple, they may be confused with metastatic malignant disease.[87] Rarely, they may occur in the spine and cause compression of the cord.[88]

---

[85] M Parisien, SJ Silverberg, E Shane, DW Dempster and JP Bilezikian, Bone disease in primary hyperparathyroidism, *Endocrinology and Metabolism Clinics of North America*, 1990, 19, 19–34.

[86] HE Meema, S Meema and DG Oreopoulos, Periosteal resorption of finger phalanges: radial versus ulnar surfaces, *Journal of the Canadian Association of Radiologists*, 1978, 29, 175–178.

[87] T Bassler, ET Wong and RK Brynes, Osteitis fibrosa cystica simulating metastatic tumor. An almost forgotten relationship, *American Journal of Clinical Pathology*, 1993, 100, 697–700.

[88] I Fineman, JP Johnson, P-L Di-Patre and H Sandhu, Chronic renal failure causing brown tumours and myelopathy, *Journal of Neurosurgery (Spine 2)*, 1999, 90, 242–246.

Diabetes

Diabetes has been mentioned in the context of DISH but it may also cause extra-spinal new bone formation in the absence of DISH, and because sensory loss may develop, osteomyelitis and neuropathic joints may also occur, especially in the foot.[89] It would not be possible to distinguish diabetes as a cause of any of these manifestations in the skeleton, however.

Anaemia

The haemolytic anaemias may have secondary effects on bone because the greatly reduced red cell life span in these conditions provokes a great expansion of the haemopoietic bone marrow in the long bones, vertebrae and the skull. There are very many haemolytic anaemias[90] but the most common are sickle cell disease[91] and thalassaemia,[92] both of which offer some protection against malaria and so are found in those countries where malaria is, or was, prevalent. Both are caused by genetic defects and both occur in the homozygous and heterozygous forms; generally only those with the homozygous form exhibit symptoms.[93] In both conditions, the characteristic lesion is a widening of the tables of the skull with a hair-on-end appearance on X-ray.[94] It is extremely doubtful that any child with a haemolytic anaemia would have survived very long but if a juvenile skeleton with thickening of the skull were found, an X-ray should certainly be taken in order to see if the typical hair-on-end appearance were present. If it were, the extraction and characterisation of haemoglobin would confirm the diagnosis.

There is considerable agreement within the palaeopathological community that cribra orbitalia – pitting on the superior wall of the orbit – is a sign of iron deficiency

[89] L Giurato and L Uccioli, The diabetic foot: Charcot joint and osteomyelitis, *Nuclear Medicine Communications*, 2006, 27, 745–749.

[90] S Mahmood and D Rees, Diagnosis and management of congenital haemoloytic anaemias, *Clinical Medicine*, 2007, 7, 625–629.

[91] Sickle cell disease may be a cause of avascular necrosis of the femoral and humeral heads and those with the disease may also contract osteomyelitis caused by species of Salmonella (C Aguilar, E Vichinsky and L Neumayr, Bone and joint disease in sickle cell disease, *Hematology and Oncology Clinics of North America*, 2005, 19, 929–941.

[92] BE Clark and SL Thein, Molecular diagnosis of haemoglobin disorders, *Clinical and Laboratory Haematology*, 2004, 26, 159–176.

[93] In both sickle cell disease and thalassaemia the genetic defects are expressed in the haemoglobin molecule which normally consists of two α and two β globin chains with a haem moiety. In thalassaemia there is reduced synthesis of either the α or the β chains while in sickle cell disease, there is a single mutation in which glutamic acid is substituted for valine in the β chains.

[94] M Azam and N Bhatti, Hair-on-end appearance, *Archives of Disease in Childhood*, 2006, 91, 735.

anaemia.[95] Cribra orbitalia is often associated with parietal porosity and both are thought to be the result of an expansion in haematopoietic bone marrow. Unfortunately for this hypothesis, there is little or no expansion of the bone marrow in iron deficiency anaemia since the red cell life span is reduced very little and it is only in those conditions in which the red cell life span is greatly reduced that marrow expansion is seen. Thickening of the tables of the skull and hair on end appearance is a rare phenomenon in iron deficiency anaemia.[96] Until there is some clinical validity to support the view that cribra can be equated with iron deficiency anaemia, it would be best to discard this notion, but, regrettably, it is too well established for there to be any likelihood that this will happen.

[95] U Wapler, E Crubézy and M Schultz, Is cribra orbitalia synonymous with anemia? Analysis and interpretation of cranial pathology in Sudan, *American Journal of Physical Anthropology*, 2004, 123, 333–339.
[96] HA Britton, JP Canby and CM Kohler, Iron deficiency anemia producing evidence of marrow hyperplasia in the calvarium, *Pediatrics*, 1960, 25, 621–628.

8

Trauma

Signs of trauma, whether accidental or deliberate (see Table 8.1) are commonly found on human remains. Fractures are the most frequent form of trauma found in assemblages recovered from urban or rural cemeteries. However, at certain times, evidence of wounding is quite common, and in later periods, signs of surgical or anatomical intervention may be apparent. Occasionally a skeleton with signs of hanging or beheading is uncovered, to the delight of all involved. Trauma may also be inflicted on the skeleton after it is buried. The weight of soil during burial will tend to flatten the skeleton so that the rib cage, the pelvic girdle and the skull may be fragmented. Further fragmentation or other damage may also occur at the hands of excavators, washers and – even dare one say – of palaeopathologists! It may be difficult to differentiate trauma that occurred at or around the time of death from that suffered after burial and there is no doubt that some peri-mortem trauma will not be recognised. Breaks to bones that occur during or after recovery should present no difficulty, however, as the broken surfaces will be of a much lighter colour than the rest of the skeleton.

In this chapter, broken and dislocated bones, wounding, some aspects of medical trauma, including trephination, and some special forms of trauma including spondylolysis and osteochondritis dissecans will be discussed.

FRACTURES AND DISLOCATIONS

A fracture is a break in the continuity of bone, cartilage or both and it is almost always associated with damage to overlying or adjacent soft tissues. A dislocation results from the complete loss of contact between two bone surfaces that should normally be in contact. A subluxation of a joint occurs when the loss of contact

Table 8.1. *Classification of trauma*

Accidental	Deliberate
Fractures Dislocations	Wounding
	Inter-personal fighting
	Battle wounds
	Assaults
	Torture
	Executions
	Hanging
	Beheading
	Shooting
	Surgical
	Amputations
	Anatomico-pathological autopsy

between the bones forming the joint is only partial. Finally, a fracture dislocation is a fracture in which there is a concomitant dislocation of a joint.

Fractures may be described or defined in several different ways. Thus, they may be simple, when there are only two fragments, or comminuted when there are more than two. They may also be closed, when the skin is unbroken or open (or compound) when the skin *is* broken; in the latter state, there is a greatly increased risk of infection. Fractures may also be categorised according to the nature of the fracture (see Table 8.2). There are also a great number of eponymous fractures much

Table 8.2. *Classification of fractures*

Type	Appearance
Transverse	Fracture at right angles to long axis of bone
Oblique	Fracture at oblique angle to long axis of bone
Spiral	Fracture winds around long axis of bone
Depressed	Skull fracture in which the table(s) of the skull are forced inwards
Crush	Vertebral fracture usually caused by a fall
Wedge	Vertebral fracture secondary to vertebral collapse such as caused by infection or malignant disease; typically seen in osteoporosis
Greenstick	Incomplete fracture seen in children
Pathological	Fracture occurring in a bone affected by some pathological process
Stress	Fracture occurring as the result of repeated loading

Table 8.3. *Some eponymous fractures*

Named fracture	Description
Bankart	Fracture of anterior rim of glenoid
Barton	Fracture of distal radius involving radiocarpal joint
Bennett	Intra-articular fracture-dislocation of base of first metacarpal
Bosworth	Fracture of fibula and posterior dislocation of talus
Chance	Transverse fracture of vertebral body and lamina
Chopart	Fracture-dislocation of midtarsal joints (talonavicular and calcaneocuboid joints)
Colles	Fracture of distal radius with dorsal displacement of distal fragment
Cotton	Fracture of medial and lateral malleoli and posterior process of tibia
Dupuytren	Bimalleolar ankle fracture
Duverney	Isolated fracture of blade of ilium
Essex-Lopresti	Fracture of head of radius with dislocation of distal radioulnar joint
Galeazzi	Fracture of radial shaft with dislocation of distal radioulnar joint
Gosselin	V-shaped fracture extending into the distal articular surface of the tibia, dividing it in two
Hill-Sachs	Impacted fracture on posterolateral aspect of head of humerus secondary to anterior dislocation of the shoulder
Holdsworth	Unstable fracture-dislocation at the thoraco-lumbar junction of the spine
Hutchinson	Oblique fracture of radial styloid process with extension into the wrist joint. Also known as chauffeur's fracture.
Jefferson	Complex burst fracture of the atlas, usually with lateral displaced of the lateral masses
Jones	Fracture at base of 5th metatarsal distal to metatarsal tuberosity
Le Fort	Of the face: fractures of the maxilla. Type I: horizontal fracture of alveolar process; type II: fracture of body of maxilla resulting in pyramidal fragment; type III: fracture in which entire maxilla is detached.
	Of the ankle: Vertical fracture of anterior medial portion of distal fibula with avulsion of anterior tibio-fibular ligament
Lisfranc	Fracture-dislocation (or fracture-subluxation) of tarsometatarsal joints
Maisonneuve	Spiral fracture of upper third of fibula and medial malleolus
Malgaigne	Fracture through ipsilateral ilium and pubic rami
Monteggia	Fracture of proximal third of ulna with anterior dislocation of radial head
Piedmont	Another name for the Galeazzi fracture
Pott	Any type of bimalleolar fracture
Pouteau	Identical with the Colles fracture
Rolando	Comminuted Y- or T-shaped fracture-dislocation of base of first metacarpal

(continued)

Table 8.3 (*cont.*)

Named fracture	Description
Segond	Small, vertical fracture of lateral aspect of proximal tibia just distal to tibial plateau
Smith	Reverse Colles fracture, that is, distal fragment is displaced towards the palm
Tillaux	Avulsion of anterior tibial tubercle at the attachment of the distal anterior tibiofibular ligament

loved by orthopaedic surgeons and to which reference is often given in orthopaedic texts; some of the better known are shown in Table 8.3.[1]

FRACTURES

The structure of bone enables it to withstand a high degree of compressive or shear forces but when the capacity to withstand a force is exceeded, the bone fractures. The force may be delivered at right angles to a bone, in which case a transverse or an oblique fracture results, or it may be a rotational force, such as occurs in the classic ski accident, in which a spiral fracture will result. Falls from a height onto the feet may result in crush fractures of the vertebrae or the pelvis, while a direct blow to the head may cause a depressed fracture. Whatever the cause, the consequences of a fracture are always the same.

Blood loss: The first response to a fracture is haemorrhage, both from the damaged bone and periosteum and from overlying soft tissues that may be injured. Blood loss can be severe – one to two litres from a fractured femur and two to four litres from a fractured pelvis – and the injured person may go into shock if the loss of blood is especially great. Individuals with blood loss will frequently feel thirsty and in the past, the risk of shock would probably have been enhanced if they had been offered water to drink by concerned bystanders as this would have further diluted the blood serum.

Displacement: When a limb bone is fractured the muscles around the fracture will go into spasm and may draw the distal fragment upwards; this is known

[1] TB Hunter, LF Peltier and PJ Lund, Musculoskeletal eponyms: who are those guys? *Radiographics*, 2000, 20, 819–836. More colloquial names and some definitions can be found in P Lee, TB Hunter and M Taljanovic, Musculoskeletal colloquialisms: how did we come up with these names? *Radiographics*, 2004, 24, 1009–1027.

as displacement and will compound any displacement that was caused by the injury itself. In some circumstances, displacement does not occur, particularly where another bone may act as a 'splint' for the damaged one. For example, in fractures of the forearm in which only one of the two bones is broken, the intact one will prevent the other becoming displaced. The same is true for fractures of the fibula in which the tibia remains intact. Similarly, if one or two ribs are fractured, the rest of the rib cage splints those that are broken and they do not usually lose their normal position.

Pain: A fractured bone causes considerable pain especially if moved, and those who have sustained a broken limb, for example, will take great care to lie still so as not to exacerbate the pain by movement.

Treatment of Fractures

The successful treatment of a fracture depends upon reducing it, and immobilising it. Reduction is achieved by putting the fractured bone back into its normal anatomical position. Nowadays this is done with the patient anaesthetised and relaxed and with X-ray guidance. In the past it was presumably done with brute force, the patient being held down by however many strong men it took, and the medical attendant pulling hard to overcome the resistance of the spasmodic muscles and the patient's natural inclination to escape from the pain. Alternatively, it may have been achieved with one of the machines that surgeons devised for the purpose.[2] It seems probable that in the absence of any other anaesthetic or analgesic that copious amounts of alcohol may have been taken, and some may even have been given to the patient. Once the limb is restored to its normal position, or to as near normal as can be achieved, it should be immobilised until healing is complete. The means of immobilisation by the application of splints has been in use for thousands of years. The period of immobilisation required to allow healing depends on a number of factors, including *inter alia* the age of the patient, the bone fractured and the quality of the bone, as will be discussed later. As a general rule, fractures of small bones such as of the hands or feet might need four to six weeks; fractures of the tibia or humerus, six to nine weeks; and fractures of the femur, nine to twelve weeks. Particularly with fractures of the leg, the period of immobilisation will be followed by a variable period of limited weight bearing which might last for another four to six weeks during which the muscles of the injured limb will need to be exercised and their tone and bulk brought back

---

[2] Illustrations of medieval machines for reducing fractures of the arm and the leg are to be found in: WA Clark, History of fractures up to the sixteenth century, *Journal of Bone and Joint Surgery*, 1937, 19A, 47–63, figures 6 and 7, respectively.

to normal. What is particularly noticeable about fractures that are found in skeletal assemblages is that the majority are well healed and in good alignment and few are found with signs of infection. This must indicate that there were in the general community, a number of individuals who had the knowledge and the skill to treat and set broken bones, and that the community was able to care for the injured individuals during their period of recovery and recuperation.

Complications of Fractures

As might be expected, there are several complications of fractures, as described in the following sections.

Death: Death is – of course – the most serious complication and is most likely to follow a serious accident in which there has been great blood loss or when some vital organ has been injured. Head injuries in which the brain is damaged or in which there is a large bleed into the skull are likely to result in death, as is a massive injury to the chest in which many ribs are broken and paradox-ical breathing caused. In this condition, a large segment of the rib cage may become detached from the remainder and be drawn inwards during inspira-tion and outwards during expiration, thus impairing the entry of air into the lungs.

Non-union: If a fracture fails to heal, this is known as non-union and the fibrous joint formed between the broken ends of the bones is known as a pseudarthrosis. This seems to occur often with forearm fractures, presumably because it was difficult to immobilise the arm, or because individuals with fractures started to use the arm before healing was complete. Failure of immobilisation is by far the most common cause of non-union, but it may also occur is some soft tissue – muscle or fat, for example – intrudes between the broken ends of the bones; fractures through pathological bone almost never heal.

Shortening and deformity:[3] If a broken limb is not properly reduced, it will heal with shortening or angulation (Figure 8.1), and the result may be a limb that shows significant deformity although it may be serviceable and usable, albeit with some difficulty. When assessing fractures in the skeleton it is always useful to determine the degree of shortening by reference to the normal contralateral bone, and to assess the degree of angulation.

Infection: All fractures are susceptible to infection but open fractures much more so than closed ones. As we have seen earlier, a wide variety of organisms may

---

[3] This is sometimes also referred to as mal-union.

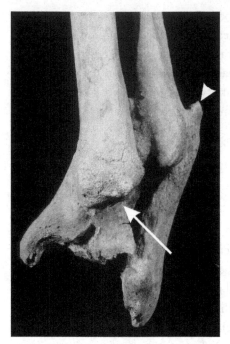

FIGURE 8.1. Healed fracture of the right ankle. The oblique fracture line (arrowed) is clearly visible and has entered the ankle joint; there is also a good deal of heterotopic ossification around the fracture. The fracture was not reduced and there is considerable angulation which would have caused some difficulty with walking during life. The remodelled proximal end of the distal fibular fragment (arrow head) would easily have been felt through the skin. There was no osteoarthritis of the ankle or knee joints so that although the individual survived the accident for several years, he did not do so for long enough for OA to supervene.

infect a wound but the end result will be the establishment of osteomyelitis for which, until very recently, the only treatment option was amputation. It is remarkable how few fractures seen in a skeletal assemblage show signs of infection, another testimony to the care with which they were treated, or to the robust natural immunity enjoyed by our ancestors in the days before we were overcome by pathological cleanliness.

Avascular necrosis: If damaged bone is cut off from its blood supply, it will die over a period of several months and the necrotic bone is eventually resorbed. This is particularly likely to happen with fractures of the femoral neck, the scaphoid, the lunate and the talus.

Femoral head: Most of the femoral head is supplied by the lateral epiphyseal artery, which is a branch of the medial circumflex artery. The lower part of the femoral head is supplied in addition by the inferior epiphyseal artery, a branch of the lateral circumflex. There is also a supply from the artery that runs in the ligamentum teres but this is extremely variable in extent. The blood vessels supplying the head of the femur run in the joint capsule and a fracture of the femoral neck is likely to disrupt them, especially if the femoral head is displaced. If the blood supply from the ligamentum teres is inadequate, as it is likely to be most of the time, then the head will become necrotic. Necrosis may also be caused by what is known as the tamponade effect, that is, by raised pressure within the joint capsule which is sufficient to disrupt the blood supply to the head of the femur.[4] Even with modern treatment about a third of displaced fractures of the femoral neck end in avascular necrosis and about a third fail to unite. Femoral neck fractures may be seen in skeletal assemblages with the loss of the head. The stump of the femoral neck may remain in articulation with the acetabulum or make a pseudarthrosis with the ilium. There is little prospect of union having taken place in the past but where the head remains, this must indicate that there was a plentiful blood supply from the ligamentum teres.

Scaphoid: The blood supply to the scaphoid comes predominantly from the radial artery. The proximal three-quarters of the bone is supplied by dorsal vessels and the distal quarter by palmar branches. The proximal pole of the scaphoid has only a limited blood supply, and large areas of it are reliant on a single vessel which may be damaged by a fracture. Osteonecrosis[5] is thought to occur in up to 40% of all scaphoid fractures.[6] Most fractures of the scaphoid occur when falling onto an outstretched hand when forced dorsiflexion of the wrist fractures through the waist of the scaphoid.

Lunate: The lunate receives its blood supply from the dorsal radiocarpal arch and the palmar intercarpal arch; the proximal pole is relatively less well supplied than the remainder of the bone. Fractures of the lunate are not common but may compromise the blood supply with subsequent necrosis.[7]

Talus: The blood supply of the talus comes from branches of the posterior tibial, peroneal and dorsalis pedis arteries, the tarsal sinus and tarsal canal branches of the posterior tibial artery being especially important. A fracture of the neck

---

[4] F G-C Bachiller, AP Caballer and LF Portal, Avascular necrosis of the femoral head after femoral neck fracture, *Clinical Orthopaedics and Related Research*, 2002, 399, 87–109.

[5] The stages in the process are described by R Schmitt, A Heinze, F Feliner, N Obletter, R Struhn and W Bautz, Imaging and staging of avascular necrosis of the wrist and hand, *European Journal of Radiology*, 1997, 25, 92–103.

[6] DM Freedman, MJ Botte and RH Gelberman, Vascularity of the carpus, *Clinical Orthopaedics and Related Research*, 2001, 383, 47–59.

[7] Osteonecrosis of the lunate is sometimes referred to as Kienböck's disease, a painful condition that often requires surgery; it is clear, however, that avascular necrosis is only one factor in the aetiology of this condition (see: C Irisarri, Aetiology of Kienböck's disease, *Journal of Hand Surgery*, 2004, 29B, 281–287). Robert Kienböck 1871–1953.

of the talus with dislocation of the subtalar or the ankle joint is likely to cause osteonecrosis of the body of the talus, and this may occur in a substantial number of cases with considerable morbidity.[8]

Osteoarthritis: Osteoarthritis following trauma is very likely to occur under two circumstances. Firstly, if the fracture heals in poor alignment so that the normal mechanics of the joint above or below the fracture are altered; and secondly, if the fracture line extends into a joint; in the latter case, osteoarthritis is almost inevitable. Since osteoarthritis will take many years to develop, its presence in the skeleton will indicate that the individual survived for some considerable time after the injury that caused the fracture.

Ankylosis: A fracture that extends into a joint, or a fracture-dislocation of a joint will almost certainly result in blood entering the joint, which greatly increases the risk that the joint will become ankylosed. Any joint that is found to be fused in the skeleton and in which there is no obvious sign of infection, or some concomitant disease such as a sero-negative arthropathy, is very likely to have been subject to injury of one kind or another.

Soft tissue injury: In addition to damage to overlying muscles, and underlying organs, blood vessels and nerves are prone to injury following a fracture. The soft tissue sites that are particularly vulnerable include the circumflex arteries, which are particularly liable to be damaged by fractures of the surgical neck of the humerus, and the brachial artery by a fracture of the elbow, for example. However, any vessel may be involved in an injury and bleeding is an inevitable concomitant of a fracture. The peripheral nerves that are near the surface and in direct relation with bones are susceptible to injury, as may be seen in Table 8.4. If the damage is slight, complete recovery is likely, but if the nerve is badly damaged or completely severed, the muscles supplied by that nerve will either be weakened or completely paralysed. Soft tissue injury may also result in heterotopic ossification, as described in Chapter 12.

Healing of Fractures

The healing of a fracture can be divided into three stages: (1) the inflammatory phase that lasts for up to 72 hours; (2) the reparative phase, that begins on about the second day post injury and lasts about two weeks; and (3) the remodelling phase that begins

---

[8] HA Vallier, SE Nork, DP Barei, SK Benirschke and BJ Sangeorzan, Talar neck fractures: results and outcomes, *Journal of Bone and Joint Surgery*, 2004, 86A, 1616–1624.

Table 8.4. *Peripheral nerves particularly susceptible to damage from an injury*

Injury	Peripheral nerve damaged
Facial fractures or other injury	Supraorbital
	Infraorbital
	Dental
Shoulder dislocation	Brachial plexus
	Axillary
Fracture of humerus	Radial
Fracture or dislocation of elbow	Median
	Ulnar
Forearm injuries	Anterior and posterior interosseous
Wrist	Median
Fractures or injuries to fingers and toes	Digital
Pelvic or hip fractures	Sciatic
Tibial fractures	Tibial
Fracture of proximal fibula	Lateral popliteal

in the middle of the reparative phase and may last for up to seven years. All three phases are characterised by the release of factors that stimulate different aspects of the process.[9]

> *The inflammatory phase:* In this phase the broken ends of the bone are sharp and a haematoma forms at the site of the fracture. Damaged tissue releases IL-1, IL-6 and PDGF which stimulate the appearance of macrophages and other cells that begin to remove tissue debris. Fibroblast growth factor (FGF) is also released which stimulates the proliferation of fibroblasts while the release of IGF-II stimulates type I collagen synthesis by osteoblasts. Finally, nitric oxide and endothelial stimulating angiogenesis factor cause local vasodilatation and new vessel formation to increase the blood supply to the affected area.

> *The reparative phase:* During the reparative phase, osteoblasts are formed within the haematoma and are induced to produce collagen by TGF-β which also stimulates mesenchymal cells to form type II collagen and proteoglycans necessary for the production of cartilage. The haematoma is converted into bridging callus by the action of cartilage and bone-forming cells, the amount of which is directly proportional to the degree of movement at the fracture site. Osteoblasts in the endosteum produce woven bone within the medullary cavity

---

[9] M Keel and O Trentz, Pathophysiology of polytrauma, *Injury*, 2005, 36, 691–709.

and periosteal osteoblasts form sub-periosteal callus. The edges of the fractured bone become rounded as they begin to be remodelled.

The remodelling phase: Bone production continues and the woven bone that formed the callus is remodelled by cutting cones that invade the site. Remodelling in fractures of cancellous bone occurs on the surfaces of the trabeculae which become thicker in the process. During this phase, the medullary canal becomes patent again and repopulated with the normal marrow cells. When the marrow is repopulated, healing is said to be complete. Remodelling can continue for up to seven years at the end of which time, there may be virtually no trace of the fracture.

Factors affecting bone healing: The principal factors affecting bone healing are age and bone quality. Thus, the young heal at a much greater rate than the old. Poor quality – osteoporotic – bone heals much more slowly than bone of normal quality. Fractures through bone that is affected by a pathological process such as Paget's disease or a bone tumour will never heal if left to its own devices. Poor nutrition will delay bone healing, especially a diet lacking in calcium, phosphorus or protein as will a disruption of the blood supply due to vascular damage, and so will loss of bone, such as may occur with a badly comminuted fracture.

The timing of fractures: An examination of the state of fractures in the skeleton should enable the palaeopathologist to provide a reasonable estimate of how long before death they were incurred. A fracture in which the edges of the fragments are still sharp will have occurred shortly before, or at the time of death. Remodelling of the fragments but with little callus formation will indicate that the individual survived at least a day or two, while if callus formation is well advanced, the survival period can be measured in weeks. A completely remodelled fracture can only mean that the individual survived the injury by several years, as will the appearance of osteoarthritis at joints involved in the injury. If a skeleton presents with several fractures, it should be possible to rank them in the order in which they occurred by their appearance.

The Epidemiology of Fractures

The rank order in which fractures occur for modern adults and for a large series of skeletons is shown in Table 8.5. In general there is a reasonable agreement between the two sets of data but there are some interesting differences. For example, rib fractures are the most common type of fracture in the skeleton in both males and females but are much less common in the contemporary population. By contrast,

Table 8.5. *Rank order of fractures in adults*

Males				Females			
Archaeological		Modern		Archaeological		Modern	
Rib	1	Wrist/hand	1	Rib	1	Radius/ulna	1
Radius	2	Tibia/fibula/ankle	2	Hand	2=	Femur	2
Ulna	3=	Radius/ulna	3	Fibula	2=	Tibia/fibula/ankle	3
Hand	3=	Foot	4	Tibia	4	Foot	4
Fibula	3=	Skull	5=	Radius	5=	Wrist/hand	5
Tibia	6	Rib	5=	Ulna	5=	Humerus	6
Skull	7=	Humerus	7=	Spine	5=	Rib	7
Clavicle	7=	Femur	7=	Clavicle	8=	Spine	8
Humerus	7=	Clavicle	9	Femur	8=	Skull	9
Spine	7=	Spine	10	Foot	8=	Pelvis	10
Femur	7=	Patella	11	Humerus	11	Clavicle	11
		Pelvis	12	Skull	12=	Patella	12
		Scapula	13			Scapula	13

Modern data extracted from: van Staa et al. (2001)[10]

fractures of the tibia are more common in the modern males while fractures of the foot, which are third equal in the modern ranking were not found at all in the skeletons. Similarly, pelvic fractures which were admittedly uncommon in modern males had no representation in the skeletal assemblage.

For the modern females, fractures of the radius and ulna are most common, presumably a reflection of the age structure of the modern population in which osteoporotic fractures are well represented. In the skeletal assemblage they are much less common – this is clearly indicated by the difference in the ranking for fractures of the femur. There is also a striking difference in the frequency of fractures of the humerus and foot, both being much more common in the modern than the skeletal females.

Some of the differences between the skeletal and the modern ranking of fractures no doubt reflects differences in age structure since there has been no attempt to perform any kind of age standardisation; and perhaps also to some extent by differences in social factors such as occupation, transport and leisure pursuits.

[10] TP van Staa, EM Denison, HGM Leufkens and C Cooper, Epidemiology of fractures in England and Wales, *Bone*, 2001, 29, 517–522.

Table 8.6. *Rank order of fractures in children*

Site of fracture	Rank order
Radius/ulna	1
Wrist	2
Humerus	3
Clavicle	4
Foot	5
Tibia/fibula	6
Skull	7
Ankle	8
Femur/hip	9
Patella	10
Ribs	11
Vertebrae	12
Scapula	13
Pelvis	14

Data from Cooper et al. (2004)[11]

Fractures in children are extremely uncommon in skeletal assemblages and this is at first sight, something of a surprise since it is reasonable to suppose that children were falling out of trees or injuring themselves in other ways in the past as much as they do today.[12] The explanation, however, may not be that difficult to determine, since if the child survived the injury into adulthood, the fracture would have completely remodelled and no signs of it would be visible on the mature skeleton. The distribution of fractures in modern children treated by their general practitioner is shown in Table 8.6[13] from which it can be seen that fractures of the humerus and clavicle are more common and fractures of the tibia less common than in modern adults.[14]

[11] C Cooper, EM Dennison, HG Leufkens, N Bishop and TP van Staa, Epidemiology of childhood fractures in Britain: a study using the general practice research database, *Journal of Bone and Mineral Research*, 2004, 19, 1976–1981.

[12] Well, actually, they don't fall out of trees very often nowadays. They are too busy sustaining repetitive strain injuries to the thumbs from the use of Playstations and their mobile phones. How palaeopathologists in the future will be able to get to grips with this, one hardly dare think.

[13] C Cooper, EM Dennison, HG Leufkens, N Bishop and TP van Staa, Epidemiology of childhood fractures in Britain: a study using the general practice research database, *Journal of Bone and Mineral Research*, 2004, 19, 1976–1981.

[14] What is not shown in the table is that the incidence of fractures in both sexes increased steadily with age, increasing approximately five-fold between the ages of 1 and 15 (B Kopjar and TM Wickizer, Fractures among children: incidence and impact of daily activities, *Injury Prevention*, 1998, 4, 194–197).

Comments of the Aetiology of Some Fractures

It is possible to infer the aetiology of some of the fractures seen in the skeleton. Osteoporotic fractures of the distal radius, femoral neck and vertebrae have been alluded to in Chapter 7. Fractures of the shaft of the radius and/or the ulna are often referred to as parry fractures, since it is assumed that the individual was using his or her arm to ward off a blow aimed at the head. Rib fractures are commonly the result of brawls or falls, in the case of the former, usually from a kick when the victim is on the floor.[15] Fractures of the metacarpals – especially the fifth – are also often sustained in a fist fight.[16] Falls may account for many fractures. The Colles fracture or a scaphoid fracture when an attempt is made to save oneself by an outstretched hand. Crush fractures may be caused by a fall onto the feet, as may the rather uncommon fracture of the tibial plateau.[17]

Stress fractures: Stress fractures are the result of repeated trauma to bones and they are often found in young men or women who engage in vigorous athletic pursuits and in older individuals engaged in a variety of occupations. The most common stress fractures and their causes are shown in Table 8.7.

The only stress fracture mentioned here is spondylolysis. This is a fracture through the pars interarticularis and is confined almost exclusively to the lumbar region,[18] with L5 bearing the brunt of the injury (Figure 8.2). The break is most often bilateral, but unilateral cases do occur and then the contralateral pedicle and lamina may be hypertrophied. Other levels of the lumbar spine are also affected and on occasion, more than one vertebra is involved. The fracture is never found in children before they can walk, nor is it found in adult patients who have never walked,[19] and it is generally thought that it is a consequence of the stresses imposed on the lower spine by locomotion although there may be contributory environmental or inherited factors as some families have a high prevalence of the condition.[20] Athletes and others who engage in vigorous

[15] M Sirmale, S Turut, E Topcu, U Yazici, S Kaya and A Tasteppe, A comprehensive analysis of traumatic rib fractures: morbidity, mortality and management, *European Journal of Cardiothoracic Surgery*, 2003, 24, 133–138.
[16] F Kermad, JF Cazeneuve, Y Hassan, B Rihan and H Boustani, Two-pin L fixation of fractures of the fifth metacarpal neck, *Acta Orthopaedica Belgica*, 2002, 68, 231–234.
[17] JO Anglen and WL Healey, Tibial plateau fractures, *Orthopedics*, 1988, 11, 1527–1534.
[18] There is a well-recognised congenital form of spondylolysis that affects the cervical region (TR Yochum, JT Carton and MS Barry, Cervical spondylolysis: three levels of simultaneous involvement, *Journal of Manipulative and Physiological Therapeutics*, 1995, 18, 411–415).
[19] NJ Rosenberg, WL Bargar and B Friedman, The incidence of spondylolysis and spondylolisthesis in non-ambulatory patients, *Spine*, 1981, 6, 35–38.
[20] K Haukipuro, N Keranen, E Koivisto, R Lindholm, R Norio and L Punto, Familial occurrence of lumbar spondylolysis and spondylolisthesis, *Clinical Genetics*, 1978, 133, 471–476.

Table 8.7. *Stress fractures by anatomical site and activity*

Anatomical site	Activity producing fracture
Distal humerus	Throwing
Ulna	Using a pitchfork
Spinous processes of lower cervical or upper thoracic vertebrae	Shovelling
Lumbar vertebrae (spondylolysis)	Athletic pursuits; gymnastics; dancing
Ribs	Carrying heavy objects; prolonged coughing
Obturator ring of pelvis	Gymnastics
Femoral neck	Dancing; long distance running; marching; gymnastics
Femoral shaft	Dancing; long distance running
Proximal fibula	Jumping
Distal fibula	Long distance running
Calcaneus	Jumping; prolonged standing
Navicular	Marching; long distance running
Metatarsal shafts	Marching; prolonged standing; dancing
Sesamoid bones of foot	Prolonged standing

FIGURE 8.2. Fourth lumbar vertebra with spondylolysis and marginal osteophyte around the vertebral body. The detached lamina has survived but this is by no means always the case and the diagnosis has sometimes to be made in its absence.

pursuits tend to have a higher prevalence of spondylolysis than those who enjoy a more sedentary way of life[21] and there is considerable variation in the prevalence in different populations.[22] On average, about 5% of the population will be found with the condition which tends to be more common in males than in females.[23] The condition may also occur as the result of acute trauma, such as may follow a fall from a height.[24]

Uncomplicated spondylolysis is clinically silent although when it is found as a coincidental finding in those who complain of back ache, it is sometimes seen as the cause.[25] Sometimes, however, the body of the spondylolytic vertebra slips forward on the one below – a condition known as spondylolisthesis which does seem to be a cause of back pain and neurological complications.[26] Whereas spondylolysis is unmistakeable in the skeleton, it is rarely possible to determine whether or not there has been any slippage unless the inferior vertebral body has become sloped due to the pressure exerted on it from the one above, or if the slipped body is fused to the one below, as was found to be the case in an individual with DISH.[27]

Osteochondritis Dissecans (OCD)

Osteochondritis dissecans (OCD) is an osteochondral fracture in which the fractured fragment may become incompletely or completely detached.[28] It may be caused by direct trauma or repetitive microtrauma such as may follow excessive normal

[21] CM Bone, Low-back pain in athletes, *Journal of Bone and Joint Surgery*, 2004, 86A, 383–386.

[22] HA Waldron, Variations in the prevalence of spondylolysis in early British populations, *Journal of the Royal Society of Medicine*, 1991, 84, 547–549.

[23] CA McTimoney and LJ Mitchell, Current evaluation and management of spondylolysis and spondylolisthesis, *Current Sports Medicine Reports*, 2003, 2, 41–46.

[24] R Cope, Acute traumatic spondylolysis. Report of a case and review of the literature, *Clinical Orthopaedics and Related Research*, 1988, 230, 162–165.

[25] Various schemes for classifying spondylolysis have been described. Although these have little application in palaeopathology, those who are interested will find them described in: MJ Herman and PD Pizzutillo, Spondylolysis and spondylolisthesis in the child and adolescent: a new classification, *Clinical Orthopaedics and Related Research*, 2005, 434, 46–54.

[26] A Ganju, Isthmic spondylolisthesis, *Neurosurgical Focus*, 2002, 13, Article 1.

[27] K Manchester, Spondylolysis and spondylolisthesis in two Anglo-Saxon skeletons, *Paleopathology Newsletter*, 1982, 37, 9–12. There are a number of systems for grading the degree of slippage based on the radiological appearances. As with those for classifying spondylolysis, the palaeopathological applications are not considerable but those who wish to look into the matter further should consult: SJ Timon, MJ Gardner, T Wanich, A Poynton, R Pigeon, RF Wildmann, BA Rawlins and SW Burke, Not all spondylolisthesis grading instruments are reliable, *Clinical Orthopaedics and Related Research*, 2005, 434, 157–162.

[28] JR Schenck, RC Goodnight and J Marc, Osteochondritis dissecans, *Journal of Bone and Joint Surgery*, 1996, 78A, 439–456.

Table 8.8. *Sites of osteochondritis dissecans, in order of frequency*

Joints affected	Most common sites
Knee	Lateral aspect of medial femoral condyle (75%); weight bearing surface of medial condyle (10%); lateral femoral condyle (10%); anterior intercondylar groove or patella (5%)
Elbow	Anterolateral aspect of capitulum
Ankle	Posteromedial aspect of dome of talus (56%); anterolateral aspect of talus (44%). May also occur on the navicular.
Hip	Femoral head. May be predated by Perthes' disease
Shoulder	Rare; occurs on head of humerus and glenoid
Wrist	Rare; mostly confined to scaphoid and in those subjected to repetitive trauma of the wrist.

compressive strain but the exact aetiology is unclear[29] although it is known that those who engage in sport or other vigorous physical activity have a higher than average prevalence.[30] The condition occurs more commonly in males than in females and tends to present in young patients, although there is a wide range of age at diagnosis. OCD occurs within joints and several may be affected; it occurs more commonly on convex than concave surfaces. The knee joint is the one most frequently involved and the lateral aspect of the medial femoral condyle is the favoured site, other joints affected include (in order of frequency) the elbow, ankle, hip, shoulder and wrist (Table 8.8).

Those with the condition may be unaware of it, or the joint may be swollen and painful with limitation of movement. Osteoarthritis is a common long-term complication. The defect varies in size but is not difficult to recognise in the skeleton. The edges of the lesion are often not remodelled and the surface of the lesion may be irregular. The condition should not be confused with other defects in the cortex which are simply normal variants; these present as holes of varying sizes (although usually small). The cortex can be followed into the hole and the floor of the defect is smooth (when it can be seen). The most common sites for these anomalies are the glenoid and the proximal surface of the first phalanx of the great toe.

[29] MA Yadao, LD Field and FH Savoie, Osteochondritis of the elbow, *Instructional Course Lectures*, 2004, 53, 599–606.

[30] S Orava and K Virtanen, Osteochondroses in athletes, *British Journal of Sports Medicine*, 1982, 16, 161–168.

DISLOCATIONS AND SUBLUXATIONS

Joints that are highly mobile often achieve their mobility at the cost of stability and nowhere is this more evident than in the glenohumeral joint which is the joint that is most frequently and easily dislocated. Stable joints such as hip, by contrast, are seldom dislocated and then only with the application of considerable force. Subluxation is often the result of joint disease as we have seen in Chapter 4.

In some situations, dislocated joints are easily – if painfully – reduced and most dislocations and subluxations are likely to leave no traces on the skeleton. The major exception to this is dislocation of the shoulder.

Dislocation of the shoulder

Dislocation of the shoulder may result from accidents, from injury sustained in vigorous physical exercise or by a fall onto an outstretched hand. In 95% of cases, the dislocation is anterior and in most cases, the head of the humerus comes to lie in front of the scapula just below the coracoid process. It is easily reduced and may go entirely unnoticed in the skeleton except for the possible presence of two lesions, the Bankart and Hill-Sachs lesions. The Bankart[31] lesion is a fracture of the anterior rim of the glenoid which may involve only the cartilaginous labrum but may also involve the bone, especially with repeated dislocations. The Hill-Sachs lesion is a compression fracture that is found on the postero-lateral aspect of the head of the humerus and is caused by impaction of the humerus on the rim of the glenoid. The fracture is wide and shallow and, again, is more common with repeated dislocations. The Hill-Sachs lesion is readily seen in the skeleton once observers are alerted to the possibility of its presence. Bankart lesions can also be seen relatively easily, especially florid types that occur with repeated dislocation. The two lesions are frequently seen in the same individual.[32]

Where there is evidence of either of these lesions, the diagnosis of dislocation of the shoulder is clear and if they were looked for more assiduously, it is probable that several cases would come to light. With other dislocations, however, there are not

[31] Arthur Sidney Blundell Bankart 1879–1951.

[32] AB Widjaja, A Tran, M Bailey and S Proper, Correlation between Bankart and Hill-Sachs lesions in anterior shoulder dislocation, *ANZ Journal of Surgery*, 2006, 76, 436–438. A lesion similar to the Hill-Sachs lesions has been described on the femoral head in a case of hip instability (RN Villar, AM Sheikh and A Arora, Hill-Sachs type lesion of the femoral head in a case of hip instability, *Arthroscopy*, 2000, 16, 858–859).

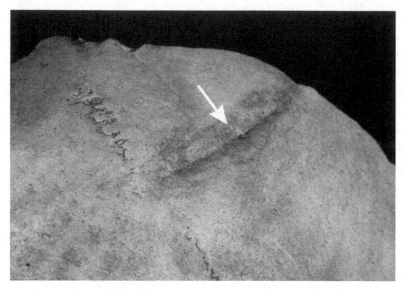

FIGURE 8.3. Skull from Anglo-Saxon male showing healed wound (arrowed) made with a straight edged weapon. The edges of the wound are completely remodelled indicating that the man survived several years after the injury.

likely to be any obvious signs and their under-reporting in the archaeological record is bound to happen. Sometimes a dislocation of a small joint is accompanied by bleeding and the joint may ankylose even though it is reduced, and with a fracture-dislocation of a joint such as the elbow, ankylosis must be a likely outcome which will be obvious to the palaeopathologist.

WOUNDING

The human propensity to inflict harm on others is quite often encountered in skeletal assemblages through signs of injury inflicted with sharp or blunt weapons (Figure 8.3). This is nowhere more evident than on the battlefield where human ingenuity has excelled itself in devising ways to do harm. Among skeletal assemblages from the general population in the United Kingdom, evidence for fighting seems most prevalent among the Anglo-Saxons and it is by no means unusual to find skeletons from Anglo-Saxon contexts with wounds to the head or other parts of the body. Whether the individuals were injured in battle, were soldiers, or those who chanced to be in the way of the action, is, of course, impossible to say. What is possible is to determine whether the individual survived the attack, and it is by no means infrequent to find a single skeleton with several wounds, some healed and some fresh, indicating those that were survived and those that were presumably fatal. The healing of a wound follows exactly the same pattern as the healing of a fracture, and in the final stage they will be remodelled with smooth, rolled edges. In a skeleton with several wounds, their timing can often be determined using the same criteria as for timing fractures.

It is during battle that the most severe wounds are likely to be encountered and many surgical techniques were pioneered or perfected in the past by military surgeons, such as Ambroise Parè (in the sixteenth century);[33] Napoleon's surgeon the Baron Dominique Jean Larrey;[34] Robert Wiseman, the Royalist surgeon in the English Civil War;[35] and the many surgeons who participated in the American Civil War.[36] The horrors of warfare, which were worsened considerably after the invention of gunpowder and the introduction of guns to the battlefield, may be gleaned from sources as widespread as the *Iliad* [37] to the photographic record of the American Civil War injuries,[38] or from assemblages recovered from battle cemeteries such as that of those who died at the Battle of Towton during the War of the Roses,[39] or the battle of Zaimokuza in Japan in 1333.[40]

GUNSHOT WOUNDS

The analysis of gunshot wounds is an important aspect of forensic medicine and pathology and only brief mention will be made of them here. Those who wish for

[33] OH Wangensteen, SD Wangensteen and CF Klinger, Wound managements of Ambroise Parè and Dominique Larrey, great French military surgeons of the 16th and 19th centuries, *Bulletin of the History of Medicine*, 1972, 46, 207–234.

[34] LA Brewster, Baron Dominique Jean Larrey (1766–1842). Father of modern military surgery, innovator, humanist, *Journal of Thoracic and Cardiovascular Surgery*, 1986, 92, 1096–1098.

[35] AD Smith, Richard Wiseman: his contribution to English surgery, *Bulletin of the New York Academy of Medicine*, 1970, 46, 167–182.

[36] One of the more colourful American Civil War surgeons was William Chester Minor who served on the Union side. After the war he moved to England where he was committed to Broadmoor having killed a man in a fit of insanity. While in Broadmoor he contributed several articles to the embryo Oxford English Dictionary before being sent back to America in 1910. He is the madman in Simon Winchester's book *The professor and the madman* (London, Harper Collins, 1998) which recounts the early history of the OED.

[37] GH Santos, Chest trauma during the battle of Troy: ancient warfare and chest trauma, *Annals of Thoracic Surgery*, 2000, 69, 1285–1287.

[38] BP Bengston and JE Kuz, *Photographic atlas of Civil War injuries*, Grand Rapids, Medical Staff Press, 1996.

[39] V Fiorato, A Boylston and C Knüsel, *Blood red roses: the archaeology of a mass grave from the Battle of Towton AD 1461*, Oxford, Oxbow Books, 2000.

[40] M Shackley, Arms and the men: 14th century Japanese swordsmanship illustrated by skeletons from Zaimokuza, near Kamakura, Japan, *World Archaeology*, 1986, 18, 247–254. See also the special issue of the *International Journal of Osteoarchaeology* (1996, 6 (1)) which contains several papers on battle and other trauma.

further information should consult a standard text.[41] The damage caused by bullets or other fired projectiles is due to the loss of kinetic energy sustained as they enter the body. The kinetic energy in turn, depends upon the weight and velocity of the projectile, the latter of which would have been relatively low under recent times.[42] Bullets entering the skull leave an entry wound and almost always an exit wound as well. Entry wounds are usually round or oval and have a sharp punched-out appearance on the external table with a bevelling on the internal table. The exit wound is larger than the entry wound and shows bevelling on the external surface.[43] There are often fractures radiating from both entry and exit wounds which may intersect. Where there is more than one gunshot wound to the head, the pattern of fractures can sometimes be used to determine the sequence[44] and direction[45] of fire. Gunshot wounds can sometimes be confused with other types of damage, and where there is doubt about the origin of the wound it is useful to X-ray the skull since in the case of a gunshot wound, there will be radiodense particles of lead around the entry and the exit wounds.

Gunshot wounds to long bones are usually comminuted, the fragments sometimes taking a 'butterfly' appearance, but a single drill hole appearance is also sometimes seen. There is generally less damage in cancellous than in cortical bone because the kinetic energy of the projectile is dissipated more readily in areas of trabecular bone.[46]

AMPUTATION

Amputation was one of the many techniques that was commonplace to the military surgeon[47] but it was also used by general surgeons, perhaps as long ago as

---

[41] See, for example, J Dix, *Color atlas of forensic pathology*, Boca Raton, CRC Press, 2000, and BJ Knight and PJ Saukko, *Knight's forensic pathology, 3rd edition*, London, Arnold, 2004.

[42] For further details see: ARW Jackson and J Jackson, *Forensic Science*, Harlow, Pearson Education, 2004, chapter 9.

[43] G Quatrehomme and MY Işcan, Characteristics of gunshot wounds in the skull, *Journal of Forensic Sciences*, 1999, 44, 568–576; G Quatrehomme and MY Işcan, Gunshot wounds to the skull: comparison of entries and exits, *Forensic Science International*, 1998, 94, 141–146.

[44] DS Dixon, Pattern of intersecting fractures and direction of fire, *Journal of Forensic Sciences*, 1984, 29, 651–654.

[45] DF Huelke and JH Darling, Bone fractures produced by bullets, *Journal of Forensic Sciences*, 1964, 9, 461–469.

[46] WU Spitz, Medico-legal investigation of death. Guidelines for the application of pathology to crime scene investigation, 3rd edition, Springfield, CC Thomas, 1993, pp 311–381.

[47] TS Helling and WK McNabney, The role of amputation in the management of battlefield casualties: a history of two millennia, *Journal of Trauma*, 2000, 49, 930–939.

2000 BC,[48] but it was not practiced widely until the eighteenth and nineteenth centuries. In the absence of anaesthesia and adequate analgesia, the operation was over
in very short order and the chances of survival were extremely poor. Robert Liston
(1794–1847), who was a surgeon at University College Hospital in London was one
of the most skilled of the early nineteenth-century surgeons. It was said of him that

> Amputations were his special delight, and . . . in his hands the use of the saw followed
> the flash of the knife so quickly that the student who turned his head for even a moment
> found that the operation was completed when he looked round again.[49]

Until the advent of anaesthesia, the operation was undertaken as quickly as possible to
minimise the suffering of the patient. As performed in the sixteenth and seventeenth
centuries, the soft tissues were cut with a single circular cut down to the bone, which
was then sawn through. Later soft-tissue flaps were devised to close the wound, and
two or three cuts would be made to sever the soft tissue. The bone would be cut
with either a single or a double cut.[50] Whatever the technique, the case mortality
rate was extremely high and few patients survived, dying either from shock at the
time, or later, because of infection and septicaemia. Not until Lister introduced his
carbolic spray did the case fatality rate approach acceptable limits (15% in his own
case).[51] The reason for the poor survival rate was that the majority of wounds quickly
became infected and, indeed, the presence of pus in the wound was taken as a sign of
healing, a belief that went back to the time of Galen who had propounded the belief
that the presence of pus was both good and laudable, a tenet that held sway well into
the nineteenth century.[52]

---

[48] DR Brothwell and V Møller-Christensen, A possible case of amputation, dated to c. 2000 BC, *Man*, 1963,
63, 192–194; AI Bloom, RA Bloom, G Kahilia, Eisenberg and P Smith, Amputation of the hand in a 3600-
year-old skeletal remains of an adult male: the first case reported from Israel, *International Journal of
Osteoarchaeology*, 1995, 5, 188–191.

[49] Liston was the first surgeon in England to perform an operation under anaesthesia. On 21 December 1846
he amputated the leg of Frederick Churchill who was suffering from osteomyelitis while the patient was
anaesthetised with ether; the operation took less than half a minute (DJ Coltart, Surgery between Hunter
and Lister as exemplified by the life and works of Robert Liston (1794–1847), *Journal of the Royal Society of
Medicine*, 1972, 65, 556–560).

[50] M Sachs, J Bojunga and A Encke, Historical evolution of limb amputation, *World Journal of Surgery*, 1999,
23, 1088–1093.

[51] SWB Newsom, Pioneers in infection control – Joseph Lister, *Journal of Hospital Infection*, 2003, 55, 246–253.

[52] Galen's *pus bonum et laudabile* was not adhered to by all those who dealt with wound in the intervening
period and, indeed, it is very difficult to see now how it could not have occurred to the surgeons of – say –
the eighteenth and nineteenth centuries that infected wounds were harmful to their patients. Some shrewd
observer might surely have noticed that those whose wounds were *not* infected were more likely to survive
that those with stinking, infected stumps. For a short history of the treatment of wounds see: AJ Thurston,
Of blood, inflammation and gunshot wounds: the history of the control of sepsis, *ANZ Journal of Surgery*,
2000, 70, 855–861.

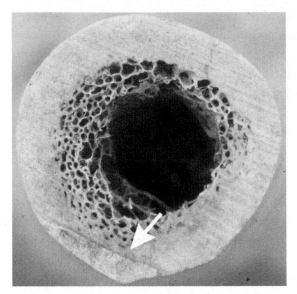

FIGURE 8.4. Distal end of amputated femur from an eighteenth century context. The kerf marks on the cut surface are clearly seen. The breakaway point has only a single surface (arrowed) showing that the surgeon made only one cut with the saw to detach the leg. There was no indication of the reason for the amputation on the bone.

Bones from amputees are most likely to be found in assemblages from hospital sites, and they may be the distal bones, that is, the part of the limb that was discarded, or the remnant of the proximal stump that was still attached to the patient (Figure 8.4). The amputated limbs are easily recognisable by the kerf made by the surgeon's saw,[53] and there is almost always a breakaway point on the distal bone which is made as the bone parts. This breakaway point will have as many sides as there were cuts with the saw, either one or two. The distal bone will – of course – show no evidence of healing, but on some rare occasions, the proximal end may do so, indicating that the patient was lucky enough to survive at least for some months after the operation, sometimes considerably longer.[54] What is seldom found, however, is evidence of the reason for the amputation. This might have included a compound fracture, osteomyelitis, a tumour of either bone or soft tissue or an aneurysm of a peripheral artery. In the middle of the nineteenth century, the most common

[53] The kerf mark is the groove made by a cutting tool; in the case of a saw, the kerf is wider than the saw blade and the physical characteristics of the kerf may often allow the type of saw used to be identified; this is particularly useful in forensic medicine. See, for example: S Symes, Morphology of saw marks in human bone: introduction and examination of residual kerf contour, In: *Forensic osteology, advances in the identification of human remains* (edited by K Reichs), CC Thomas, Springfield, 1998, pp 389–409.

[54] SA Mays, Healed limb amputations in human Osteoarchaeology and their causes: a case study from Ipswich, UK, *International Journal of Osteoarchaeology*, 1996, 6, 101–113.

indication for amputation at the London Hospital by far was trauma resulting from injuries at work. The case fatality rate was very high and almost half the patients died following the operation.[55]

TREPHINATION

Trephination, of the deliberate removal of pieces of bone from the skull,[56] has been known from the earliest times and examples are to be found throughout the world, from Europe,[57] North America,[58] Mexico[59] and most notably, from Peru.[60] There is no means of knowing why the operation was first carried out but a number of suggestions have been made, including to relieve headache, cure epilepsy or let out evil spirits.[61] The operation would have required a good deal of stoicism on the part of the patient since it would have involved cutting and reflecting the scalp from the underlying bone, achieved no doubt by the shedding of much blood, given the vascularity of the scalp, and then removal of bone, utilising one of several methods. The most common method involved scraping away the bone using a stone or metal implement, cutting out a square or rectangle of bone with four separate cuts; or drilling and removing a circle or ellipse of bone. The last method might

[55] EJ Chaloner, HS Flora and RJ Ham, Amputations at the London Hospital 1852–1857, *Journal of the Royal Society of Medicine*, 2001, 94, 409–412.

[56] There is sometimes some confusion about the terms used for this operation; both trephination and trepanation are used and are synonymous, at least in the palaeopathological context, although they have separate derivations. Trephination *sensu strictu* refers to the removal of a circular piece of bone using an instrument with a circular, saw-toothed blade, known as a trephine. Trepanation, on the other hand, has its roots in the Greek word, trepa (τρῦπα), meaning a hole.

[57] J Piek, G Lidke, T Terberger, U von Smekal and MR Gaab, Stone age skull surgery in Mecklenburg-Vorpommern: a systematic study, *Neurosurgery*, 1999, 45, 147–151.

[58] JL Stone and ML Miles, Skull trepanation among the early Indians of Canada and the United States, *Neurosurgery*, 1990, 26, 1015–1019.

[59] M Velasco-Suarez, J Bautista Martinez, R Garcia Oliveros and PR Weinstein, Archaeological origins of cranial surgery: trephination in Mexica, *Neurosurgery*, 1992, 31, 313–318.

[60] S Rifkinson-Mann, Cranial surgery in ancient Peru, *Neurosurgery*, 1988, 23, 411–416.

[61] Let no-one think that the practice has died out in modern times; it is still quite widely practiced. One patient described by Margetts had no fewer than five operations, initially for a headache following a blow to the head, and virtually the whole of his calvarium had been removed. So anxious were they about his safety, with so little between his brain and the outside world, that he was fitted with a plastic skull cap to wear under his hat (EL Margetts, Trepanation of the skull by medicine-men of primitive cultures, with particular reference to present-day native East African practice, In: *Diseases in antiquity* (edited by D Brothwell and AJ Sandison), Springfield, CC Thoms, 1967, pp 673–701). There are also those who drill holes in their skulls using an electric drill, usually in total ignorance of the anatomy of structures within their head; one such individual succeeded in drilling into the sagittal sinus producing a spectacular haemorrhage. He survived but needed surgery to clear up the mess (JP Wadley, GT Smith and C Shieff, Self-trephination of the skull with an electric power drill, *British Journal of Neurosurgery*, 1997, 11, 156–158).

employ ring-drilling to produce a series of contiguous small holes and removing the contained piece of bone, presumably by levering it outwards, or the use of a single, large drill hole.[62]

The dangers in the procedure scarcely need spelling out, but the operators must soon have learned to avoid the areas overlying the sagittal sinus or the middle meningeal artery, and most lesions are found in the frontal or parietal bones. Some skulls have several holes in them and it may be that these are skulls on which trainees practiced prior to taking up their art on the living. Holes made with cutting tools or drills are easy to recognise but those made by scraping may sometimes be confused with other pathological lesions and there may be some difficulty in arriving at a definitive diagnosis.[63] The clue often lies in the fact that holes in the skull produced by scraping tend to be relatively large, and have edges bevelled away from the outer table. They will also lack any fracture lines that might be associated with impact trauma. They may show signs of inflammation or infection, and they may also show signs of healing and remodelling although, of course, the hole is never filled.

THE AUTOPSY

Dissection of the human body seems not to have been practiced with any regularity until the seventeenth century, partly because of the difficulty in obtaining and preserving bodies for any length of time. The Greek and Roman anatomists generally contented themselves with studies on animals. Galen, the most influential of the ancient physicians save Hippocrates, apparently had only two human skeletons to study, and by extrapolating his findings on animals to humans, made a number of errors that were perpetuated until the times of Vesalius.[64] Throughout the medieval period, there are sporadic references to the autopsy but the practice was hampered, if not actually forbidden, by the attitude of the church. St Augustine was strongly opposed to dissection, for humanitarian and aesthetic, rather than religious reasons, but the decree promulgated at the Council of Tours in 1163 that *ecclesia abhorret a sanguina* was widely interpreted to mean that the clergy should not perform surgery on either the living or the dead. In 1299, Pope Boniface VIII forbade the cooking

---

[62] The various techniques are well illustrated in: D Campillo, Neurosurgical pathology in prehistory, *Acta Neurochirurgica (Wien)*, 1984, 70, 275–290.

[63] MH Kaufmann, D Whitaker and J McTavish, Differential diagnosis of holes in the calvarium: application of modern clinical data to palaeopathology, *Journal of Archaeological Science*, 1997, 24, 193–218.

[64] C Singer, *A short history of anatomy and physiology from the Greeks to Harvey*, New York, Dover Books, 1957.

of bodies to separate the flesh from the bones, which was done to bring home the bones of those who died on the Crusades. Although the ban was specific in its instructions, many considered that *any* dissection was thereby prohibited. When autopsies were undertaken, they were often done for forensic reasons. Mondino de Luzzi's influential *Anathomia*, based at least in part on human dissection, appeared in the fifteenth century and was frequently reprinted during this and the following century. The greatest single advance in the study of anatomy, however, came with the publication of the great work by Andreas Vesalius, *De corporis humani fabrici*, published in 1543 with wonderful woodcuts, some of which were made by Stephan van Calcar, who had been a pupil of Titian. This book, which finally overthrew the Galenical system of anatomy was based on dissection and is one of the most influential of medical books ever published.[65]

Many autopsies were performed for pathological reasons in the early modern period and volumes of autopsy reports (or *specilegia*) were published at the end of the seventeenth century but none was grander than the *Sepulchretum sive anatomia practica* of Theophillus Bonet (1620–1689) that contained over 3000 autopsy protocols. This was a largely uncritical work, however, and the new era of empirical medicine, that is, one that was based on observation rather than deduction was exemplified by the publication of Giovanni Morgagni's *De sedibus et causis morborum*, published in Morgagni's eightieth year, in 1762. This book can be said to have ushered in the great period of pathological anatomy, exemplified in England by the work of John Hunter and his various pupils in the eighteenth century, by Bichat, Corvisart, Laennec and Louis in Paris in the early nineteenth in the aftermath of the Revolution, and by Skoda and Rokitanski in Vienna during the later nineteenth.[66]

An autopsy may either be partial or complete. In a partial autopsy the viscera in the abdomen and/or chest are examined, but the skull is not opened, whereas it is when the autopsy is complete. Where the autopsy was confined to an examination of the abdomen, there may be no signs on the skeleton. On the other hand, when the heart and lungs were examined, it would have been necessary to cut through the rib cage and this should be evident on the skeleton. To undertake a complete autopsy, the calvarium was removed with a saw and this is very obvious on the skeleton

[65] For the history of the autopsy see, LS King and MC Meehan, A history of the autopsy. A review, *American Journal of Pathology*, 1973, 73, 514–544; RB Hill and RE Anderson, The recent history of the autopsy, *Archives of Pathology and Laboratory Medicine*, 1996, 120, 702–712.

[66] ER Long, *A history of pathology*, New York, Dover Books, 1965; RC Maulitz, *Morbid appearances. The anatomy of pathology in the early nineteenth century*, Cambridge, Cambridge University Press, 1987.

FIGURE 8.5. Skeleton from late eighteenth or early nineteenth century context with the calvarium removed, the classic sign of an autopsy. The spinal column had also been removed, presumably so that the central nervous system could be examined. The reason for the autopsy was not evident from the skeleton.

(Figure 8.5). Autopsy material becomes relatively more common after the eighteenth century and a study of the cuts on the skull may often give some indication of the skill of the operator. Skulls may be found showing tentative saw cuts and – usually – several definite cuts; sometimes it can be seen that the calvarium was levered off, leaving an irregular, fractured edge. In some cases, the laminae of the vertebrae are sawn through to remove the spinal cord, presumably with the brain, so that the central nervous system could have been studied. As with amputations, there is usually nothing on the skeleton to indicate why the autopsy was undertaken, whether it was for forensic, pathological or anatomical purposes.[67]

---

[67] There are some occasions where this is *not* the case, however. For example, bones with evidence of autopsy cuts were recovered from Benjamin Franklin's house in London, which had been the site of William Hewson's anatomy school from 1772–1774, and were clearly part of material that had either been used for demonstrations to Hewson's pupils, or preparations they had made themselves (S Hillson, T Waldron, B Owen-Smith and L Martin, Benjamin Franklin, William Hewson and the Craven Street bones, *Archaeology International*, 1998–1999, 2, 14–16).

LEGALISED TRAUMA

Trauma may be deliberately inflicted on an individual by the law to punish, degrade or kill and many ways have been devised to do all these. In the United Kingdom, common criminals were put to death by hanging but the nobility generally preferred to have their lives ended by decapitation with the sword or the axe for reasons that defy a ready explanation.

Beheading

Beheading results in characteristic damage to the skeleton and there is usually no difficulty in deciding when it has taken place. Finding a skeleton with its head between its legs ought generally to alert the excavator to the possibility and the suspicion will be confirmed by finding that one or the other of the cervical vertebrae has been transacted. There is sometimes a cut mark on the back of the mandible, the mastoid process or the first rib. When an axe rather than a sword has been used by the executioner, crush fractures of the transverse processes may also be found.[68] The most exhaustive survey of decapitated burials in Britain is contributed by Harman and her colleagues who found that the blow was usually struck from the back to the front, and that the cut generally passed through the upper cervical vertebrae although sometimes C7 or even T1 were involved.[69]

Hanging

Death by hanging has always been the most common method by which criminals were executed in the United Kingdom. Until the nineteenth century, hanging was performed with a running noose and the victim suspended from a gallows or some other convenient structure such as the branch of a tree. The victim was either hoisted up by the rope which was tied, leaving him in place, or he might be placed on a cart with the noose around his neck and the cart withdrawn, leaving him dangling until he strangled to death. During the later medieval period and into the eighteenth century, the victim climbed a ladder with a noose around his neck, the executioner

[68] S Ulrich-Bochsler, Skettale Befunde bei historischen Enthauptungen im Kanton Bern, *Archiv für Kirminologie*, 1988, 181, 76–83.

[69] M Harman, TI Molleson and JL Price, Burials, bodies and beheadings in Romano-British and Anglo-Saxon burials, *Bulletin of the British Museum of Natural History (Geology)*, 1981, 35, 145–188.

fastened the rope to a cross beam on the gallows and he was then turned off the ladder to dangle until he died. Hanging with a running noose results in death by cerebral anoxia brought about by compression of the carotid arteries, by vagal inhibition or by closure of the airway. It is said that unconsciousness supervenes rapidly although those who confidently assert this have no first-hand evidence to support their claim, but the pulse may continue to beat for several minutes and those who attended public hangings would have observed the victim apparently struggling for many minutes also although the struggles may have been reflex muscle spasms in an already unconscious individual. In the nineteenth century, a trap-door was built into the gallows through which the victim dropped. With this method of execution, death was said to be both humane and instantaneous.

Hanging with a running noose produces no lesions on the skeleton[70] but skeletons are recovered from sites where it is known that executions took place. The finding of bodies buried at such spots, especially where it seems that their hands were bound behind them, is suggestive that they were those of executed criminals. Occasionally, careful excavation of skeletons from such sites may reveal that the fingers were flexed, as may occur in those in fear or in great pain.[71] During the excavations in Nubia in the early 1900s, the skeletons of one hundred men were found in two trenches, many with ropes around their necks. They had clearly been executed by the Romans. However, there were no signs of damage to the neck although in some cases the sutures at the base of the skull had been pulled apart, the dislocation having taken place on the side on which the knot in the rope had been placed.[72] Hanging with a drop may cause a characteristic fracture-dislocation of the axis, the so-called hangman's fracture. The body of the axis and the odontoid peg stay fixed to the atlas and this block is then dislocated upwards and forwards to crush the spinal cord.[73] Another type of fracture

[70]   The skeleton of Mary Bateman who was hanged in 1809 was formerly in the anatomical museum of the University of Leeds medical school and that of the infamous William Burke was preserved in the medical school in Edinburgh – he was hanged in 1829 on the evidence of his former colleague, William Hare. The skeletons of both Bateman and Burke were examined by AJE Cave in 1941 and neither had any lesions on the skull or the cervical vertebrae (The earliest English example of bilateral cervical rib, *British Journal of Surgery*, 1941, 29, 47–51). The Hunterian Museum of the Royal College of Surgeons of London has the remains of three felons executed in the eighteenth century and their skeletons too, show no evidence of their unfortunate experience.

[71]   Two skeletons recovered from Galley Hill in Surrey were found with their hands behind them – apparently tied – and with tightly flexed fingers and it was suggested that both had been hanged (T Waldron and G Waldron, Two felons from Surrey, *London Archaeologist*, 1988, 5, 443–445).

[72]   F Wood Jones, The examination of the bodies of 100 men executed in Nubia in Roman times, *British Medical Journal*, 1908, i, 736.

[73]   This lesion has been well described and illustrated by F Wood Jones (The ideal lesion produced by hanging, *Lancet*, 1913, i, 53). Wood Jones' interest in hanging was stimulated by his examination of the Nubian skeletons found with ropes around their necks and it is said that on his return from Egypt he continued his

has also been described, however, in a study of 34 executed murderers who were hanged and buried at three separate prisons in Britain between 1882 and 1945. In this type, the right side of C2 was fractured through the neural arch, but on the left side, the fracture line ran in an antero-posterior direction across the superior articular facet joint, immediately lateral to the vertebral body. It is possible that both types of fracture may be found in the skeleton, but only in those who were hanged with the benefit of a drop. Evidence of hanging in earlier periods will of necessity have to be inferential.

researches on the lesions produced by hanging by suspending cadavers taken from the anatomy room in the lift shaft of St Thomas's Hospital where he was then working. No ethical committees to hinder research in those days!

9

Tumours

Although the word tumour simply means a swelling, in the minds of most people it has unpleasant connotations as it is frequently taken as a synonym for cancer, which it is not. Without any further elaboration, a tumour is simply a new growth and on this account it is sometimes also known as a neoplasm, and the process by which it arises, as neoplasia. Tumours may be classified as either primary or secondary, or as either benign or malignant. A primary tumour is one that originates in the tissue in which it is found, whereas a secondary tumour is one that has arisen in a different tissue from that in which it is found. A benign tumour does not spread beyond the tissue in which it originates. By contrast, the characteristic of a malignant tumour is that it *does* spread beyond its tissue of origin. Malignant tumours are often a cause of death whereas this is generally not the case with benign tumours, although there are exceptions as we shall see. A secondary tumour is malignant by definition, but a primary tumour may be either benign or malignant.

EPIDEMIOLOGY OF BONE TUMOURS

Primary bone tumours are uncommon and benign tumours are much more common than malignant. Malignant primary tumours of bone account for less than 1% of all malignant tumours and are more common in males than in females except in late childhood when there is a very slight female excess. The male excess becomes increasingly apparent with increasing age. The majority of primary malignant tumours occur in those aged 60 and over, and a quarter occur in those aged over 75 (see Table 9.1). Many of these tumours in the elderly are due to the occurrence of malignant change in bone affected by Paget's disease. There is a small peak of primary malignant tumours in children during adolescence when there is an increase in the rate of osteosarcoma; even so, the numbers involved are very

Table 9.1. *Cumulative percentage of incidence of bone tumours by age and quartiles*

Age (years)	Cumulative percent
0–39	25
40–59	50
60–74	75
75+	100

It can be seen that the quartiles are achieved more rapidly with increasing age. Thus the first quartile occupies 40 years, the second 19 years, the third 14 years, and the fourth, approximately 10. Half of all tumours occur over the age of 60.

Data are for the United Kingdom 2003 and for both sexes combined.

small with a peak of about 10 cases per million. There has been no discernible increase in the rate of bone cancers in the United Kingdom over the past quarter century.[1]

There is a widely held belief that cancer is a modern phenomenon, possibly related to increasing exposure to environmental or occupational carcinogens, or personal habits such as smoking or coffee drinking.[2] Relatively few cases of malignant disease have been reported in the palaeopathological literature, as Calvin Wells noted many years ago.[3] Using a model developed with an historical population from England and Wales, it was possible to predict how many cases of malignant bone disease might be expected in a skeletal assemblage. The result showed that less than 2% of male skeletons would be expected to show evidence of cancer and between 4 and 7% of the females. In a single case study, the estimates were not significantly different from those actually observed.[4] A more recent study of human remains from Egypt (dating between 3200 and 500 BC) and from a post-medieval ossuary in southern Germany, used data from the same historical population and found no significant difference

---

[1] These data are available from www.info.cancerresearchuk.org and are correct for 2003.

[2] R Doll and R Peto, The causes of cancer: quantitative estimates of avoidable risks of cancer in the United States today, *Journal of the National Cancer Institute*, 1981, 66, 1191–1308.

[3] Wells wrote, 'It is with carcinoma that the greatest difference is found between modern and ancient patterns of malignant disease ... Evidence of the disease from early burial grounds is rare' (*Bones, bodies and disease*, London, Thames and Hudson, 1964, p 73). See also MS Micozzi, Disease in antiquity. The case of cancer, *Archives of Pathology and Laboratory Medicine*, 1991, 115, 838–844.

[4] T Waldron, What was the prevalence of malignant disease in the past? *International Journal of Osteoarchaeology*, 1996, 6, 463–470.

between the numbers observed and the numbers in the reference population.[5] These data suggest that the small number of tumours found in skeletal assemblages is principally an artefact of the relatively small number of very old individuals present, but that the age- and sex-specific prevalences may not have varied much over a considerable period of time.

THE DIAGNOSIS OF TUMOURS IN HUMAN REMAINS

Many tumours in bone may not be visible on direct inspection and there is no doubt that the cull would be increased if adult skeletons – particularly those of elderly individuals – were routinely X-rayed. But even with radiography, the diagnosis is by no means straight forward and this is an area in which help from clinical specialists is likely to be of the greatest assistance to the palaeopathologist. Resnick, for example, has written that, 'It is with regard to tumors and tumor-like lesions that the interpreter of skeletal radiographs faces the greatest diagnostic challenges. It is essential to know the age of the patient and to have a good knowledge of the sites likely to be affected by the potential lesions.'[6] He also wrote that, 'In no other area of musculoskeletal diagnosis is the cooperation of the orthopedic surgeon, radiologist, and pathologist more important. Any of the three specialists working independently of the other is more likely to err.'[7] If the task is difficult for present-day clinicians with all the methods of investigation at their disposal, consider how much more difficult it is going to be for the palaeopathologist, often working alone and most often with nothing more than visual inspection as a guide. It is, therefore, imperative that help from a skeletal radiologist or a pathologist is obtained if a definitive diagnosis is to be attempted at all; without them, it is doubtful that a precise classification of a tumour will be possible in many – perhaps the majority – of cases.

BENIGN TUMOURS

Benign tumours of bone may arise from bone, cartilage or the soft tissues around the bone (see Table 9.2). Only the most common will be described here. Meningiomas

[5] AG Nerlich, H Rohrback, B Backmeier and A Zink, Malignant tumors in two ancient populations: an approach to historical tumor epidemiology, *Oncology Reports*, 2006, 16, 197–202.

[6] D Resnick and G Niwayama, *Diagnosis of bone and joint disorders, 2nd edition*, Philadelphia, WB Saunders, 1988, p 3617.

[7] *Ibid*, p 3602.

Table 9.2. *Most common sites involved by benign bone tumours*

Tumour	Sites most commonly affected in order of frequency
Tumours arising from bone	
Osteoma	**Skull, frontal sinus**, mandible, maxilla, external auditory meatus
Enostosis (bone island)	**Pelvis, proximal femur**, ribs, humerus, tibia
Osteoid osteoma	**Femur, tibia**, foot, hand, humerus
Osteoblastoma	**Vertebrae**, femur, mandible, maxilla, tibia, foot
Tumours arising from cartilage	
Chondroma	
Enchondroma	**Hand**, femur, humerus, foot
Periosteal chondroma	**Humerus, femur, hand**, tibia, foot
Chondroblastoma	**Femur, humerus, tibia**, foot
Osteochondroma	**Femur, humerus, tibia**, foot, hand, pelvis
Tumours arising from other tissues	
Haemangioma	**Vertebrae, skull**, ribs, mandible, maxilla, foot
Non-ossifying fibromas	**Femur, tibia**, fibula, humerus
Bone cysts	
Simple	**Humerus, femur**, tibia, fibula
Aneurysmal	**Tibia, femur, vertebrae**, humerus, pelvis, foot, fibula, hand

Sites at which the majority of tumours occur are shown in bold. Data from several sources.

which are recognised in the skeleton by their effects on the inner table of the skull are discussed in Chapter 11.

Tumours Arising from Bone[8]

Osteomas: Osteomas are overgrowths of normal bone that are formed in the periosteum. They are common, usually small and easy to recognise, and generally have no clinical significance. Although they may occur on any bone, they are found most frequently on the frontal bone[9] and in the sinuses, especially

---

[8] Tumours are named by combining the name of the tumour in which they arise with the suffix 'oma'. Thus an osteoma is a tumour that arises in bone and a chondroma, one that arises in cartilage. A carcinoma, which is the most common type of malignant tumour is one that arises in squamous epithelium such as lines the airways, the gut or the milk ducts of the breasts.

[9] TR Patel and GL Borah, Frontal bone periosteal osteomas, *Plastic and Reconstructive Surgery*, 2004, 114, 648–651.

Table 9.3. *Age of presentation and sex preference for benign bone tumours*

Tumour	Age at presentation	Sex preference
Osteoma	All ages	M = F
Enostosis	All ages	M = F
Osteoid osteoma	2nd and 3rd decades	M > F
Osteoblastoma	2nd and 3rd decades	M > F
Enchondroma	3rd and 4th decades	M = F
Periosteal chondroma	< 30	M > F
Chondroblastoma	2nd & 3rd decades	M > F
Osteochondroma	< 20	M = F
Haemangioma	≥ 40	F > M
Non-ossifying fibromas	< 20	M > F
Simple bone cyst	< 20	M > F
Aneurysmal bone cyst	< 20	F ≥ M

M = male

F = female

the frontal sinuses.[10] They may also be found in the external auditory meatus in those who swim or dive in cold water.[11] Osteomas are found at all ages but are most common over the age of 40 (Table 9.3) and will be encountered frequently in any skeletal assemblage (Figure 9.1).

Enostosis: Also known as bone islands, these tumours are composed of normal compact bone and they occur most commonly in the pelvis and proximal femur. There is no sex difference in prevalence and they occur at all ages. They are likely to come to light in the skeleton as an incidental finding when bones are X-rayed for other purposes. On X-ray they present as single or multiple sclerotic areas, with an average size of about 15 mm. Spicules of bone extend from the lesion (so-called 'thorny' radiation) into the surrounding trabecular bone creating a feathered, or brush-like border.[12] They are not clinically significant but may be mistaken for skeletal metastases.

Osteoid osteoma: This tumour is composed of an inner vascular core of osteoid surrounded by sclerotic woven bone. Radiologically they appear as small foci (average size about 15 mm) with a translucent centre surrounded by a zone

[10]   R Eller and M Sillers, Common fibro-osseous lesions of the paranasal sinuses, *Otolaryngologic Clinics of North America*, 2006, 39, 585–600.
[11]   DF Harrison, The relationship of osteomata of the external auditory meatus to swimming, *Annals of the Royal College of Surgeons of London*, 1962, 31, 187–201.
[12]   A Greenspan, Bone island (enostosis): current concept – a review, *Skeletal Radiology*, 1995, 24, 111–115.

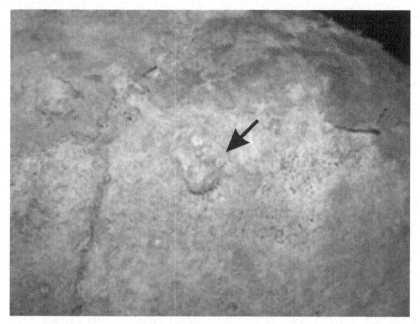

FIGURE 9.1. Frontal bone showing the presence of a small button osteoma (arrowed).

of uniform sclerosis. This appearance is virtually pathognomonic. They occur most commonly in the femur and tibia, and may be located in the cortex or in trabecular bone. In the cortex there may be cortical thickening with overlying periosteal new bone and this may present a clue to its presence. They are most frequently encountered between the ages of 7 and 25 and there is a male excess of approximately 3:1. These tumours are clinically significant and cause pain, especially at night.[13]

Osteoblastoma: Osteoblastomas are tumours formed from well-vascularised connective tissue within which there is active production of osteoid and woven bone. Like osteoid osteomas, to which they are clearly related, they occur mostly in the young, and most cases occur in individuals between the ages of 10 and 30; males are affected twice as often as females. The vertebral column is the most frequent site of occurrence. They cause expansion of the bones in which they occur and radiologically they may show lysis, sclerosis or a combination of both. The appearances are by no means characteristic and they would be very difficult to diagnose accurately in the skeleton. They are larger than osteoid

[13] P Kitsoulis, G Mantellos and M Vlychou, Osteoid osteoma, *Acta Othopaedica Belgica*, 2006, 72, 119–125.

osteomas and may reach a maximum of several centimetres and they show invasive characteristics in a proportion of cases.[14]

Tumours Arising from Cartilage

Enchondroma: Enchondromas are cartilaginous tumours that may be single or multiple. The single tumours occur most frequently in the hands, most commonly in the proximal phalanges and there is a distinct preference for the fifth ray of the hand. The terminal phalanges and the carpal bones are infrequently involved.[15] They usually present in the twenties or thirties and there is no sex difference in prevalence and are asymptomatic except that they may cause swelling of the affected bone. Their radiological appearance is characteristic; the lesion is intramedullary, well defined with a lobulated appearance and endosteal erosion.

Multiple enchondromas (enchondromatosis) are uncommon and two forms are often distinguished: Ollier's disease and Maffucci's syndrome.[16] In Ollier's disease the lesions are asymmetric, predominantly affecting one side of the body. The condition presents in childhood and affects the femur, tibia and hands. The bones are swollen and other skeletal deformities may be apparent.[17] Maffucci's syndrome is, in effect, Ollier's disease with the added complication of soft tissue haemangiomas. The bones of the hand are most commonly affected but the long bones may also be involved and may be subject to pathological fractures. The condition again presents in childhood and malignant transformation is common, occurring in up to a third of all patients.[18] The distinction between these two conditions is probably no longer justifiable and it seems most likely that they are part of the spectrum of a single disease entity.[19]

Periosteal chondroma: Periosteal chondroma tumours are most common in those who are less than thirty years of age and are found about twice as often in men as in women. They develop beneath the periosteum and predominantly occur

[14] DR Lucas, KK Unni, RA McLeod, MI O'Connor and FH Sim, Osteoblastoma: a clinicopathologic study of 306 cases, *Human Pathology*, 1994, 25, 117–134.
[15] R Caulke, The distribution of solitary enchondromata at the hand, *Journal of Hand Surgery*, 2002, 27, 444–445.
[16] Louis Xavier Édouard Léopald Ollier 1830–1900; Angelo Maffucci 1847–1903.
[17] T Miyawaki, Y Kinoshita and T Tizuka, A case of Ollier's disease of the hand, *Annals of Plastic Surgery*, 1997, 38, 77–80.
[18] RP Kaplan, JT Wang, DM Amron and L Kaplan, Maffucci's syndrome: two case reports with a literature review, *Journal of the American Academy of Dermatology*, 1993, 29, 894–899.
[19] CD Mellon, JE Carter and DB Owen, Ollier's disease and Maffucci's syndrome: distinct entities or a continuum? *Journal of Neurology*, 1988, 235, 376–378.

in the femur and humerus. In their sub-periosteal position they may cause cortical erosion and periosteal new bone formation in the affected bones[20] but they would present very considerable diagnostic problems in the skeleton.

Chondroblastoma: Chondroblastoma is a rare cartilaginous tumour that originates in the epiphysis of the long bones, especially the femur, humerus and tibia[21] and occurs most commonly in the second and third decades of life; it is about twice as common in males as in females.[22] Histologically it is formed from chondroblastoma cells, osteoclast like giant cells and sometimes contains reactive osteoid.[23] The tumour may cause local pain, swelling and tenderness, and restriction of movement. Occasionally it may also pursue a much more aggressive course with widespread metastases.[24] The lesion may be recognised in the skeleton if it causes a swelling, or sometimes a hole, in the bone. It may also come to light as an incidental finding on X-ray when it appears as a lytic lesion with well-defined margins, spherical or oval in shape, usually not more than 5 or 6 cm in maximum extent, and it may be outlined by a sclerotic margin.

Osteochondroma: Osteochondromas are bony excrescences covered with cartilage that arise from the surface of bone. They are the most common benign bone tumour and are found most frequently on the femur, humerus and tibia, especially the areas with the most rapid growth such as the distal femur, and the proximal humerus and tibia. They may be single or multiple,[25] and arise spontaneously or following injury and they need to be differentiated from heterotopic ossification traumatica (HOT) and this may sometimes prove problematic, especially as they will lack the cartilaginous cap in the dry bones. The cortex of the osteochondroma is continuous with the cortex or the trabeculae of the affected bone, a fact that can best be confirmed on X-ray; this is not the case with HOT. The tumours take a variety of shapes, and they may be pendunculated or sessile. The metaphysis of the bone on which they occur may also be slightly expanded.

[20] MM Lewis, S Kenan, SM Yabut, A Norman and G Steiner, Periosteal chondroma. A report of ten cases and review of the literature, *Clinical Orthopaedics and Related Research*, 1990, 256, 185–192.
[21] DS Springfield, R Capanna, F Gherlinzoni, P Picci and M Campanacci, Chondroblastoma. A review of seventy cases, *Journal of Bone and Joint Surgery*, 1985, 67A, 748–755.
[22] RE Turcotte, AM Kurt, FH Sim, KK Unnit and RA McLeod, Chondroblastoma, *Human Pathology*, 1993, 24, 944–949.
[23] F Masui, S Ushigome, K Kamitani, K Asanuma and K Fujii, Chondroblastoma: a study of 11 cases, *European Journal of Surgical Oncology*, 2002, 28, 869–874.
[24] AJ Ramappa, FY Lee, P Tang, JR Carlson, MC Gebhardt and HJ Mankin, Chondroblastoma of bone, *Journal of Bone and Joint Surgery*, 2000, 82A, 1140–1145.
[25] Multiple osteochondromatosis is a hereditary developmental condition and will be considered in chapter 10.

Osteochondromas are probably developmental anomalies, rather than true tumours although on rare occasions they may undergo malignant change and then exhibit the features of a true neoplasm.[26] In life, the tumours are recognised as painless swelling and very rarely they may regress spontaneously;[27] they may fracture if those who have them engage in vigorous physical activity.[28]

> *Haemangioma:* Haemangiomas are tumours formed of vascular tissue that occur most commonly in soft tissues. In bone they are uncommon and found most often in the spine, skull and facial bones.[29] In life they rarely present symptoms although they may occasionally cause spinal cord compression or back pain.[30] They are generally found in middle age and are more common in females than in males.

When present in the skull, haemangiomas may produce a swelling which would be obvious in the skeleton but in other sites they are most likely to be noted as an incidental finding when the vertebrae, for example, were X-rayed for some other purpose. They have a characteristic radiological appearance, producing a coarse, vertical, trabecular pattern (the so-called corduroy look), In the skull, haemangiomas produce lytic lesions, with a trabeculated interior and scalloped margins.[31]

> *Non-ossifying fibromas:* Non-ossifying fibromas tumours are composed of connective tissue cells and occur most commonly in the long bones in children, most often the femur,[32] where they are almost always found as an incidental radiological finding.[33] Males are affected about twice as often as females. They do

[26] CO Fuselier, T Binning, D Kuschner, WW Kirchwehm, JR Rice, V Hetherington, RL Kahl, DC Hanley, A West and J Gray, Solitary osteochondroma of the foot: an in-depth study with case reports, *Journal of Foot Surgery*, 1984, 23, 3–24.
[27] Y Revilla, MC Lozano, G Gonzalex and A Martinez, Evanescent exostoses. A new case, *European Journal of Radiology*, 1999, 29, 270–272.
[28] P Carpintero, F Leon, M Zafra, M Montero and FJ Berral, Fractures of osteochondroma during physical exercise, *American Journal of Sports Medicine*, 2003, 31, 1003–1006.
[29] Other types of vascular anomaly are described by JJ Choi and MD Murphy, Angiomatous skeletal lesions, *Seminars in Musculoskeletal Radiology*, 2000, 4, 103–112.
[30] MW Fox and BM Onofrio, The natural history and management of symptomatic and asymptomatic vertebral haemangiomas, *Journal of Neurosurgery*, 1993, 78, 36–45.
[31] CR Tremlin, JB Stambough and JL Stambough, Acute spinal cord compression caused by vertebral hemangioma, *Spine Journal*, 2004, 4, 595–600.
[32] J Caffey, On fibrous defects in cortical walls of growing tubular bones, *Advances in Pediatrics*, 1955, 7, 13–15.
[33] Non-ossifying fibromas are often referred to in the literature, both clinical and palaeopathological as fibrous cortical defects and it is by no means clear what the connection between the two is since there is no precise definition for either. A distinction has been made between the two on the basis of size and natural history; fibrous cortical defects are generally less than 3 cm in size and most heal spontaneously although some may enlarge and evolve into non-ossifying fibromas. Both conditions need to be differentiated from cortical avulsive injuries that are related to repetitive stress at the site of muscle insertions (D Resnick and G Greenway, Distal femoral cortical defects, irregularities, and excavations, *Radiology*, 1982, 143, 345–354). It

not occur in children before they can walk, suggesting that the strain exerted on the muscles during walking may be important in their development. They will appear as small defects in the distal shaft of one of the long bones with a sclerotic margin on X-ray and they may be multiple.[34] They are generally asymptomatic although large defects may be the site of a pathological fracture.[35]

Simple bone cysts: Simple (unicameral) bone cysts are common lesions found most frequently in the long bones, especially in the proximal humerus and femur. Most are discovered in those aged below twenty and they occur about twice as frequently in males as in females. They may cause slight swelling of the bone and they may be the site of a pathological fracture.[36] Radiologically they appear as lytic areas within a bone with the long axis parallel to the long axis of the bone, with cortical thinning and a narrow sclerotic margin; they may sometimes be multiloculated.

Aneurysmal bone cyst: Aneurysmal bone cysts are blood-filled cysts which usually present in the first two decades of life and have a slight female preponderance.[37] Their aetiology is by no means clear. They are found most often in the tibia, femur and vertebrae and cause slight to moderate expansion of the affected bone with cortical thinning. Radiologically the tumour presents as an eccentric lytic area, often with trabeculation, the inner surface of which is generally well defined and there may or may not be a sclerotic rim. The cortex is thinned and appears to be ballooned and periosteal new bone is often present.[38]

MALIGNANT TUMOURS

Malignant tumours of bone may be primary or secondary. Secondary tumours are much more common than primary and although almost any malignant tumours

should be clear from this that the diagnosis of these defects in the skeleton may be a matter of considerable difficulty and to refer to them all as cortical defects (unspecified) may be about as far as most of us would feel we were able to go. For other fibrous tumours see: SE Smith and MJ Kransdorf, Primary musculoskeletal tumors of fibrous origin, *Seminars in Musculoskeletal Radiology*, 2000, 4, 73–88.

[34] RA Blau, DL Zwick and RA Westphal, Multiple non-ossifying fibromas. A case report, *Journal of Bone and Joint Surgery*, 1988, 70A, 299–304.

[35] C Hoeffel, M Panuel, F Plenet, L Mainard and JC Hoeffel, Pathological fracture in non-ossifying fibromas with histological features simulating aneurysmal bone cyst, *European Radiology*, 1999, 9, 669–671.

[36] R Baig and JL Eady, Unicameral (simple) bone cysts, *Southern Medical Journal*, 2006, 99, 966–976.

[37] A Leithner, R Windhager, S Lang, OA Haas, F Kaiberger and R Kotz, Aneurysmal bone cyst. A population based epidemiologic study and literature review, *Clinical Orthopaedics and Related Research*, 1999, 363, 176–179.

[38] HJ Mankin, FJ Hornicek, E Ortiz-Cruz, J Villafuerte and MC Gebhardt, Aneurysmal bone cyst: a review of 150 patients, *Journal of Clinical Oncology*, 2005, 20, 6756–6762.

that originate in extra-skeletal sites may metastasise to bone, some exhibit a much greater tendency to do so than others as we shall see.

Primary Malignant Bone Tumours

As with the benign bone tumours, malignant tumours can arise from any of the tissues that constitute bone but there are some tumours that arise from the haematopoietic tissues that – by virtue of their position in the bone marrow – can also affect bone (see Table 9.4). None of the primary bone tumours is very common, in total only comprising less than 1% of all malignant tumours. Only the more common of these tumours will be described.

The Periosteal Response to Malignant Bone Tumours

The periosteum responds in almost every case of primary malignant bone disease, and in some cases of benign tumour, but the types of response are varied, depending in part on the nature and speed of growth of the tumour. With a slow-growing, expansile lesion such as a simple bone cyst, a thick layer of periosteum may be formed, separated from the cortex of the bone. The thickness of the periosteal layer will increase as the tumour increases in size. As a rapidly growing tumour such as an osteosarcoma penetrates through the cortex it may lift the periosteum to produce a triangular elevation with formation of new bone under the elevated periosteum. This is known to the radiologists as Codman's triangle.[39] Alternatively, a rapidly growing tumour may induce the formation of multiple layers of periosteal new bone, forming an onion-skin like appearance. Radiating spicules of periosteal new bone at different angles to the long axis of the affected bone, and mixed with tumour tissue may form the so-called sun-burst appearance, or they may form at right angles to the surface of the bone, in the hair-on-end appearance. The sun-burst is typical of an osteosarcoma while the hair-on-end appearance is more often seen with Ewing's sarcoma.[40]

> *Osteosarcoma:* Osteosarcoma is the most common primary tumour of bone and it occurs most commonly in adolescents during the period of maximum bone

---

[39] Ernest Armory Codman 1869–1940.

[40] AE Wenaden, TA Szyszko and A Saifuddin, Imaging of periosteal reactions associated with focal lesions of bone, *Clinical Radiology*, 2005, 60, 439–456. This paper has many helpful illustrations which demonstrate these different types of periosteal new bone formation.

Table 9.4. *Malignant primary tumours of bone*

Tumour	Sites most commonly affected in order of frequency	Age at presentation	Sex preference
Osteosarcoma	**Femur**, **tibia**, humerus	2nd and 3rd decade; 60+	M > F
Ewing's sarcoma	**Femur**, **pelvis**, **tibia**, humerus, fibula, ribs, vertebrae, scapula	5–30	M ≥ F
Chondrosarcoma	**Pelvis**, femur, humerus, tibia, ribs, scapula	30–60	M > F
Fibrosarcoma	**Femur**, tibia, **humerus**, **pelvis**, mandible, maxilla	3rd–5th decades	M = F
Angiosarcoma	**Tibia**, **femur**, **humerus**, **vertebrae**, pelvis, foot, ribs	3rd–5th decades	M > F
Lymphoma Non-Hodgkin's Hodgkin's	**Femur**, **tibia**, **fibulaSpine**, **pelvis**, **ribs**, **femur**, **sternum**	All ages	M > F
Leukaemia Acute Chronic	Any **Femur**, **humerus**	All ages 50+	M > F
Myelomatosis	**Skull**, **pelvis**, **ribs**	6th decade onwards	M > F

Sites at which the majority of tumours occur are shown in bold. Data from several sources.
M = male
F = female

growth. The majority occur in the long bones, especially the femur, tibia and humerus. The knee is a particularly favoured site. The main cell type is osteoblast derived and the appearance of the lesion depends upon both its location within the bone and the amount of bone being produced by the tumour cells. The majority of the tumours start within the bone, most commonly at the metaphysis and as they progress, they burst through the cortex to produce large soft tissue masses. Periosteal reaction is invariable either in the form of a Codman triangle, or a sun-burst appearance. The bony lesions are typically a mixture of lysis and sclerosis, purely lytic or sclerotic forms being unusual. The tumours present in the skeleton as large masses, often of spiculated bone and an X-ray will show tumour tissue within the medullary cavity and the cortex. The typical sun-burst appearance may be present on X-ray but its absence does not rule out the diagnosis. These tumours are generally very friable and care must be taken when excavating them and during all the post-excavation stages if they are not to be badly damaged. The role of cytokines and other factors in the aetiology and development of these tumours is being evaluated[41] as are possible genetic factors.[42] Osteosarcomas metastasise by haematogenous spread and the lungs are a major target organ. They are often highly resistant to treatment and would have been uniformly fatal in the past.

There are some rarer types of osteosarcoma which arise on the surface of the bone, and there are three different types, parosteal, periosteal and the so-called, high-grade surface osteosarcoma. They all tend to arise in a rather older age group than the conventional osteosarcomas and they have different biological characteristics, the parosteal and periosteal tumours having the best prognosis.[43] Parosteal tumours are slow growing and may achieve a very large size. They occur in the long bones almost exclusively, the metaphysis of the femur, humerus and tibia being the favoured sites. They are usually lobulated and there is often a distinct plane of cleavage between the tumour and the underlying cortex. Periosteal tumours remain in the cortex of the affected bone – usually the femur or tibia – often with an exuberant periosteal reaction; the medullary cavity is rarely involved. The high-grade surface tumours have a broad attachment to the affected bone. There is normally no plane of cleavage between the tumour and the cortex and radiating spicules of periosteal bone are uncommon.[44]

> *Osteosarcoma in Paget's disease:* A small proportion of individuals (between 1 and 5%) with extensive Paget's disease of bone (males more frequently than females) develop osteosarcoma. The principal sites are the pelvis, proximal femur, proximal humerus and skull. The lesions are highly malignant, tend to be mainly osteolytic, and the survival rate is very poor.[45]

[41] H Yoshikawa, T Nakase, A Myoui and T Ueda, Bone morphogenic proteins in bone tumours, *Journal of Orthopedic Science*, 2004, 9, 334–340; JB Hayden and BH Hoang, Osteosarcoma: basic science and clinical implications, *Orthopaedic Clinics of North America*, 2006, 37, 1–7.

[42] M Kansara and DM Thomas, Molecular pathogenesis of osteosarcoma, *DNA and Cell Biology*, 2007, 26, 1–18.

[43] AK Raymond, Surface osteosarcoma, *Clinical Orthopaedics and Related Research*, 1991, 270, 140–148.

[44] K Okada, KK Unni, RG Swee and FH Sim, High grade surface osteosarcoma. A clinicopathologic study of 46 cases, *Cancer*, 1999, 85, 1044–1054.

[45] HJ Mankin and FJ Hornicek, Paget's sarcoma: a historical and outcome review, *Clinical Orthopaedics and Related Research*, 2005, 438, 97–102. Rarely, other types of tumour develop in Pagety bone, including fibrosarcomas, chondrosarcomas and giant cell tumours (H Haibach, C Farrell and FJ Dittrich, Neoplasms arising in Paget's disease of bone: a study of 82 cases, *American Journal of Clinical Pathology*, 1985, 83, 594–600).

Ewing's Sarcoma

Ewing's sarcoma is the second most common malignant tumour of bone in children and adolescents. The highest incidence of the disease is in late childhood and early adolescence and it has a relatively poor survival rate.[46] It is a small round cell tumour that occurs most frequently in the lower part of the body, most tumours arising in the pelvis, femur and tibia. In the great majority of cases there is a chromosomal abnormality affecting chromosomes 22q12 and 11q24.[47] It is an aggressive tumour, osteolytic in nature, showing cortical erosion and a brisk periosteal reaction, often of the onion-skin or hair-on-end type. Pathological fractures are common, especially of the femur.[48]

Chondrosarcoma: Chondrosarcomas may arise de novo or in pre-existing chondromas. They are usually intra-medullary (central) but some may appear on the surface of the bone. The long bones and the pelvis are the most common sites and they generally appear between the ages of thirty and sixty and there is a slight male excess. Chondrosarcomas are bulky tumours, sometimes growing to a considerable size. They tend to erode the cortex, a point that distinguishes them from the benign enchondroma. Aggressive tumours tend to be calcified but they have no absolutely characteristic features and are often difficult to diagnose in the absence of histology. The more aggressive tumours are locally invasive and may metastasize to other organs; survival in these cases is poor.[49] The genetics of these tumours has been recently reviewed by Terek.[50]

Fibrosarcoma: Fibrosarcoma is a rare tumour composed of fibrous tissue and neither bone nor cartilage is present. They most commonly present in the third to fifth decades and there is a male excess. The long bones and the pelvis account for the majority of tumours, and they are particularly common about the knee. The majority of lesions are central but periosteal tumours also occur.[51] They are large, destructive tumours which seem to provoke little response in the affected

[46] CA Stiller, SS Bielack, G Jundt and E Steliarova-Foucher, Bone tumours in European children and adolescents, *European Journal of Cancer*, 2006, 42, 2124–2135.
[47] M Paulussen, B Frohlic and H Jurgens, Ewing tumour: incidence, prognosis and treatment options, *Paediatric Drugs*, 2001, 3, 899–913.
[48] LM Wagner, MD Neel, AS Pappo, TE Merchant, CA Poquette, BN Rao and C Rodriguez-Galindo, Fractures in pediatric Ewing sarcoma, *Journal of Pediatric Hematology and Oncology*, 2001, 23, 568–571.
[49] J Bruns, M Elbrach and O Niggemeyer, Chondrosarcoma of bone: an oncological and functional follow-up study, *Annals of Oncolocy*, 2001, 12, 859–864.
[50] RM Terek, Recent advances in the basic science of chondrosarcoma, *Orthopaedic Clinics of North America*, 2006, 37, 9–14.
[51] AG Huvos and NL Higinbotham, Primary fibrosarcoma of bone. A clinicopathologic study of 130 patients, *Cancer*, 1975, 35, 837–847.

bone. Thus they are seen on X-ray as lytic areas which may have destroyed the cortex but with little if any sclerosis or periosteal new bone. Pathological fractures are common as are metastases and survival is not good even with modern treatment.[52]

Angiosarcoma: Angiosarcomas are rare. They are formed of irregular vascular channels lined with abnormal endothelial cells, hence their alternate name of haemangioendothelioma. They occur most often in the third to fifth decades, are more common in men and are found predominantly in the long bones. The tumours are usually multifocal, multiple tumours often occurring in the same bone. They vary in size and their radiological appearance is also variable, but they usually present as well-defined multiple lytic lesions with little sclerosis or periosteal new bone. There may also be cortical thinning and expansion of the affected bone(s) and they often mimic other malignant bone disorders.[53]

Lymphomas: The lymphomas arise from the cells of the lymphatic system. They can conveniently be classified into two broad groups, the Hodgkin's and non-Hodgkin's types.[54] Bony involvement tends to be more common in those with Hodgkin's lymphoma than in the other types.[55] They occur at all ages and there is generally a male excess, which increases with increasing age. In the non-Hodgkin's types, children are more likely to have bony involvement than adults whereas the converse is true for Hodgkin's lymphoma. The long bones tend to be mainly involved in the non-Hodgkin's type and they become affected through haematogenous spread, or spread from local lymph nodes. Lesions may be single or multiple and are lytic with a rather moth-eaten appearance, with a variable proportion showing sclerosis and periosteal new bone formation.[56] In

[52] PJ Papagelopoulos, E Galanis, FJ Frassica, FH Sim, DR Larson and LE Wold, Primary fibrosarcoma of bone. Outcome after primary surgical treatment, *Clinical Orthopaedics and Related Research*, 2000, 373, 88–103.

[53] DE Wenger and LE Wold, Malignant vascular lesions of bone: radiologic and pathologic features, *Skeletal Radiology*, 2000, 29, 619–631.

[54] One of the non-Hodgkin's types is Burkitt's lymphoma which is caused by infection with the Epstein-Barr virus (SB Pattle and PJ Farrell, The role of Epstein-Barr virus in cancer, *Expert Opinion on Biological Therapy*, 2006, 6, 1193–1205). It is particularly prevalent in East Africa and bony changes are largely confined to the mandible (OW Mwanda, R Rochford, AM Moormann, A Macnell, C Whalen and ML Wilson, Burkitt's lymphoma in Kenya: geographical, age, gender and ethnic distribution, *East African Medical Journal*, 2004, 8 (Supplement), S68 – S77).

[55] In the majority of cases, skeletal involvement is secondary to tumours that affect the lymphatic system but very rarely, the skeleton may be the primary site of a lymphoma, both Hodgkin's and non-Hodgkin's types (C Gebert, J Hardes, H Ahrens, H Buerger, W Winkelmann and G Gosheger, Primary multifocal osseous Hodgkin's disease: a case report and review of the literature, *Journal of Cancer Research and Clinical Oncology*, 2000s, 131, 163–168; P Kitsoulis, M Vlychou, A Papadou-Bai, G Karatzias, A Charchanti, NJ Agnantis and M Bai, Primary lymphomas of bone, *Anticancer Research*, 2006, 26, 325–337).

[56] H Rosenthal, R Kolb, KF Gratz, A Reiter and M Galanski, Ossäre Manifestationen beim Non-Hodgkin-Lymphom im Kindes- und Jugendalter, *Der Radiologe*, 2000, 40, 737–744.

Hodgkin's lymphoma the principal sites are the spine, pelvis, ribs, femur and sternum. The lesions may be sclerotic, lytic or a combination of both. Spread from adjacent lymph nodes may result in scalloping of the anterior surface of the vertebral body. The lytic lesions are generally poorly defined and about a third show some periosteal reaction.[57]

Leukaemia: Leukaemia is the name given to a group of malignant diseases that affect the white blood cells. The tumours arise in the bone marrow and so bony involvement is almost inevitable in all cases. They are classified as acute and chronic and may be either lymphocytic or granulocytic depending on which white cell line is affected. The acute leukaemias occur in both children and adults but chronic leukaemia is an adult disease. There is a small peak of incidence in children below the age of five but leukaemia can occur at all ages although the incidence increases considerably with increasing age and in the adult types, males are more often affected than females.

Bony changes are more common in acute than in chronic leukaemia and changes in children are more frequent than in adults. Children with acute leukaemia frequently have osteopaenia[58] and may have a radiolucent band at the metaphysis of the long bones, and lytic lesions with periosteal new bone formation.[59] A small proportion of children develop transverse metaphyseal fractures usually bilateral and in the lower limb bones.[60] Lytic changes may be found in almost any bone but sclerotic change is unusual. The changes in adults with acute leukaemia are similar to those in children, including osteopaenia, discrete lytic lesions and – less commonly – translucent metaphyseal bands.

The changes in chronic leukaemia are less common and less florid than in acute leukaemia but may include osteopaenia, small discrete lytic lesions, especially in the femur and humerus.[61]

Myelomatosis: Myelomatosis is a plasma cell tumour that produces widespread skeletal change. It is predominantly a disease of the elderly, most cases occurring after the age of fifty, the incidence increasing with increasing age. Males are more often affected than females. Osteolytic lesions are the norm, occurring most

[57] BL Pear, Skeletal manifestations of the lymphomas and leukemias, *Seminars in Roentgenology*, 1974, 9, 229–240.

[58] JH Davies, BAJ Evans, MEM Jenney and JW Gregory, Skeletal morbidity in children with acute lymphoblastic leukaemia, *Clinical Endocrinology*, 2005, 63, 1–9.

[59] DG Gallagher, DJ Phillips and SD Heinrich, Orthopedic manifestations of acute pediatric leukemia, *Orthopedic Clinics of North America*, 1996, 27, 635–644.

[60] D Manson, RF Martin and WP Cockshott, Metaphyseal impaction fractures in acute lymphoblastic leukemia, *Skeletal Radiology*, 1989, 17, 561–564.

[61] SI Schable, L Tyminski, RD Holland and GM Rittenberg, The skeletal manifestations of chronic myelogenous leukemia, *Skeletal Radiology*, 1980, 5, 145–149.

often in the spine, ribs, skull, pelvis and femur. The lesions tend to be uniform in size and sclerosis is unusual. In the spine, the lesions tend to be restricted to the vertebral bodies with the posterior elements being spared which helps to distinguish myeloma from metastatic bone disease.[62]

The lysis is caused by the activation of osteoclasts by increased receptor activity of RANK-L and decreased OPG expression, thereby stimulating osteoclast formation and activation.[63] Early in the disease, there is a compensatory increase in osteoblast function but this is later decreased by the secretion of osteoblast inhibitory factors.[64] The decrease in osteoblast function means that the lesions show no attempt at healing or remodelling.[65] The prognosis of the disease is poor and is related to the patient's genotype.[66]

One interesting feature of the myeloma cells is that they secrete large quantities of monoclonal antibodies usually IgG or IgA although in a small proportion of cases, only light chains are secreted.[67] It is sometimes difficult to differentiate between the lesions of multiple myeloma and metastatic bone disease but the difficulty can be resolved if myeloma protein can be extracted from the affected bone.[68]

METASTATIC BONE TUMOURS

Metastatic bone tumours are much more common than primary tumours and spread to bone occurs via four main routes: through the blood vascular system, both the arterial and venous systems; by direct spread from a tumour adjacent to a bone; through the lymphatic system; and through the cerebrospinal fluid in those with

---

[62] HG Jacobson, MH Poppel, JH Shapiro and S Grossberger, The vertebral pedicle sign: a roentgen finding to differentiate metastatic carcinoma from multiple myeloma, *American Journal of Roentgenology*, 1958, 80, 817–821.

[63] O Sezer, Myeloma bone disease, *Hematology*, 2005, 10 Supplement 1, 19–24.

[64] O Hjertner, T Standal, M Borset, A Sundan and A Waage, Bone disease in multiple myeloma, *Medical Oncology*, 2006, 23, 431–441.

[65] N Giuliani, Rizzoli and GD Roodman, Multiple myeloma bone disease: pathophysiology of osteoblast inhibition, *Blood*, 2006, 108, 3992–3996.

[66] JJ Keats, T Reiman, AR Belch and LM Pilarski, Ten years and counting: so what do we know about t(4;14)(p16:q32) multiple myeloma, *Leukemia and Lymphoma*, 2006, 47, 2289–2300.

[67] R Bataille and J-L Harousseau, Multiple myeloma, *New England Journal of Medicine*, 1997, 336, 1657–1664. Some myelomas secrete IgM and more rarely, IgD; IgD myelomas tend to occur in younger individuals and are particularly aggressive (D Sinclair, IgD myeloma: clinical, biological and laboratory features, *Clinical Laboratory*, 2002, 48, 617–622).

[68] C Cattaneo, K Gelsthorpe, P Phillips, T Waldron, JR Booth and RJ Sokol, Immunological diagnosis of multiple myeloma in a medieval bone, *International Journal of Osteoarchaeology*, 1994, 4, 1–2.

Table 9.5. *Frequency with which primary tumours metastasise to bone*

Site of primary	Frequency of skeletal metastasis (%)
Bladder	13–26
Breast	57–73
Colon and rectum	6–11
Kidney	23–45
Lung	19–32
Mouth	14–21
Ovary	6
Prostate	57–84
Stomach	2–18
Testis	10–20
Thyroid	19–50
Uterus (neck and body)	8–22

Data based on autopsy studies from several sources and summarised in table 93–1 of Resnick and Niwayama (1988).[69]

tumours of the brain. Although virtually any malignant tumour can metastasise to bone, in practice, some show a much greater propensity to do so than others. Carcinomas of the breast, lung, prostate, kidney and thyroid are particularly liable to do so but the majority of tumours are due to spread from the first three since they are the most numerous. In males, carcinoma of the prostate and the lung account for the majority of bony secondaries while in females, carcinoma of the breast is by far the most common cause. The frequency with which the various tumours metastasise shows considerable variation depending on the method used to detect them – radiology, bone scan, MRI scan or autopsy. The range, based on autopsy studies, is shown in Table 9.5. The most common sites for secondary bone tumours are the spine, pelvis, proximal femur and the skull, although virtually any bone may be involved.

Secondary bone tumours tend to be predominantly lytic or sclerotic, that is, they stimulate either the osteoclast, osteoblast or both. Breast and lung secondaries are mainly lytic in character, while prostatic secondaries are mainly sclerotic (Figure 9.2). It is becoming evident that secondary tumours dysregulate the RANK/RANKL/OPG

[69] D Resnick and G Niwayama, *Diagnosis of bone and joint disorders, 2nd edition*, Philadelphia, WB Saunders, 1988, p 3617.

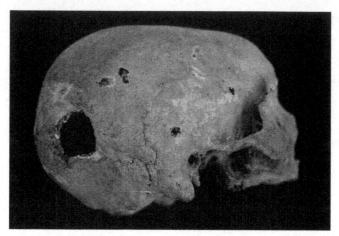

FIGURE 9.2. Skull of elderly female from eighteenth century context showing the presence of several holes, including one large one in the occipital region. They all had undercut edges and an X-ray showed the presence of several more lytic lesions. These were all secondary tumours, most likely spread from a primary carcinoma of the breast.

system,[70] and also secrete factors that stimulate osteoclasts[71] and osteoblasts.[72] In addition, active factors are released from the bone matrix following osteolytic activity,[73] and there is also evidence that tumour cells express chemokine receptors which attach to ligands present in target organs including the bone marrow.[74] The end result is for the tumour cells to enhance the activity of bone-forming or bone-resorbing cells and for this activity to increase through a series of positive feed-back mechanisms.

> *Breast cancer:* Breast cancer does occur in males but very rarely. In females, although most cases present between the ages of fifty and sixty-five a significant number of cases also present in the thirties and fourties and the incidence is increasing in all age groups. The disease is more common in the developed countries, probably reflecting a difference in aetiological factors between these

[70] M Baud'huin, L Duplomb, C Ruiz Velasco, Y Fortun, D Heymann and M Padrines, Key roles of the OPG-RANK-RANKL system in bone oncology, *Expert Reviews of Anticancer Therapy*, 2007, 7, 221–232.

[71] TA Guise, WM Kozlow, A Heras-Herzig, SS Padalecki, JJ Yin and JM Chirgwin, Molecular mechanisms of breast cancer metastases to bone, *Clinical Breast Cancer*, 2005, 5 Supplement 2, S46–S53.

[72] ET Keller and J Brown, Prostate cancer bone metastases promote both osteolytic and osteoblastic activity, *Journal of Cellular Biochemistry*, 2004, 91, 718–729.

[73] TA Guise and JM Chirgwin, Transforming growth factor-beta in osteolytic breast cancer bone metastases, *Clinical Orthopaedics and Related Research*, 2003, 415 Supplement, S32–S38.

[74] A Zlotnik, Involvement of chemokine receptors in organ-specific metastases, *Contributions to Microbioloogy*, 2006, 13, 191–199.

Table 9.6. *Crude incidence of tumours that commonly metastasise to bone*

Site of primary	Crude incidence per 10^5	
	Male	Female
Breast	1.2	143.7
Lung	74.7	50.5
Adenocarcinoma*	11.3	7.6
Prostate	109.6	
Kidney	13.9	8.6
Thyroid	1.4	3.7
Myeloma	7.0	5.6

* The incidence of adenocarcinoma is calculated assuming that it is 15%, of the total of all lung tumours.

and the developing countries.[75] It is by far the most common cause of metastasis to bone in females (Table 9.6). The lesions are mainly lytic and occur most frequently in the femur, the axial skeleton and the skull. The lytic lesions are of variable size and show undercut edges with no evidence of healing or remodelling and sclerosis is not common. Tumours in young women often follow a particularly rapid course[76] and at all ages, the disease would have been uniformly fatal in the past. There is no reason to suppose that breast cancer was not present in the past and, indeed, there is evidence for it dating back at least to the early Christian period in Nubia.[77]

Lung cancer: The majority of cases of lung cancer occur over the age of 60 and it is virtually unknown under the age of 40. At all ages there is a considerable male excess. About a fifth of the tumours are of the small cell type; the remainder are non-small cell types, including adenocarcinomas that make up about 15% of all cases in the United Kingdom. The major cause of lung cancer is smoking[78] but the association is much less obvious with adenocarcinomas than with the other types. It is interesting that the incidence of adenocarcinoma is on the increase[79]

[75] MD Althuis, JM Dozier, WF Anderson, SS Devesa and LA Brinton, Global trends in breast cancer incidence and mortality 1973–1997, *International Journal of Epidemiology*, 2005, 34, 405–412.
[76] C Shannon and IE Smith, Breast cancer in adolescents and young women, *European Journal of Cancer*, 2003, 39, 2632–2642.
[77] E Strouhal, A case of metastatic carcinoma from Christian Sayala (Egyptian Nubia), *Anthropologischer Anzeiger*, 1993, 51, 97–115.
[78] MD Williams and AB Sandler, The epidemiology of lung cancer, *Cancer Treatment and Research*, 2001, 105, 31–52.
[79] J Subramanian and R Govindan, Lung cancer in never smokers: a review, *Journal of Clinical Oncology*, 2007, 25, 561–570.

and it is presumably this type that would have been most common in most periods in the past. Secondaries are mainly lytic and occur most frequently in the vertebrae, ribs and skull. The cervical vertebrae are likely to be affected when a tumour is present in the apex of the lung, the so-called Pancoast tumour.[80]

Prostate cancer: Prostate cancer is a disease of elderly men, the majority of cases presenting after the age of sixty but the incidence increases in every succeeding decade and the aetiology remains largely unknown although genetic factors seem to be important in about 40% of cases.[81] Prostatic secondaries are typically sclerotic and spread to the pelvis and lumbar vertebrae, principally through the venous plexus of Batson.[82] In some cases, periosteal new bone is formed on the surface and rarely presents as a sun-burst appearance.[83] The disease was certainly present in the past and has even been described in cremated remains dating back to the first century AD,[84] but the few cases described in the literature have usually all been detected because of the widespread presence of periosteal new bone.[85]

Kidney cancer: Spread to the skeleton from a kidney tumour is common and the lesions are predominantly lytic, affecting the spine, pelvis, ribs and femurs. The lesions are usually multiple but solitary lesions are not uncommon. The disease is more common in males than in females. Most cases of kidney cancer occur between the ages of fifty-five and eighty and the incidence seems to be rising in all parts of the world for reasons that are not understood.[86]

Thyroid cancer: Thyroid cancer is found at all ages and most cases occur between the ages of thirty and sixty but it may also be found in children and the incidence rises rapidly between the ages of five and fifteen;[87] there is a female excess at

---

[80] Henry Khunrath Pancoast 1875–1939.

[81] AW Hsing and AP Chokkalingam, Prostate cancer epidemiology, *Frontiers in Bioscience*, 2006, 11, 1388–1413.

[82] This plexus of veins which lies outside the abdominal cavity and communicates with the veins in the spinal canal was described by Oscar Vivien Batson (1894–1979) and postulated as the means by which tumours could easily spread to the vertebrae. There has been much discussion about the validity of this hypothesis but the evidence seems to be in favour of it; see, for example: AA Geldof, Models for cancer skeletal metastasis: a reappraisal of Batson's plexus, *Anticancer Research*, 1997, 17, 1535–1539.

[83] RA Bloom, E Libson, JE Husband and DJ Stoker, The periosteal sunburst reaction to bone metastases. A literature review and report of 20 additional cases, *Skeletal Radiology*, 1987, 16, 629–634.

[84] G Grevin, R Lagier and CA Baud, Metastatic carcinoma of presumed prostatic origin in cremated bones from the first century AD, *Virchows Archiv*, 1997, 431, 211–214.

[85] T Waldron, a nineteenth-century case of carcinoma of the prostate, with a note on the early history of the disease, *International Journal of Osteoarchaeology*, 1997, 7, 241–247.

[86] JK McLaughlin, L Lipworth and RE Tarone, Epidemiological aspects of renal cell carcinoma, *Seminars in Oncology*, 2006, 33, 527–533.

[87] HR Harach and ED Williams, Childhood thyroid cancer in England and Wales, *British Journal of Cancer*, 1995, 72, 777–783.

all ages. Thyroid cancer is another tumour whose incidence appears to be increasing, more in some histological types than others.[88] The skeletal lesions predominate in the axial skeleton and are lytic in character.

Diagnosing Secondary Tumours

Lytic lesions in the skeleton are generally difficult to overlook but they need to be differentiated from other causes of holes in the bone, including post-mortem damage and trauma. It is usually not very difficult to do so because the lesions resulting from metastases have undercut edges and show no evidence of healing or remodelling. Holes resulting from trauma may often show evidence of remodelling if the victim survived for any length of time after the event and will not have undercut edges. Gunshot wounds will show the characteristic bevelling on the inner or outer table depending on whether the hole is an entry or an exit wound. With post-mortem damage, the damaged edge will almost always be of a lighter colour than the remainder of the bone. Sclerotic secondaries are much more difficult to detect although suspicion may be aroused if the pelvic bones or individual vertebrae appear to be heavier than normal, for example. In all such cases, the bones should be X-rayed when the presence of areas of sclerosis will be apparent if metastases are present. X-rays of bones with lytic lesions will invariably show many lucent areas which represent metastases that are not visible macroscopically.

Lytic lesions in a female skeleton will most likely have been caused by carcinoma of the breast, while in a male skeleton, lung cancer is much the most likely diagnosis. Although kidney and thyroid tumours show a marked tendency to metastasise to bone, their incidence is much lower than the other tumours and so they are less likely to be present on this account (see Table 9.6). There is nothing to distinguish them with any certainty from the other lytic tumours, however, or from myelomatosis for that matter, and in the end, the final decision has to be made on probabilistic grounds. In the case of myeloma, there is some hope in arriving at a definitive answer if it proves possible to extract immunoglobulin from the affected bone, but as with other diagnostic tests applied to bone, only a positive result counts. A negative does not necessarily rule out the diagnosis since this may be due to loss of protein from the bone or to poor technique, a cause never to be forgotten.

[88]   RM Reynolds, J Weir, DL Stockton, DH Brewster, TC Sandeep and RW Strachan, Changing trends in incidence and mortality of thyroid cancer in Scotland, *Clinical Endocrinology*, 2005, 62, 156–162.

It is worth remembering that it is in the diagnosis of tumours in the skeleton that radiology is likely to prove the most useful, both in increasing the number of lesions found by X-raying bones that appear to be expanded, that have discrete areas of periosteal new bone on them or have holes that cannot be explained by trauma or post-excavation damage. The help of a skeletal radiologist is essential if much sense is to be made of the X-rays. Skeletal pathologists are likely to be less helpful because their expertise lies primarily in diagnosing bone tumours from their histology and it is unlikely in the extreme that any material that would interest them will survive. Even with all the help that one can muster, however, it is almost certain that a substantial number of the tumours that may be found in the skeleton will not receive a definitive diagnosis.

10

Disorders of Growth and Development

There is considerable interest in growth and development, both historical and anthropological. Growth and development is an area to which the study of skeletal assemblages is able to make a significant contribution. Final achieved height is determined to a great extent by genetic factors[1] and by the influence of hormones, most importantly growth hormone and thyroxin, but in populations which share a similar genetic makeup, the state of nutrition during the period of active growth during puberty is the most significant factor.[2] Thus, it is often taken as a surrogate for the comparison of nutritional status in different skeletal assemblages.[3]

NORMAL GROWTH

As is well known, the growth of the skeleton does not proceed in a uniform manner from birth to adulthood, but there are two major linear growth spurts during childhood: the first during the first two years of life, and the second which begins at puberty. From birth to age one, growth proceeds at a rate of between 18–25 cm, and from one to two, at 10–13 cm per year. The pubertal growth spurt, which is generally supposed to be the most rapid, actually proceeds at the rather more stately pace of 6–13 cm per year. It is, however, more prolonged and is the period during which most height is gained. The importance of genetic factors is well illustrated by the fact that tall parents tend to have tall children, and short parents, short children. However, as first demonstrated by Frances Galton in 1886, the children of tall parents actually

[1] MA Preece, The genetic contribution to stature, *Hormone Research*, 1996, 45, Supplement 2, 56–58.
[2] DM Styne, The regulation of pubertal growth, *Hormone Research*, 2003, 60, 22–26.
[3] It is important to remember in this respect, however, that it is only nutritional status during the period of active growth in puberty that can be compared.

tend to be *shorter* than their parents, while those of short parents tend to be *taller* than their parents. Galton referred to this phenomenon as regression to the mean.[4]

Historians and physical anthropologists both have had a keen interest in the height of past populations, the historians basing their conclusions largely on data derived from measurements of army recruits or the aristocracy, and in North America, on slave populations. Differences have, of course, been found, with several cycles of changes in height noticed both in Europe and North America and attempts have been made to relate these to availability of food, wars and other environmental or social influences.[5] There was a steady increase in mean height in all the developed countries and in those parts of the developing world that have adopted a western style of life and diet from the start of the twentieth century but in England, there has been almost no change in the mean height of men or women between 1993 and 2003.[6]

Final achieved height is calculated from the skeleton using the maximum length of the limb bones, entering the length into whichever of the published regression equations is preferred by the investigator.[7] Most tend to use the equations published by Trotter and Gleser[8] but whichever are used, the result does not equate exactly with the height during life and comparison with modern heights derived from the direct measurement of the living is not strictly permissible. Comparison between skeletal populations, however, *is* perfectly valid so long as the same regression equations (and the same bone) are used for the purpose. The major disadvantage with estimating heights from archaeological assemblages is that mean height obtained is the resultant of the variations that may have taken place over the length of time represented by

[4] Frances Galton 1822–1911. Actually, in his paper he used the term *mediocrity* rather than median, but the median was what he was describing. For this and other comments on this statistical nicety see: JM Bland and DG Altman, Statistic notes: regression towards the mean, *British Medical Journal*, 1994, 308, 1499.

[5] Two of the most important historical sources are: J Komlos, *Nutrition and economic developments in the 19th century*, Princeton, Princeton University Press, 1989, and R Floud, K Wachter and A Gregory, *Height, health and history*, Cambridge, Cambridge University Press, 1990. An excellent and succinct account of the subject is given by T Cuff, *Historical anthropometrics* to be found at eh.net/encyclopedia/article/cuff.anthropetric.

[6] The mean height of men in 2003 was 175.0 cm, and of women, 161.4 cm. For the complete data set see: K Sproston and P Primatesta (editors), *Health survey of England 2003*, London, The Stationary Office, 2005.

[7] In most cases, investigators will use any surviving long bone to make an estimate of height but because this introduces considerable errors into the calculation of the mean, it is best to use the same bone in all cases, even though this will reduce the number of estimations that can be made. The femur is probably the best bone to standardise on, and – in fact – there is little virtue in doing anything more than restricting any comparison to the mean maximum length of the femur, thus doing away with the notion that actual heights are being compared (T Waldron, A note on the estimation of height from long-bone measurements, *International Journal of Osteoarchaeology*, 1998, 8, 75–77).

[8] Of the various equations and their modifications that Trotter and Gleser published, the ones that are probably most widely used appeared in 1970 under Mildred Trotter's name alone: Estimation of stature from intact long limb bones, In: *Personal identification in mass disasters*, edited by TD Stewart, Washington, Smithsonian Institution, pp 71–97.

the period during which the assemblage was buried and any short-term fluctuations will necessarily be missed. It is known that changes in height may take place over very short periods. For example, there was a rapid fall in the mean height of English men during the eighteenth century in the wake of the Industrial Revolution while, by contrast, the mean height of men increased over the last two or three decades of the nineteenth century following improvements in nutrition. Such rapid changes in height are beyond the scope of the examination of human remains, unfortunately.

Growth rates: Growth rates in children are influenced by a number of factors, of which the total energy and protein content are the most important, but there is also a need for certain essential elements, including calcium, phosphorus, iron, copper and zinc.[9] Adequate secretion of growth hormone and thyroxin are also required for growth to proceed at a normal rate, while a number of childhood diseases, including infectious disease and rickets will slow down growth if only temporarily. It would be very interesting to know the speed at which children developed in the past as this would provide some insight into the state of nutrition at different historical periods. We do know that children in the past tend to be 'short-for-dates' compared with their modern counterparts, that is to say, they appear to be shorter than modern children of comparable age[10] and probably continued to grow for some years longer than contemporary children and adolescents in order to achieve their final height.[11] Growth rates in modern children are determined using a follow-up study. In this type of epidemiological study, a group of children – a cohort – is identified and their height is measured at the start of the study, and at various intervals in the so-called follow-up period. The average rate of growth per year can then be calculated and the results of such studies are widely used by paediatricians to determine both normal and abnormal rates of growth in their patients. For reasons that will be discussed further in Chapter 13, it is not possible to conduct such a study in palaeopathology and if it is desired to calculate growth rates in the past, recourse can only be made to a cross-sectional type of study. The procedure here is simply to measure the length of one or more long bones from the skeletons of children whose ages have been determined using the

[9] LH Allen, Nutritional influences on linear growth: a general review, *European Journal of Clinical Nutrition*, 1994, 48 Supplement 1, S75 – S89; A Prentice and CJ Bates, Adequacy of dietary mineral supply for human bone growth and mineralisation, *Ibid*, S161 – S176.
[10] H Goode, T Waldron and J Rogers, Bone growth in juveniles: a methodological note, *International Journal of Osteoarchaeology*, 1993, 3, 321–323. See also, B Bogin, *Patterns of human growth*, Cambridge, Cambridge University Press, 1999.
[11] JM Tanner, *A history of the study of human growth*, Cambridge, Cambridge University Press, 1981.

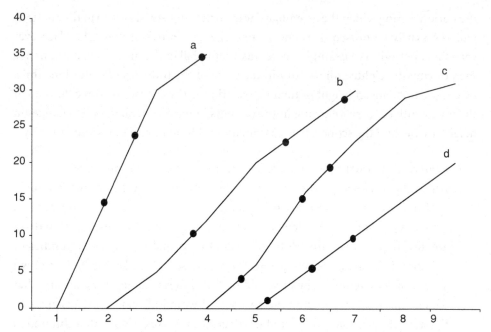

FIGURE 10.1. Diagram to show four hypothetical cohorts of children having been born at different times (shown in arbitrary units on the x-axis) and with slightly different growth rates (shown in arbitrary units on the y-axis). Children available for study (shown as solid circles on A, B, C and D) will come from the whole assemblage and would originally have formed part of one of other of the original cohorts. The curve constructed from these points will not truly represent *any* of the growth rates of the cohorts that make up the assemblage.

best means possible, and then plotting the results on a graph from which the annual rates of growth of the bones, rather than the actual height, can be determined. Very great care must be taken, however, when drawing inferences from such results since, technically, it is not permissible to measure dynamic events from a cross-sectional study; the reason for this can be seen by reference to Figure 10.1.

Figure 10.1 represents a skeletal assemblage that spans a number of years shown by arbitrary numbers along the horizontal axis. The children that are found in the assemblage are from an unknown number of cohorts, however defined. Four of these cohorts, A, B, C and D, are shown in the figure, having been born at different times and all growing at somewhat different rates (the y-axis shows the increments in growth in arbitrary units). The palaeopathologist wishing to study the growth of the children in the cohort cannot, of course, differentiate between the cohorts and so takes measurements from all juvenile skeletons as are available, in other words, taking a cross-sectional approach. The children studied will come from all periods represented in the assemblage and will have originally belonged to several cohorts. The circles in Figure 10.1 represent some of the children studied, and it is noted that they are members of one or other of the cohorts shown. The growth curve constructed from the results will include data from children scattered throughout the period and will not truly represent *any* of the actual growth curves and this cross-sectional growth curve will not be able to distinguish any fluctuations that may have taken place over the study period. It follows that any comparison with modern growth rates will be completely invalid.

ABNORMAL GROWTH AND DEVELOPMENT

Abnormalities in the growth and development are manifested most often by a failure to achieve normal height, or, less often, to grow considerably beyond it. These conditions are usually referred to as dwarfism and gigantism, respectively, although the former term is being discarded nowadays as being somewhat pejorative; it is kept here since it is used in a strictly biological sense.

DWARFISM

Dwarfism is the term used to describe abnormally short stature (below the 5th percentile on a growth chart or 3 standard deviations or more from the mean height for age) and it may result from a number of conditions. The four most common causes of dwarfism are achondroplasia, Turner's syndrome, lack of growth hormone (sometimes called pituitary dwarfism) and inadequate nutrition. The first two conditions are associated with skeletal abnormalities whereas the last two are not.

Dwarfs have always been objects of attention and even veneration. There are very many depictions of dwarfs in art[12] and at least one famous artist – Toulouse-Lautrec – was himself a dwarf.[13] They seem to have been particularly favoured in ancient Egypt and there are numerous depictions of dwarfs in wall paintings in tombs, and there were two dwarf gods, Ptah and Bes.[14] The fascination with dwarfs was by no means restricted to the ancient world and several kings and queens of England had them

[12] J Haworth and A Chudley, Dwarfs in art, *Clinical Genetics*, 2001, 59, 84–87.
[13] It is probable that Toulouse-Lautrec suffered from pyknodysostosis (P Maroteaux, Toulouse-Lautrec's diagnosis, *Nature Genetics*, 1995, 11, 363–363).
[14] C Kozma, Dwarfs in ancient Egypt, *American Journal of Medical Genetics*, 2006, 140A, 303–311.

attached to their court; Van Dyck's picture of Queen Henrietta Maria with her dwarf Sir Jeffrey Hudson is very well known, while in America, General Tom Thumb (the stage name of Charles Sherwood Stratton) made a very substantial living as part of Barnum's circus.[15]

Pituitary Dwarfism

Normal growth requires the production of growth hormone by the pituitary gland. The hormone is secreted by one of several groups of cells in the anterior pituitary that produce hormones in response to stimulating factors released from the hypothalamus.[16] Lack of growth hormone is one form of hypopituitarism which may occur as a solitary deficit or accompanied by deficits in other hormones including TSH or ACTH.[17] Individuals lacking in growth hormone are substantially shorter than normal but are in normal proportion and there is usually nothing else about the skeleton that might provide additional help with the diagnosis, although in a small number of cases, the pituitary fossa may be smaller than normal.[18] What causes the lack of growth hormone is not known but there is a form of the condition found in Pakistan, in which there is a nonsense mutation in the growth hormone-releasing hormone (GHRH) receptor gene.[19]

Pituitary dwarfism should be relatively easy to diagnose in the adult skeleton since it will have normal proportions but be of significantly small stature. In a child, it might not be possible to distinguish it from one whose growth had been stunted by severe malnutrition, except that the latter might show evidence of osteoporosis. Being able to show that a particular skeleton was of significantly small stature – as opposed to being at the extreme lower end of the distribution curve – would require reference data. This would be relatively straightforward for adult skeletons, since the mean height and standard deviation, or the maximum lengths of a long bone, preferably of the femur of the adult skeletons in the assemblage would provide the reference. For children it would be necessary to use age-specific limb bone lengths

[15] Both Jeffrey Hudson and Charles Stratton seem to have been pituitary dwarfs.
[16] The other hormones are thyroid stimulating hormone (TSH), adrenocorticotrophic hormone (ACTH), luteinizing hormone (LH), follicle stimulating hormone (FHS) and prolactin.
[17] SWJ Lamberts, WW de Herder and AJ van der Lely, Pituitary insufficiency, *Lancet*, 1998, 352, 127–134.
[18] Y Inoue, Y Nemoto, K Fujita, H Aoki, K Tekemoto, Y Tsukamoto, J Oda and Y Onoyama, Pituitary dwarfism: CT evaluation of the pituitary gland, *Radiology*, 1986, 159, 171–173.
[19] HG Maheshwari, BL Silverman, J Dupuis and G Baumann, Phenotype and genetic analysis of a syndrome caused by inactivating mutation in the growth hormone-releasing hormone receptor: dwarfism of Sindh, *Journal of Clinical Endocrinology and Metabolism*, 1998, 83, 4065–4074.

of normal children in the assemblage and here the difficulty might be in finding sufficient numbers to provide the necessary means and standard deviations, or calculated heights if this was considered to be preferable.[20] It would be permissible to amalgamate data from several assemblages from the same geographical area and time period if these were needed to boost the numbers. If even this were difficult, then the only alternative may be to utilise data from modern children although this would be the least favourable option.

Turner's Syndrome

Turner's syndrome is a condition which occurs only in females and was described by Turner in 1938.[21] The syndrome is caused by the absence, or partial absence, of one of the X chromosomes. It is uncommon, occurring in about 1 in 2,500 live births. Affected individuals are short, usually between 140–143 cm in height,[22] with a characteristic webbed neck and low hair line.[23] They are subject to a number of cardiovascular and renal anomalies while skeletal changes include delayed epiphyseal fusion, osteoporosis, cubitus valgus (turned out elbows), cranio-facial abnormalities, including retrognathic jaws,[24] and shortening of the metacarpals and metatarsals. There is increased shortening in the hands, from the distal phalanges to the metacarpals which is said to be characteristic of the condition.[25]

Achondroplasia

Achondroplasia is the most common of the non-lethal skeletal dysplasias and it may be helpful to make some general remarks about this group of conditions as a whole before considering it in detail.

[20] Recent regression equations for calculating the height of children aged 3–10 are given by SL Smith (Stature estimation of 3–10-year old children from long bone lengths, *Journal of Forensic Sciences*, 2007, 52, 538–546).
[21] HH Turner, A syndrome of infantilism, congenital webbed neck, and cubitus valgus, *Endocrinology*, 1938, 23, 566–574. (Henry Hubert Turner, 1892–1970.)
[22] The short stature is due in part to the absence of the SHOX (Short stature HOmeoboX) gene which is present on the X chromosome. Homeobox genes are responsible for normal development (SK Leka, S Kitsiou-Tzeli, A Kalpini-Mavrou and E Kanavakis, Short stature and dysmorphology associated with defects in the SHOX gene, *Hormones*, 2006, 5, 107–118).
[23] BH Doswell, J Visootsak, AN Brady and JM Graham, Turner syndrome: an update and review for the primary paediatrician, *Clinical Pediatrics*, 2006, 45, 301–313.
[24] MR Perkiomaki, S Kyranides, A Niinima and L Alvesalo, The relationship of distinct craniofacial features between Turner syndrome females and their parents, *European Journal of Orthodontics*, 2005, 27, 48–52.
[25] E Laurencikas, E Soderman, M Davenport, H Jorulf and L Savendahl, Metacarpophalangeal pattern profile analysis as a tool for early diagnosis of Turner syndrome, *Acta Radiologica*, 2005, 46, 424–430.

Skeletal dysplasias: The skeletal dysplasias are a rare, but extremely interesting group of conditions[26] and on this account, have been very widely studied by clinicians and geneticists alike. Several hundred have now been described and classified[27] and the genetic defect is now well understood[28] and a skeletal gene database has been set up to provide information about them.[29] The skeletal dysplasias have an incidence of about $10–24/10^5$ births but of these almost a quarter are stillborn and another third die within the first year of life. The most common of the skeletal dysplasias are shown in Table 10.1 and these together account for approximately 80% of the total.

The dysplasias are characterised by the following:

- Abnormal shape or size of the skeleton;
- Increased or decreased number of skeletal elements; and
- Abnormal bone texture as the result of an increase or decrease in bone remodelling and mineral deposition.

Shortening of the extremities is a frequent feature of the skeletal dysplasias. The trunk is usually normal although the thorax may be narrow due to shortening of the ribs. The shortening of the extremities is classified as follows:

- Micromelic – shortening of the whole limb;
- Rhizomelic – shortening of the proximal segment;
- Mesomelic – shortening of the middle segments; and
- Acromelic – shortening of the distal segment.

Abnormalities of the digits are relatively common. Polydactyly is the condition in which there are more than five fingers or toes. If the extra digit is on the radial or tibial side it is said to be pre-axial, if it is on the ulnar or fibular side, it is post-axial. Syndactyly refers to the fusion of digits, while clinodactyly refers to deviation of the fingers which would be difficult to detect in the skeleton.

There may be a number of changes in the skull including scaphocephaly (a long, flat skull) and brachycephaly (a short, broad skull). The sutures may close prematurely (craniosynostosis) resulting in a variety of different shapes, and there

[26]   CJ Papadatos and CS Bartsocas, *Skeletal dysplasias*, New York, Alan Liss, 1982.

[27]   CM Hall, International nosology and classification of constitutional disorders of bone (2001), *American Journal of Medical Genetics*, 2002, 113, 65–77.

[28]   K Ozono, Recent advances in molecular analysis of skeletal dysplasias, *Acta Pediatrica Japonica*, 1997, 39, 491–498.

[29]   L Jia, NC Ho, SS Park, J Powell and CA Francomano, Comprehensive resource: skeletal gene database, *American Journal of Medical Genetics*, 2001, 106, 275–281. Further details about the genetics of individual conditions can be found on the OMIM (Online Mendelian inheritance in Man) website: www.ncbi.nih.gov/omim.

Table 10.1. *Some of the more common skeletal dysplasias*

Dysplasia	Lethality	Incidence per live births	Mode of transmission
Thanatophoric dysplasia	Fatal	1:10,000	Autosomal recessive
Achondroplasia	Homozygous type fatal	1:10,000–25,000	Autosomal dominant
Osteogenesis imperfecta	Fatal form (type II)	1:20,000–50,000	Autosomal dominant; type III autosomal recessive
Achondrogenesis	Usually fatal	1:40,000	Autosomal recessive
Asphyxiating thoracic dysplasia (Jeune's disease)	Usually fatal	1:70,000	Autosomal recessive
Chondroplasia punctata	Fatal form	1:10,000	Autosomal dominant; Lethal type, autosomal recessive
Chondrodermal dysplasia (Ellis-van Creveld disease)	50% fatality in infants	1:60,000	Autosomal recessive
Campomelic dysplasia	Usually fatal	1:200,000	Autosomal recessive

Data from several sources. Note that the incidence will depend to a large extent on the population being sampled.
Description of the non-fatal types is given in the text.

may be frontal bossing, while Wormian bones are a feature of some of the dysplasias, notably osteogenesis imperfecta. The orbits may appear closer together than normal (hypotelorism) or further apart (hypertelorism) and the mandible may be smaller than normal (micrognathia).[30] The changes in the skull are discussed in more detail in the following section.

We return now to achondroplasia. This is an autosomal dominant condition that results from a defect in the fibroblast growth factor receptor (FGFR) 3 gene located on chromosome 4p.[31] This defect results in defective enchondral ossification although

[30] These abnormalities are well described with excellent illustrations by P Jeanty and G Valero, The assessment of the fetus with a skeletal dysplasia; this article can be downloaded from: www.thefetus.net.
[31] The specific defect in the majority of cases is a glycine for arginine transposition; in a small number of cases there is a glycine for cytosine transposition.

periosteal ossification is not affected.[32] The physical appearance is characterised by prominent rhizomelia with stubby hands, a large head with frontal bossing and a narrow foramen magnum, a depressed nasal bridge, short vertebrae, squared pelvic wings, a narrow spinal canal and an exaggerated lumbar lordosis. Apart from the fatal homozygous type, life expectancy is normal.[33] In a typical case, the diagnosis should not be difficult in the skeleton and cases have been described but it has not proved possible reliably to extract the defective FGFR3 gene from this material.[34]

> *Osteogenesis imperfecta (OI)*: Osteogenesis imperfecta (OI) is the name given to a group of conditions that are typified by osteoporosis with abnormal fragility of the skeleton (Table 10.2) and which are sometimes referred to collectively as brittle bone disease. It is an uncommon condition with an incidence between 1:20,000–1:50,000 but many mild forms probably go undetected. The vast majority of cases of OI are caused by dominant mutations in the type I collagen genes, COL1A1 and COL1A2.[35] Four phenotypes were originally described by Sillence and his colleagues[36] but since then types V, VI and VII have been added to the litany and it is conceivable that this is by no means the end of the list.[37] Type I is the most common form in which affected individuals have fragile bones, blue sclerae and progressive deafness due to premature otosclerosis. Life expectancy is normal but type II is lethal. Patients with other types may

---

[32] E Lemyre, EM Azouz, AS Teebi, P Glanc and MF Chen, Bone dysplasia series. Achondroplasia, hypochondroplasia and thanatophoric dysplasia: review and update, *Canadian Association of Radiologists Journal*, 1999, 50, 185–197.

[33] Those with homozygous achondroplasia generally die in early infancy from respiratory difficulties caused by upper airways obstruction or deformities of the thoracic cage. Some also have compression of the medulla which can, in some cases, respond to surgery (N Moskowitz, B Carson, S Kopits, R Levitt and G Hart, Foramen magnum decompression in an infant with homozygous achondroplasia, *Journal of Neurosurgery*, 1989, 70, 126–128).

[34] CM Pusch, M Broghammer, GJ Nicholson, AG Nerlich, A Zink, I Kennerknecht, L Backmann and N Blin, PCR-induced sequence alterations hamper the typing of prehistoric bone samples for diagnostic achondroplasia mutations, *Molecular Biology and Evolution*, 2004, 21, 2005–2011.

[35] VG Tedeschi, M Mottes, M Camilot, S Viglio, F Antoniazzi and L Tatò, Osteogenesis imperfecta: clinical, biochemical and molecular findings, *Clinical Genetics*, 2006, 70, 131–139.

[36] DO Sillence, A Senn and DM Danks, Genetic heterogeneity in osteogenesis imperfecta, *Journal of Medical Genetics*, 1979, 16, 101–116.

[37] FH Glorieux, F Rauch, H Plotkin, L Ward, R Travers, P Roughley, L Lalic, DF Glorieux, F Fassier and NJ Bishop, Type V osteogenesis imperfecta: a new form of brittle bone disease, *Journal of Bone and Mineral Research*, 2000, 15, 1650–1658; FH Glorieux, LM Ward, F Rauch, L Lalic, PJ Roughley and R Travers, Osteogenesis imperfecta type VI: a form of brittle bone disease with a mineralization defect, *Journal of Bone and Mineral Research*, 2002, 17, 30–38; LM Ward, F Rauch, R Travers, G Chabot, EM Azouz, L Lalic, PJ Roughley and FH Glorieux, Osteogenesis imperfecta type VII: an autosomal recessive form of brittle bone disease, *Bone*, 2002, 31, 12–18. The genetic basis of these types of OI does not seem to have been determined to date.

Table 10.2. *Main features of the major types of osteogenesis imperfecta*

Type of osteogenesis imperfecta	Mode of inheritance	Major clinical radiological features	Genetic defect
Type I	Autosomal dominant	Osteoporosis; fractures; Wormian bones; blue sclerae; discoloured teeth; cardiovascular anomalies; otosclerosis	Type I collagen genes
Type II	Autosomal dominant	Short, deformed limbs; deformed skull; deep grey-blue sclerae; fatal	Type I collagen genes
Type III	Autosomal recessive	Multiple fractures; progressive deformity of skull, long bones, spine, chest and pelvis; large vault of skull with small jaw; short stature; kyphoscoliosis; sclerae blue in infancy.	Type I collagen genes
Type IV	Autosomal dominant	Multiple fractures; small stature; bowed legs; normal sclerae.	Type I collagen genes

have skeletal deformities, short stature, bowed limbs and scoliosis. In all types, fractures are common, most frequently in the lower limbs and they are usually transverse. The fractures may heal normally but the callus formation may sometimes mimic an osteosarcoma and pseudarthrosis also occurs. Wormian bones are common in the skull. In some cases the OI is associated with dentinogenesis imperfecta in which the deciduous and permanent teeth are blue, brown or opalescent and the pulp chambers and root canals are obliterated by abnormal dentin.[38] Marked osteoporosis, evidence of multiple fractures and Wormian bones in the skull, perhaps combined with short stature, bowing of the limb bones should suggest the diagnosis, and a small number of cases has been described in the palaeopathological literature.[39]

[38] LS Levin, The dentition in osteogenesis imperfecta syndromes, *Clinical Orthopaedics and Related Research*, 1981, 159, 64–74.
[39] PH Gray, A case of osteogenesis imperfecta, with associated dentinogenesis imperfecta, dating from antiquity, *Clinical Radiology*, 1970, 21, 106–108; C Wells, Osteogenesis imperfecta from an Anglo-Saxon burial ground at Burgh Castle, Suffolk, 1965, 9, 88–89.

Chondroplasia punctata (chondrodysplasia punctata): The non-lethal type of chondroplasia punctata is inherited as an autosomal dominant, is more common in males than females and is caused by a dysfunction in the peroxisomes.[40] The skull is asymmetrical with frontal bossing and there is asymmetric mild shortening and bowing of the long bones, scoliosis, clubfoot and stippling of the epiphyses, especially the proximal humerus on X-ray. Life span is normal in this type.

Chondrodermal dysplasia (Ellis-van Creveld disease): Chondrodermal dysplasia is characterised by short stature, acromesomelia and polydactyly mainly affecting the hands.[41] The shortening of the limbs is most pronounced in the hands where the distal and middle phalanges are shorter than the proximal phalanx. The extra digit on the hands is on the ulnar side (post-axial). The iliac crests and sciatic notches are small and the fibula is disproportionately shorter than the tibia. Dental anomalies are common, including small or abnormally shaped teeth, and congenitally missing teeth.[42] The genetic fault lies in a mutation in the EVC and EVC2 genes.[43]

Hereditary multiple exostoses (HME): Hereditary multiple exostoses (HME) is an autosomal dominant condition (also sometimes referred to as diaphyseal aclasis) with an incidence of 1:50,000. It is caused by mutations in the EXT (exostosin) genes, EXT1 on chromosome 8 and EXT2 on chromosome 11[44] which causes an error in the regulation of normal chondrocyte proliferation and maturation.[45] There is a wide spectrum of expression but the clinical manifestations include short stature, discrepancies in limb length and subluxation of the wrist joint. The number of exostoses (osteochondromas) is variable, but tends to increase up to about the age of 12 and as many as one hundred may be present. The exostoses take a variety of shapes and may occur in any location but they are particularly common around the knee, the fibula and the humerus.

---

[40] SJ Steinberg, G Dodt, GV Raymond, NE Braverman, AB Moser and HW Moser, Peroxisome biogenesis disorders, *Biochimica et Biophysica Acta*, 2006, 1763, 1733–1748.

[41] E George, D DeSilva, E Lieber, K Raziuddin and M Gudavalli, Ellis van Creveld syndrome (chondrodermal dysplasia, MIM 22550) in three siblings from a non-sanguineous mating, *Journal of Perinatal Medicine*, 2000, 28, 425–427.

[42] A Cahuana, C Palma, W Gonzalez and E Gean, Oral manifestations in Ellis-van Creveld syndrome: report of five cases, *Pediatric Dentistry*, 2004, 26, 277–282.

[43] SW Thompson, VL Ruiz-Perez, HJ Blair, S Barton, V Navarro, JL Robson, MJ Wright and JA Goodship, Sequencing EVC and EVC2 identifies mutations in two-thirds of Ellis-van Creveld syndrome patients, *Human Genetics*, 2007, 120, 663–670.

[44] C Alvarez, S Tredwell, M De Vera and M Hayden, The genotype-phenotype correlation of hereditary multiple exostoses, *Clinical Genetics*, 2006, 70, 122–130.

[45] JR Stieber and JP Dormans, Manifestations of hereditary multiple exostoses, *Journal of the American Academy of Orthopaedic Surgeons*, 2005, 13, 110–120.

The ulna may be short and bowed, somewhat resembling the Madelung deformity. The metacarpals may also be shortened and deformed. The femurs show coxa valga with a thickened, irregular neck and the distal metaphysis may be widened. In rare cases, the pelvis and its outlet may be obstructed by exostoses, giving rise to difficulties in pregnancy and labour.[46] There is a relatively high risk that the osteochondromas may undergo sarcomatous change. The risk is usually given as 1–2% but in one family the risk of malignancy developing was 8.3%.[47] The presence of multiple exostoses with or without the other accompanying signs should make the diagnosis in the skeleton about as straightforward as these things can be.[48]

Osteopetrosis: Osteopetrosis is caused by a failure of the osteoclasts to resorb bone. There are several variants some of which are autosomal recessive and some autosomal dominant, the latter variants being more benign than the former (see Table 10.3). The incidence is not known with any certainty but is probably in the range of 1;100,000–500,000. The malignant infantile autosomal recessive type is rare and characterised by dense sclerotic bones which fracture easily. The bone marrow cavities are obliterated causing deficient haematopoiesis, recurrent infections and early death. Individuals with the recessive intermediate type are of short stature and prone to fractures. The bones show widespread sclerosis, especially of the skull base, widening of the metaphyses, 'bone-within-bone' appearance, and pathological fractures. In infants the appearances may be somewhat reminiscent of rickets and there may be radiolucent areas in the metaphyses. The three autosomal dominant forms are relatively mild and have a much better prognosis and the condition is often found co-incidentally. An autosomal dominant form was the first to be described by Albers-Schönberg[49] and the condition is still referred to as Albers-Schönberg disease, especially in the older texts. Radiographs will show diffuse sclerosis, especially in the cranial vault as a solitary finding (type I). Generalized sclerosis, especially of the end plates of the vertebrae separated by a line of decreased density giving a sandwich, or 'rugger-jersey' type of appearance (type II); in this type fractures

[46] CL Wiklund, RM Pauli, D Johnstone and JT Hecht, Natural history of hereditary multiple exostoses, *American Journal of Medical Genetics*, 1995, 55, 43–46.

[47] A Kivioja, H Ervasti, J Kinnunen, I Kaitila, M Wolf and T Bohling, Chondrosarcoma in a family with multiple hereditary exostoses, *Journal of Bone and Joint Surgery*, 2000, 82, 261–266.

[48] A case of HME was found by Beighton and his colleagues among the skeletons housed in the Pathologisch-anatomisisches Bundesmuseum in Vienna. The case was that of a man who died in 1842 of a ruptured aortic aneurysm, probably syphilitic in origin (P Beighton, E Sujansky, B Patzak and KA Portele, Genetic skeletal dysplasias in the Museum of Pathological Anatomy, Vienna, *American Journal of Medical Genetics*, 1993, 47, 843–847).

[49] Heinrich Ernst Albers-Schönberg 1865–1921.

Table 10.3. *Main features of the major types of osteopetrosis*

Type of osteopetrosis	Mode of inheritance	Major skeletal radiological features	Genetic defect*
Malignant infantile	Autosomal recessive	Dense sclerosis, multiple fractures, wide metaphyses, early death	TCIRG1 CLCN7 OSTM1
Intermediate	Autosomal recessive	Mild sclerosis, short stature, multiple fractures	CLCN7
Benign type I	Autosomal dominant	Diffuse sclerosis, no fractures	LRP5
Benign type II	Autosomal dominant	Bone-in-bone appearance, rugger-jersey spine, fractures	CLCN7
Benign type III	Autosomal dominant	Sclerosis of distal skeleton and skull	?

Based on Balemans et al. (2005).[50]

* The names of these genes, and any others mentioned in the text, can be found on the Human Genome Organisation's web site at www.gene.ucl.ac.uk/nomenclature.

are common. In type III, there is sclerosis of the distal limb bones and skull but the axial skeleton shows little involvement. The primary genetic defects are known for the majority of types of osteopetrosis and several genes are involved.[51] The condition is not likely to turn up in a skeletal assemblage with any regularity and is most likely to be found as an incidental finding. It would be prudent to X-ray any bones of children otherwise thought to have rickets so that the chance to see a rarity is not missed.

Dyschondrosteosis (DCO; Léri-Weill disease[52]): Dyschondrosteosis is an autosomal dominant condition (incidence 1:200,000) in which mesomelic short stature is associated with the Madelung deformity of the radius. The final achieved height in cases of DCO is generally not markedly reduced and changes in the lower

[50] W Balemans, L Van Wesenbeeck and W Van Hul, A clinical and molecular overview of the human osteopetrosis, *Calcified Tissue Research*, 2005, 77, 263–274.

[51] M C de Vernejoul and O Bénichou, Human osteopetrosis and other sclerosing disorders: recent genetic developments, *Calcified Tissue International*, 2001, 69, 1–6; W Balemans, L Van Wesenbeeck and W Van Hull, A clinical and molecular overview of the human osteopetroses, *Calcified Tissue International*, 2005, 77, 263–274.

[52] André Léri 1875–1930; Jean A Weill b 1903.

limbs tend to be less severe than in the arms. Females are more commonly, and more severely affected than males.[53] It is caused by a heterozygous mutation in the SHOX gene on the sex chromosomes.[54] If the SHOX mutation is heterozygous, then the more severe Langer form of mesomelic dwarfism results.[55] Here the dwarfism is more pronounced, there is both rhizomelic and mesomelic limb shortening, and the mandible is hypoplastic. Hypoplasia of the ulnas and fibulas is very marked and the radii and tibias are short, thick and noticeably curved.[56]

Madelung deformity of the radius: The Madelung deformity of the radius was first described in 1878 and is characterised by a short radius that curves distally both towards the ulna and backwards. The head of the ulna is prominent and projects backwards from the wrist and the carpal bones tend to have a triangular arrangement.[57] Osteoarthritis is a common late complication. The Madelung deformity may occur as an isolated phenomenon and is more common in females than males. It is most commonly found in association with DCO, but it may be found in some other dysplasias including achondroplasia, HME and Turner's syndrome and it may rarely follow trauma.[58]

Even though it is not likely to occur very often in the archaeological record, the Madelung deformity should be readily recognised in the skeleton[59] and, when it does, it is most likely to be associated with DCO.[60]

[53] C Dawe, R Wynne-Davies and GE Fulford, Clinical variation in dyschondrosteosis. A report on 13 individuals in 8 families, *Journal of Bone and Joint Surgery*, 1982, 64B, 377–381.

[54] AA Jorge, SC Souza, MY Nishi, AE Billerbeck, DC Liborio, CA Kim, IJ Arnhold and BB Mendonca, SHOX mutations in idiopathic short stature and Leri-Weill dyschondrosteosis: frequency and phenotype variability, *Clinical Endocrinology*, 2007, 66, 130–135.

[55] S Benito-Sanz, NS Thomas, C Huber, DG Del Blanco, M Aza-Carmona, JA Crolla, V Maloney, J Argente, A Campos-Barros, V Cormier-Daire and KE Heath, A novel class of pseudoautosomal region1 deletions downstream of SHOX I is associated with Leri-Weill dyschondrosteosis, *American Journal of Human Genetics*, 2005, 77, 533–544.

[56] A Baxova, K Kozlowski, I Netriova and D Sillence, Mesomelic dysplasia: Langer type, *Australasian Radiology*, 1994, 38, 58–60. A type of DCO has been described in which the features of the Leri-Weill and Langer types seemed mixed, suggesting that there is likely to be a broad spectrum of phenotypes associated with SHOX mutations (T Bieganski, K Bik, V Cormier-Daire, C Huber, G Nowicki and K Kozlowki, Severe, atypical form of dyschondrosteosis (report of two cases), *European Journal of Pediatrics*, 2005, 164, 539–543).

[57] AS Arora and KC Chung, Otto W Madelung and the recognition of Madelung's deformity, *Journal of Hand Surgery*, 2006, 31, 177–182. (Otto Wilhelm Madelung, 1846–1926.)

[58] MI Vender and HK Watson, Acquired Madelung-like deformity in a gymnast, *Journal of Hand Surgery*, 1988, 13, 19–21.

[59] There is an abnormal ligament (Vicker's ligament) in many cases of Madelung deformity that tethers the lunate in a proximal position between or below the radius and ulna. It is attached to the medial side of the distal radius and may be recognised in the skeleton by the appearance of a cortical defect in this position. (D Vickers and G Nielsen, Madelung deformity: surgical prophylaxis (physiolysis) during the late growth period by resection of the dyschondrosteosis lesion, *Journal of Hand Surgery*, 1992, 17B, 401–407.)

[60] T Waldron, A case of dyschondrosteosis from Roman Britain, *Journal of Medical Genetics*, 2000, 37, e27.

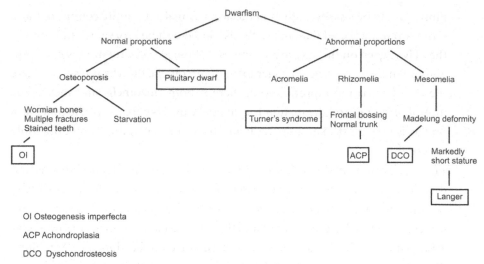

OI Osteogenesis imperfecta

ACP Achondroplasia

DCO Dyschondrosteosis

FIGURE 10.2. Scheme for differentiating between the more common forms of dwarfism.

Other Forms of Dwarfism

It is important to remember that short stature may be normal in the sense that it occurs in an individual who is at the extreme left-hand end of the normal distribution for height. Before a short skeleton is labelled as that of a dwarf, care must be taken to ensure that it falls outside the fifth centile of the appropriate age and sex standardised distribution, or more than three standard deviations from the mean. Dwarfism as the result of inadequate nutrition is most likely to present as a skeleton with normal proportions but with no other stigmata although osteoporosis may be apparent on X-ray. The lack of some essential elements – even with an otherwise apparently adequate diet – may result in retardation of growth, most notably a lack of iodine which is common in some parts of the world and results in hypothyroidism and the production of goitres and mental impairment.[61] Zinc deficiency may also result in stunted growth in some cases[62] but it would not be possible to differentiate this cause of dwarfism on morphological grounds, although it could conceivably be detected if bone zinc levels were determined in appropriate cases.[63]

---

[61] The skeletal changes in hypothyroidism are described in Chapter 7.

[62] AS Prasad, AR Schulert, A Miale, Z Farid and HH Sandstead, Zinc and iron deficiency in male subjects with dwarfism and hypogonadism but without ancylostomiasis, schistosomiasis or severe anemia, *American Journal of Clinical Nutrition*, 1963, 12, 437–444.

[63] A scheme to help differentiate between some of the more common types of dwarfism is shown in Figure 10.2.

Gigantism

An abnormally tall skeleton may be no more than that of an individual at the extreme right-hand end of the height distribution. There is no formal definition of a giant, but – by analogy with dwarfism – one might suppose it is an individual who lies more than three standard deviations from the mean of the appropriate age and sex standardised height. The most common cause of gigantism is excessive excretion of growth hormone (GH) from the anterior pituitary by a GH secreting adenoma. If the tumour develops before the epiphyses have fused, the result is gigantism, if after the epiphyses have fused, the result is acromegaly.

> *Gigantism:* Growth hormone exerts its effects on multiple organs and systems and many of its effects are mediated via IGF-1 (which was originally referred to in the older literature as somatomedin) and other factors.[64] In gigantism due to over-secretion of GH the body proportions are not abnormal but the bones are massive and epiphyseal fusion is long delayed. In some cases the tumour may cause the pituitary fossa to become enlarged and this may be seen directly, if the skull is broken, or by X-raying the skull.[65]

One of the most famous giants was Charles Byrne whose skeleton is in the Hunterian Museum of the Royal College of Surgeons of London. He was known as the Irish giant and earned his living exhibiting himself but died at the early age of 22. He was very anxious that he should not fall into the hands of the anatomists when he died and left a large sum of money to ensure that he was buried at sea. An even larger sum, however, saw to it that his body was diverted to John Hunter's dissection rooms where he was rendered to the form in which he can be seen today.[66]

> *Acromegaly:* The oversecretion of GH once the epiphyses have fused affects many organ systems including the skeleton[67] and the joints.[68] The frontal sinuses and

[64] T Ueland, Bone metabolism in relation to alterations in systemic growth hormone, *Growth Hormone and IGF Research*, 2004, 14, 404–417.

[65] To measure the pituitary volume from an x-ray both lateral and antero-posterior views are required. The volume (in mm³) is then $= \frac{1}{2} (L \times D \times W)$ where L = maximum lateral length; D = maximum lateral depth; and W = maximum ap width. The mean pituitary volume is 594 mm³ but with a very wide range from 240–1092 mm³. The method is described by G Di Chiro and KB Nelson, The volume of the sella turcica, *American Journal of Roentgenology*, 1962, 87, 989–1008.

[66] R Richardson, A potted history of specimen-taking, *Lancet*, 2000, 355, 935–936. An X-ray of the skull shows an enlarged pituitary fossa indicating that Byrne did indeed have a pituitary tumour.

[67] F Bogazzi, C Cosci, C Sardella, E Martino and M Gasperi, Acromegaly: effects on bone metabolism and mass, *Journal of Endocrinological Investigation*, 2005, 28 (Suppl), 33–35.

[68] A Colao, R Pivonello, R Scarpa, G Vallone, C Ruosi and G Lombardi, The acromegalic arthropathy, *Journal of Endocrinological Investigation*, 2005, 28 (Suppl), 24–31.

the supraorbital ridges are enlarged, and there is prognathism of the mandible. The pituitary fossa is likely to be enlarged and the tufts of the terminal phalanges of the hands and feet may be considerably enlarged and both the hands and feet are larger than normal. The vertebral bodies may show such extensive osteophytosis as to resemble DISH, and some show an increase in the concavity of the posterior border. The arthropathy, which is a common cause of morbidity,[69] has some features of OA including (in life) joint space narrowing, and marginal osteophytes.

In the skeleton, the diagnosis would depend on finding a skeleton with an enlarged jaw and supraorbital ridges, large hands and feet and, if possible, radiographic evidence of an enlarged pituitary fossa.

Disorders of Skull Growth

Disorders of skull growth cause it to be either very small or very large, or of abnormal shape due to the premature closure of the sutures. These conditions are referred to as microcephaly, macrocephaly and craniosynostosis, respectively.

Microcephaly and macrocephaly: Microcephaly and macrocephaly are generally said to be present when the head is either two standard deviations below or above the appropriate age and sex-standardised mean; some paediatricians prefer to use a definition of minus three standard deviations to diagnose microcephaly.[70]

Microcephaly: Approximately 2% of the general population have a small head, that is, two standard deviations below the mean, but only about 0.1% are more than three standard deviations below. The condition may present as an isolated phenomenon, or associated with other abnormalities when it is known as syndromic. If present at birth, it is termed primary, and secondary if it develops later in childhood; there are a number of genetic and environmental causes and it may also occur with pansynostosis.[71]

Macrocephaly: Macrocephaly may be due to a larger than normal brain mass (familial megencephaly), but most cases are caused by raised intracranial pressure or hydrocephalus, both the last conditions having a variety of causes. Hydrocephalus accounts for most cases and is the result of an excessive volume

[69] J Ayuk and MC Sheppard, Growth hormone and its disorders, *Postgraduate Medical Journal*, 2006, 82, 24–30.
[70] This distinction is clinically important since most children with a head in the range -2 to -3 SD have no intellectual impairment, whereas those whose head is 3 or more SD below the mean, mostly do have some mental impairment.
[71] D Abuelo, Microcephaly syndromes, *Seminars in Pediatric Neurology*, 2007, 14, 118–127.

of cerebro-spinal fluid (CSF) in the brain, leading to progressive enlargement of the ventricles of the brain, the subarachnoid spaces or both.[72] For skull enlargement to occur, hydrocephalus (or other cause) must be present before the sutures fuse, and untreated, would eventually lead to death.

Florid cases of microcephaly and macrocephaly are very obvious on simple examination but to diagnose those that are less extreme requires normative data against which to compare that skull circumference. Ideally, these data should be derived from other skeletons from the same assemblage, or those from other assemblages from similar times and places. In the last resort, modern growth charts can be used.

Cranio-synostosis: This is caused by premature fusion of one or more of the six major sutures of the skull.[73] The incidence is variable, between 3–14/10,000 births, and males are affected more frequently than females.[74] The fused plate of bone fails to grow further but there is compensatory over-growth at other sutures, and there are often abnormalities of the skull base.[75] The condition is referred to as simple when only one suture is involved, and compound, when two or more are affected. Premature fusion may occur in the presence or absence of other abnormalities, syndromic[76] and non-syndromic forms,[77] respectively. The abnormality in skull shape depends upon which of the sutures is prematurely fused, and the principal changes are shown in Table 10.4. In life, craniosynostosis may be complicated by raised intracranial pressure but the intracranial volume is not reduced.[78]

Cleft Palate

Cleft palate is the most common of a number of orofacial clefts, and its aetiology includes both environmental and genetic factors.[79] It occurs in about 1 in 1–2,000

[72] AT Vertinsky and PD Barnes, Macrocephaly, increased intracranial pressure, and hydrocephalus in the infant and young child, *Topics in Magnetic Resonance Imaging*, 2007, 18, 31–51.

[73] These are the metopic, sagittal, left and right coronal, and left and right lambdoid.

[74] S Singer, C Bower, P Southall and J Goldblatt, Craniosynostosis in Western Australia, 1980–1994: a population-based study, *American Journal of Medical Genetics*, 1999, 83, 382–387.

[75] JB Delashaw, JA Pershing and JA Jane, Cranial deformation in craniosynostosis. A new explanation, *Neurosurgical Clinics of North America*, 1991, 2, 611–620.

[76] There is a very large number of these syndromic forms. See, for example, MM Cohen, Craniosynostosis update 1987, *American Journal of Medical Genetics Supplement*, 1988, 4, 99–148.

[77] JK Williams, RG Ellenbogen and JS Gross, State of the art in craniofacial surgery: nonsymdromic craniosynostosis, *Cleft Palate-Craniofacial Journal*, 1999, 36, 471–485.

[78] H Kabbani and TS Raghuveer, Craniosynostosis, *American Family Physician*, 2004, 69, 2863–2870; S Sgouros, Skull vault growth in craniosynostosis, *Childs Nervous System*, 2005, 21, 861–870.

[79] BL Eppley, JA van Aalst, A Robey, RJ Havlik andAM Sadove, The spectrum of orofacial clefting, *Plastic and Reconstructive Surgery*, 2005, 115, 101e–114e.

Table 10.4. *Principal changes in the skull in craniosynostosis*

Type of craniosynostosis	Sutures prematurely fused	Principal changes in the skull
Scaphocephaly	Sagittal	Elongation of the skull with bitemporoparietal narrowing and frontal and occipital bossing.
Trigonocephaly	Metopic	Elongate, pointed forehead with a ridge in the centre of the forehead; parieto-occipital bossing.
Frontal plagiocephaly	Left or right coronal	Flattening of forehead on affected side with contralateral frontal bossing.
Brachiocephaly	Bilateral coronal	Skull assume an almost circular shape with a prominent frontal bone and flattened occiput and anterior displacement of the vertex.
Occipital plagiocephaly	Left or right lambdoid	Ipsilateral occipitoparietal flattening with contralateral parietal bossing and contralateral frontal bossing.

births although there is considerable racial variation[80] and the left side is more often affected than the right. In life, the cleft may be partial or complete, in which case it involves the maxilla and the lip. In the skeleton the condition will be readily apparent by a defect in the hard palate which may or may not involve the anterior margin.

Developmental Disorders of the Hips

There are three developmental disorders of the hips that affect children and adolescents and which may persist into adulthood without appropriate treatment, as would have been the case for the greater part of the period with which palaeopathologists are concerned. The conditions are congenital hip dysplasia, slipped capital femoral epiphysis and Perthes' disease.

---

[80]   KKH Gundlach and C Maus, Epidemiological studies on the frequency of clefts in Europe and world-wide, *Journal of Cranio-Maxillofacial Surgery*, 2006, 34, Supplement 2, 1–2.

Congenital hip dysplasia (CHD): Congenital hip dysplasia (CHD) has superseded the old term, congenital dislocation of the hips because it is not always present at birth and does not always result in dislocation. At birth about 2% of neonates have clinical evidence of hip instability but by three months, only one infant in 1000 has evidence of dislocation. There are several known risk factors including family history, breech presentation and post-natal swaddling.[81] Girls are many times more likely to be affected than boys. The left hip is affected about four times more commonly than the right but the condition may also be bilateral.[82] There is an association between CHD and idiopathic clubfoot[83] and with congenital muscular torticollis;[84] in both cases the increased risk is sufficiently great not to have arisen by chance although the mechanism is not fully understood.

In the infant, the acetabulum is shallow and the femoral head is undeveloped with variable degrees of subluxation.[85] The condition can be corrected with appropriate treatment and this must be achieved to avoid late sequelae, including early onset secondary arthritis resulting from subluxation or complete dislocation, and dysplasia of the acetabulum.[86] There was not much prospect of corrective treatment until comparatively recently. Cases of CHD present to the palaeopathologist from time to time and should not be difficult to diagnose. In a typical case one or both acetabula will be hypoplastic or obliterated altogether. There are likely to be pseudoarthroses on the ilium, and the femoral heads are likely to be hypoplastic. The pseudarthrosis are often large, surrounded by new bone and they will frequently be eburnated as will the femoral heads. Where secondary osteoarthritis develops this can be taken as an indication that the individual was able to walk, although almost certainly with a waddling gait, and survived for many years into adulthood.

Slipped capital femoral epiphysis (SCFE): Slipped capital femoral epiphysis (SCFE) has been recognised since the sixteenth century, having been described by

[81] CE Backe, J Clegg and M Herron, Risk factors for developmental dysplasia of the hip: ultrasonographic findings in the neonatal period, *Journal of Pediatric Orthopedics*, 2002, 11B, 212–218.

[82] K Rosendahl, T Merkestad and RT Lie, Developmental dysplasia of the hip: prevalence based on ultrasound diagnosis, *Pediatric Radiology*, 1996, 26, 635–639.

[83] BT Carney and EA Vanek, Incidence of hip dysplasia in idiopathic clubfoot, *Journal of Surgical and Orthopaedic Advances*, 2006, 15, 71–73.

[84] J von Heideken, DW Green, SW Burke, K Sindle, J Denneen, Y Haglund-Akerlind and RF Widmann, The relationship between developmental dysplasia of the hip and congenital muscular torticollis, *Journal of Pediatric Orthopedics*, 2006, 26, 805–808.

[85] There are three types of CHD, classified *inter alia* by the degree of subluxation or dislocation; the changes described in the text would be most likely to follow a type III dislocation (PM Dunn, Congenital dislocation of the hip (CDH): necropsy studies at birth, *Proceedings of the Royal Society of Medicine*, 1969, 62, 1035–1037).

[86] CB Cady, Developmental dysplasia of the hip: definition, recognition, and prevention of late sequelae, *Pediatric Annals*, 2006, 35, 92–101.

Ambroise Paré (1510–1590). It manifests itself around the onset of puberty, particularly in overweight males who are about three times as likely to have the condition as females.[87] It is the result of a fracture through the growth plate and has an incidence of about $1/10^5$ of the population. In life it generally presents with hip or – in about a quarter of cases – with knee pain and alterations in gait. The aim of treatment is to stabilise the fracture so that the blood supply to the femoral head is not compromised with the risk of osteonecrosis. The condition has no preference as to side and is bilateral in about a quarter of cases. It is not clear what causes the fracture,[88] although trauma and activity are thought to play a part. Whatever the aetiology, the result is that the epiphysis is displaced posteriorly and medially with a reduction in the anteroposterior neck-shaft angle.[89] Late sequelae include osteonecrosis with a small femoral head and buttressing of the femoral neck, possible limb shortening as the result of premature fusion of the epiphysis, severe varus deformity with shortening and broadening of the femoral neck and early-onset osteoarthritis.[90]

The condition can be recognised in the skeleton by the malalignment of the femoral head on the neck of the femur, perhaps accompanied by other late sequelae, including osteoarthritis.[91]

Perthes' disease:[92] Perthes' disease is a form of idiopathic avascular necrosis of the femoral head that occurs in children, with symptoms usually appearing between the ages of four and eight years of age. Boys are affected about four

---

[87] M Poussa, D Schlenzka and T Yrjonen, Body mass index and slipped capital femoral epiphysis, *Journal of Pediatric Orthopedics*, 2003, 12, 369–371.

[88] The fracture is a type I in the Salter-Harris classification.

[89] The anteroposterior angle is the angle between a line drawn through the middle of the long axis of the femur and one at right angles to the growth plate measured on a radiograph. Normal values for this angle are 146–147° while in patients with SCFE the values are 127–134° (C Santili, MC de Assis, FI Kusabara, IL Romero, CM Sartini and CA Longui, Southwick's head-shaft angles: normal standards and abnormal values observed in obesity and in patient with epiphysiolysis, *Journal of Pediatric Orthopedics*, 2004, 13, 244–247).

[90] CA Boles and CY el-Khoury, Slipped capital femoral epiphysis, *Radiographics*, 1997, 17, 809–823.

[91] SCFE with osteoarthritis may be difficult to distinguish from the changes that take place in the femoral head in primary OA with superomedial migration of the femoral head when the superior aspect of the femoral head becomes flattened and marginal osteophyte accumulates on the interior aspect of the head. These changes are referred to as a tilt deformity (D Resnick, Patterns of migration of the femoral head in osteoarthritis of the hip. Roentgenographic-pathologic correlation and comparison with rheumatoid arthritis, *American Journal of Roentgenology*, 1975, 124, 62–74).

[92] This condition was described independently in 1910 by Perthes in Germany, Calvé in France and Legg in Boston and thus is also known Legg-Calvé-Perthes disease. It may also appear – incorrectly – as Perthes' disease, and sometimes as coxa plana. (Georg Clement Perthes 1869–1927; Jacques Calvé 1875–1954; Arthur Thornton Legg 1874–1939.)

times as often as girls and the condition is bilateral in between 10 and 20% of cases. The condition has an incidence of approximately 1 in 1200 children.

The condition passes through four stages: (1) the onset of avascular necrosis; (2) fragmentation of the head of the femur; (3) revascularisation and regeneration; and (4) healing. In some cases healing and regeneration are complete and it may not be possible to recognise the condition in later life but in others, changes are evident in the proximal femur. There are various radiographic means of classifying Perthes' disease which are used to predict the final outcome[93] but none is suitable for palaeopathology.

Late changes seen in Perthes' disease include: a smooth flattening of the femoral head sometimes associated with a shallow acetabulum; shortening and widening of the femoral neck with a varus deformity; enlargement of the femoral head and neck (coxa magna);[94] a mushroom deformity of the femoral head;[95] shortening of the limb on the affected side[96] and secondary osteoarthritis.[97] The smoothly flattened femoral head with a short neck is most likely to suggest the diagnosis to the palaeopathologist but it is by no means difficult to confuse Perthes' disease with SCFE. One radiological sign that may occasionally be helpful is the appearance of cystic lesions in the femoral head which are considered characteristic of SCFE.[98]

Fibrous Dysplasia

Fibrous dysplasia is a developmental anomaly in which the osteoblasts fail to differentiate and mature, this leads to well-defined intra-medullary lesions in which the bone is replaced by fibrous tissue and calcified cartilage. These areas are radiolucent on X-ray and they are described in life as having a ground-glass appearance. Four

[93] See, for example, AM Ismail and MF Macnicol, Prognosis in Perthes' disease. A comparison of radiological predictors, *Journal of Bone and Joint Surgery*, 1998, 80B, 310–314.

[94] SM Rowe, ES Moon, EK Song, JY Seol, JK Seon and SS Kim, The correlation between coxa magna and final outcome in Legg-Calvé-Perthes disease, *Journal of Pediatric Orthopedics*, 2005, 25, 22–27.

[95] The mushroom deformity of the femoral head occurs in other conditions, and most frequently in osteoarthritis (MH Perlman, M Schweitzer, R Tyson and D Resnick, The mushroom femoral head. A radiographic investigation, *Investigative Radiology*, 1992, 27, 891–897).

[96] Leg shortening in Perthes' disease is not very marked, on average only about 2.5 cm (A Grzegorzewski, M Synder, P Kozlowski, W Szymczak and RJ Bowen, Leg length discrepancy in Legg-Calvé-Perthes disease, *Journal of Pediatric Orthopedics*, 2005, 25, 206–209).

[97] T Yrjonen, Long-term prognosis of Legg-Calvé-Perthes disease: a meta-analysis, *Journal of Pediatric Orthopedics*, 1999, 8, 169–172.

[98] FN Silverman, Lesions of the femoral neck in Legg-Perthes disease, *American Journal of Roentgenology*, 1985, 144, 1249–1254.

Table 10.5. *Distribution of lesions in different types of fibrous dysplasia*

Type of fibrous dysplasia	Sites affected in order of frequency
Monostotic	Rib, femur, tibia, cranio-facial bones, humerus, vertebrae
Polyostotic	Femur, tibia, ribs, skull, facial bones, upper extremities, lumbar spine, clavicle, cervical spine
Cranio-facial	Frontal, sphenoid, maxilla, ethmoids
Cherubism	Maxilla, mandible

types are recognised: monostotic (only a single bone is affected), polyostotic (several bones affected), craniofacial which may complicate either of the first two types or occur in isolation, and cherubism, an autosomal dominant condition with variable penetrance that occurs in children and is more severe in males than in females. The majority of cases (70–80%) are monostotic; the pattern of distribution in the various types is shown in Table 10.5.

In life, the condition may cause pain and deformation of the affected bones and pathological fractures are common. In the polyostotic form, the weight-bearing bones may become bowed and there may be a coxa vara deformity of the femoral neck and proximal femur giving rise to the so-called shepherd's crook deformity[99] and, if the vertebrae are affected, there may be kyphosis. Malignant transformation is known, but is rare.[100] The molecular basis of the condition is now well understood[101] and this has led to improvements in treatment.[102] Polyostotic fibrous dysplasia may be accompanied by various endocrine disturbances and café au lait spots on the skin when it is referred to as McCune-Albright syndrome[103] but it would be impossible to differentiate this from the normal variant in the skeleton.[104]

[99] PJ Livesley, JC McAllister and a Catterall, The treatment of progressive coxa vara in children with bone softening disorders, *International Orthopaedics*, 1994, 18, 310–312.

[100] SM Yabut, S Kenan, HA Sissons and MM Lewis, Malignant transformation of fibrous dysplasia. A case report and review of the literature, *Clinical Orthopaedics and Related Research*, 1988, 228, 281–289.

[101] PJ Marie, Cellular and molecular basis of fibrous dysplasia, *Histology and Histopathology*, 2001, 16, 981–988.

[102] RD Chapurlat and PJ Meunier, Fibrous dysplasia of bone, *Bailliere's Best Practice and Research. Clinical Rheumatology*, 2000, 14, 385–398.

[103] TS Hannon, K Noonan, EA Steinmetz, EA Eugster, MA Levine and OH Pescovitz, Is McCune-Albright syndrome overlooked in subjects with fibrous dysplasia of bone? *Journal of Pediatrics*, 2003, 142, 532–538.

[104] There is another rare condition in which changes similar to those seen in fibrous dysplasia are found in the cortex of the long bones. This was first described as a separate entity in 1976 and termed osteofibrous dysplasia (M Campanacci, Osteofibrous dysplasia of long bones, a new clinical entity, *Italian Journal of Orthopedics and Traumatology*, 1976, 2, 221–237). More recent molecular studies have shown that the genetic abnormalities in fibrous dysplasia are not present in osteofibrous dysplasia, providing good evidence that the two conditions do indeed have a separate aetiology (A Sakamoto, Y Oda, Y Iwamoto and M Tsuneyoshi, A comparative study of fibrous dysplasia and osteofibrous dysplasia with regard to $G_s\alpha$ mutation at the Arg^{210} codon, *Journal of Molecular Diagnostics*, 2000, 2, 67–72).

In the skeleton, fibrous dysplasia may be considered by finding expansile swellings on one or more bones or healed fractures. X-rays of affected bones should show lucent areas with endosteal scalloping and sometimes, a thick sclerotic border, the so-called rind sign.[105] The condition may also be found as an incidental finding. However it is brought to light, the help of a skeletal radiologist should always be sought before committing a diagnosis to paper.

Kyphosis and Scoliosis

Kyphosis refers to a forward curvature in the spine in the anteroposterior plane.[106] It is most commonly a result of a destructive disease of the vertebral bodies such as tuberculosis, osteomyelitis, brucellosis or malignant disease, or secondary to trauma, especially to vertebral fractures that occur in osteoporosis. It may also occur in the context of scoliosis.

Scoliosis refers to a lateral curvature of the spine. There are several causes of scoliosis[107] and there is also an association with the Klippel-Feil syndrome[108] (see below) but the most common type, accounting for up to 80% of all cases, is the so-called idiopathic form.[109] Three types of idiopathic scoliosis are described: infantile scoliosis which occurs before the age of three and resolves spontaneously; juvenile scoliosis which occurs between the ages of three and puberty and which is usually progressive; and adolescent scoliosis which is the most common form, and occurs more often in females than in males, the prevalence increasing with increasing age from six to twelve;[110] the overall prevalence is up to 4.5%.[111]

Scoliosis is a complicated deformity since, in addition to the lateral curvature, there is also rotation of the vertebrae. As the disease progresses, the vertebral bodies and spinous processes rotate towards the concavity of the curve, the posterior parts

[105] WH Jee, KH Choi, BY Choe, JM Park and KS Shinn, Fibrous dysplasia: MR imaging characteristics with radiopathologic correlation, *American Journal of Roentgenology*, 1996, 167, 1523–1527.

[106] The thoracic spine has a normal kyphosis while the lumbar spine exhibits a backward curvature which is known as a lordosis.

[107] RG Burwell, Aetiology of idiopathic scoliosis: current concepts, *Pediatric Rehabilitation*, 2003, 6, 137–170.

[108] MN Thomsen, U Schneider, M Weber, R Johannisson and FU Niethard, Scoliosis and congenital anomalies associated with the Klippel-Feil syndrome type I-III, *Spine*, 1997, 15, 396–401.

[109] BV Reamy and JB Slakey, Adolescent idiopathic scoliosis: review and current concepts, *American Family Physician*, 2001, 64, 111–116.

[110] AJ Stirling, D Howel, PA Millner, S Sadiq, D Sharples and RA Dickson, Late-onset idiopathic scoliosis in children six to fourteen years old. A cross-sectional prevalence study, *Journal of Bone and Joint Surgery*, 1996, 78A, 1330–1336.

[111] E Rogala, D Drummond and J Curr, Scoliosis: incidence and natural history, *Journal of Bone and Joint Surgery*, 1996, 78A, 314–317.

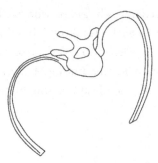

FIGURE 10.3. Diagram of a cross-section of the spine in scoliosis. The posterior part of the ribs on the convex side are pushed backwards while the anterior part is pushed anteriorly. This results in the characteristic humped back and narrowing of the thoracic cage. The lamina and spinal canal on the concave side are narrower than on the contralateral side and the spinous process is rotated towards the concave side.

of the ribs on the convex side are pushed backwards causing the characteristic hump in the chest and narrowing of the thoracic cage; the anterior parts of the ribs are pushed anteriorly (Figure 10.3). The lamina and spinal canal on the concave side of the curve are narrower than on the contralateral side. The ribs are often thinner than normal and the vertebrae are wedged towards the concave side and osteophytes are often present together with osteoarthritis of the costo-vertebral joints. There are a number of vertebral anomalies that may cause scoliosis including partial or complete unilateral failure of formation, resulting in wedged or hemi-vertebrae, and failure of segmentation which may be partial or complete.

The degree of curvature is measured on X-ray using the Cobb method (Figure 10.4). In this method, the proximal and distal end vertebrae are delineated, these being the vertebrae at the upper and lower limits of the curve and which tilt most towards its concavity. A line is drawn along the upper end plate of the proximal body and the lower end plate of the distal body and the angle of interest is the angle between these two lines. The Cobb angle can easily be determined on skeletons with scoliosis after the vertebrae have been articulated and fixed in position.[112]

The severity of scoliosis varies from a slight non-progressive curvature that requires no intervention to those in whom the curve measures more than 40 degrees by the Cobb method and who would nowadays be considered for surgery. In those with a substantial deformity, severe cardiac and respiratory complications may arise

---

[112] There are various ways of doing this, but one which I have found useful if to cut a section of plastic pipe insulation and pass it up (or down) through the spinal canal. The vertebrae can then be arranged in their anatomical position for radiography.

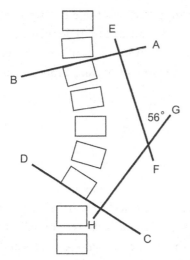

FIGURE 10.4. To determine the degree of spinal curvature from a radiograph by the Cobb method, the angle formed between the line (AB) drawn along the upper surface of the vertebral body at the uppermost part of the curve and that (CD) drawn along the inferior surface of the vertebral body at the lowermost part is measured. This angle is often far to the left of the radiograph and it is more convenient instead to measure the angle formed by dropping lines perpendicular to AB and DC, EF and GH as shown in the in the diagram.

in later life;[113] back pain is common, but most people with the condition function well and have a normal life expectancy.[114] The socio-economic consequences of the condition may be considerable, however, and some studies have shown that those with scoliosis are likely to unemployed and are self-conscious or embarrassed by their condition.[115] In the past, opportunities for employment may also have been limited and it is likely that those with severe scoliosis would descend into vagrancy or beggary unless they enjoyed the support of their community.

Cases occur in skeletal assemblages and there is no difficulty whatsoever in recognising them for what they are; however, in some assemblages they seem to be somewhat under-represented. At Christ Church, Spitalfields, for example, the crude prevalence was less than 1% but by contrast, Wells reported on an assemblage of 50 skeletons recovered from the church of St Michael-at-Thorn in Norwich. Only eight had well-preserved spines and of these, two had scoliosis, both females. Given that

[113] MA Braithwaite, Cardiorespiratory consequences of unfused idiopathic scoliosis, *British Journal of Diseases of the Chest*, 1986, 80, 360–369.

[114] SL Weinstein, LA Dolan, KF Spratt, KK Peterson, MJ Spoonamore and IV Ponseti, Health and function of patients with untreated idiopathic scoliosis: a 50-year natural history study, *Journal of the American Medical Association*, 2003, 289, 559–567.

[115] JV Fowles, DS Drummond and S L'Ecuyer, Untreated scoliosis in the adult, *Clinical Orthopaedics and Related Research*, 1978, 134, 212–217.

Norwich had been a centre of weaving, Wells supposed that these two women had been employed as weavers and that this has been the cause of their deformity.[116] The more obvious explanation that these were cases of idiopathic scoliosis who gravitated towards a large centre of population in the hope of finding support was not considered.

Klippel-Feil Syndrome

The original syndrome described by Klippel and Feil in 1912 was a triad comprising a short neck, low hairline and limited movement of the neck.[117] It has since come to be applied to any congenital fusion of two or more of the cervical vertebrae.[118] In this condition the vertebrae are completely fused, that is to say, both the bodies and the posterior elements are fused, and in this way it can be distinguished from other forms of fusion in which the posterior elements remain unfused. Various other anomalies may be associated with the condition, including scoliosis, as noted above.[119]

Other Spinal Anomalies

Several other anomalies can be noted in the spine and although they cannot always be considered pathological, are usually considered under this rubric by bone specialists and for this reason, a brief account of them will be given.

Cervical rib: The anterior element of the transverse process of the seventh cervical vertebra is the homologue of the rib in the thoracic region and it sometimes develops to form a cervical rib of variable length. The condition is usually bilateral and occurs in up to 1% of the population.[120] It usually presents no problems during life but does occasionally obstruct or damage the subclavian

[116] C Wells, Weaver, tinker or shoemaker? *Medical and Biological Illustration*, 1967, 17, 39–47.
[117] Maurice Klippel (1858–1942); André Feil (b 1884).
[118] The condition can be classified into a number of types depending on the number of fused segments; see, for example, DD Samartzis, J Herman, JP Lubicky and FH Shen, Classification of congenitally fused cervical patterns in Klippel-Feil patients: epidemiology and role in the development of cervical spine-related symptoms, *Spine*, 2006, 31, E7908–804.
[119] MR Tracy, JP Dormans and K Kusumi, Klippel-Feil syndrome: clinical features and current understanding of etiology, *Clinical Orthopedics and Related Research*, 2004, 424, 183–190.
[120] E McNally, B Sandin and RA Wilkins, The ossification of the costal element of the seventh cervical vertebra with particular reference to cervical ribs, *Journal of Anatomy*, 1990, 170, 125–129.

artery leading to symptoms in the ipsilateral hand or arm.[121] In the skeleton, the cervical rib will be loose and it is easy to confuse it with the eleventh or twelfth thoracic ribs, especially is the ribs are damaged. If it seems that there are thirteen ribs, however, the seventh cervical vertebra should be examined for an articular facet since cervical ribs are more common than thirteen thoracic ribs.

Spina bifida occulta: Spina bifida occulta is the term used to describe a sacrum in which all the laminae are unfused.[122] It is clinically insignificant and is not to be confused with the condition of spina bifida in children in which the defect occurs in the lumbar spine and which may be accompanied by herniation of the contents of the spinal cord into an external sac with severe neurological consequences. This condition would have been invariably fatal in the past. The mildest form of the condition in infants is also called spina bifida occulta which may be silent but may be apparent in some children by the presence of a tuft of hair or a dimple over the defect in the underlying vertebra. On this account it is strongly recommended that some other term is used to describe the innocuous condition in the sacrum; bifid sacrum might be preferable but long usage of the usual phrase suggests it is not likely easily to be abandoned.

Bifid sacrum is one of the easiest conditions to recognise in the skeleton. The prevalence is considerable, 8% in one skeletal assemblage[123] and 11% in a series of unselected radiographs.[124]

Transitional vertebrae: The L5/S1 junction of the spine tends to be unstable and the transverse process of the lower lumbar vertebra is frequently enlarged to resemble the lateral mass of the sacrum. The enlargement may be unilateral or bilateral, and one or both sides may be fused to the sacrum, giving rise to eight variations,[125] none of which can be missed in the skeleton. As with bifid sacrum, the condition has no clinical significance.

Six lumbar vertebrae: Another aspect of the instability of the lumbro-sacral junction is the presence of six lumbar vertebrae. Some consider this to be an atavistic condition, mimicking the situation in the early hominins but not all agree with

[121] GM Patton, Arterial thoracic outlet syndrome, *Hand Clinics*, 2004, 20, 107–111.

[122] This definition is by no means universally agreed and there are many different classifications; see: TL Albrecht, SD Scutter and M Henneberg, Radiographic method to assess the prevalence of sacral spinal bifida occulta, *Clinical Anatomy*, 2007, 20, 170–174.

[123] G Saluja, Spina bifida in human skeletal remains from Ireland, *Journal of Anatomy*, 1986, 146, 259.

[124] JF Brailsford, Deformities of the lumbrosacral region of the spine, *British Journal of Surgery*, 1929, 16, 562–567.

[125] These are: left unfused, right unfused; left fused, right fused; left fused, right unfused; right fused, left unfused.

this view.[126] Recognising the condition ought to present no problems although the tyro may be confused and wonder if there has been an intrusion from another skeleton. This confusion can be easily resolved by articulating the lumbar spine to show that they all fit together nicely. About 3% of the general population have six lumbar vertebrae[127] but, again, the condition has no clinical significance.[128]

[126] M Häusler, SA Martelli and T Böni, Vertebrate numbers of the early hominid spine, *Journal of Human Evolution*, 2002, 43, 621–643.

[127] LT Ford and FG Goodman, X-ray studies of the lumbrosacral spine, *Southern Medical Journal*, 1966, 59, 1123–1128.

[128] There are a number of instances in the literature in which an increase in the prevalence of bifid sacrum has been found in skeletons with spondylolysis or, conversely, a decrease in the prevalence in the presence of transitional vertebrae. These associations were examined in a case-reference study and were not confirmed (T Waldron, A case-referent study of spondylolysis and spina bifida and transitional vertebrae in human skeletal remains, *International Journal of Osteoarchaeology*, 1993, 3, 55–57). By contrast, there does seem to be an association between having six lumbar vertebrae and transitional vertebrae and there is some evidence that those with six lumbar vertebrae are more susceptible to spondylolysis.

11

Soft Tissue Diseases

For the examination of soft tissue diseases, mummies come into their own, subject to the limitations that were mentioned briefly in Chapter 1 and which may need to be expanded upon here. The principal constraint is that, in most parts of the world, mummified remains are greatly in the minority and most palaeopathologists will spend most of their working lives dealing with human remains that have no soft tissue attached to them. There is then the problem that even in those cultures in which mummification, either direct or indirect, was the major means of disposing of their dead, the bodies may often lack the internal organs, and where they are present, it may be difficult to examine them without subjecting the mummy to an autopsy or to endoscopic examination. A full autopsy is – understandably – often not permitted because it is, by its nature, destructive and many archaeologists and museum curators are reluctant to permit valuable exhibits to be partially or completely destroyed. Modern imaging techniques such as CAT or MRI scanning permit non-destructive examination to be made but they are expensive and by no means available to all investigators, and certainly not on a large scale without special funding. Even when available, the results may not always be instructive because of changes in the tissues resulting either from the mummification or from natural decay. Finally, it is seldom possible to amass sufficient data from the examination of mummies for the application of epidemiological methods, and in most cases results are almost always based on small numbers and very often on single cases which may have little value beyond confirming that a particular human disease was present in the past, a fact that may or may not have much intellectual content.

It has to be recognised, however, that mummies exert a particular fascination, not only for the general public, but also to those who study human remains professionally. Indeed, what many would consider to be the first significant contributions to palaeopathology were made by Ruffer[1] who studied Egyptian mummies. The Paleopathology Association was founded in 1973 by Aidan Cockburn and his colleagues after they had examined the mummy of PUM-II.

References to investigations in mummies abound in the palaeopathological literature and many books have been written about them. In recent years, reports have appeared of the presence of several parasitic infestations in mummies, including pinworm,[2] ascaris, trichuris and mites,[3] antigens to *E histolytica* in desiccated faeces,[4] flukes and hookworm,[5] Leishmaniasis[6] and cysticercosis.[7] Syphilis and

[1] Ruffer was born in France but qualified in medicine in England. He studied at the Pasteur Institute in Paris for a short while when Pasteur was still active and, on returning to England, was appointed Director of the British Institute of Preventive Medicine in 1891. He acquired diphtheria while studying the bacillus and had such severe paralytic sequelae that he resigned his post and went to Egypt to convalesce. He was eventually appointed professor of bacteriology in Cairo and began his study of Egyptian mummies, publishing many papers on the subject. He was knighted in 1916 and died at sea in 1917, when returning from a conference in Salonika. He is widely credited with having coined the word palaeopathology, which first appeared in a paper of 1913 (On pathological lesions found in Coptic bodies, *Journal of Pathology and Bacteriology*, 1913, 18, 149–162) but in fact he was ante-dated by Robert Wilson Schufeldt. Ruffer's papers were collected after his death by RL Moodie (*Studies in the palaeopathology of Egypt*, Chicago, University of Chicago Press, 1921). Rather surprisingly, there has never been a full biography of Ruffer but some details of his life can be found in Moodie's biographical sketch in the collected works (pp xiii–xvi) and in the short paper by AT Sandison (Sir Marc Armand Ruffer (1859–1917), *Medical History*, 1967, 11, 150–155). Schufeldt was also an interesting character, although completely different from Ruffer. The son of an admiral, he served some time in the US Navy before studying medicine at Cornell and joining the army. His main interest, however, was ornithology and he published well over 1500 papers on this and other subjects including his Notes on palæopathology, published in 1893 in *Popular Science Monthly* (42, 679–684). In a foot-note to that paper he described palaeopathology as '. . . a term here proposed under which may be described all diseased and pathological conditions found fossilized in the remains of extinct or fossil animals.' Schufeldt wrote an autobiography which he ended ten years before his death, leaving another biographer to fill the gap (RW Schufeldt, Life history of an American naturalist, *Medical Life*, 1924, 31, 67–76; 105–115; 138–149; 193–203; 307–326; EE Hume, Robert Wilson Schufeldt (1850–1934) In: *Ornithologists of the United States Army Medical Corps*, Baltimore, Johns Hopkins Press, 1942, pp 390–412). Schufeldt also published a complete bibliography up to 1920 which by then had reached 1565 the first papers having appeared in 1881. What a treasure he would have been for the RAE. For those who want to be astonished see: RW Schufeldt, Complete list of my published writings, with brief biographical notes, *Medical Review of Reviews*, 1920, 26, 17–23; 70–75; 123–130; 200–206; 249–257; 314–320; 368–377; 437–447; 495–498.
[2] PD Horne, First evidence of enterobiasis on ancient Egypt, *Journal of Parasitology*, 2002, 88, 1019–1021.
[3] MR Hidalgo-Argüello, N Díez Baños, J Fregeneda Grandes and E Prada Marcos, Parasitological analysis of Leonese royalty from Collegiate-Basilica of St Isodoro, Leon (Spain): helminths, protozoa, and mites, *Journal of Parasitology*, 2003, 89, 738–743.
[4] ML Gonçalves, VL da Silva, CM de Andrade, K Reinhard, GC da Rocha, M Le Bailly, F Bouchet, LF Ferreira and A Araujo, Amoebiasis distribution in the past: first steps using an immunoassay technique, *Transactions of the Royal Society of Tropical Medicine and Hygiene*, 2004, 98, 88–91.
[5] L Sianto, KJ Reinhard, M Chame, S Chaves, S Mendonça, ML Gonçalves, A Fernandes, LF Ferreira and A Araújo, The finding of *Enchinostoma* (Trematoda: Digenea) and hookworm eggs in coprolites collected from a Brazilian mummified body dated 600–1,200 years before present, *Journal of Parasitology*, 2005, 91, 972–975.
[6] AR Zink, M Spigelman, B Schraut, CL Greenblatt, AG Nerlich and HD Donoghue, Leishmaniasis in ancient Egypt and upper Nubia, *Emerging Infectious Diseases*, 2006, 12, 1616–1617.
[7] F Bruschi, M Masetti, MT Locci, R Ciranni and G Fornaciari, Short report: cysticercosis in an Egyptian mummy of the late Ptolemaic period, *American Journal of Tropical Medicine and Hygiene*, 2006, 74, 598–599.

papillomavirus have been found together in a sixteenth-century Italian female mummy,[8] myelomeningocele in a Peruvian child,[9] a case of megacolon perhaps secondary to Chagas' disease,[10] nodules on the liver of a child from Korea,[11] juvenile cirrhosis[12] and an Egyptian mummy was presumed to have died from myocardial infarction on the basis of finding elevated levels of cardiac troponin in abdominal tissue.[13] Because it is so easily accessible, the skin of mummies has always attracted a good deal of attention and the structure has been closely examined,[14] and various skin diseases noted,[15] including smallpox and eczema.[16] And, of course, Ötzi can seldom be left out of the reckoning, and the menu of his last meals (red deer and cereals, preceded by ibex, dicotyledans and cereals) has been made known to satisfy an impatient world.[17]

This is a considerable list, but perhaps a greater number of soft tissue diseases can also be determined from the stigmata left on the skeleton than one perhaps first thinks. Several have already been alluded to in earlier chapters, including heterotopic ossification, intervertebral disc disease, Schmorl's nodes, periosteal new bone on the pleural surface of the ribs from peripheral lung lesions or on the distal tibia resulting from varicose ulcers, rotator cuff disease and some of the inflammatory conditions of ligaments and tendons. Secondary bone tumours too are merely the skeletal reflection of tumours arising in soft tissues. In addition to these, however, it is also possible to make inferences about some cardio-vascular and neurological lesions, and to detect a variety of stones that arise in the gall-bladder, kidney or bladder.

---

[8] G Fornaciari, K Zavagilia, L Giusti, C Vultaggio and R Ciranni, Human papillomavirus in a 16th century mummy, *Lancet*, 2003, 362, 1160.

[9] FJ Carod-Artal and CB Vázquez-Cabrera, Myelomeningocele in a Peruvian mummy from the Moche period, *Neurology*, 2006, 66, 1775–1776.

[10] K Reinhard, TM Fink and J Skiles, A case of megacolon in Rio Grande valley as a possible case of Chagas disease, *Memórias do Instituto Oswaldo Cruz*, 2003, 98 Supplement 1, 165–172.

[11] SB Kim, JE Shin, SS Park, GD Bok, YP Chang, J Kim, YH Chung, YS Yi, MH Shin, BS Chang, DH Shin and MJ Kim, Endoscopic investigation of the internal organs of a 15th-century child mummy from Yangju, Korea, *Journal of Anatomy*, 2006, 209, 681–688.

[12] R Ciranni and G Fornaciari, Juvenile cirrhosis in a 16th century Italian mummy. Current technologies in pathology and ancient human tissues, *Vichow's Archiv*, 2004, 445, 647–650.

[13] R Miller, DD Callas, SE Kahn and V Ricchiuti, Evidence of myocardial infarction in mummified human tissue, *Journal of the American Medical Association*, 2000, 284, 831–832.

[14] BS Chang, CS Uhm, CH Park, HK Kim, GY Lee, HH Cho, MJ Kim, YH Chung, KW Song, DS Lim and DH Shin, Preserved skin structure of a recently found fifteenth-century mummy in Daejeon, Korea, *Journal of Anatomy*, 2006, 209, 671–680.

[15] EJ Lowenstein, Paleodermatoses: lessons learned from mummies, *Journal of the American Academy of Dermatology*, 2004, 50, 919–936.

[16] KS Leslie, NJ Levell and SL Dove, Cutaneous findings in mummies from the British Museum, *Journal of Visual Communication in Medicine*, 2005, 28, 156–162.

[17] F Rollo, M Ubaldi, L Ermini and I Marota, Ötzi's last meals: DNA analysis of the intestinal content of the Neolithic glacier mummy from the Alps, *Proceedings of the National Academy of Sciences of the United States of America*, 2002, 99, 12594–12599.

CARDIO-VASCULAR LESIONS

Skeletal evidence of cardio-vascular disease comes from the impressions left by abnormal blood vessels, either aneurysms or enlarged collateral vessels that develop in response to a coarctation of the aorta.

> *Aneurysms:* Aneurysms are dilations of a portion of an artery that may be congenital or secondary to a disease such as atherosclerosis or syphilis, or to trauma. There are four sites where aneurysms are most likely to affect bone, the arch of the aorta, the descending aorta, the vertebral artery in its passage through the transverse foramina of the cervical vertebrae and the popliteal artery behind the knee.

The ascending aorta or the aortic arch are the classic sites for the development of syphilitic aneurysms although they may also rarely involve the innominate artery.[18] They are much less common now that there is effective treatment for syphilis but were by no means rare in the era before antibiotics. The classic effect on bone is sternal erosion which mainly affects the manubrium, close to the origin of the innominate artery, and the right clavicle,[19] but it may also cause pressure defects in the second and third ribs.[20] The defect is smooth, variable in size and may even erode completely through the sternum. Without treatment, the aneurysm will eventually rupture causing the instant death of the individual. In assemblages that come from periods or places where syphilis was known to be prevalent (18th- and 19th-century London, for example), a close look at the posterior surfaces of the manubria, especially those from older individuals, might well prove rewarding.

> *Descending and abdominal aorta:* The descending aorta begins at the level of the fourth thoracic vertebra and is continuous with the abdominal aorta at the diaphragm, ending at the level of the fourth lumbar vertebra where it divides into the two common iliac arteries. In its thoracic and abdominal course it lies to the left-hand side of the bodies of the vertebrae. Aneurysms of the aorta may occur in any part of its course but tend to be in the lower parts of the vessel.

---

[18] In this case they do not affect bone (SM Tadavarthy, WR Castaneda-Zuniga, J Klugman, JB Shachar and K Amplatz, Syphilitic aneurysms of the innominate artery, *Diagnostic Radiology*, 1981, 139, 31–34).

[19] RJ Weisser and RJ Marshall, Syphilitic aneurysms with bone erosion and rupture, *West Virginia Medical Journal*, 1976, 72, 1–4; NK Bodhey, AK Gupta, KS Neelakandhan and M Unnikrishnan, Early sternal erosion and luetic aneurysm of thoracic aorta: report of 6 cases and analysis of cause-effect relationship, *European Journal of Cardio-thoracic Surgery*, 2005, 28, 499–501.

[20] H Nakane, Y Okada, S Ibayashi, S Sadoshima and M Fujishima, Brain infarction caused by syphilitic aneurysm. A case report, *Angiology*, 1996, 47, 911–917.

Nowadays they are most often due to atherosclerosis but they may also be found in Behçet's disease,[21] and may be caused by the spread of infection from adjacent vertebrae.[22] Conversely, the aneurysm may affect the vertebrae in such a way as initially to simulate a pyogenic infection[23] and they also may be confused with malignant disease of the spine.[24] The lesion involves the anterior parts of the vertebral bodies, may affect more than one vertebra, and has smooth, scalloped edges. The size of the lesion will depend on the extent of the overlying aneurysm but up to half the vertebral body may be destroyed by the constant pulsatile pressure from the aneurysm.

The vertebral artery: The vertebral artery originates from the subclavian and generally enters the transverse foramina of the cervical vertebrae at the level of C6. It enters the skull through the foramen magnum to form the basilar artery (with its opposite partner). Aneurysms may form on any part of the vertebral artery, and they may be traumatic or non-traumatic in origin. Only those that form on the section within the transverse foramina leave an impression on the skeleton, however. They are generally unilateral and most commonly are found at the level of C2 where their presence is indicated by a smooth defect in the body of the affected vertebra, usually with a sclerotic margin on X-ray.[25] If such a lesion is found, the task is to determine whether it is really the result of an aneurysm or the result of tortuosity of the artery. During its course through the transverse foramina, the artery may become coiled or looped and this may cause pressure defects in the adjacent vertebral body. The lesion is identical with that caused by an aneurysm and, in addition, both may affect the pedicle or cause widening of the transverse foramen or the intervertebral foramen.[26] Lesions due to tortuosity show a marked preference for the left hand

[21] A El Machraoui, F Tabache, A El Khattabi, A Bezza, A Abouzahir, D Ghafir, V Ohayon and MI Archane, Abdominal aortic aneurysm with lumbar vertebral erosion in Behçet's disease revealed by low back pain: a case report and review of the literature, *Rheumatology*, 2001, 40, 472–473. Hulusi Behçet 1889–1948.

[22] The infection responsible is often tuberculosis (Y Takahashi, Y Sasaki, T Shibata and S Suefiro, Descending thoracic aortic aneurysm complicated with severe vertebral erosion, *European Journal of Cardio-thoracic Surgery*, 2007, 31, 941–943) but other infections may also be culpable (J Naktin and J DeSimone, Lumbar vertebral osteomyelitis with mycotic abdominal aortic aneurysm caused by highly penicillin-resistant *Streptococcus pneumoniae*, *Journal of Clinical Microbiology*, 1999, 37, 4198–4200).

[23] RH Choplin, N Karstaedt and NT Wolfman, Ruptured abdominal aortic aneurysm simulating pyogenic vertebral spondylitis, *American Journal of Roentgenology*, 1082, 138, 748–750.

[24] K Wang and M Hodges, Erosion of lumbar vertebral bodies due to abdominal aortic aneurysm, *American Journal of Roentgenology*, 1982, 138, 1317–1318.

[25] T Waldron and D Antoine, Tortuosity or aneurysm? The palaeopathology of some abnormalities of the vertebral artery, *International Journal of Osteoarchaeology*, 2002, 12, 79–88.

[26] RW Lindsey, J Piepmeier and K Burkus, Tortuosity of the vertebral artery: an adventitious finding after cervical trauma, *Journal of Bone and Joint Surgery*, 1985, 67A, 806–808.

side and most occur at the level of C4 or C5 – lower than the lesion from an aneurysm.[27]

Popliteal artery: The popliteal artery is a continuation of the femoral artery and can readily be palpated in the popliteal fossa behind the knee. The popliteal artery lies on the posterior surface of the distal femur and divides into the anterior and posterior tibial arteries at the lower border of the popliteus muscle. Because of its relatively unprotected position, the popliteal artery is prone to damage, either from a fracture of the distal femur or from other injury. The result may be complete disruption of the artery or the formation of an aneurysm.[28] Popliteal aneurysms were relatively common in the eighteenth century as an occupational hazard for coachmen, who presumably traumatised the artery on the corner of their hard seats in the front of the coach and it was first successfully treated by John Hunter who ligated the popliteal artery proximal to the aneurysm, leading to the development of a collateral circulation that was able to supply the leg.[29]

A popliteal aneurysm may produce scalloping of the distal femoral shaft,[30] or destruction of the femoral condyle with periosteal new bone formation, simulating a malignant tumour.[31] Archaeological examples are rare but one case found in a disarticulated assemblage was confirmed by comparison with an authenticated specimen of eighteenth century date from a museum collection.[32]

Coarctation of the aorta: Coarctation of the aorta is a congenital constriction in the vessel at the point where the embryonic ductus arteriosus inserts just distal to the left subclavian artery. Blood flow is impaired distal to the constriction and collateral vessels develop to ensure that the trunk and lower limbs are adequately supplied. One consequence is hypertrophy of the intercostal arteries which

[27] FJ Palmer and M Sequiera, Cervical vertebral erosion and vertebral tortuosity: an angiographic study, *Australasian Radiography*, 1980, 24, 20–23.

[28] An aneurysm may also be a rare complication of a congenital exostosis (A Cardon, S Aillet, J Ledu and Y Kerdiles, Pseudo-aneurysm of the popliteal artery by femoral exostosis in a young child, *Journal of Cardiovascular Surgery*, 2001, 42, 241–244).

[29] DC Schechter and JJ Bergan, Popliteal aneurysm: a celebration of the bicentennial of John Hunter's operation, *Annals of Vascular Surgery*, 1986, 1, 118–126. A dissection of one of Hunter's cases is on view at the Royal College of Surgeons of England. There is a view that Hunter was preceded in his treatment of this condition by the French surgeon, Dominique Anel (1679–1730), who is said to have performed the operation some 75 years before Hunter (CA Sloffer and G Lanzino, Historical vignette. Dominique Anel: father of the Hunterian ligation? *Journal of Neurosurgery*, 2006, 104, 626–629).

[30] GJ Ross, LV Ross, WH Hartz and RM Fairman, Case report 723, *Skeletal Radiology*, 1992, 21, 190–193.

[31] K Erler, MT Ozdemir, E Ogus and M Basbozkurt, Does false aneurysm behave like a sarcoma? Distal femoral arterial false aneurysm simulated a malignant mesenchymal tumor. A case report and review of the literature, *Archives of Orthopedic and Trauma Surgery*, 2004, 124, 60–63.

[32] J Wakely and A Smith, A possible eighteenth century to nineteenth century example of a popliteal aneurysm from Leicester, *International Journal of Osteoarchaeology*, 1998, 8, 56–60.

produces a characteristic notching of the ribs. It was once thought that this was pathognomonic of coarctation but it is now known that, although coarctation is the most common cause, there are a number of others, mostly cardiovascular in origin.[33] The notching is within the subcostal groove in which the neuro-vascular bundle runs and is close to the costal angle. It may be observed in very young children[34] and the first (and to date, only) palaeopathological case was described in skeletal remains of Etruscan origin.[35]

NEUROLOGICAL LESIONS

Some neurological disorders have been referred to in other chapters, including nerve root compression in inter-vertebral disc disease, the neurological effects of polio and leprosy, various causes of neuroarthropathy, and the potential for nerve damage following fractures of particular bones. Other conditions that might be detected by their effects on bone include two tumours – meningiomas and acoustic neuromas, neurofibromatosis, and this also seems to be the best place to mention true dysraphism.

Meningioma: Meningiomas are tumours that are thought to arise from arachnoid cap cells which are specialised cells found in the arachnoid granulations.[36] It is not certain that only cap cells can form meningiomas[37] but nevertheless, these tumours are found in the anatomical sites where arachnoid granulations occur most frequently, that is, the superior sagittal sinus, the basal cisterns, the trans-verse sinus, and the other dural sinuses.[38] Although meningiomas are generally considered to be benign – in the sense that they do not metastasise – they may cause death by increasing intracranial pressure if they become sufficiently large, and they may also rarely metastasise, with the lungs, abdominal viscera and skeleton being the favoured sites.[39] Bony reaction in the skull occurs in up to

[33] Leading article, Rib notching, *British Medical Journal*, 1064, 2, 1152.
[34] RA Ferris and JM LoPresti, Rib notching due to coarctation of the aorta: report of a case initially observed at less than one year of age, *British Journal of Radiology*, 1974, 47, 357–359.
[35] R Ciranni and G Fornaciari, The aortic coarctation and the Etruscan man: morphohistologic diagnosis of an ancient cardiovascular disease, *Vichow's Archiv*, 2006, 449, 476–478. The illustrations in this paper are particularly helpful.
[36] G Parisi, R Tropea, S Giuffrida, M Lombardo and F Giuffre, Cystic meningiomas. Report of seven cases, *Journal of Neurosurgery*, 1986, 64, 35–38.
[37] P McL Black, Meningiomas, *Neurosurgery*, 1993, 32, 643–657.
[38] R Murtagh and C Linden, Neuroimaging of intracranial meningiomas, *Neurosurgery Clinics of North America*, 1994, 5, 217–233.
[39] B Rawat, AA Franchetto and J Elavethil, Extracranial metastases of meningioma, *Neuroradiology*, 1995, 37, 38–41.

two-thirds of patients and the changes may be osteolytic or osteoblastic.[40] A rare form of primary interosseous meningioma, without dural connections, may be confused with Paget's disease.[41]

Meningiomas account for about a quarter of all primary intracranial tumours[42] but are said to have a low incidence of between $2-4/10^5$ and there is a two-fold excess of females with the condition.[43] The aetiology of these tumours is unknown but somatic mutations of a tumour-suppressor gene for meningioma on the long arm of chromosome 22 have been found in some patients.[44]

Three major radiological signs are characteristic of meningioma: an increase in vascular channels in bone, hyperostosis and erosion. When the tumour arises in the vault, one or more of the branches of the middle meningeal artery may be enlarged and this may be associated in some cases with enlargement of the foramen spinosum, through which the artery passes. The increased density seen on skull X-ray when hyperostosis is present may affect both the inner and outer tables and the appearance may be similar to that seen in an osteosarcoma.[45]

In the skeleton, meningiomas can be recognised by the combination of a pressure defect on the inner table of the skull which is associated with an impression formed by a large aberrant vessel arising from the middle meningeal supply (Figure 11.1). These signs may be recognised in a skull X-ray, but much more readily if the skull is broken, or the interior of the skull is examined with an endoscope, but they may also be recognised if there are hyperostotic changes on the outside of the skull.[46] The tumour may sometimes cause a pressure defect in the external table of the skull and then the hole in the head will indicate the need for further investigation. It is probable that the prevalence of meningiomas is higher than generally quoted in the clinical

[40] SM Yamada, S Yamada, H Takahashi, A Teramoto and K Matsumoto, Extracranially extended meningothelial meningiomas with a high MIB-1 index: a report of two cases, *Neuropathology*, 2004, 24, 66–71.

[41] RS Crawford, BK Kleinschmidt-DeMasters and KO Lilligei, Primary interosseous meningioma. Case report, *Journal of Neurosurgery*, 1995, 83, 912–915.

[42] EB Claus, ML Bondy, JM Schildkraut, JL Wiemelts, M Wrensch and PM Black, Epidemiology of intracranial meningioma, *Neurosurgery*, 2005, 57, 1088–1095.

[43] M Body and BL Ligon, Epidemiology and etiology of intracranial meningiomas: a review, *Journal of Neuro-Oncology*, 1996, 29, 197–205; FG Davis, V Kupelian, S Freels, B McCarthy and T Surawicz, Prevalence estimates for primary brain tumours in the United States by behaviour and major histology groups, *Neuro-Oncology*, 2001, 3, 152–158.

[44] K Akagi, H Kurahashi, N Arita, T Hayakawa, M Monden, T Mori, S Takai and T Nishisho, Deletion mapping of the long arm of chromosome 22 in human meningiomas, *International Journal of Cancer*, 1995, 17, 178–182.

[45] D Sutton, The abnormal skull, In: *A textbook of radiology and imaging* (edited by D Sutton), London, Churchill Livingstone, 1987, pp 1455–1483.

[46] See, for example, the case described (twice) by Anderson (T Anderson, A medical example of meningiomatous hyperostosis, *British Journal of Neurosurgery*, 1991, 5, 399–404, and An example of meningiomatous hyperostosis from medieval Rochester, *Medical History*, 1992, 36, 207–213).

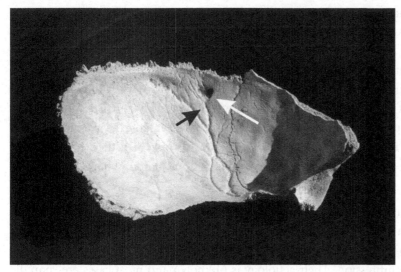

FIGURE 11.1. Internal surface of male skull showing a pressure lesion (white arrow) that has eroded through the external table. The lesion is fed by a large aberrant vessel (black arrow) from the middle meningeal distribution and almost certainly was a meningioma.

literature for the simple reason that only those that are of a sufficiently large size to produce symptoms will bring the patient to the attention of the neurosurgeons and prevalence or incidence studies based on hospital admissions will tend to under-estimate the true frequency. The few studies that have been carried out on skeletal assemblages suggest a prevalence that is several orders of magnitude greater than that found in modern studies. For example Campillo found five cases among 3000 skulls[47] giving a prevalence of 0.17% (95% CI 0.05–0.38%) while from a site in Hertfordshire, three cases were found in a small group of 167 medieval burials;[48] the prevalence at this site was 1.60% (95% CI 0.55–4.61%). Where the true prevalence of this condition lies must presently remain uncertain, but it would be a relatively simple exercise to investigate the matter by examining a large numbers of skulls.

Acoustic neuroma (Vestibular schwannoma): Acoustic neuromas are also benign tumours, in this case arising from the Schwann cells that cover the eighth cranial nerve.[49] These tumours typically arise inside the internal auditory canal in the petrous temporal bone in which situation they are described as being

---

[47] D Campillo, The possibility of diagnosing meningiomas in palaeopathology, *International Journal of Osteoarchaeology*, 1991, 1, 225–230.

[48] T Waldron, An unusual cluster of meningiomas? *International Journal of Osteoarchaeology*, 1998, 8, 213–217.

[49] The eighth nerve has two components, the vestibular and the cochlear nerve. The vestibular nerve innervates the semi-circular canals and is responsible for balance, while the cochlear nerve innervates the cochlea and is responsible for hearing. The vestibular nerve is also composed of two nerves, the inferior and superior vestibular nerves; acoustic neuromas arise most commonly from the inferior vestibular nerve

intracanalicular. As they grow they protrude from the canal into the cerebello-pontine angle and they may then compress the eighth nerve and also the seventh (facial) nerve which runs with the eighth in the internal auditory canal, and the anterior inferior cerebellar artery. With further growth, the fifth (trigeminal) nerve may be involved and the brainstem may become compressed; the final stage in development occurs when the fourth ventricle collapses and hydrocephalus ensues. As the tumour grows, it will enlarge the internal auditory canal,[50] including the internal auditory meatus by which the nerve exits the middle ear on the posterior surface of the petrous temporal bone.

Acoustic neuromas are rare tumours with an estimated incidence of between 1 and 20 cases per million[51] but this is almost certainly a considerable underestimate since many will go undetected if they do not cause significant symptoms of deafness or brain stem compression. Their aetiology is unknown and most cases are sporadic but a small proportion (<5%) are associated with neurofibromatosis 2 (NF2). The sporadic cases are almost always unilateral while those associated with NF2 are usually bilateral and may occur at a very young age;[52] the mean age of presentation in sporadic cases is between forty-five and sixty-four years and there is some evidence that the condition is becoming more frequent, and not simply as the result of better detection of cases.[53]

Acoustic neuromas are only likely to come to the palaeopathologist's attention if there is a considerable disparity between the size of the two internal acoustic meati although if it were possible to arrange for CT scanning of the skull, differences in the size of internal auditory canal might also suggest the diagnosis. If the diagnosis of acoustic neuroma is correct, then the condition has a very ancient lineage, having been suggested as a possible cause of changes in the right temporal bone of the Singa calvarium which is dated to >130 ka (kilo years).[54] Before being too confident about

(A Komatsuzaki and A Tsunoda, Nerve origin of the acoustic neuroma, *Journal of Laryngology and Otology*, 2001, 115, 376–379).

[50] A Tsunoda, O Tersaki, H Muraoka, A Komatsuzaki and Y Kimura, Cross-sectional shapes of the internal auditory canal in patients with acoustic neuromas, *Acta Otolaryngolica*, 2001, 121, 627–631.

[51] MF Howitz, C Johansen, M Tos, S Charabi and JH Olsen, Incidence of vestibular schwannoma in Denmark, 1977–1995, *American Journal of Otology*, 2000, 21, 690–694.

[52] T Miyakawa, N Kamada, T Kobayashi, K Hirano, K Fujii, Y Sasahara, Y Nagai and H Shinkai, Neurofibromatosis type 2 in an infant with multiple plexiform schwannomas as first symptom, *Journal of Dermatology*, 2007, 34, 60–64.

[53] JM Propp, BJ McCarthy, FG Davis and S Preston-Martin, Descriptive epidemiology of vestibular schwannomas, *Neuro-Oncology*, 2006, 8, 1–11.

[54] F Spoor, C Stringer and F Zonneveld, Rare temporal bone pathology of the Singa calvaria from Sudan, *American Journal of Physical Anthropology*, 1998, 107, 41–50.

the diagnosis in a skeleton, however, it would be absolutely necessary to have *both* petrous temporal bones for comparison.

> *Neurofibromatosis:* The two types of neurofibromatosis are now recognised to be clinically and genetically distinct[55] and only type 1 (NF1), also known as von Recklinghausen's disease affects bone.[56] The disease has a prevalence of at least 1 in 5000[57] and has an autosomal dominant mode of inheritance, the genetic defect being a mutation in the neurofibromin gene on chromosome 17q.[58] It is characterised by tumours of the peripheral nerves and skin pigmentation (café au lait spots). Bone abnormalities arise because of overgrowth or destruction of bone caused by the underlying neurofibromas. Osteoporosis is common, particularly of the load bearing bones,[59] and pathological fractures, especially of the tibia, with impaired healing and the development of a pseudarthrosis are frequent. Scoliosis affects one in ten of those with NF1, most commonly involving the lower cervical or upper thoracic spine. Typically there is a short curve, with distortion of the vertebrae and ribs and severe rotation.[60] In addition to the skeletal abnormalities, many other organ systems are affected.

Diagnosing NF1 in the skeleton would present many difficulties and it might be impossible to distinguish it from other skeletal dysplasias since the combination of abnormal bone growth, osteoporosis, scoliosis and pseudarthrosis are seldom likely to occur together. One attempt has been made to make the diagnosis in a Greek statue[61] although both the provenance and the diagnosis have been called into question[62] and the latter, at least, seems highly implausible. Joseph Merrick, the so-called Elephant Man, was for many years considered to have suffered from

---

[55]   RE Ferner, Neurofibromatosis 1 and neurofibromatosis 2: a twenty first century perspective, *Lancet Neurology*, 2007, 6, 340–351.

[56]   Friedrich Daniel von Recklinghausen 1833–1910.

[57]   SM Huson, DAS Compston, P Clark and PS Harper, A genetic study of von Recklinghausen's neurofibromatosis in south east Wales: prevalence, fitness, mutation rate, and effect of parental transmission on severity, *Journal of Medical Genetics*, 1989, 26, 704–711.

[58]   Neurofibromin is a tumour suppressor which is found in high concentrations in the nervous system (MM Daston, H Scrable, M Nordlund, AK Sturbaum, LM Nissen and N Ratner, The protein product of the neurofibromatosis type 1 gene is expressed at highest abundance in neurons, Schwann cells, and oligodendrocytes, *Neuron*, 1992, 8, 415–428).

[59]   T Kuorilehto, M Poyhonen, R Bloigu, J Heikkinen, K Vaananen and J Peltonen, Decreased bone mineral density and content in neurofibromatosis type 1: lowest local values are located in the load-carrying parts of the body, *Osteoporosis International*, 2005, 16, 928–936.

[60]   AH Crawford and N Bagamery, Osseous manifestations of neurofibromatosis in childhood, *Journal of Pediatric Orthopaedics*, 1986. 6, 72–88.

[61]   NK Ragge and FL Munier, Ancient neurofibromatosis, *Nature*, 1994, 368, 815.

[62]   D Gourevitch and MK Grmek, Enigmatic statue, *Nature*, 1994, 372, 228.

neurofibromatosis but latterly the diagnostic opinion has veered in favour of the Proteus syndrome[63] which is itself, associated with some skeletal anomalies.[64]

> *Spinal dysraphism (neural tube defect; spina bifida):* Spinal dysraphism is a term that includes a number of congenital spinal anomalies that result from defective closure of the neural tube early in fetal life and they all have in common the absence of some of the neural arches in the lower spine.[65] Spinal dysraphism may be open or closed.[66] Closed spinal dysraphism (CSD; spina bifida occulta) is a common condition and may affect up to 5% of the population and most usually involves L5 or S1. The condition is often clinically silent although in addition to the absence of several neural arches there are cutaneous abnormalities, such as lipoma, haemangioma, dermal sinus or a hairy patch overlying the lesion.

Open spinal dysraphism (OSD; spina bifida cystica or aperta) is subdivided into three groups: (1) meningocele without nerve tissue in the sac; (2) myelomeningocele in which spinal nerve tissue forms part of the sac and (3) rachischisis, in which there is a widely patent dorsal opening of the spine with or without residual cord tissue. Rachischisis is usually associated with anencephaly and is almost always rapidly fatal. Myelomeningocele is usually fatal within the first year of life if untreated and would have been universally fatal until quite recent times. The prevalence of myelomeningocele (and other neural tube defects) is about $115/10^5$ births but there is considerable geographical variation.[67]

It is not likely that children with OSD would have survived long in the past and it would be difficult to determine whether any infants in a skeletal assemblage actually had had the condition since the lamina may well not have fused together and it would be difficult to construct the entire spine for examination. Adults who had CSD would be recognised by a wide dorsal defect in the spine with an increased interpeduncular distance.[68]

> *Diastematomyelia:* Sometimes found in association with spina bifida, diastematomyelia is a rare condition in which the spinal cord is split into two by

---

[63] JA Tibbles and MM Cohen, The Proteus syndrome: the Elephant Man diagnosed, *British Medical Journal,* 1986, 293, 683–685.

[64] JT Tuner, MM Cohen and LG Biesecker, Reassessment of the Proteus syndrome literature: applications of diagnostic criteria to published cases, *American Journal of Medical Genetics,* 2004, 130A, 111–122.

[65] JG McComb, Spinal and cranial neural tube defects, *Seminars in Pediatric Neurology,* 1997, 4, 156–166.

[66] P Tortori-Donati, A Rossi and A Cama, Spinal dysraphism: a review of the neuroradiological features with embryological correlations and proposal for a new classification, *Neuroradiology,* 2000, 42, 471–491.

[67] EUROCAT Working Group, Prevalence of neural tube defects in 20 regions of Europe and the impact of prenatal diagnosis, 1980–1986, *Journal of Epidemiology and Community Medicine,* 1991, 45, 52–58.

[68] The distance between the medial borders of the pedicles.

the presence of a spicule of bone, fibrous tissue or cartilage oriented in the antero-posteriorly in the spinal canal, most often in the lumbar region.[69] It would be such fun to find a case, and would be an easy publication, and so it is worth carefully examining the spine of children in an assemblage in the hope of contributing the first historical case.

STONES AND CYSTS

Stones occur in both the biliary and urinary systems and are common, so the chances of finding them in burials are reasonably good, but only if the area of the skeleton where the abdominal and pelvic viscera were in life is sieved. Some care and experience will be needed to distinguish human from geological stones. The only cysts that might be encountered are those that result from hydatid disease, that is, infection with the dog tapeworm, *Echinococcus granulosus*.[70]

> *Gall stones:* Gall stones are extremely common, affecting about 10% of those over forty, and 30% of those over seventy.[71] They may be found either in the gall bladder itself or in the extra- or intra-hepatic bile ducts; the conditions are known, respectively, as choledocholithiasis or hepatolithiasis. Between 10 and 15% of those with gall bladder stones also have stones in the bile ducts.[72] The stones are composed either mainly of cholesterol, or of pigment. Cholesterol stones contain about 70% of cholesterol and when cut, have a radial structure and lines can be seen radiating from the centre of the stone to the periphery. They often have pigment at their centre and they range in colour from white to yellow. Pigment stones contain mostly calcium bilirubinate, the usual proportion being in the range 40–60%, with about 25–30% cholesterol. Most pigment stones are greenish-brown but there is a black variety which contains considerably more pigment and less cholesterol and they may also contain calcium carbonate and calcium phosphate. When pigment stones are cut, the brown stones have concentric layers of pigmented and non-pigmented material while black stones have a homogenous dark appearance throughout.[73]

[69] L Basauri, A Palma, A Zuleta, F Holzer and R Poblete, Diastematomyelia. Report of 10 cases, *Acta Neurochirurgica*, 1979, 51, 91–96.

[70] Hydatid disease is discussed in Chapter 6.

[71] BD Schirmer, KL Winters and RF Edlich, Cholelithiasis and cholecystitis, *Journal of Long Term Effects of Medical Implants*, 2005, 15, 329–338.

[72] S Tazuma, Epidemiology, pathogenesis, and classification of bile stones (common bile duct and intrahepatic), *Best Practice and Research Clinical Gastroenterology*, 2006, 20, 1075–1083.

[73] S Kim, S-J Myung, SS Lee, S-K Lee and M-H Kim, Classification and nomenclature of gallstones revisited, *Yonsei Medical Journal*, 2003, 44, 561–570.

Risk factors for the different types of stone vary somewhat. For cholesterol stones, major risk factors include being female and having a high body mass index.[74] This is reflected in the common medical saying that those with gall stones tend to be fat, fair, fertile and forty. Patients with cholesterol stones also tend to be younger than those with pigment stones, thus, patients under forty tend to have cholesterol stones, while those over seventy tend to have pigment stones and are also much more likely to have cirrhosis of the liver.[75]

Kidney and bladder stones: Stones may be found in all parts of the urinary tract and vary in size from a pin head to larger than a cricket ball; the largest ever recorded having been removed from the bladder of Sir Walter Ogilvie in 1808 and weighing in at 1.36 kg.[76] They also vary considerable in shape; bladder stones are often ellipsoidal with a well-defined nucleus and definite layers but they may also be asymmetric or tetrahedonal, especially if there are several stones packing together. Kidney stones are usually much more variable in shape, depending in which part of the kidney they develop. They are most commonly composed of calcium oxalate but may rarely be composed of uric acid, cystine, or triple phosphate (struvite stones).[77]

There is considerable variation in the prevalence of urinary stones, both geographical and historically. Calcium oxalate stones are nowadays much more common in the developed countries whereas stones composed of ammonium urate and calcium oxalate – so-called 'primitive stones' – are common in the middle and far east. These differences are largely dietary in origin but some genetic factors also seem to be involved.[78] In the developed countries, the prevalence of stone formation appears to be increasing, especially in females, and again, diet and related obesity have been blamed.[79]

Bladder stones have been causing symptoms since antiquity and a number of operations were devised to remove them. These involved entering the bladder either

[74] C Schafmayer, J Hartleb, J Tepel, S Albers, S Freitag, H Volzke, S Buch, M Seegar, B Timm, B Kremeer, UR Folsch, F Fandrich, M Krawczak, S Schreiber and J Hampe, Predictors of gallstone composition in 1025 symptomatic gallstones from Northern Germany, *BMC Gastroenterology*, 2006, 6, 36.

[75] AK Diehl, WH Schwesinger, DR Holleman, JB Chapman and WE Kurtin, Clinical correlates of gallstone composition: distinguishing pigment from cholesterol stones, *American Journal of Gastroenterology*, 1995, 90, 967–972.

[76] K Lonsdale, Human stone, *Science*, 1968, 159, 1199–1207. The mechanisms by which stones are formed are discussed by F Grases, A Costa-Bauzá and L García-Ferragut (Biopathological crystallization: a general view about the mechanism of renal stone formation, *Advances in Colloid and Interface Science*, 1998, 74, 169–194).

[77] MS Parmar, Kidney stones, *British Medical Journal*, 2004, 328, 1420–1424.

[78] A Trinchieri, Epidemiology of urolithiasis, *Archivio italiano di urologia, andrologia*, 1996, 68, 203–249.

[79] CD Scales, LH Curtis, RD Norris, WP Springhart, RL Sur, KA Schulman and GM Preminger, Changing gender prevalence of stone disease, *Journal of Urology*, 2007, 177, 979–982.

through the perineum or suprapubically, but with either approach, the risk of complications and death was extremely high.[80] During the latter part of the eighteenth century and throughout the nineteenth century, Norfolk had the reputation for the highest incidence of bladder stone in Great Britain and a notable school of lithotomists grew up there.[81]

Both kidney stones and bladder stones give rise to a considerable morbidity, causing pain and haematuria, infections and, in the case of bladder stones, urinary retention. Both kidney stones[82] and bladder stones[83] have been reported in human remains, including one from Norwich, although not from the period when the condition was at its peak.[84] More would probably be found if the soil from human graves was routinely sieved.

---

[80] H Ellis, A history of bladder stone, *Journal of the Royal Society of Medicine*, 1979, 72, 248–251.

[81] Between 1772 when the first patients were admitted to the Norfolk and Norwich Hospital, and 1909, 1,498 cases of bladder stone were operated on and 1,453 stones from these operations survive in the museum of the hospital, augmented by 204 others donated from other sources. The history of the Norfolk school can be read in: A Batty, The Norwich school of lithotomy, *Medical History*, 1970, 14, 221–259. At that date, the stones were still available for study.

[82] R Ciranni, L Giusti and G Fornaciari, Prostatic hyperplasia in the mummy of an Italian renaissance prince, *Prostat*, 2000, 45, 320–322.

[83] F Szalai and É Jávor, Finding of a bladder stone from the Avar Period in Southeast Hungary, *International Urology and Nephrology*, 1987, 19, 151–157.

[84] T Anderson, A recently discovered medieval bladder stone from Norwich, with a review of British archaeological bladder stones and documentary evidence for their treatment, *BJU International*, 2001, 88, 351–354.

12

Dental Disease

Teeth generally survive well and provide an important source of information not only about dental disease, but also the use of teeth as tools, and social habits such as artificial deformation. Tooth wear is widely used as means of ageing skeletons.[1] The diseases considered here include dental caries, ante-mortem tooth loss, periodontal disease, dental abscesses, calculus and enamel hypoplasia. A brief account will also be given of dental tumours.

CARIES

Caries[2] is the most common cause of oral pain and tooth loss.[3] It has almost certainly affected humankind from earliest times, although the site of the disease on the tooth has changed in relation to changes in the diet. Briefly, before the introduction of sugar into the diet, caries tended to appear at the cemento-enamel junction, or the appositional surfaces. Once sugar was widely available it affected the fissures on the molars more frequently than elsewhere, and this is the pattern that continues to this day although the widespread fluoridation of drinking water has reduced the prevalence of caries very considerably.[4] Those who can remember how painful caried teeth can be will not be surprised that attempts at treatment have an extremely long history.

---

[1] For further details, see S Hillson, *Dental anthropology*, Cambridge, Cambridge University Press, 1996.

[2] Caries is derived from a fifth declension Latin noun, *caries*, meaning decay and it has the same form in the singular as in the plural; species is another word with similar etymology.

[3] RH Selwitz, AI Ismail and NB Pitts, Dental caries, *Lancet*, 2007, 369, 51–59.

[4] These changes were elegantly described by WJ Moore and ME Corbett in a series of four classic papers that are required reading for all those interested in the subject: The distribution of dental caries in ancient British populations. I. Anglo-Saxon period, *Caries Research*, 1971, 5, 151–168; II. Iron Age, Romano-British and Mediaeval periods, *Ibid*, 1973, 7, 139–153; III. The 17th century, *Ibid*, 1875, 9, 163–175; IV: The 19th century, *Ibid*, 1976, 10, 401–414.

Fillings have a long usage often involving soft and easily malleable materials such as lead or tin, and amalgam fillings – a solution of one or more metals in mercury – were introduced in the early nineteenth century while nowadays, mercury-free fillings are gaining increasingly in popularity.[5] The study of human assemblages can add considerably to the knowledge of the history of practical dentistry and a typology of dental fillings has an obvious application in forensic anthropology.[6] There is no reason to doubt that ways to extract painful teeth were devised from remote antiquity and a number of fearsome instruments were invented for the purpose.[7] Unfortunately for palaeopathologists, there is no certain means of determining whether teeth lost before death were extracted or not.[8]

The development of caries is a multi-factorial process[9] that requires three things: a bacterial film (plaque), the presence of a fermentable carbohydrate and the production of acid. The bacteria that live on teeth are largely streptococci and lactobacilli[10] and they are encapsulated in an organic matrix that is known as a biofilm. They metabolise fermentable carbohydrates to produce weak organic acids that may eventually cause the local pH to fall below the level necessary to demineralise the tissues of the tooth. In its early stages, the demineralisation can be reversed by the uptake of calcium, phosphate or fluoride, but if these elements diffuse out of the tooth, then decay and cavitation ensue. Caries will develop or not depending on the balance between remineralisation and demineralisation.[11] Remineralisation is more likely to occur when the pH is restored by the saliva whereas demineralisation is encouraged by the persistence of the biofilm.

---

[5] Further details can be found in, for example: W Hoffman-Axthelm, *History of dentistry*, Chicago, Quintessence Publications, 1981. For a more journalistic read see: BW Weinberger, *The excruciating history of dentistry: toothsome tales and oral oddities from Babylon to braces*, New York, St Martin's Press, 1998.

[6] Three examples of dental practice in the late eighteenth to twentieth centuries can be found in DK Whittaker and AS Hargreaves, Dental restorations and artificial teeth in a Georgian population, *British Dental Journal*, 1991, 171, 371–376; RA Glenner, P Willey, PS Sledzik and EP Junger, Dental fillings in Civil War skulls: what do they tell us? *Journal of the American Dental Association*, 1996, 127, 1671–1677 and CW van Wyk, F Theunissen and VM Phillips, A grave matter – dental fillings of people buried in the nineteenth and twentieth centuries, *Journal of Forensic Odonto-stomatology*, 1990, 8, 15–30.

[7] Some probably did much more harm than good and the fact that individuals would nevertheless submit to their use, indicates the lengths to which they would go to get some relief from their pain. One of the most notorious extraction implements was the dental key which although a relative quick way to remove a caried molar, probably caused more injuries than all other implements combined. (JM Hyson, The dental key: a dangerous and barbarous instrument, *Journal of the History of Dentistry*, 2005, 53, 95–96.)

[8] DA Lunt, Evidence of tooth extraction in a Cypriot mandible of the Hellenistic or early Roman period, c. 150 BC to 100 AD, *British Dental Journal*, 1992, 173, 242–243.

[9] O. Fejerskov, Changing paradigms in concepts of dental caries: consequences for oral health care, *Caries Research*, 2004, 38, 182–191.

[10] The organisms present are mostly *Streptococcus mutans*, *Strep sobrinus* and various *Lactobacillus* species.

[11] JDB Featherstone, The continuum of dental caries – evidence for a dynamic disease process, *Journal of Dental Research*, 2004, 83, C38–C42.

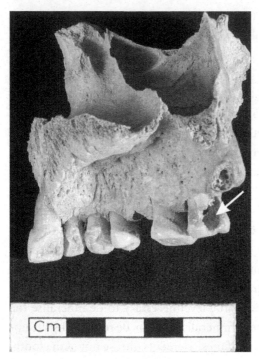

FIGURE 12.1 Male skull from medieval period showing massive caries (arrow) of right second molar.

Dental caries is typically seen first as a white or brown spot on the enamel which – unless reversed – will continue to develop and will destroy the enamel and the underlying dentine to form a cavity (Figure 12.1). The lesions vary in extent and may be found on any exposed tooth surface, and both deciduous and permanent teeth can be affected, and the prevalence of caries increases with age. If the root canal is exposed, infection may enter and form a periapical abscess or granuloma.

All types of caries should be recorded and there are several schemes for doing so;[12] methods of reporting the frequency of caries, and other dental disease are described in Chapter 13.

ANTE-MORTEM TOOTH LOSS

Teeth may be lost for a variety of reasons, including periodontal disease, trauma, extraction or scurvy, but periodontal disease accounts for the majority.[13] Tooth loss

[12] Perhaps the most widely used of the schemes for recording caries is that due to WJ Moore and ME Corbett (Distribution of dental caries in ancient British populations: I. Anglo-Saxon period, *Caries Research*, 1971, 151–168). For a more recent scheme see: S Hillson, Recording dental caries in archaeological human remains, *International Journal of Osteoarchaeology*, 2001, 11, 249–289.

[13] AK Al-Shammari, AK Al-Khabbaz, JM Al-Ansari, R Neiva and HL Wang, Risk indicators for tooth loss due to periodontal disease, *Journal of Periodontology*, 2005, 76, 1910–1918.

is nowadays more common in women than in men and increases with age,[14] and it frequently results in difficulties with chewing and malnutrition.[15]

It is simple to recognise whether a missing tooth has been lost before or after death. If the loss is post-mortem, then the socket will appear pristine with no evidence of remodelling, whereas, if the loss is ante-mortem, the socket will show some degree of remodelling. Where more than one tooth has been lost ante-mortem, it is possible to tell the order in which they were lost by the state of remodelling. Where the loss occurred several years before death, the jaw may be completely remodelled and in those who are completely edentulous, the mandible particularly may loose considerable bulk through resorption of bone and appear much smaller than normal.[16]

There is often no means of deciding how the teeth were lost although where there is extensive periodontal disease, it is reasonable to suppose that this was the major cause of any missing teeth. Similarly if the tooth loss is associated with evidence of trauma to the jaws, then it would not be unreasonable to assume that both can be attributed to the same cause.

The number of missing teeth must be counted, recorded and used as part of the assessment of total dental disease.

PERIODONTAL DISEASE

Periodontal disease is extremely common and in its mildest form – gingivitis – is said to affect between 50 and 90% of the population.[17] There are many other diseases that affect the periodontium – the tissues surrounding and supporting the teeth – but the inflammatory conditions of gingivitis and periodontitis are much the most common and both are caused by pathogenic bacteria in the dental plaque. Many bacteria are associated with periodontal disease including *Porphyromonas gingivalis*, *Tannerella forsythensis*, *Treponema denticola* and *Actonobacillus actinomycetemcomitans* (especially in young people), while some viruses and fungi, including *Candida albicans* have also been implicated.[18] The presence of bacteria, however, is a necessary but not sufficient cause of periodontal disease, a susceptible host is also required,

---

[14] FN Hugo, JB Hilgert, M da L de Sousa, DD da Silvan and GA Pucca, Correlation of partial tooth loss and edentulism in the Brazilian elderly, *Community Dentistry and Oral Epidemiology*, 2007, 35, 224–232.

[15] E Musacchio, E Perissinotto, P Binotto, L Sartori, F Silva-Netto, S Zambon, E Manzato, MC Corti, G Baggio and G Crepaldi, Tooth loss in the elderly and its association with nutritional status, socio-economic and lifestyle factors, *Acta Odontological Scandinavica*, 2007, 65, 78–86.

[16] J Pietrokovski, R Starinsky, B Arensburg and I Kaffe, Morphologic characteristics of bony edentulous jaws, *Journal of Prosthodontics*, 2007, 16, 141–147.

[17] GC Armitage, Periodontal diagnoses and classification of periodontal disease, *Periodontology 2000*, 2004, 34, 9–21.

[18] BL Pihlstrom, BS Michalowicz and NW Johnson, Periodontal diseases, *Lancet*, 2005, 366, 1809–1820.

the susceptibility probably being due to bleeding of the gums in response to the accumulation of plaque.[19] Both the host and the bacteria release cytokines that initiate the inflammatory process and this may result in the destruction of the alveolar bone.[20] The result is the formation of soft tissue pockets between the gums and the tooth root with loosening of the tooth, pain and discomfort and eventual loss of the tooth. Once a periodontal pocket forms and becomes filled with bacteria the process is largely irreversible. The link between systemic diseases such as cardiovascular disease, diabetes and pulmonary disease is clear, and since some of these are potentially fatal,[21] this may have been the reason that so many people were reported as having died of 'teeth' in the London Bills of Mortality.[22]

In the skeleton, periodontal disease is recognised by the recession of the alveolar margin which is also likely to show evidence of inflammation and remodelling, including pitting and new bone formation and the formation of a cylindrical cavity around the roots of affected teeth which must be differentiated from a periapical cavity (see below). Two types of bone loss can be recognised on X-ray and by simple inspection, horizontal and vertical,[23] but this distinction is not always made when reporting it in the skeleton. Clinically, the condition is said to be important when the depth of the periodontal pocket exceeds 3 mm, and when reporting periodontal disease in the skeleton it is best to measure the depth of the alveolar recession from the cemento-enamel junction to the alveolar margin. This can be done with a periodontal probe[24] which has markings at different intervals, with callipers, or with a simple homemade device. Either the average depth, or the range of depth (from least to greatest) can be recorded, or simply the number of individuals in whom at least one depth exceeds 3 mm.

DENTAL CALCULUS

Dental calculus is simply mineralised plaque, the predominant constituent of which is calcium phosphate. There are two forms of calculus, supra- and sub-gingival

---

[19] DF Kinane, Aetiology and pathogenesis of periodontal disease, *Annals of the Royal Australasian College of Dental Surgeons*, 2000, 15, 42–50.

[20] RC Page, The pathology of periodontal diseases that may affect systemic disease: inversion of a paradigm, *Annals of Periodontology*, 1998, 3, 108–120.

[21] RC Page, The etiology and pathogenesis of periodontitis, *Compendium of Continuing Education in Dentistry*, 2002, 23, 11–14.

[22] JH Clarke, Toothaches and death, *Journal of the History of Dentistry*, 1999, 47, 11–13.

[23] GS Goaz and SC White, *Oral radiology, principles and interpretations*, St Louis, Mosby, 1994.

[24] There are two types of markings on dental probes, the Williams markings which have circumferential lines at every millimetre or the Marquis markings which have alternating shades every 3 mm; instruments with Williams markings are much the more preferable.

depending on whether the calculus is on the crown of the tooth or the exposed roots and both forms are to be found in most adults. It develops in an alkaline environment[25] and so it tends to be found most often on the lingual surfaces of the lower anterior teeth, since this is the most alkaline area of the mouth. There is a close correlation between dental hygiene and the occurrence of calculus and populations that do not practice regular hygiene may have very extensive calculus formation[26] and this is evident in some assemblages.

When examined with the EM, remains of bacteria can be seen in calculus and there may be a wide array of other materials including pollen grains, fragments of plant remains, and animal hairs. All have been described in calculus from prehistoric human remains.[27] It is probably not the case, however, that the constituents of the diet could ever be accurately inferred from a study of calculus.

In life, calculus is firmly attached to the surface of the teeth, but it loosens during burial and may easily become detached. This process will be greatly accelerated by taking a toothbrush to the teeth and the use of a stiff brush to clean teeth – or indeed, any part of the human skeleton – should be avoided, and preferably banned.

Calculus is easily recognised as a greyish-white deposit on the teeth and it is probably not necessary to do more than simply record its presence or absence in the mouth (Figure 12.2). Since there is an inverse relationship between the degree of calculus and dental hygiene it may be possible to infer something about the latter from the former, and so some grading system from – say – minimal to extensive, could be justified.

There is theoretically an inverse relationship between calculus and caries; since the former depends on mineralisation (which requires and alkaline environment) and the latter on demineralisation (which requires an acid one), the two processes are incompatible. Both are frequently found together in the mouth, however, but if calculus forms over a caried tooth, the caries will be halted.

PERIAPICAL CAVITIES

It is by no means uncommon to find cavities at the apex of a tooth, which is frequently associated with other dental disease, including caries. The cavity is usually recognised

[25] C Dawes, Recent research on calculus, *New Zealand Dental Journal*, 1998, 94, 60–62.
[26] DJ White, Dental calculus: recent insights into occurrence, formation, prevention, removal and oral health effects of supragingival and subgingival deposits, *European Journal of Oral Science*, 1997, 105, 508–522.
[27] K Dobney and D Brothwell, Dental calculus: its relevance to ancient diet and oral ecology, In: *Teeth and anthropology* (edited by E Cruwys and RA Foley), BAR, Oxford, 1986, pp 52–82.

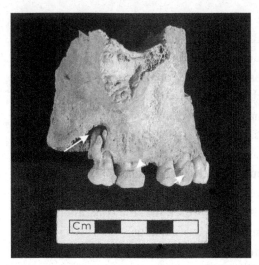

FIGURE 12.2 Male skull from medieval period showing dental calculus (short arrow), apical granuloma (long arrow) of right second molar and alveolar disease (arrow head).

because the anterior alveolar wall has been destroyed, leaving the cavity exposed. It is usual to describe such cavities as abscess cavities, but in fact, there are three types of periapical lesions that may present, cysts, granulomas and abscesses, of which half are granulomas, about a third abscesses and the remainder, cysts.[28] All result from infection of the dental pulp but the final outcome depends upon the virulence of the infection and the host's reaction to it. The dental pulp may be infected with a great variety of micro-organisms, both aerobic and anaerobic, but once infected, the infection can travel in one way only: along the root canal and through the apical foramen where it will induce an inflammatory response in the periapical tissues. The first response is the formation of a granuloma which will eventually lead to the development of a smooth-walled cavity with a diameter that is typically less than 3 mm. Granulomas commonly develop into cysts, in which the granulation tissue is replaced by fluid; a cyst has the same morphological characteristics as a granuloma, that is, it is circumscribed and smooth walled, but it typically larger than a granuloma (> 3 mm in size). An abscess forms when pus collects in the cavity of a granuloma. An acute abscess will affect the soft tissue surrounding the tooth and the pus will track through the bone to the soft tissues where it will burst, discharging pus, usually into the mouth. In the case of a chronic infection, the abscess may achieve a considerable size and form a fistula in the surrounding bone through which the pus will drain.

---

[28] PN Ramachandran Nair, G Pajarola and HE Schroeder, Types and incidence of human periapical lesions obtained with extracted teeth, *Oral Surgery, Oral Medicine, Oral Pathology, Oral Radiology, and Endodontics,* 1996, 81, 93–102.

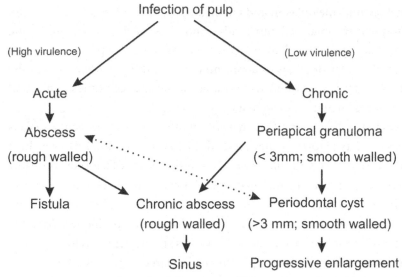

FIGURE 12.3 Scheme for differentiating different forms of apical lesions.

The fistula may be into the mouth or into the maxillary sinus, for example. It is impossible to differentiate an acute abscess from a periapical granuloma since both tend to be less than 3 mm in size, unless the walls of the cavity appear roughened, in which case it is more likely to be an acute abscess. A chronic abscess cavity will be larger and will be accompanied by a fistula; only the presence of the fistula makes the diagnosis certain.[29] (The relationship between these various lesions is shown in Figure 12.3.)

Despite appearances, apical granulomas, cysts and chronic abscesses usually cause only mild pain and have no systemic effects. Acute abscesses, on the other hand, are very painful and there is usually a feeling of general malaise. On rare occasions the effects are much more serious and become potentially life threatening.[30]

DEVELOPMENTAL DEFECTS OF ENAMEL

Dental enamel is closely related to hydroxyapatite but contains a number of impurities, such as carbonate substituting for phosphate in the crystal lattice. Enamel crystals are secreted by the ameloblasts together with a number of enamel proteins

[29] G Dias and N Tayles, 'Abscess cavity' – a misnomer, *International Journal of Osteoarchaeology*, 1997, 7, 548–554.
[30] SJ Thomas, C Hughes, C Atkinson, AR Ness and P Revington, Is there an epidemic of admissions for surgical treatment of dental abscesses in the UK? *British Medical Journal*, 2008, 336, 1219–1220.

including amelogenin, ameloblastin and enamelin. The enamel crystals grow in an incremental way and are organised into bundles known as prisms, each prism having cross-striations that represent a daily increment in growth. More prominent cross-striations occur a regular intervals of about nine days and these are known as the striae of Retzius.[31] The striae of Retzius terminate at the surface of the enamel and form a series of steps known as perikymata.[32]

Disturbances in the formation of enamel are common and can be seen as defects which can take a variety of forms. Causes include birth trauma,[33] low birth weight,[34] infections and a variety of systemic illnesses.[35] In addition genetic factors are probably involved,[36] and there is also a rare inherited defect known as amelogenesis imperfecta (AI) which occurs at a rate of between 0.6 and 1.4/1000.[37] Caries, attrition and trauma may all hide the defects and, given the varied and non-specific aetiology, the probability of attributing the correct cause (or causes) to the defects is low.[38]

The defects in enamel may appear as pits, furrows or large areas of missing enamel. The furrow form defects are usually referred to a linear enamel hypoplasia which are recognised on the tooth as increased spacing between perikymata. Clinically, it is the more severe types of enamel defect that attract attention,[39] whereas archaeologists tend to concentrate very much on the linear type of defect which is usually taken as an indication of some kind of systemic stress.[40] Enamel hypoplasia is both of considerable antiquity[41] and very common, affecting up to half of all children in

[31] Gustaf Magnus Retzius 1842–1919. He was the son of Anders Retzius (1796–1860) who devised the cranial index.
[32] JP Simmer and J C-C Hu, Dental enamel formation and its impact on clinical dentistry, *Journal of Dental Education*, 2001, 65, 896–905.
[33] WK Seow, Enamel hypoplasia in the primary dentition: a review, *ASDC Journal of Dentistry for Children*, 1991, 58, 441–452.
[34] JM Fearne, EM Bryan, AM Elliman, AH Brook and DM Williams, Enamel defects in the primary dentition of children weighing less than 2000g, *British Dental Journal*, 1990, 168, 433–437.
[35] JJ Pindborg, Aetiology of developmental enamel defects not related to fluorosis, *International Dental Journal*, 1982, 32, 123–134.
[36] S Taji, T Hughes, J Rogers and G Townsend, Localised enamel hypoplasia of human deciduous canines: genotype or environment? *Australian Dental Journal*, 2000, 45, 83–90.
[37] B Bäckman, Inherited enamel defects, In: *Dental enamel* (edited by DJ Chadwick and G Cardew), Ciba Foundation Symposium 205, Chichester, Wiley, 1997, pp 175–186.
[38] WK Seow, Clinical diagnosis of enamel defects: pitfalls and practical guidelines, *International Dental Journal*, 1997, 47, 173–182.
[39] K Mathu-Muju and JT White, Diagnosis and treatment of molar incisor hypomineralization, *Compendium*, 2006, 27, 604–611.
[40] T King, LT Humphrey and S Hillson, Linear enamel hypoplasias as indicators of systemic physiological stress: evidence from two known age-at-death and sex populations from postmedieval London, *American Journal of Physical Anthropology*, 2005, 128, 547–549.
[41] D Guatelli-Steinberg, CS Larsen and DL Hutchinson, Prevalence and the duration of linear enamel hypoplasia: a comparative study of Neandertals and Inuit foragers, *Journal of Human Evolution*, 2004, 47, 65–84.

some communities.[42] If the dentition is complete it is possible to date the defects with considerable accuracy by matching up the defects in the crowns of different teeth.[43]

> *Fluorosis:* Fluoride ions occur naturally in most drinking waters and they readily become incorporated into the dental enamel of developing teeth.[44] If the concentration is above about 0.5 ppm in the drinking water, defects in the enamel may be noted. These range from white lines or larger white patches to yellow-brown staining at higher concentrations; the molars are more often affected than the incisors.[45]

ECTOPIC TEETH AND MORPHOLOGICAL VARIATION

Teeth may sometimes be found in unusual places, and they are referred to as being ectopic. They are found in a variety of positions within the mouth and also sometimes within the maxillary sinus,[46] or the nasal cavity.[47] Teeth may also be transposed, that is, there is an interchange in the normal position of two permanent teeth. Most often the maxillary canine transposes with the first premolar or, more rarely, with the lateral incisor.[48] Finally, impacted teeth may migrate through the lower jaw; this is a rare event involving most often, the lateral incisor, canine and second premolar.[49]

Variations in the morphology of the teeth are very common[50] and may occur in both the permanent and deciduous dentition.[51] Variants include microdontia,

[42] AH Goodman, LH Allen, GP Hernandez, A Amador, LV Arriola, A Chávez and GH Pelto, Prevalence and age at development of enamel hypoplasias in Mexican children, *American Journal of Physical Anthropology*, 1987, 72, 7–19.

[43] S Hillson, *Teeth*, Cambridge, Cambridge University Press, 2005, pp 169–176.

[44] C Robinson, S Connell, J Kirkham, SJ Brookes, RC Shore and AM Smith, The effect of fluoride on the developing tooth, *Caries Research*, 2004, 38, 268–276.

[45] Other intrinsic and extrinsic causes of tooth discolouration are reviewed by A Watts and M Addy (Tooth discolouration and staining: a review of the literature, *British Dental Journal*, 2001, 190, 309–316).

[46] T Baykul, H Doğru, H Yasan and M Cina Askoy, Clinical impact of ectopic teeth in the maxillary sinus, *Auris, Nasus, Larynx*, 2006, 33, 277–281.

[47] MT Cobourne, KL Bloom, KE Harley and SR Porter, An unusual dental cause of nasal discharge: a case report, *International Journal of Paediatric Dentistry*, 1996, 6, 187–189.

[48] Y Shapira and MM Kuftinec, Maxillary tooth transpositions: characteristic features and accompanying dental anomalies, *American Journal of Orthodontics and Dentofacial Orthopedics*, 2001, 119, 127–134.

[49] Y Shapira and MM Kuftinec, Intrabony migration of impacted teeth, *Angle Orthodontics*, 2003, 73, 738–743.

[50] T Ooshima, R Ishida, K Mishima and S Sobue, The prevalence of developmental anomalies of teeth and their association with tooth size in the primary and permanent dentitions of 1650 Japanese children, *International Journal of Paediatric Dentistry*, 1996, 6, 87–94.

[51] There is some dispute as to whether anomalies in the deciduous teeth and the permanent teeth are related. See, for example, RS Whittington and CS Durward, Survey of anomalies in primary teeth and their correlation with the permanent dentition, *New Zealand Dental Journal*, 1996, 92, 4–8, and HJ Edgar and

macrodontia, peg-shaped teeth and variations in the form of the dental crowns or roots. Over thirty such variations have been described by dental anthropologists and there are some elaborate scoring systems.[52] None of the variations is strictly pathological although – as already noted – changes in dental morphology may accompany some systemic diseases.

DENTAL TUMOURS

Tumours may arise from any of the odontogenic tissues and may be either benign[53] or malignant,[54] although malignant tumours are rare. A number of cystic lesions may also occur of which the dentigerous cyst is the most common.[55] Many odontogenic tumours are asymptomatic but they may become sufficiently large to cause pain and swelling, facial disfigurement and other dental problems.[56]

> *Benign tumours:* Odontomas account for two-thirds of all benign dental tumours. They include various dental tissues, including dentine and enamel and half are associated with impacted teeth. They form between the roots of teeth and may cause resorption of adjacent teeth and they are usually discovered on X-ray.[57] Ameloblastomas may also be associated with impacted teeth. They are slowly growing tumours and typically present between the ages of thirty and fifty as a painless mass in the jaw, the mandible being much more frequently involved than the maxilla.[58] The mass may erode through the jaw and involve local soft

LR Pease, Correlations between deciduous and permanent tooth morphology in a European American sample, *American Journal of Physical Anthropology*, 2007, 133, 726–734, for a positive and a negative view, respectively.

[52] They are well and voluminously described by R Scott and CG Turner, *The anthropology of modern human teeth: dental morphology and its variation in recent human populations*, New York, Cambridge University Press, 1997.

[53] JA Regezi, Odontogenic cysts, odontogenic tumors, fibroosseous, and giant cell lesions of the jaws, *Modern Pathology*, 2002, 15, 331–341.

[54] PJ Slootweg, Malignant odontogenic tumors: an overview, *Mund- Kiefer- und Gesichtschirurgie*, 2002, 6, 295–302.

[55] BL Dunfee, O Sakai, R Pistey and A Gohel, Radiologic and pathologic characteristics of benign and malignant lesions of the mandible, *Radiographics*, 2006, 26, 1751–1768.

[56] SJ Theodorou, DJ Theodorou and DJ Sartoris, Imaging characteristics of neoplasms and other lesions of the jawbones. Part 1. Odontogenic tumors and tumorlike lesions, *Clinical Imaging*, 2007, 31, 114–119.

[57] JA Regezi, DA Kerr and RM Courtney, Odontogenic tumors: analysis of 706 cases, *Journal of Oral Surgery*, 1978, 36, 771–778.

[58] RA Zwahlen and KW Grätz, Maxillary ameloblastomas: a review of the literature and of a 15-year database, *Journal of Craniomaxillofacial Surgery*, 2002, 30, 273–279.

tissues and it may also erode the roots of adjacent teeth and the tumours may be difficult to differentiate from malignant lesions without the aid of histology.[59] Cementoblastomas are rare but may most often be found at the apex of the first mandibular molars;[60] on X-ray they appear as rounded, well demarcated sun-burst opacities with a radiolucent rim.[61]

Malignant lesions: Odontogenic carcinomas are rare but aggressive with cortical destruction. Ameloblastomas may rarely undergo malignant change and they may achieve considerable size with a great deal of bony destruction.[62] As with other tumours, there is great difficulty in arriving at a definitive diagnosis, especially in the absence of any histology, and in suspected cases, the help of a dental radiologist and pathologist is likely to be of the greatest assistance.

DENTAL CYSTS

A solitary bone cyst may be the result of trauma which has led to bleeding into the bone, while primordial cysts result when a dental follicle fails to develop and undergoes cystic degeneration. Neither is likely to be recognised in the absence of radiography.

The most common type of cyst (apart from the periapical cyst discussed above) is the dentigerous cyst. This forms within the lining of the dental follicle and fluid accumulates between the follicular epithelium and the crown of the developing tooth. Dentigerous cysts occur most often around an unerupted third molar, usually in the mandible. Although they are usually painless, they may expand to considerable size and cause expansion of the jaws.[63] Bilateral cysts are very rare and generally occur in the context of some systemic disease.[64] Dentigerous cysts are rare in young

[59] M Minami, T Kaneda, H Yamamoto, K Ozawa, Y Itai, M Ozawa, K Yoshikawa and Y Sasaki, Ameloblastoma in the maxillomandibular region: MR imaging, *Radiology*, 1992, 184, 389–393.

[60] RB Brannon, CB Fowler, WM Carpenter and RL Corio, Cementoblastoma: an innocuous neoplasm? A clinicopathologic study of 44 cases and review of the literature with special emphasis on recurrence, *Oral Surgery, Oral Medicine, Oral Pathology, Oral Radiology and Endodontics*, 2002, 93, 311–320.

[61] T Kaneda, M Minami and T Kurabayashi, Benign odontogenic tumors of the mandible and maxilla, *Neuroimaging Clinics of North America*, 2003, 13, 495–507.

[62] AL Weber, C Bui and T Kaneda, Malignant tumors of the mandible and maxilla, *Neuroimaging Clinics of North America*, 2003, 13, 509–524.

[63] RJ Scholl, HM Kellett, DP Neumann and AG Lurie, Cysts and cystic lesions of the mandible: clinical and radiologic-histopathologic review, *Radiographics*, 1999, 19, 1107–1124.

[64] DQ Freitas, LM Tempest, E Sicoli and FC Lopes-Neto, Bilateral dentigerous cysts: review of the literature and report of an unusual case, *Dentomaxillofacial Radiology*, 2006, 35, 464–468.

children[65] and may rarely undergo malignant change,[66] sometimes in very young children.[67]

[65]   AL Counts, LA Kochis, J Buschman and TD Savant, An aggressive dentigerous cyst in a seven-year-old child, *ASDC Journal of Dentistry for Children*, 2001, 68, 268–271.

[66]   T Yasuoka, K Yonemoto, Y Kato and N Tatematsu, Squamous cell carcinoma arising in a dentigerous cyst, *Journal of Oral and Maxillofacial Surgery*, 2000, 58, 900–905.

[67]   SH Gulbranson, JD Wolfrey, JM Raines and BP McNally, Squamous cell carcinoma arising in a dentigerous cysts in a 16-month-old girl, *Otolaryngology-Head and Neck Surgery*, 2002, 127, 463–464.

13

An Introduction to Epidemiology

Having recognised and diagnosed disease in an assemblage, the palaeopathologist will wish to transmit the findings to an audience and in doing so, will almost certainly want to present the frequency with which the various diseases have occurred in the material being studied. These frequencies might then be compared with others from other sites to see how they might have changed over time and place, but it is unlikely that they will be directly comparable with modern-day frequencies for reasons that will be explained later. In this chapter, some methods for presenting and comparing data will be described. Those who would like to explore these matters in greater detail are referred elsewhere.[1]

DISEASE FREQUENCY

There are two main measures of disease frequency, incidence and prevalence, and they differ in some important respects notwithstanding, that the terms are often used interchangeably, even by those who should know better.

Incidence is the number of new cases that arise in a population at risk over a specified time; thus:

$$I = \frac{n}{N}$$

where I = incidence, n = number of new cases, and N = population at risk. Incidence always has a time base, and is usually expressed as so many cases per 10^5

---

[1] There are some useful introductory texts to epidemiology, the most helpful of which are probably: D Coggon, G Rose and DJP Barker, *Epidemiology for the uninitiated*, 5th edition, London, BMJ Books, 2003; R Bonia, R Beaglehole and TJ Kjellström, *Basic epidemiology*, 2nd edition, Geneva, WHO, 2006. Palaeoepidemiology is considered in: T Waldron, *Palaeoepidemiology. The measure of disease in the human past*, Walnut Creek, Left Coast Press, 2007.

per month, or year, whichever is the most suitable time frame for the disease under consideration.

Prevalence, on the other hand, is simply the number of cases in the group being studied; that is:

$$P = \frac{n}{N}$$

where P = prevalence, n = number of cases, and N = number in the study group. Prevalence has no time base and on this account is not strictly a rate, although it is still almost always referred to as such.

The relationship between incidence and prevalence is given approximately as follows:

$$P \approx I \times D$$

where P = prevalence, I = incidence, and D = the duration of the disease.[2] It can readily be seen that for diseases that have a very short duration, such as many of the childhood infections, prevalence and incidence may be approximately equal, whereas for diseases with a long duration – such as osteoarthritis – the prevalence will be several times the incidence.

Incidence

The incidence of a disease is determined by means of a follow-up, or cohort study. In this type of study, a population – sometimes referred to as a cohort[3] – is defined and then followed up over a period during which, the number of new cases of the disease is counted. The study population and the length of the follow-up period are both largely determined by the nature of the disease under consideration. For example, studying the incidence of measles in children aged five to ten would require that the cohort was comprised of such children and the follow-up period would be for a few months during the time when the infection was most likely to occur, that is in late winter and early spring. On the other hand, determining the incidence of

---

[2] A more accurate relationship would need to take account of those who are lost to the population in question, either through migration, death or recovery, and those who enter the population from outside who may or may not have the disease of interest.

[3] A cohort was originally a unit (composed of six centuries) of the Roman army. Epidemiologically it was first defined as all those born on the same date: nowadays it has the much more general meaning used in the text.

Table 13.1. *Hypothetical data for study of archaeology and skin cancer*

Cohort	Skin cancer	No skin cancer	Total
1. Field archaeologists	13	762	770
2. Non-archaeologists	3	870	873
3. Other archaeologists	4	910	914

Relative risk for cohorts 1:2 = 4.9 (95% CI 1.4–17.1%)
Relative risk for cohorts 1:3 = 3.8 (95% CI 1.2–11.6%)
Relative risk for cohorts 2:3 = 0.8 (95% CI 0.2–3.5%)

heart disease in middle-aged men would require that the study group was selected from those fitting into that category and the follow-up period would be substantially longer, most likely at least a year. In both cases, those who already had the disease under study would not be entered into the cohort because, by definition, they could not be *new* cases.[4] The incidence would then be simply calculated as shown in the first equation above.

Relative risk (risk ratio): A follow-up study can also be used to estimate the risk of developing a particular condition following some kind of exposure, or indulging in a certain habit. Many studies of this kind have been carried out to investigate the effects of smoking, for example. Let us suppose that we are concerned that exposure to sunlight on archaeological digs may increase the risk of skin cancer. We might recruit two cohorts, one of archaeologists, and one of non-archaeologists and determine how many of them developed skin cancer over a certain period.[5] We might be more sophisticated and have an additional cohort, that is, of archaeologists who did not carry out field work and use them as an extra reference group. Let us further suppose that we are actually able to carry out the study, and that we obtain the results as shown in Table 13.1. From this table we can see that the risk of developing skin cancer if

---

[4] Modern epidemiologists are tending to relax this requirement somewhat, considering that a second heart attack, for example, *is* a new episode, albeit not the first. This could not be permitted where having the disease once confers immunity from a second attack, as would almost certainly be the case in the measles example.

[5] Since we are hypothetically studying a disease that takes many years to develop, we would probably wish to carry out what is known as an historical cohort study, or a retrospective cohort study. In this case, we would construct our cohort from archaeologists who were working – say – thirty or forty years ago and determine how many had developed skin cancer over this period. For further details of this technique see any of the texts referred to in note 1 of this chapter.

you are a field archaeologist is 13/770 and if you not an archaeologist at all, it is 3/873; the relative risk (RR), therefore, is:

$$\frac{(13/770)}{(3/873)} = \frac{(13 \times 873)}{(3 \times 770)} = \frac{11349}{2310} = 4.9$$

Thus, the field archaeologists have an approximately five times risk of developing skin cancer compared with the non-archaeologists. It is actually better to include the 95% confidence interval (CI) when giving any epidemiological data and in this case, the risk is 4.9 with a 95% CI of 1.4–17.1%.[6] If the field archaeologists are compared with the non-field archaeologists, then the relative risk is 3.8 (95% CI 1.2–11.6%).[7]

These data, if real, would suggest that field archaeologists have a risk of contracting skin cancer that is about five times that of non-archaeologists and a relative risk of such a magnitude would excite considerable media attention and, no doubt, brief fame for the investigators. More importantly, the likelihood of further grants to repeat and refine the work. Before getting unduly concerned, however, it is worth considering what the *absolute risk* is. The non-archaeologists have an incidence of skin cancer of 3.5 per 1000 while the field archaeologists' incidence is about 17 per 1000 which means there would be an extra 13.6 cases per 1000 archaeologists, indicating that even with a large relative risk, the great majority of archaeologists will still *not* get skin cancer. Absolute risks are almost always smaller than the corresponding relative risks would appear to indicate and on this account, are seldom stressed by either researchers or media.

Prevalence

Prevalence is estimated very simply by counting the number of individuals in a study population with the disease of interest, and the means of doing so is by carrying out what is known as a cross-sectional study. For example, suppose we wish to study asthma among university students. We would identify a university which would agree to collaborate, recruit as many students from the student body as we deemed necessary and then determine by some means or other, which of them had asthma.

---

[6] The 95% CI is the value between which the estimate would fall on 95 of 100 occasions. The fact that neither of the 95% CIs for the relative risk include unity, indicates that the risk is statistically significant, that is $p < 5\%$.

[7] The relative risk for the non-archaeologists and the other archaeologists is 0.8 (95% CI 0.2–3.5%). Since, in this case, the 95% CI includes unity, this difference is not significant.

We might do this by asking them to complete a questionnaire, or by carrying out lung function tests if we had the means to do so. We might then find that of 3764 students who had taken part in the study, 298 had asthma, giving a prevalence of 7.9% (95% CI 7.1–8.8); this is referred to as the point prevalence. It might occur to us, however, that some of the students with asthma could have been absent during the time of the study because they were unwell and we might, therefore, decide to repeat the study. This time we manage to recruit 3657 students, and of these, 312 have asthma. The prevalence on this occasion is 8.5% and the 95% CI 7.7–9.5%. The mean of the two estimates gives us a better indication of the 'true' prevalence, which is now 8.2% (95% CI 7.6–8.9%), and this mean is referred to as the period prevalence.

It should be obvious that of these two measures of disease frequency, only prevalence can be estimated for disease occurring in human remains since there is no way at all that one can determine either the population at risk, or the number of new cases.[8] In effect, every time one examines a skeletal assemblage, one is carrying out a cross-sectional study and any estimates of disease frequency are point prevalence.

Unfortunately, most skeletal assemblages span a very long period, often several centuries, which means that it is impossible to detect any short term fluctuations that might have occurred, since the prevalence obtained is simply the mean over the whole period. Further, it is unlikely that the prevalence obtained from a skeletal assemblage reflects the prevalence that obtained among the living population from which the skeletons were drawn, except in the case of those diseases that do not contribute to death. Even where it seems reasonable to conclude that the prevalence is equivalent to that in the once living population, unfortunately the data cannot be directly compared with those from modern populations.[9]

---

[8] It is also regrettably the case that it is impossible to estimate any of the other rates that are of interest to modern epidemiologists. For example, it would be of the greatest interest to calculate stillbirth rates or infant mortality rates for a skeletal assemblage, but since both depend upon knowing the number of *live* births for the denominator, this cannot be done, unless these data are known from other sources such as parish records.

[9] The reason that it is not possible to compare the prevalence of disease in an assemblage with modern prevalences is due to the different techniques that are used in modern epidemiology. To begin with, it is very unusual for modern epidemiologists to use the complete population at their disposal and they will almost always use a sample drawn more or less at random and extrapolate the results to the whole population. And their target populations will also vary considerably; thus they may study a population sample; a sample drawn from a general practice register (or registers); a hospital based population, either in-patient or out-patient; or a factory or industry population. The group chosen for study is often nowadays referred to as the study-base and it is important to know the origin of the study-base before making comparisons between modern studies. The other difficulty that will arise is that different methods may be used to diagnose the disease being considered: the diagnosis may be based on clinical examination; autopsy findings; X-ray results; or questionnaires. Again, the method of ascertaining cases must be known before making comparisons of any sort; it must be clearly understood that the basis of comparison is to compare like with like and this is by no means always as easy as it sounds. Even if it is not possible to

Table 13.2. *Age-specific prevalence of a disease in two hypothetical populations*

Age group (years)	A			B		
	n	N	P	n	N	P
25–	0	112	0	0	61	0
35–	3	137	2.2	1	72	1.4
45–	16	217	7.4	5	111	4.5
55–	28	301	9.3	12	207	5.8
65–	64	452	14.2	47	263	17.9
Total	111	1219	9.1	65	477	13.6

n = number of cases
N = total number in age group
P = prevalence (%)
Common odds ratio = 0.93 (A:B)

The prevalence that we have been discussing so far is known as the crude prevalence, because it takes no account of the structure of the study-base, and, therefore, is not a suitable statistic to use for comparative purposes. The reason is obvious. Many diseases are either age or sex dependent and unless the structure of the two populations being compared is similar in age and sex, error is bound to be introduced. One way around this problem is to calculate age and sex-specific prevalences and then directly compare these. This process is rather complicated and involves too many comparisons. A better way is to use either direct or indirect standardisation, or to calculate the common odds ratio. Whatever method is used, the end result is a summary statistic that can be compared and tested for significance. It is perfectly permissible to standardise archaeological prevalences, but probably the most satisfactory solution is to compute the common odds ratio. I will briefly describe this method.[10]

Consider the two populations shown in Table 13.2 where the age-specific prevalences for the disease under study are shown. The crude prevalence in B is 13.5%,

compare archaeological data with modern data quantitatively, it is, nevertheless, valid to make qualitative comparisons. For example, we know that the prevalence of osteoarthritis increases with age and that the condition tends to be slightly more common in females than in males, at least in the older age groups. Now although prevalences found in a skeletal assemblage cannot be directly compared with modern data they should, however, reflect the trends in the modern data. Thus, if it was found that the prevalence of osteoarthritis *decreased* with increasing age, or was much higher in males than in females, this should throw considerable doubt on the validity of the archaeological data, and it would be best to ignore them and move onto something else.

[10] Methods of standardisation are described – often at considerable length – in all texts on modern epidemiology, and those who wish to find out about them are encouraged to consult them.

compared with 9.1% in A, suggesting that the disease is more frequent in B than in A. Except for the oldest age group, however, the prevalence is greater in B than in A, which is somewhat counter-intuitive. To compare the prevalences using the common odds ratio we can proceed as follows. The odds ratio[11] for the 35-year-olds is:

$$\frac{3}{134} \Big/ \frac{1}{71} = \frac{3 \times 71}{134} = 1.59$$

We can continue the process for each of the age groups (ignoring the youngest as the prevalence in both populations is zero) and arrive at the following:

$$\frac{213 + 1696 + 5460 + 13824}{134 + 1055 + 3276 + 18236} = \frac{21193}{22701} = 0.93$$

The common odds ratio is thus very close to unity, indicating that there is no significant – or indeed, any other – difference between the two populations with respect to this particular disease, the apparent increased prevalence in B being largely due to the high prevalence in the oldest age group.[12] One drawback with the common odds ratio, or any other method of standardisation is that it can be used only to compare two populations; if it is required to compare more than two, then this must be done in pairwise steps, A:B; A:C; and B:C, for example.

Outcome variables

One other potential source of difficulty when making comparisons relates to the outcome variables under consideration. With skeletal assemblages, the outcome variable is most likely to be a disease but it may be a normal variant, such as six lumbar vertebra, or a congenital abnormality such as transitional vertebra. For the comparison to be valid, the means by which the outcome variables are ascertained must be the same, that is to say, the diagnostic criteria (in the case of a disease) must be the same for all the populations being compared. Let us suppose that we wish to compare the prevalence of rheumatoid arthritis in two modern populations as reported in the clinical literature. We will already have checked to make sure that the populations are similar in age and sex (or that some summary statistic has been used

---

[11]   The odds of having the disease are 3/(137 − 3); do not confuse with the *risk* of having it, which is 3/137.

[12]   In this example, the common odds ratio is obtained comparing the prevalence of A with the prevalence of B; to compare the prevalence of B with that of A, the simplest way is to take the reciprocal of the common odds ratio already obtained, which is 1.08. There is, of course, still no difference between the two, but the magnitude of the common odds ratio will differ depending on which prevalences are first put into the equation.

to allow for any differences) and we find that the prevalence in one population is twice that in the other. This would certainly be interesting and would prompt a search for factors that might explain it. The statistician with whom we are discussing these results over coffee asks naively whether the method of diagnosing the disease was the same in both studies and when we check this carefully again we find that in one population the disease was diagnosed on the basis of a clinical examination, and in the second, on the basis of X-ray changes. As clinical signs appear earlier than the X-ray changes it is little surprise that the prevalence in the clinical study seems greater than in the radiological, and we hastily take the paper we have prepared out of the post.

The way in which epidemiologists try to achieve consistency with respect to outcome variables is to use operational definitions which have been alluded to in earlier chapters. As we have seen, diagnosis in palaeopathology differs in many respects from either clinical or radiological diagnosis and different criteria have to be used, although these must obviously be clinically based. The criteria for making an operational definition *must* be agreed before a study is undertaken and *must* be strictly adhered to. There is a tendency for diagnostic creep[13] to occur in a study in which the number of cases seems to be dismally small, and so it is best to prepare a check list of those criteria that must be satisfied before an operational definition is made, making sure that *only* those cases that fulfil the criteria as defined are admitted to the study. Unfortunately, as we have already seen, diagnosis in palaeopathology is not likely to be very accurate and it is *very* likely that different palaeopathologists will arrive at different conclusions, even when faced with the same material. Before making any comparisons with published studies, it is vital that you know what criteria were used to make the diagnosis; if they differ from yours, then any comparison will be invalid. Equally unfortunately, there are virtually no operational definitions that have been universally – or even minimally – agreed for use in palaeopathology and this does make comparative work extremely problematic. One of the purposes of this book is to stress the use of operational definitions and perhaps persuade others to use them, in the suggested or modified form.

Missing Data

It is almost unheard of that all the skeletons in an assemblage to be intact and so when calculating prevalence, some allowance has to be made for missing data;

---

[13] Diagnostic creep occurs when stringent criteria are gradually relaxed to increase the number of cases recruited into a study.

this is particularly important when deciding on the denominator in a calculation.[14] Imagine that we have an assemblage of 380 adult skeletons and 11 have osteoarthritis (OA) of the elbow. We might assume that the prevalence is:

$$11/380 = 2.9\% \ (95\% \ CI \ 1.6 - 5.1\%).$$

We find from our notes, however, that 40 of the skeletons have no elbows and we reason, quite rightly, that they cannot appear in the denominator, and so our calculation now looks like this:

$$P = 11/340 = 3.2\% \ (05\% \ CI \ 1.8 - 5.7\%).$$

The prevalence is slightly higher than before, as we would expect. A further complication arises, however, when we check our notes for a second time and discover that there are 67 skeletons with a single elbow, and we decide that they, too, must be eliminated from the calculation. At the third attempt, then, having subtracted the 67 single elbowed skeletons from the denominator above, the calculation seems to be:

$$P = 11/273 = 4.0\% \ (95\% \ CI \ 2.3 - 7.1\%).$$

Finally, one more check shows that 3 of the 67 skeletons with one elbow actually have OA of the one that is extant, and so they can go in the denominator; our final calculation is therefore:

$$P = 11/276 = 3.9\% \ (95\% \ CI \ 2.2 - 7.0).$$

In this case then, when calculating the prevalence of OA, the denominator is the number of paired joints present, plus the number of single joints with the disease. The numerator is, of course, the total number of diseased joints. With non-paired elements, the situation is more straightforward since the denominator is always likely to be the number of extant elements.

Overall Prevalence

Many prevalence calculations will use the number of particular elements – joints, vertebrae, femurs – as the denominator but it would be useful to know what the

---

[14] The first step in making a prevalence calculation is to decide on the denominator which is very unlikely to be the total number of skeletons in the assemblage although it is obvious when reading some of the literature that this is the denominator frequently used. In calculating the prevalence of joint disease, the denominator is the number of joints, not the number of skeletons; for tuberculosis of the spine, it will be the number of spines, and so on. It is sometimes very difficult to decide on the denominator and in any report, the decision should be stated.

overall prevalence is, that is, the extent of disease amongst the assemblage as a whole. The means of determining this will depend upon the nature of the disease under consideration, and whether it is unifocal or multifocal.

As a typical unifocal disease we might take tuberculosis. In most cases, the spine is affected and this can be considered as a single unit for these purposes. In other cases, however, there may be evidence of extra-spinal disease but the lesions are most likely to be solitary and affect only a single element. The overall prevalence in this case, may be arrived at simply by adding together all the prevalences for the separate elements. For example, suppose there is an assemblage in which 7 of 174 spines (4.0%) have tuberculosis, 2 of 116 wrists (1.7%), and 1 of 154 knees (0.7%). The overall prevalence is simply the sum of these three, or 6.4%.[15] This method can be applied to any unifocal (or monostototic) condition.

With a multifocal disease such as most of the joint diseases, however, the situation is much more complicated. The overall prevalence cannot be obtained by the addition of the prevalences for each single joint because this would mean that skeletons with multifocal disease would appear in the denominator more than once. One solution has been suggested which involves constructing a matrix of joints, present and absent, diseased and normal, and then calculating the overall prevalence from the matrix. Those who wish to pursue this further should consult the original paper.[16]

Denominator-free Methods

Denominators give rise to problems in modern epidemiology as well as in palaeoepidemiology and a number of so-called denominator-free methods have been devised to overcome these problems. Of these denominator-free methods, ranking and proportional morbidity or mortality will be considered here.

Ranking

Suppose that we have examined a number of assemblages from different periods and we think that there is a difference in the distribution of OA between them. We could compare the prevalence of the individual joints but we could also rank order the

---

[15] Note that it is *not* the sum of all the diseased elements divided by the total number of each element (which is this case would give a prevalence of 2.3%) since many skeletons will then appear more than once in the denominator.

[16] A Law, A simple method for determining the prevalence of disease in a past human population, *International Journal of Osteoarchaeology*, 2005, 15, 146–147.

Table 13.3. *Rank order of joints affected by osteoarthritis from two different periods*

Rank order	Early period	Late period
1	Spine	Shoulder
2	Shoulder	Spine
3	Hand	Wrist
4	TMJ	Hand
5	Knee	Hip
6	Elbow	Foot
7	Wrist	Ankle
8	Hip	TMJ
9	Ankle	Knee
10	Foot	Elbow

TMJ = temporomandibular joint

sites by their frequency of occurrence and save ourselves the bother of all the sums involved, and also of deciding which denominators to use. The assemblages come from two broad periods, Romano-British and Anglo-Saxon, and the eighteenth and early nineteenth centuries; we will call them early and late, respectively, for convenience. The rank order in which the various joints are affected is shown in Table 13.3 and even a brief examination of the table will reveal some substantial differences. The next question to ask then is, are these differences likely to arisen simply by chance, and this can be checked using Spearman's rank correlation coefficient (r_s or ρ).[17] For the data in the table, $r_s = 0.42$ which indicates that there is a weak positive correlation between the two rankings and therefore the differences are not significant.

Proportional Morbidity or Mortality Ratio

In modern epidemiology, it is more common to compute the proportional mortality ratio rather than the proportional morbidity ratio, because mortality statistics are easier to come by. The method for calculating the ratio is similar irrespective of whether it is mortality or morbidity under consideration, however, and can be illustrated by a consideration of the data in Table 13.4. It can be seen from this table that heart disease accounts for the highest proportion of deaths in both populations,

---

[17] There are other tests for testing the significant of differences in ranking, but Spearman's coefficient is the simplest to calculate.

Table 13.4. *Specific causes of death as a proportion of all causes for two populations*

Cause of death	C		D	
	Number of deaths	Proportion of all deaths	Number of deaths	Proportion of all deaths
Cancer	27000	18	35100	27
Heart disease	48000	32	62400	48
Respiratory disease	13500	9	3900	3
Neurological disease	7500	5	7800	6
Trauma	40500	27	6500	5
All other causes	13500	9	14300	11
TOTALS	150000	100	130000	100

but that trauma seems to be much less frequent in D than in C. The proportional mortality of trauma in each population can be calculated simply as:

$$PM = \frac{\text{Number of deaths due to trauma}}{\text{Total number of deaths}} \times 100$$

where PM = proportional mortality.

The proportional mortality in the two populations can be compared to compute the proportional mortality ratio (PMR) which in this case, is:

$$PMR = \frac{\text{Proportion of trauma in C}}{\text{Proportion of trauma in D}} = \frac{27}{5} \times 100 = 540$$

This is the simplest case, but the PMR can also be calculated by deriving an expected number of deaths and comparing it with the number observed. Returning to Table 13.4, it can be seen that if the rate of trauma in D were applied to C, then the number of trauma cases expected would be 7500,[18] whereas the number observed is 40500. If

$$PMR = \frac{\text{Observed}}{\text{Expected}} \times 100$$

then,

$$PMR = \frac{40500}{7500} = 540 \ (95\% \ \text{CI} \ 535 - 545).[19]$$

[18] Obtained by applying the proportion of deaths in D (5%) to the total number of deaths in C; thus 5% of 150000 is 7500.

[19] An alternative to calculating the PMR is the mortality odds ratio which was introduced by OS Miettenen and JD Wang (An alternative to the proportionate mortality ratio, *American Journal of Epidemiology*, 1981, 114, 144–148) because of some reservations they had about the PMR. Those who wish to learn more about this should consult the original paper.

There are a number of limitations to the use of the PMR the most substantial of which is that since the proportion of deaths must necessarily add up to 100, any increase in the proportion of deaths from one cause must be accompanied by a decrease in the proportion of deaths from one or more other causes. From a simple examination of the data, it may not be obvious whether an apparently increased proportion is real. To confirm an increase requires that the cause-specific death rates are known, and it usually because they are *not* known that the PMR is calculated in the first case.

It is not possible to carry out mortality studies in palaeopathology but under some circumstances, proportional *morbidity* studies can be carried out. Consider two assemblages in the first of which there were 12 transitional vertebrae among a total of 205 other conditions, while in the second, there were 7 in a total of 312 other conditions. The PMR in this case is 171 and this confirms the excess in the first assemblage without the requirement to calculate and compare prevalences.[20]

Calculating the PMR is about as simple a procedure as can be imagined and the difficulty in using it in palaeopathology is likely to arise when deciding what does, or does not constitute a disease, or a condition. There may be little difficulty with gross pathology – a fractured femur, for example – but things will not be so simple with conditions in which there is no dichotomous state of 'present' or 'absent'. There may be considerable difference between observers as to what constitutes an abnormal (or pathological) degree of periosteal new bone formation, for example, and the only safe way to proceed is to establish criteria for making a diagnosis (preferably by using operational definitions) before the study starts, and adhere to them throughout the study. If more than a single observer is involved in the study, then each must agree to the criteria and some form of inter-observer error test should be carried out before the study data are collected to ensure that coding is consistent.[21]

Analytical Epidemiology

So far, we have considered epidemiological methods that are essentially descriptive in character and although they are important, they do not necessarily provide information about the cause of disease and for this purpose so-called analytical methods are employed. The most important and powerful of these methods is the case-control

---

[20]   The morbidity odds ratio is 2.71 (95% CI 1.05–7.00). Since the CI does not include unity (just), the difference between the two proportions is statistically significant ($p < 5\%$).

[21]   Both inter- and intra-observer error can be formally tested; the most usual way of doing so is to calculate the kappa (κ) statistic.

Table 13.5. *Results of a hypothetical case-control study*

		Case	Control	
Exposure	+	25	325	350
	−	11	339	350
		36	664	700

Odds ratio = 2.37 (95% CI 1.1–54.90)

(or case-referent) study and since this has some applications to palaeopathology, it will be described briefly here.

The starting point of a case-control study is the notion that there is an association between a particular disease and what might loosely be considered as an exposure of some kind; this might be toxic dust in a factory, smoking, coffee drinking, living next to a nuclear power station and so on. From this notion a formal hypothesis might emerge which can be tested with a case-control study. The procedure is very simple – in theory. Individuals with the disease of interest are recruited and they form the cases; a number of individuals *without* the disease are also recruited and they form the controls. Once this is done, the number of individuals with the putative harmful exposure is determined and of these, some will be cases and some will be controls. If the exposure is associated with the disease, then there are likely to be more exposed cases than exposed controls and this is formally tested by calculating the odds ratio. Consider the example shown in Table 13.5. In this hypothetical study, 350 cases and 350 controls have been recruited; of these 25 cases and 11 controls have been exposed to the putative causal agent, and the odds ratio, therefore is:

$$OR = \frac{25}{325} \Big/ \frac{11}{339} = \frac{25 \times 339}{11 \times 325} = 2.37 \, (95\% \text{ CI } 1.15 - 4.90)$$

Odds ratios in excess of 2 are usually considered to be substantial enough to take seriously and since the 95% confidence interval does not include 1, the ratio is a significant one (statistically, at least). The result of this study would, therefore, lead us to suppose that there is an aetiological link between the exposure and the disease.[22]

---

[22] The jump from association to causation must be taken with caution; there are many examples in epidemiology of spurious associations being misinterpreted as causation, usually with the view of obtaining further research grants. The most important contribution to this debate remains Bradford Hill's presidential address to the Epidemiology Section of the Royal Society of Medicine (The environment and disease. Association or causation? *Journal of the Royal Society of Medicine*, 1965, 58, 295–300). In this paper, Bradford Hill suggested a number of features that should be taken into account when attempting to answer the question posed by the title of his paper. These were: strength of the association, consistency, specificity, temporality, toxicological gradient, plausibility, coherence, experiment and analogy.

Matching: When choosing controls for a case-control study, the question arises of
how far they should be matched with the cases? The theory behind matching
cases and controls was that by doing so, they would be as similar as possible with
the exception of the exposure that was being investigated. The tendency in modern epidemiology now, however, is to take a more relaxed view about matching
since over-exact matching may hide some important differences between the
cases and the controls. Matching is important when studying diseases that are
age- or sex-related; it would not be sensible, for example, not to match on
sex or age when studying prostate cancer or breast cancer, but it may not be
important for some other conditions – spondylolysis, for example. In most
studies, matching concentrates on eliminating, or controlling for, confounders.
These are strictly speaking, factors that are related to the exposure under study
and which also produce the same outcome; in practice, the definition is used
more loosely simply to refer to factors that produce the same outcome. For
example, in any study of lung or heart disease, it would be important to match
on smoking habits since smoking is known to affect both.[23] Before deciding on
matching, therefore, it is necessary to know something of the natural history
of the disease being studied and to consider whether there are any confounders
that might need controlling for.

Number of controls: Increasing the number of controls helps to prevent getting
a false negative result in a case-control study; the degree to which one can be
confident that a false negative result has *not* been obtained is known as the
power of the study. Increasing the number of controls increases the power of
the study, although there is a limit to this rule, and generally speaking, the
power of the study is not increased by having more than five controls per case.[24]

Case-control Studies in Palaeopathology

There will be limited opportunities to employ case-control studies in palaeopathology but as an example, take the suggestion that individuals with DISH are more likely
to have intervertebral disc disease (IVD) than those without. To test this hypothesis

---

[23] It is by no means unusual for those who plan studies either to overlook confounders or not to recognize
them until the time comes to analyse the data. Fortunately, there is at least a partial fix in the form of the
Mantel-Haenszel chi-squared test which can be stratified to allow for confounding. Further details can be
found in the texts mentioned at the start of this chapter.

[24] Obtaining a false negative result is known technically as a type II error; the type I error is the converse;
that it to say, a false positive result is obtained. It is possible to calculate before starting a study how many
controls will be needed; this will vary, of course, according to the power that you wish to give to it.

we will take IVD as the outcome, and DISH as the putative exposure. Cases can be recruited retrospectively or prospectively, that is, they can be recruited from records of past assemblages, or recruited as one comes across them when examining new assemblages; the former is much the quickest way of doing so. Since DISH is both age and sex related it is necessary to match for both variables and we will select three controls per case from the same assemblage as the case. We have operational definitions for IVD which we use when admitting a case to the study, and we use an operational definition for DISH when deciding how many of the cases and controls have the condition. The results might be that we have 135 cases of IVD and 270 controls; 15 cases are found to have DISH and so are 53 of the controls. The odds ratio, therefore, is 0.51 with a 95% confidence interval of 0.28–0.95. Since the confidence interval does not include 1, we can say that this is a significant difference and we can safely say – based on these data – that there is no association between having DISH and developing IVD. What we cannot legitimately say is that *not* having DISH predisposes towards IVD since this was not the hypothesis we set out to test and we would need another study to do so.

Planning a Study

Regardless of the type of study, it must be carefully planned in advance to make sure that time and resources are not wasted. The purpose of the study must be clearly stated since this will dictate the method to be used. Outcome measures and, for case-control studies, exposures (in the broadest sense) must be defined and criteria agreed for recruiting cases and controls to the study. These criteria and the operational definitions of outcome measures must be strictly adhered to by all observers throughout the study. There is a tendency to relax entry criteria and loosen operational definitions if there are difficulties in recruiting numbers to a study and this creep must be resisted. It is best to have a sheet outlining both entry criteria and operational definitions which is completed for each member of the study-base so that it can be seen that the rules have been followed. If measurements or observations are to be made, then specific recording sheets should be devised and fully completed. Negative *and* positive results must be recorded in all cases. If there is some degree of subjectivity about any of the observations, then all the observers should be trained and an inter-observer (and preferably an intra-observer) error test performed *before* the main study begins. Where there are large discrepancies between observers, then the cause must be determined and corrected before the study data are collected. Ideally the type of statistical analysis to be applied to the data should be decided at the planning stage – this is usually not difficult with a study of human remains as the choice is rather limited – and other types of analysis should not subsequently be used. It is very helpful to involve a statistician in the planning stage of a study to ensure that sufficient data of the right sort are collected; most case-control studies, for example, do not have sufficient power and it is not much use, having found a negative result, to ask a statistician to find a positive result for you.[25]

A Note about Teeth

There are some particular problems about recording the prevalence of caries and teeth lost before death. Because the examination of teeth is such an important part of any palaeopathological study, the problems need a brief mention here.

In modern dentistry, the frequency of dental disease in the permanent teeth is reported using the DMFT index, in which the number of caried or diseased teeth (D), the number missing as the result of caries (M), the number filled (F) and the total number (T) is recorded.[26] The index is obtained simply by adding D, M and F and dividing by T. The mean index is usually quoted for populations although other indices have also been suggested.[27]

The DMFT obviously has limited application to assemblages of human remains because there will be no filled teeth (although this may well change in the future are more and more recent burials are uncovered), and it is by no means certain that all teeth lost ante-mortem were lost as the result of caries. On this account it is usually suggested that the number of caried teeth is reported as the proportion of the total number of teeth present in the assemblage. This is not a very helpful measure, however, because the result is biased due to the fact that molars survive better than the anterior teeth[28] and the molars are the most likely to be affected by

---

[25] This activity is sometimes known as a type IX error and will not endear you to your statistical colleagues.

[26] There is a more detailed index in which the DMF is calculated for each tooth surface; this is known as the DMFS index. For this purpose, molars and pre-molars are considered to have five surfaces and the front teeth to have four. The maximum value of the DMFS for 28 teeth is 128. The scheme is applicable to archaeological teeth and details are given in: World Health Organisation, *Oral health surveys*, 3rd edition, Geneva, WHO, 1987.

[27] It is usually found that DMF index is skewed to the right and the presence of substantial numbers of individuals with a very low index will lower the mean. To help overcome this bias, it has been suggested that the Significant Caries Index (SiC) be used; this is the mean DMFT of the third of the study group with the highest caries score (D Brathall, Introducing the Significant Caries Index together with a proposal for a new global oral health goal for 12-year olds, *International Dental Journal*, 2000, 50, 378–384). When examining milk teeth, the *deft* index is used where *e* refers to the number of teeth extracted because of caries while the other initials are the same as those used for the permanent teeth.

[28] S Hillson, *Dental anthropology*, Cambridge, Cambridge University Press, 1996, pp 280–284.

caries. The mean caries index (DT) can be determined and expressed as a mean for that part of the assemblage with extant teeth, and the same can be done for missing teeth (MT). The DT is a more useful summary statistic than simply reporting the number of caried teeth as a proportion of the total, and this can be done for each tooth type is desired. What is much more interesting clinically, however, it to know what proportion of individuals had dental disease, irrespective of the number of teeth affected per individual.

For dental abscesses the best method is simply to report the number of individuals in whom they are present, and present this as a proportion of the total number with teeth extant; some may also feel the need to report the mean number of abscesses. When it comes to alveolar disease, it is simplest to record the number of individuals with a loss of alveolar bone that exceeds 3 mm as measured from the cemento-enamel junction to the crest of the alveolar margin for at least one tooth.

SELECT BIBLIOGRAPHY

AC Aufderheide and C Rodriguez-Martin, encyclopedia of human paleopathology, Cambridge, Cambridge University Press, 1998.

JH Beaty and JR Kasser, Rockwood and Wilkin's fractures in children, 6th edition, Philadelphia, Lippincott Williams and Wilkins, 2006.

JP Bilezikian, LG Raisz and GA Rodan, Principles of bone biology, 2nd edition, San Diego, Academic Press, 2002.

KD Brandt, M Doherty and LS Lohmander, Osteoarthritis, Oxford, Oxford University Press, 2003.

D Brothwell and AJ Sandison, Diseases in antiquity, Springfield, CC Thomas, 1967.

RW Bucholz, JD Heckman and CM Court-Brown, Rockwood and Green's fractures in adults, 6th edition, Philadelphia, Lippincott Williams and Wilkins, 2006.

J Cohen and WG Powderley, Infectious diseases, 2nd edition, Philadelphia, Mosby, 2004.

O Dutour, G Pálfi, J Berato and J-P Brun, The origin of syphilis in Europe, before or after 1493? Paris, Centre Archéologique du Var, 1994.

H Ellis, Clinical anatomy, 11th edition, Oxford, Blackwell Publishing, 2006.

MJ Favus, Primer on the metabolic bone diseases and disorders of mineral metabolism, 6th edition, Washington, D.C., American Society for Bone and Mineral Research, 2006.

DM Grieg, Surgical pathology of bone, Edinburgh, Oliver and Boyd, 1931.

A Hakim, Oxford handbook of rheumatology, Oxford, Oxford University Press, 2006.

AL Kaplan, JJ McCartney and DA Sisli, Health, disease and illness. Concepts in medicine, Washington, DC, Georgetown University Press, 2004.

D Male, J Brostoff, DB Roth and I Roitt, Immunology, 7th edition, Philadelphia, Elsevier Mosby, 2006.

H Moscovitch, Black's medical dictionary, 4th edition, London, A & C Black, 2005.

DJ Ortner, Identification of pathological conditions in human skeletal remains, 2nd edition, San Diego, Academic Press, 2003.

G Pálfi, OI Dutour, J Deak and I Hutás, Tuberculosis, past and present, Budapest, Golden Book Publisher, 1999.

D Resnick, Diagnosis of bone and joint disorders, 4th edition, Philadelphia, WB Saunders, 2002.

PA Revell, Pathology of bone, Berlin, Springer-Verlag, 1986.

R Souhami, Bailliere's clinical oncology, Volume 1, no 1, Bone tumours, Oxford, Bailliere Tindall, 1987.

JW Spranger, PR Brill and A Poznanski, Bone dysplasias. An atlas of genetic disorders and skeletal development, 2nd edition, Oxford, Oxford University Press, 2002.

Index

antra of Highmore, 114
aorta, 224–5
    coarctation of, 226–7
        rib notching in, 227
apical granuloma, *see* periapical cavities
apoptosis, 15, 18
arthritis mutilans, 64
articular cartilage, 24
    in osteoarthritis, 27–8
AS, *see* ankylosing spondylitis
autopsy, 162–4
    complete, 163
    partial, 163
    signs of in the skeleton, 163–4
avascular necrosis, 144–5
    in Perthes disease, 213
    in slipped capital femoral epiphysis,
        212
    of femoral head, 145
    of lunate, 145–6
    of scaphoid, 145
    of talus, 146

bamboo spine, 59
Bankart lesion, 155
bare area (within a joint), 25
Bayes's theorem, 2, n2
Behçet's disease, 225
beheading, 165
bejel, *see* endemic syphilis
bipartite patella, 22
bladder stones, *see* kidney and bladder
        stones
bone balance, 19
bone cysts, 177
bone formers (or forming), 30, 72–3
    definition of , 72
bone mass, 17
    maximum (or peak), 17
bone matrix, 14
bone mineral density (BMD), 118–9
bone morphogenic proteins (BMP), 18
bone remodelling, 18
    in Paget's disease, 125
    following fracture, 148

bone remodelling unit (BRU), 18
Bouchard's nodes, 37
brachycephaly, 198, 210
breast cancer, 186–7
Brodie's abscess, 88
brown tumours, 135
Brucella abortus, 96
brucellosis, 96–7
    periosteal new bone in, 96
    spine in, 96
bunionette, 71
bunions, 70–1
    differentiation from gout, 71

calcaneal spur, 62
calcitonin, 16
calculus, *see* dental calculus
callus, 13, 148
cancellous bone, 12
caries, 236–9
    development of, 237
    effects on teeth, 239
caries sicca, 105–6
case-control (case-referent) studies, 261–3
    in palaeopathology, 263–4
cement line, 13
cervical rib, 218–9
Charcot joints
    in leprosy, 100
    in syphilis, 106
CHD, *see* congenital hip dsyplasia
chondroblastoma, 175
chondrodermal dysplasia, 202
chondroplasia (chondrodysplasia) punctata,
        202
chondrosarcoma, 181
chronic recurrent multiple osteomyelitis,
        89
cleft palate, 202
clinodactyly, 198
cloacae, 85, 93
Cobb angle, 216
Codman's triangle, 178
collagen, 14, 42, 132, 148, 200
common odds ratio, 254

CPSIA information can be obtained
at www.ICGtesting.com
Printed in the USA
LVOW04s0715050118
561939LV00011B/392/P